PLUNKY

PLUNKY
Juju Jazz Funk & Oneness

James "Plunky" Branch

coolgrovepress

Copyright © 2015 J. Plunky Branch

All rights reserved under the International and
Pan-American copyright conventions. Published in the United States by
Cool Grove Press, an imprint of Cool Grove Publishing, inc., New York.
512 Argyle Road, Brooklyn, NY 11218
http://www.coolgrove.com
All inquiries to info@coolgrove.com

Publisher's Cataloging-in-Publication
(Provided by Quality Books, Inc.)

Plunky, author.
  Plunky : Juju jazz funk and Oneness / James "Plunky"
Branch. -- First edition.
  pages cm
  Includes bibliographical references.
  LCCN 2015955775
  ISBN 978-1-887276-45-0

  1. Plunky. 2. Saxophonists--United States--
Biography. 3. Musicians--United States--Biography.
4. Musicians--Political activity--United States.
5. Autobiographies.   I. Title.

ML419.P65A3 2015   781.65092
                              QBI15-600222

coolgrovepress ny

Foreword/Dedication

Every life is a cycle – from birth to death, dust to dust. Every life is a trip, a journey from someplace to some place. And if the journey isn't orbital, its path is at least an arc, a part of a circle. Some lives burn bright enough to light up the sky in a flash, like comets. Some lives soar or arch over longer, larger, higher heavens, like suns. They are stars that attract adoring, orbiting planets and followers and imitators and historians to tell their stories and make them legends. Some lives are even bigger than that. Like massive quasars, god-like, they become the stuff of myths, the substance of archetypical stories of a whole people, inspiring generations and millennia. There are also local lives: countless miniature twinkling lights, candles, neon lights, incandescent street lamps. These are tiny sparklers who emit guiding beams important to the cities, towns, neighborhoods and families where they reside. These little lights illuminate and pinpoint views in what otherwise might be a dark void. Little lights are big and bright if you're close enough to them. Little lights shine individually and collectively. Alone, each is unique. Together, they are a non-blinding force. United and directed, a collection of little lights is a galaxy of goodness.

This is dedicated to the exceptional local lights: musicians, artists, organizers, teachers, and others who sparkle where they are, because they are supposed to. And to all the phenomenal artists who have inspired me, and to all my friends and fans who have lifted me and elevated my light as if it were a beacon, thank you.

TABLE OF CONTENTS

FOREWORD/DEDICATION vii
PREFACE xi

CHAPTERS
1. MY MUSIC PHILOSOPHY, POLITICS & PURPOSE 1
2. FROM RVA TO COLUMBIA UNIVERSITY 6
3. AFTER COLUMBIA – WHAT A TRIP! 23
4. THE ARMY 35
5. SAN FRANCISCO JUJU 41
6. BACK TO THE BIG APPLE 51
7. ONENESS OF JUJU IN RVA 60
8. FAMILY & PLUNKY & ONENESS 74
9. BLACK FIRE! 84
10. BRANCHES OF THE ARTS 96
11. WHAT A TRIP – AFRICA AND BEYOND 105
12. EVERY WAY BUT LOOSE 115
13. AFRICAN VENTURES 125
14. THE NINETIES ALBUMS 140
15. JOURNEY OF A LIFETIME JOURNAL 154
16. A EUROPEAN TOUR WITH BOBBY BYRD 185
17. 2000'S RECORDINGS 233
18. UNDER THE RADAR TRIP TO CUBA 241
19. UNDER THE RADAR TRIP TO CUBA II 269
20. 2000 INTERNATIONAL TOURING, GIGS & TRIPS 298
21. MARTINI KITCHEN & BUBBLE BAR 313
22. 40TH YEAR ANNIVERSARY DOCUMENTARY FILM 321
23. THE LAST ALBUMS/ FIRE 325
24. LESSONS LEARNED/ WHAT WORKED FOR ME 333
25. EPILOGUE – COMPLETED CIRCLES 344

APPENDICIES

A.	ACKNOWLEDGEMENTS :	358

B. JOURNALS OF INTERNATIONAL TOURS
I.	Journal of the 2001 UK Tour	359
II.	Journey to MIDEM 2002	365
III.	Journal of Two Weeks to Rio	381
IV.	Journal of Our Tour De France 2006	394
V.	Journal of the DRIVE IT Tour in France 2008	406
VI.	Journal of a Weekend in Paris 2010	421
VII.	Journal of a Trip to Montreal	426
VIII.	My Capital Jazz Cruise	430

C.	DISCOGRAPHY	448
D.	ONENESS MUSICIANS	451
E.	MOMENTOUS GIGS, VENUES AND COLLABORATORS	456
F.	CREDITS	462

ix

Preface

Everybody's got a story to tell. This is mine. In the span of 68 years I have been a musician, poet, dropout, administrator, film maker, teacher, tennis bum, producer, hippie and international traveler. I have performed countless gigs, written over 400 songs, produced 25 albums and 42 music videos. I've also toured in Europe, been to Africa six times, visited Cuba twice while producing a documentary film; have been the subject of two documentaries, and celebrated 45 years as an independent artist. I've had so many enlightening experiences that I have decided to share some of the details of my story. I hope that you and others will enjoy wading through what I have experienced as a collector of memories.

Plunky – 1973

Chapter 1

My Music Philosophy Politics and Purpose

"Wisdom, peace and love through music" is my signature phrase. It sums up my purposes and goals for my music and my career in six words. My mantra could be: *"Information, insights and inspiration through creativity."* Or, it could be *"Political, social and business advancement through culture,"* but that would be seven words.

I am J. Plunky Branch, saxophonist, producer, songwriter and bandleader from Richmond, Virginia (RVA). I have shared stages with some of the biggest names in black music, had hundreds of collaborations, and generated critical acclaim. I love funk, jazz and message music. I am inspired by the music of George Clinton, John Coltrane, and Bob Marley. But while music has been my vehicle of choice, it was initially a choice of practicality, convenience and default, rather than the pull of muses, natural talent or irresistible impulse.

This may seem odd because I have been characterized as being so passionate in my performances. People say my love for performing radiates from the stage and touches my audiences. This is likely due to my adopted African music philosophy. I believe the investment of sincere energy and dedication to nia (Swahili for purpose) are the most important measures of a musical performance's value and "goodness." In the aesthetics of black music, the emphasis is on the "how" rather than the "what." It's the earnest energy and the emotional investment that make a performance soulful; so I give my all, every time I perform.

There is also the belief that the declared objectives regarding the effects on the audience become self-fulfilling. When we declare that we want to inspire the listeners, and we believe we can, and act (perform) as if we feel it; we will likely inspire listeners. If I say "we want to funk you up," and give my all to making the groove funky enough, it will funk things up. If I write an instrumental song and call it "Forever In A Moment" and I invest my spirit in the playing of the song, some folks are likely to feel the romance and timelessness of the melody and the moment. When John Coltrane played "A Love Supreme" or Bob Marley sang "Redemption Song" we were moved by the power of their stated intentions, their faith and their commitment. Nommo (Swahili – name, the word) creates. "In the beginning was the word…" Creating begins with the word (nommo) and the work is completed and distinguished by its naming (nommo). Like in some churches some congregates might say I am naming and claiming my blessing. If you can conceive it (think it, name it) and believe it (have enough faith, see it), then you can receive it. So my talent as a horn player or singer is enhanced by my investment of sincere effort.

The significance of my notes, tone and lyrics is augmented by my stated intention to demonstrate that music can have positive political, social and even spiritual effects on me, the other musicians, the audience, and society at large.

"Writing the story of your own life is a bit like drilling your own teeth."
—Gloria Swanson, 1899 - 1983

I am writing my autobiography to share my views and experiences. I am a local musician who has had some international touring ventures. My career has been a manifestation of my belief that wherever you are, success can be earned by utilizing your strengths, by collaborating with people with complementary skills, and by knowing that disciplined effort and perseverance furthers. Well, that sums it all up nicely. And maybe I don't need to write anymore…

But as you can already tell, brevity is not my strong suit. My life has been long and my experiences extremely varied. And I have enough vanity to think that my stories matter; so here I go…

"With the power of soul anything is possible!" – Jimi Hendrix

Music is, above all, about joy; or it should be. It can soothe, make you jump and shout, or carry you to other places and times. But music is also about sharing; it is about connecting, and being social. For me it's about having fun, making love and being moved. Socially, music is always about raising consciousness and motivating a group, a room, a people or a generation to move – forward.

"Nearing the end, I can better understand the beginning."
— J. Plunky Branch

Two things that had an enormous impact on my social consciousness were the civil rights movement and the counter-culture movement, including the riotous demonstration and campus take-over at Columbia University in 1968. I grew up and went to public schools in the very segregated city of Richmond, Virginia (RVA). (It is worth noting that in 1959, nearby Prince Edward County, Virginia chose to close its public schools altogether rather than integrate them.) During my youth I didn't know any white people. Okay, I did know Mr. Jack, the Jewish owner of the store on the corner. And there were Kate and her brother, Smokey, the two very young white kids who were neighbors for a brief time when we moved into their neighborhood. Oh yeah, there was Mr. Tirs, the Slavic man who taught Russian in my high school. But that was essentially it. I didn't look at, converse with, or interact with white people, except at grocery or department stores, or to avoid them on city streets.

The sit-ins of the civil rights movement moved me. I wanted to go downtown to participate in the efforts to desegregate our department store lunch counters, but my parents thought it was too dangerous and I was too young, even as a 10th grader. But those efforts and the reports on the nightly news of the demonstrations and non-violent protests across the South were tear-inducing and inspirational. The leaders of the movement, Dr. Martin Luther King, Stokley Carmichael, Dr. Ralph Abernathy, Medgar Evers, Rosa Parks and all the rest, were my heroes.

The music of the times informed and motivated my generation. And message music was our soundtrack as we worked our way through the great debates of our time (non-violence vs. self-defensive aggression; integration vs. black nationalism; capitalism vs. socialism; Negro, colored, Black or Afro-American; nigger vs. nigga vs. ban the word. Black Power!). Our music supported, taught and inspired us.*

Black music has always been one of the ways black history has been documented, from the griots in Africa to the jazzmen in the Harlem Renaissance; from the protest songs of the civil rights era to the hip-hop at the close of the 20th century. Certainly, music has documented my personal journey.

In the 1960s & 70s message music told us what was going on. Black popular music mirrored the moods and aspirations of the community, and some of the music was overtly political. During my early adult years, jazz musicians and thought leaders, particularly the proponents of the more avant garde, free jazz, "new music," increasingly turned to political and African cultural themes for inspiration. And I was motivated to become a musician and contribute to this legacy from the protest songs of the civil rights era to the hip-hop at the close of the 20th century.

*SOME MESSAGE MUSIC SONGS, PROTEST R&B AND BLACK EMPOWERMENT MUSIC

Curtis Mayfield: Keep On Pushing (1964), People Get Ready (1965), We're A Winner (1967)
James Brown: I'm Black & I'm Proud (1968), The Big Payback (1973)
Sly & the Family Stone: Every Day People (1968), Stand (1969)
Last Poets: Niggers Are Scared of Revolution (1970)
Gil Scott Heron: The Revolution Will Not Be Televised 1970, Winter In America (1974)
Marvin Gaye: What's Going On (1971)
Bob Marley: I Shot the Sheriff (1973), Get Up Stand Up, Redemption Song
Fela Kuti: Africa 70 Afro-Beat music with political themes
Hugh Masekela: Grazing in the Grass (1968), The Union of South Africa (1971), I am Not Afraid (1974)
The O'Jay's: Ship Ahoy, For the Love of Money, Don't Call Me Brother (1973), Message in the Music (1976)
Parliament-Funkadelic: Chocolate City (1975), Mothership Connection (1975)
John Coltrane: Alabama (1963), A Love Supreme (1965)
Pharaoh Sanders: The Creator Has A Master Plan (1969), Black Unity (1972)
Archie Shepp: The Magic of Juju (1967), Attica Blues (1972), Cry of My People (1973), Kwanza (1974)
Public Enemy, Boogie Down Production, Poor Righteous Teachers in the 1980s & 90s

SOME OF MY ADDITIONAL FAVORITE RECORDINGS AND
SONGS OF ALL TIME

John Coltrane: Ballads, Giant Steps, Chasing the Trane, Blue Trane, Naima, Transitions, My Favorite Things, Afro Blue, A Love Supreme, and any other album
Dave Brubeck: Take Five, Strange Meadow Lark, Blue Rondo ala Turk
Horace Silver: Song For My Father, Cape Verdean Blues, Lonely Woman, Nutville, Senor Blues
Miles Davis: Kind of Blue, Nefertiti, Bitches Brew, On the Corner, and any other album
Jill Scott: Who Is Jill Scott, and any other album
Richard Smallwood: I Love the Lord, Center Of My Joy, Total Praise, A Secret Place
Jimi Hendrix: All Along the Watchtower, Voodoo Child, Foxy Lady
The Beatles: Rubber Soul, The White Album, Sgt. Pepper's Lonely Hearts Club Band, The Fool on the Hill, In My Life, The Long And Winding Road, Yesterday, and many others
Luther Vandross: If Only for One Night, A House is Not a Home, So Amazing, Anyone Who Had A Heart, Never Too Much, and any other
Doug & Jean Carne: Infant Eyes, Arise and Shine, Spirit of the New Land
Thelonious Monk: Monks Dream, Round Midnight, Epistrophy, Ruby My Dear, and any other
Steel Pulse: Earth Crises
Mongo Santamaria: Afro Blue
Crosby, Stills and Nash: Crosby, Stills & Nash
Eddie Palmieri: Azucar, Harlem River Drive
Stevie Wonder: Music of My Mind, Talking Book, Songs in the Key of Life, Hotter Than July, Signed Sealed Delivered, All I Do,
Dexter Gordon: "Soy Califa"
Roy Ayers: "Everybody Loves the Sunshine"
Charles Mingus: Goodbye Porkpie Hat, Fables of Faubus
Pharoah Sanders: Thembi, Astral Traveling
Wayne Davis: Wayne Davis
Julius Hemphill: Dogon AD
Grover Washington: Wine Light, Mr. Magic

⌘⌘⌘

Chapter 2

Richmond to Columbia University

I was born July 20, 1947, into a family that was as typical and as unique as most. My parents, James and Beulah Branch, and I lived in a clap board house on the Southside of Richmond with my father's parents and an aunt and her husband. The living conditions were poor, in a rickety house with drafty crowded rooms, no indoor bathrooms, a stove in the middle room for heat, and a wood/coal stove in the kitchen where we also bathed in a big tin tub on Saturday nights. But the house and the family were held together with plenty of love.

As the first born male, I was named James E. Branch, Jr., after my father; but my father was also responsible for my nickname. The story is that when I was an infant, he would play with me and toss me in the air saying, "Plunky, plunky, plunky!" and I would laugh gleefully. When people came to visit, he told them if you want to see the baby smile, just say "Plunky," and they did, and I did. And I have been Plunky ever since.

When my grandparents died, they were replaced in the house by the births of my two younger brothers, Gregory (Khari) and Philip (Muzi), with whom I would grow up, and work, and remain close for all of my life.

My parents were the only members of their families to finish college, and they would work diligently for 30 years, he as an IRS bureaucrat and she as a teacher for Richmond Public Schools, until retirement. My father was a stern, almost mean, taskmaster. He was extremely tight with his money and his emotions and he demanded strict adherence to his every command. My mother was pretty much the opposite: soft, nurturing, generous to a fault, and expressively loving.

As a child it was hard for me to understand my father's frugality. He scrimped, sacrificed and saved religiously. He was extremely disciplined when it came to planning for the future. He wore the same two suits for years, though he bought us new clothes for school and for Easter every year. He bought, paid for and stored new furniture even before he found the house he would buy on the other side of town. He hated to owe anyone, so he never

Three Branch boys: Philip (Muzi), Gregory (Khari) & James (Plunky)

used credit cards; instead using lay-away plans or opting to save his money until he had accumulated enough to pay cash. I am not sure how he stomached having a mortgage, but I do know that by the time he died in 1997, he left my mother with a financially unencumbered home and substantial savings.

I started taking piano lessons from Mrs. Graham, my church organist, when I was six or seven. I showed great progress and advanced quickly. I remember playing the sheet music for "March of the Toys" very early on, and everyone marveled at my talent. My father played the piano we had in our living room. The ramshackle house had no indoor toilet, only an outhouse, but we did have a big, old, heavy, black, upright piano that my father played on special occasions. He could play any song we requested, but he only played on holidays or birthdays or those rare times when we had company. I practiced on that piano and considered it mine.

When we moved from the Southside to the upscale Byrd Park neighborhood in the West End of Richmond, we could not get the piano out of the old house, so we had to leave it. And since we moved all the way across town and didn't have a car, my piano lessons with Mrs. Graham were discontinued. Years later my mother would admit that she didn't really want me to play the piano because she thought it was too effeminate and feared playing it could turn me into a flamboyant Liberace. Funny.

In the fourth grade the whole class took beginning music lessons on Tonettes, little plastic song flutes. I showed some aptitude and it was recommended that I move up to taking band class. I played clarinet. My mother was very supportive, renting, and then buying me the instrument that I would play through high school.

In middle school I was selected for the all-city concert band and that was so cool to get out of classes to go across town and meet other kids from all over the city. (In that ensemble I met Jackie Peters who would become my 10th grade girlfriend, college classmate, fellow soul and African music lover, tennis enthusiast, and a lifelong friend.) In high school I played the oboe, bassoon and tympani drums, but as first chair first clarinetist, the single reed horn was clearly my preference. I was the concert maestro for the concert band and the elected president of the marching band.

High School marching band was one of the most fun activities ever, especially during football season. We performed at pep rallies, in the stands during the games, and most importantly, on the field during halftime. We would travel to out-of-town games on the band bus and had fun singing, playing songs, carousing with the cheerleaders and majorettes and generally having the times of our lives.

Our halftime shows involved marching in precision formations to traditional marches and also partying to current R&B songs. Our band director, Joseph Kennedy, Jr., was a fantastic professional musician, and he would write the arrangements of songs we requested for our halftime shows. We always ended our shows with a hot, current hit song and our fans would scream and shout that our band was the best. (Of, course it didn't hurt that our football team rarely lost a game during my three years in high school and it didn't hurt that we had future NFL Hall of Famer, Willie Lanier, playing linebacker for us. So the Mighty Green Dragons of Maggie L. Walker High School had the best team and the best band of all the Black schools in the state!)

Mr. Kennedy played jazz and classical violin. He was the first black to integrate the all-white Richmond Symphony Orchestra. He toured with

Benny Carter and with pianist, Ahmad Jamal, especially during the summer months, and he would come back in the Fall and tell us about some of his experiences.

All my public school music teachers were working jazz musicians, who moonlighted in clubs and venues around the region. My early teachers, Johnny Peyton and Dave Williams, were both saxophonists of local renown. (In 1977 I would replace Mr. Peyton as his long term substitute teacher at Mosby Middle School and J. F. Kennedy High School, where I directed the small, but energetic and talented, marching and concert bands. Years after that, Johnny Peyton made a comeback when he created the Renaissance Big Band, a 17-piece ensemble playing classic swinging jazz. I had the honor of playing tenor sax with that band directed by Johnny Peyton, my first band teacher, and sitting next to alto saxophonist Dave Williams, who was my second band teacher. Talk about full circle…)

The soundtrack for my teen years was provided by the local black radio stations that played soul, blues, and gospel music. We listened to Junior Walker and the All Stars, James Brown, Booker T & the MG's, all of Motown, plus Otis Redding, Clyde McPhatter, Etta James, Little Ester, Chubby Checker, the Impressions, the Drifters, and many others. Local soul bands played at our dances and at the clubs. Very often the national artists we listened to on the radio would come through town, touring on the chitterling circuit, sometimes using local groups as opening acts or even as their back-up bands. I joined Jackie Peters' group, Jackie and the Citations, but after only one or two gigs I had to quit because my parents wouldn't let me hang out and I was often on punishment for not maintaining all A's on my report cards.

Music was actually my second love. Chemistry was first. I was always interested in science, and at age nine, I found my father's college chemistry book and was hooked. I studied it and loved the symbols, formulas and charts. I think it made me feel smart and special, like being a member of some secret, esoteric society; so I was going to be a scientist.

In high school I was president of the Chemistry Club. In the 11th grade my project, "The Identification of Metallic Ions by Paper Chromatography" won first place in the local and third place in the state science fair. I attended science conferences at University of Virginia and was offered a scholarship to go there. I did well on all the qualifying standardized tests, had exceptional grades and took advanced courses math and science. I got a 610 on my

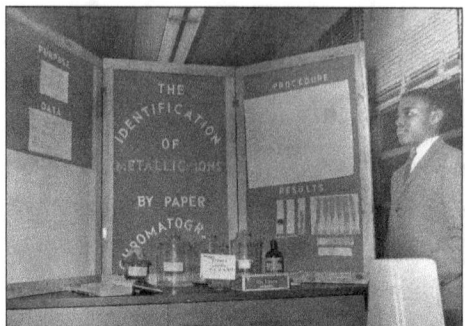

My high school science project

High school graduation, 1965

Chemistry SAT and I was sure that science was to be my career path. I was also offered a full scholarship to Howard University in Washington, D.C. and to other colleges. My first choice was to attend Amherst College in Massachusetts but when I was only accepted onto their waiting list, I opted to go to Columbia University because of the prestige of it being an Ivy League school and the attraction of living in New York City.

Before my family moved from Southside, we lived near a big DuPont manufacturing plant outside of which was a sign with the company logo and the slogan: "Better things for better living through chemistry." I thought I would grow up to be a chemist, work for DuPont, and invent some new plastic, product or process that would make living easier or better for everyone. A noble purpose, I thought.

My chemistry career path was followed only until my second year of college at Columbia. Two things derailed my science aspirations: organic chemistry class and left wing politics. By my sophomore year I had learned that organic chem was a bitch, and chemists were all being co-opted by the military industrial complex to work on making napalm and all manner of weapons of mass destruction to be visited upon the people of Southeast Asia, Africa and the rest of the third world. I was fully deprogrammed and indoctrinated (some would say, enlightened) by the left-wing political, anti-war viewpoints of my fellow students, for whom civil rights, eliminating the draft system, and ending the Viet Nam War were causes to be championed.

At Columbia we had many long, vociferous debates about the war, racism, socialism, and cutting-edge progressivism vs. the status quo. During the mid-sixties, these topics were hotly debated, especially since there were incidents, upheavals and movements in the news that portended the possibilities of massive social change. There was talk of non-violent activism and even the possibility of revolution in the air.

In my incoming freshman class there were 16 blacks and that number effectively doubled black undergraduate population on campus. We were tested and nurtured by our ivy-towered campus situation. We were bright, newly freed of direct parental control, and we were representing our race. Though small in number we were vocal and committed to determining what the right activist path was for us: the passive resistance of Dr. Martin Luther King and SCLC; vs. the self-defense of Stokley Carmichael and SNCC; vs. the "by any means necessary" push of Malcolm X and the Nation of Islam. Integration, Black nationalism, socialism, black capitalism were topics of discussion for us blacks.

We were challenged by our studies and current events to examine systems of government and economics that might be viable in an ever changing international environment. Over time I developed my own views. (For example: I saw democratic socialism as an economic operating system based on collectivism, deciding by democratic government action to provide for the general welfare of the citizenry by operating education, public works, roads, mail, public transportation, common defense, community safety, health care and systems for legal redress. In the 1950s and '60s, the U.S. grew a middle-class using what I would call socialist programs, like the G.I. Bill for education and home ownership, and by taxing the highest income bracket at rates of up to 90%. The debate can be made as to what percentage of GDP social programs must constitute before the economy ceases to be capitalist. Clearly most economies will be liberal hybrids, combinations of elements of both capitalism and socialism. Civil societies are grand experiments to see if we can collectively ride the arcs made by the pendulum swinging back and forward toward workable, sustainable models. There are macroeconomics, micro economics and there are adversarial systems, all of which have to be managed and coordinated. The challenge is to develop and amend economic systems that utilize incentives to motivate competitiveness while restricting selfish abuses and class disparities.)

In addition to being exposed to these political and social ideas, I was also getting a deeper look into jazz. In Richmond I was introduced to jazz by hearing a smattering on the radio, seeing snippets on television, and by my music teachers who were all jazz musicians who wanted us to have some appreciation for the music. When I was in high school my father joined the Columbia Records Tape Club, monthly ordering albums for our reel-to-reel tape recorder. After he had gotten most of what he liked (Johnny Mathis, Barbara Streisand, Lena Horne, Andre Previn, Lou Rawls, etc.) he let me order some albums. I got Dave Brubeck, Miles Davis, John Coltrane, Jimmy Smith and James Brown. These albums changed my life, introducing me to jazz as a personal, introspective listening experience, and germinating my appreciation for improvisation, esoteric repertoires, and being hip and cool.

While attending Columbia, living in New York, hearing jazz all the time and seeing it live, the music overwhelmed me. I loved it. My best friend at college was Kent Parker who was from Brooklyn, New York. We had much in common: we loved the ladies, we were hip, we were into football, we liked to party, and we liked jazz music. Kent was a jazz aficionado. He and his father had an extensive album collection that included all things Blue Note and beyond. At their home on Brooklyn Avenue, in his own room, Kent had a Grundig stereo system with super speakers that made listening to the music a phenomenal experience. We would go there on weekends to look at, I mean read, Playboy magazines, prepare dance routines for partying we would be doing and listening to and discussing Hank Mobley, Lee Morgan, Jackie McLean, Lambert-Hendricks-and-Ross, Dexter Gordon, and the rest of the hard-boppers. Horace Silver was our main man. We listened to "Song For My Father" so much that we could sing every note to every solo on it. Joe Henderson's tenor sax on that song was a classic, near perfect rendition. Kent and I once went to a party on campus, dressed alike and "performed" that song along with the record on the dance floor. Sounds corny, but no, you had to have been there to see us score.

In my freshman year I was briefly in the Columbia University Marching Band. It was a student run operation whose motto was "The Cleverest Band in the World." Their idea of clever was being crazy and irreverent. At football game halftimes they would run chaotically onto the field making noise, and then proceed to play music satirizing current events and personalities. It was all very cerebral and often immature, and certainly not soulful. The football team never won a game while I was there. I couldn't handle being in a crazy, undisciplined band playing for a losing team. I did play for the pep band at the basketball games. We played at the home games and some away games, including at Madison Square Garden for the Holiday Basketball Tournament. But that was the extent of my music playing that first year at Columbia.

In my sophomore year, I started a band, the Soul Syndicate, billed as "14 pieces of driving soul!" We were all Columbia undergrads: drums, two guitars, bass, four horns, and a five man singing group. Later, we added Archie, a non-student from Harlem, to play conga drums and percussion. I played tenor sax. Clarinets were just not cool enough for a soul band. Plus, in the middle of most of the R&B songs on the radio, there was a saxophone solo; and I wanted to be the guy that played that solo.

The Soul Syndicate was a classic cover band playing soul music. Most of our repertoire consisted of medleys of James Brown songs and a medley of Temptations songs. But any other hit soul songs might be thrown in to the mix. I was the leader who called the tunes, scheduled rehearsals, booked the gigs and managed the group. Kent Parker was our James Brown singer. The key man, however, was probably, the bassist, Rich Steinman, a classical cello player who loved soul music and who could write and arrange horn parts and vocal harmonies. Rich had a fantastic ear and he could listen to a record and then sit right down and write out the parts for all the musicians.

When the Soul Syndicate performed on campus we caused quite a sensation. We were a mixed group, dressed in black with white ties looking like mobsters, playing tightly arranged renditions of R&B hits. We played for dances on campus and became quite the rage. We were a novelty and we were good.

We performed a Columbia homecoming weekend concert with blues guitarist Buddy Guy. On our last set he came out and jammed with us, later saying that he really enjoyed playing in front of such a big band. From that gig we got a gig playing for the prom of a New Jersey prep school that was so posh and exclusive that even the janitor was white.

Around that same time another novelty act was put together by one of the

Soul Syndicate at Columbia University circa 1967: Top row, l. to r. Kent Parker, Charlie Jones, Al Dempsey, Al Waller, Eugene Buckingham; middle: Adam Bottom row l. to r. Joe Witkin, John Herbert, Harold Brooks, Plunky, Paul Berman, Rich Steinman, Archie Donadell

white fraternities on campus to play "doo wop" songs at a themed dance they were sponsoring. That group, Sha Na Na, would go on to parlay their '50s rock & roll revivalism to fame, a national television series, merchandising, and touring successes.

While the Soul Syndicate would not equal Sha Na Na's level of exposure, our group did play on a number of campuses and clubs around New York. We would play at the Cheetah, a chic disco club on 58th Street in downtown Manhattan. For us it was a big deal getting the gig there. Because we would bring in lots of college kids to our shows, we became one of the house bands at the Cheetah, appearing with another soul group called Johnny Maestro & the Brooklyn Bridge. The Cheetah had a large circular revolving stage and the two bands would set up back-to-back on the stage. We would play our respective one-hour sets and at the end we would play a previously agreed-on song together while the stage would spin the other group to face the front. The music would be non-stop and the club employed their house dancers to start and keep the party going.

On campus and around the city the Soul Syndicate earned a reputation for playing authentic soul music and giving energetic, tight shows. We were not unique but we were quite different. In actuality, we simply duplicated what I had experienced with the local bands in Richmond, but we did it on an Ivy League campus in New York City. Most of the other guys in the band went on to graduate and became doctors, lawyers, social workers, professors and activists.

With my band and other activities on campus, my student life devolved into non-stop sex, drugs, rock & roll and jazz. My girlfriend, Jackie F., was the finest sister at Barnard. She had model good looks, a refined upbringing, and she was super intelligent. (Beauty, fineness and smarts have become the signature traits of all my long term lovers. Pretty faces, fine bodies and master's degrees. I know what I like.) I treated Jackie poorly (and I am not proud of it), but she fell in love with me, enchanted by my bad boy image. I was hipper than most of the preppy guys on campus and people came to me for all sorts of advice on social and love life. I had swag.

l. to r. Eugene Buckingham, Al Dempsey, Kent Parker, Harold Brooks (sax)

From the beginning I almost never went to class. When I got to Columbia the school had a policy of mandatory class attendance. Freshmen were only allowed four unexcused absences without being put on probation. A second semester of multiple class cutting meant suspension. In my freshman year I cut 211 classes.

My freshman advisor was the dean of the school. He had advised me to take a light load of introductory classes so I could adjust to the college environment. The classes I took were light weight courses that I had had in high school; so without attending classes at all I was still able to get four B's and a

C. After the first semester I was called in to see the dean about my class cutting. When he saw my grades, instead of putting me on probation, he decided he would look into changing the policy to one of voluntary class attendance. And by the end of that year, that's what he did.

In retrospect I can see that his low expectation of me and my acceptance of a low demand course load combined to allow me too much time for extracurricular activities on campus. I got into socializing and partying; playing bridge, pool and poker for money; experimenting with recreational drugs and going to the movies and clubs in downtown New York until all hours of the night.

The light work load at school gave me too much time to test the limits of my new found freedom. I was no longer in small city RVA but in the wide open, wildest city in the world, NYC.

What I learned, among other things, is that education, learning anything, becoming proficient in anything, will always cost something. To take college courses you pay tuition. Learning to play poker might cost you a lot of money while you learn how to win. Learning to play saxophone will cost you hours of practicing in the shed. Learning about drugs could cost you lots of money, hangovers, bad trips, bad deals or even some hard time. Learning about women and sex could cost you… but it might be a lot of fun while you pay.

I had bunches of girls and eventually I would lose Jackie because of my affairs. I didn't know how much she meant to me until I lost her. Losing her turned me into a lovelorn poet. I would spend hours sitting on a bench in the median of Broadway pining for her and writing paeans to love. That episode taught me that you don't know what the blues is until you've had a love you've lost. I learned that love is of penultimate importance. But that wouldn't stop my oats-sowing, philandering ways.

I also learned that there are several ways to transition from adolescence to adulthood. In Africa you might be sent to "finishing school" out in the bush with some elders to receive your manhood training. In other societies you might go serve time in the military to become a man. College is another way you go through that passage into being a grown person. Some guys take longer to grow up than others.

But some of the most important things I learned during this period of my life were in the areas of politics and the history of human development. Reading Franz Fanon, James Baldwin, and manifestos on various "isms" and political movements changed my world view. Hearing the civil rights leaders on television and hearing Malcolm X on Harlem street corners challenged my thinking, my inactivity and my commitment. Debates with fellow students, black and white, some of the brightest minds of the generation, convinced me of the inadequacy of my previous education and experiences to inform my opinions on these serious issues. The conservative views of my parent's generation and the way of life in the South were insufficient for moving forward toward broader horizons. The times, they were a-changing, and so was I.

One thing for sure, I wasn't in Richmond anymore and becoming a chemist to work for DuPont and supporting the military was no longer the career path I was navigating. I thought I might become a writer, a poet or musician. I tried my hand at entrepreneurial activities. Of course, I was directing my band. But I wasn't pursuing my studies. In January of 1968, the start of the second semester of my junior year, I dropped out of school.

In April of that year Martin Luther King was assassinated. Two weeks after that, Columbia's campus erupted in a rebellion. In the weeks leading up to the outbreak and campus takeover, there were debates and demonstrations about Columbia University's plan to construct a new gymnasium in Morningside Park, the area that separates the campus from Harlem. The symbolism of the great white university seizing territory from the black community was made all the more egregious with the assassination of Dr. M. L. King. So in protest the Student Afro-American Society (SAS) and the Students for a Democratic Society (SDS), the white activist organization, took over and occupied the dean's offices located in Hamilton Hall, for a brief time holding the dean hostage.

After the building was occupied and the dean had been released, there were great debates as to the next strategic moves. The SDS group wanted to take "revolutionary" actions like destroying records and equipment. The blacks wanted to make a non-violent political statement of solidarity with Harlem. The whites wanted to expand the focus of the demonstration to include the Viet Nam War and other global issues. The black students wanted to keep the focus on black civil rights issues. So it was decided that the whites would leave Hamilton Hall and go take over other campus buildings, including the president's office in Low Law Library.

Though I was no longer an enrolled student, I was still very actively involved socially, musically and politically. When we took over Hamilton Hall,

I was assigned to man the telephone switchboard because working with the old-style, plug-in wires to connect calls had been one of my work-study jobs as a freshman. During the early hours and days of the takeover I never left my post, answering and forwarding calls through what was the main switchboard for the school's administration.

We were getting calls from civil rights leaders like Stokley Carmichael and H. Rap Brown and from other Harlem leaders showing solidarity with our efforts. Because April was the time that acceptance letters went out to the incoming freshman class, I was also fielding calls from frantic parents inquiring about what the takeover might mean for their young sons' future at Columbia. I told them that there might not be a next school year or campus at all.

As the days of the rebellion wore on there were negotiations with the administration about how it would end. The SDS group vowed to go out with a violent confrontation with the "pigs." The right wing "jocks" wanted to go in and bust the head of the SDS "pukes." The blacks were told if they left peacefully they would not be attacked and would not be expelled. We were also warned that any "outside agitators" would be prosecuted to the fullest extent of the law. Because I was no longer enrolled, I did not have any standing to be there, so after five days; I slipped out under the cover of darkness, hours before the mass arrests and the violent confrontation between the police and SDS.

The Columbia rebellion in April 1968 ended in mass arrests when the black students were herded out of Hamilton Hall and with an intense and violent police action against the white students. Some of the black student leaders were beaten, apparently targeted by the police. The white students were stampeded and assaulted by riot gear equipped police, some on horseback. Afterward the campus looked like a war zone and some believed the revolution was at hand.

The Columbia rebellion of 1968 was a significant event in that era. It was one of the very first campus takeovers at a major university. It placed Columbia along with the University of California at Berkeley as two of the most important bastions of student anti-war activity and progressive political thought. That April 1968 action set off a wave of campus anti-war demonstrations that would lead up to the National Guard shootings at Kent State in 1970. Those demonstrations also led to the eventual ending of the war in Viet Nam and the elimination of the draft system of conscription. The Columbia rebellion has been the subject of numerous articles, books and at least one four-hour documentary film.

In April 2008, the 40 year anniversary of the Columbia protest, a weekend conference was held on campus as a reunion to reflect on and reexamine the issues and outcomes of the campus rebellion of all those years ago. I was only able to attend for the last day-and-a-half of the three-day program of events.

Here are my random thoughts written after the "Columbia 1968 + 40" event:

Full circle is a meaningful route to travel, especially when its arc spans 40 years. Revisiting one's roots can have the revitalizing effect of jogging the memory and clarifying some things buried under the accumulated dust.

The occasion of the 40th anniversary of the 1968 Columbia University student protests, which resulted in over 700 arrests and scores of injuries, brought me back to the campus. I didn't realize how much I had forgotten, how far I had moved on, or how profoundly I have been affected by my (our) experiences there.

I had thought about not going to the reunion. I had a gig with my band in Richmond on Friday night, so I had to miss the fireworks of that night's "What Happened?" event on campus. I wondered how and if it could be worth the drive, the expense and time to just put in an appearance on Saturday. But boy what an enjoyable, exciting and enlightening time I had in my brief time at the Columbia 1968 + 40 event! Faces, places and anecdotes brought back a flood of memories.

I missed the Saturday afternoon luncheon in Harlem, which everybody said was "da bomb!" But I made it to the Saturday night Voices of 1968 event that featured writers reading their works from and about their experiences during those turbulent and formative times. I was moved by the power of their words. Although it was largely a White literary event, it was like church for me, the church of the holy inspired activism. It was like a homecoming. And, it was gratifying to hear how different factions perceived and felt the proceedings of the protest week and its aftermath.

All of the writers were brilliant and insightful. I was moved by a woman who read a poetic work about lying on the paved stones of the campus walk to block the entrance of the mounted police to protect her building-occupying compatriots, while knowing she was pregnant with her first born. I was stunned to hear from a writer whose father had been killed during that period by the dark forces of the police state. I was inspired by the story of professors who formed a protective ring around the Low library to protect the protesters from the right wing "jocks" who wanted to beat up the "pukes." I smiled at the thought of those writers who attempted to write poems in the midst of a rebellion. I was awed by the defiance of those who were undaunted by the harsh putdown of the protest and went on to pursue revolutionary aims by forming the Weather Underground, taking a Bob Dylan song lyric more seriously than even he probably intended.

In the Saturday night audience were several members of my inner cadre of friends: Arnim Johnson, Ray Gaspard, Kent (Rashid) Parker, Alexis Scott-Reeves. I was happy to see the revolutionary poet Ngoma, a Richmond native who did not attend Columbia, but showed up because he knew the event had value and meaning.

I was stunned and moved to see Ntozake Shange move ever so haltingly down the aisle with the aid of a walker, reminding me that no matter how young of mind and spirit I am on the inside, I am, we are, now a part of the old guard. Still avant, but older, nonetheless.

After reading her poem, Ntozake made her way out of the auditorium. I rushed to see if I could be of assistance and to let her know I was there and appreciated her work and the past we share. I was asked to go get her a cab and found myself out on Amsterdam Avenue, this April night dressed in black and trying in vain to hail a taxi. A young twenty-something white girl came up behind me and asked if she could help. She was able to get a cab to stop and she told me that she was a grad student doing her dissertation on Ntozake's writings.

I realized how important writers have been in my life. All my girlfriends at Columbia were and are writers and publishers, and I never before made that connection. Thulani, one of the organizers of the commemorative event who deserves all our unadulterated gratitude, was a superlative poet even 40 years ago. I often refer to her as my first wife because we lived together for the five years, bridging the 1968 strike and the years when I was a fugitive from the FBI as an anti-war deserter from the army, our time in San Francisco as supporters of Angela Davis, the Soledad Brothers and my earliest years as an avant-garde jazz musician and Strata-East Records producer, among a host of other things and activities. She was my support system for which I could never express enough gratitude and love.

I got goose pimples talking to Paul Berman, who played trombone beside me all those months in the Soul Syndicate, and hearing him reminisce about me leading the band into battle and encouraging new levels of creativity. He has since become a professional writer who was at one time on staff with Thulani at the Village Voice. Paul asked me to remind Cicero Wilson, back then one of the leaders of Student Afro-American Society (SAS) and drummer in our band, how Paul had arranged a meeting between Cicero, the leaders of SAS and Mark Rudd and the leaders of SDS on the night before the April 1968 protest. Paul thinks that he may have been the only person who could have facilitated such a powwow. He recalled that the student leaders met that night for several hours and had concluded the meeting believing that most likely nothing would happen that next fateful day.

When we took over Hamilton Hall I volunteered to man the switchboard, handling all phone communications in and out of the building for over 56 straight hours. One of my work-study jobs had been operating the switchboard in Furnald Hall in my freshman year so I knew the equipment. I left Hamilton Hall before the arrests because I had quit school in January and I would have been treated as an "outside agitator" had I been arrested. I would be drafted into the army later that year.

Frankly, I had forgotten that we were so radical. While in recent years I have cited my segregated Southern childhood, my public school education, my high school socializing, and my Black family and the sixties civil rights events as the most formative experiences contributing to my current political and social views, in fact, it was my years during and just after my matriculation at Columbia, 1965 – 1973, that radicalized me and made me a revolutionary artist.

I had forgotten that Jack Kerouac, Allen Ginsberg, Tom Hayden, Phil Ochs and so much of the Beat Generation, hippie culture and the white radical left were associated with Columbia. One writer related that he had few years ago tried to get his government files from that era and was told that he couldn't have them because they were a part of an ongoing criminal investigation. The audience laughed.

I went to the Omega House later on Saturday night to be reminded how strong the bonds between us Black people are, how we party with a purpose and how we are a family. The news headlines - the Jeremiah Wright story, the Sean Bell verdict and this Columbia reunion of protesters - reminded me that those of us in the most progressive wing of our movement have to continue to struggle. But in this YouTube age we must know that timing, strategic planning and coordinated efforts are often trumped by images, demeanor and television set designs. We progressives are being asked to suppress our agenda, soften our voices and wait until after the elections to agitate for more media time. Yet the killings in our community do not wait. We are asked to bear yet another heavy price for the possibility of a grand PR coup, the historical forward step of a Black president.

Lessons from the weekend headlines: we may know the truth and can preach it, but pride still goeth before the fall. We may have a Black man running for president but the police with impunity are still gunning down unarmed Black men.

The Sunday morning memorial service at Earl Hall was well attended and moving. We called the names and remembered our fallen comrades. I played "Amazing Grace" and "Take My Hand, Precious Lord" and got two standing ovations. Once again, I brought soul music to Columbia campus proceedings.

On Saturday afternoon I visited Furnald Hall, my old dorm, and remembered how many hours I spent camped out in that lobby, playing bridge, in debates or just holding court like some southern social advisor. While walking past South Lawn I watched a group of current students playing touch football and remembered playing so many of those games myself 40 years ago, with Kent Parker throwing long touchdown passes to me as I speedily outran the white boys way back then. On this 2008 afternoon, the football bounced over the hedge; I retrieved it and tossed it back to the only Black guy on the field. Full circle.

⌘⌘⌘

Chapter 3

After Columbia – What a Trip!

I am, by calling, a dealer in words; and words are, of course, the most powerful drug used by mankind. — Rudyard Kipling

I dropped out of Columbia in January 1968. I was disillusioned and disoriented.

After some weeks of bumming around I moved into a Barnard College women's dormitory suite with my girlfriend, Barbara, and her four roommates. It was a bit of a risky inconvenience for them; but for me, the vagabond, it was better than some of the other crash pads and slum apartments I had otherwise habited during the time before moving into the dorm.

Barbara was an arty, politically astute young black woman from Hampton, Virginia. She was a year younger than I and she had fallen for my swagger and my music. Though I acted like the alpha male around her, she was smart, versatile and destined to be an accomplished writer. She and I were both poets and revolutionaries, sharp-witted with soft cores. I was her knight in shining armor and she was my protector. We would stay together for over five years, through thick and thin, through tribulations and adventures.

Though I was the musician, Barbara schooled me about jazz. She knew the music at deeper levels; and she introduced me to the likes of Charlie Mingus, Thelonious Monk, Nina Simone, Billie Holiday, Max Roach, Sunny Murray, Sun Ra and beyond. I was Plunky; but she treated me like I was Dexter Gordon or Junior Walker or Maceo. She loved my music and my poetry and I loved hers. With her smarts, hipness and spunk, she could fit in anywhere I might go. She respected everything I did, and she liked or tolerated everyone who hung around me. Except for Bruce B.

Bruce was a Columbia classmate who was as different from me as day from night. We met in our freshman year and became a kind of an odd couple. He was a weird, white guy from Long Island into rock & roll; and I was a hip, black guy from the South, and very much into soul and jazz. But he and I could hang out, listen to music, walk and talk for hours on end.

Between 1966 and '68 we listened to rock music, all kinds of rock music: British rock, folk rock, psychedelic rock and the rock of groups like the Beatles, Rolling Stones, the Byrds, The Band, Bob Dylan, Buffalo Springfield, Crosby, Stills & Nash, Neil Young, Jimi Hendrix, Sly Stone, etc. And we experimented with a wide range of different drugs, including the psychedelics.

Tripping on acid was life changing. Hallucinating on LSD was more than fascinating, it was mind blowing. Acid altered your vision, turning lights into glowing prismatic spheres, and turning anything in motion into moving shapes with comet tails trailing behind. Tripping could be mentally numbing or exhilarating. It could cause a kind of psychosis, turning a bad trip into a timeless journey into paranoia. It could also seem spiritually empowering, giving one the impression that whatever was imagined could be made real, at will.

But often acid just made us do stupid things. Like the time Bruce and I sat down on the sidewalk on Broadway with our backs leaning against the mathematics building believing and telling passers-by that we were holding it up. Or later, during that same trip, the two of us stood on the yellow lines in the middle of Amsterdam Avenue facing uptown with cars whizzing by on either side, believing we were actually skiing down the eight block slope running from 118th Street to 125th. Another time we went to the beach, stood on a floating giant piece of a wooden pier, and drifted out to sea on our way to Europe or Africa; and then miraculously drifted back in to shore.

For all the fun & games, beautiful visions, and expansive mental excursions associated with psychedelic experiences, there were also down sides. For every one of the soaring flights into fanciful nirvanas, there were the crashes of coming back down to reality. Some of the trips ended in debilitating, depressing returns to the realization that the paradises were all just drug induced stupors that cost money, hours and maybe some of your brain cells.*

---

*January, 2015 - A new wave of research on the medical applications of psychedelic drugs has suggested that these substances may hold considerable promise as therapeutic interventions for a number of mental health conditions. And according to another new study, use of "classic" psychedelics — psilocybin (magic mushrooms), LSD and mescaline — may also be an effective suicide prevention measure. A growing body of

The late sixties and early 1970s were crazy times, made crazier by all the drugs. Sex, Drugs and rock & roll was a phrase commonly used to describe the scene. For me it would have been Sax, drugs and rock & soul. These activities were fun, and to some extent fundamental. Music and sex were perpetual and pervasive. Marijuana was omnipresent and cocaine was readily available. For a time herb was smoked before and after, and sometimes during everything: before and after almost every meal, rehearsal, gig, listening session, sex episode and drive to anyplace. Marijuana was used to enhance tastes, sensations and creativity; and it increased appreciation and enjoyment of music. I wondered if my own music creativity actually depended on being high; but happily once I stopped smoking I found that I could be just as imaginative and even more disciplined when straight. (Now, later in my career, I don't use any intoxicants, not even a glass of wine, when I am performing or creating; though I might reward myself when the workday or week's tasks are all done.)

But, drugs and other mind altering potions have likely always been a part of the musicians' and artists' arsenal as triggers and gateways to muses. Traditional Africans may have used special potions and smokeables. Native Americans used peyote and sacred mushrooms. Edgar Allen Poe may have used heroin. The Grateful Dead and Aldous Huxley took acid. Hemmingway drank. Gertrude Stein and Alice B. Toklas ingested marijuana. Louis Armstrong smoked herb daily. Who knows, Sly Stone and George Clinton may have smoked and snorted some of everything; and I love their funk.

In August 1968 (five months after the Columbia campus rebellion), students demonstrated in Chicago during the Democratic Party National Convention. The mood among the progressives had been both somber and agitated due to the assassinations of Martin Luther King in April and Robert Kennedy in June and the intense opposition to the Viet Nam War. The radicalization and mobilization of hundreds of student groups, including SDS and the Youth International Party (**YIPPIES**) led to the massive anti-war demon-

---

research has shown that psychedelics may have promise as therapeutic interventions for a range of psychological conditions, including anxiety, depression, obsessive-compulsive disorder and post-traumatic stress disorder. The findings were published in the journal Psychopharmacology.

strations outside the Democratic convention. The riotous demonstrations were violently put down by the Chicago police and National Guard troops and it was all shown live on national television.

This was a seminal event in an extraordinary decade for the civil rights and anti-war movements. The riots in Chicago led to the indictment of eight of the protest organizers; and, a year later the trial and conviction of the "Chicago Seven." (Initially the group was called the Chicago Eight, but the lone black defendant, Black Panther Bobby Seal, was tried separately after being charged with contempt of court for calling the judge a "fascist dog," a "honky" and a "racist pig." Bobby Seal would be bound, gagged and chained to a chair in the courtroom and later sentenced to four years for contempt of court.)

This was the birth of the "new left," a loose coalition of counterculture proponents challenging the social, economic and cultural basis of American society. It was certainly not all fun and games; the movement had shown that it could spark violent interactions.

Naively, I romanticized the model of revolution as a means to reboot and set things right. The history of the U.S. is replete with so many transgressions against people of color and blacks in particular that I thought that tearing the whole system down might be the only way for redress. But my idealized vision of revolution did not fully take into account the physical pains, violence, and economic destruction that such a civil war would bring. Riots in black neighborhoods, on college campuses and in the streets outside the Chicago political convention gave me a glimpse of the chaos that would befall our cities in a revolution, and I didn't like it. Even on television.

Two weeks after the Chicago riots, Bruce and I drove across country from New York to San Francisco. What a trip!

A cheap way to travel across country was to use an auto drive-away system, delivering a car by driving it to a destination. In September of 1968 we had been on the waiting list for a car to be delivered to California all summer long, but we were not fortunate enough to get a car going to that very popular destination. But the company told us they had a car that needed to be delivered to Las Cruses, New Mexico. We looked at the map and said that it was close enough for us. So we decided we'd take the car to New Mexico, and then hitch-hike the rest of the way to San Francisco.

To our great surprise, the car we had to deliver was a new, black, shiny, convertible Corvette Stingray. It belonged to an Air Force captain who had, soon after he bought the car, been sent overseas for two years. He had recently been re-stationed at the base in Las Cruses and he wanted to have his car brought out there to him. Wow! And what a fantastic car it was. And little did he know it would be driven by two hippie-type young guys, one black and one white. Bruce and I were driving across country in a convertible sports car, like Robert Culp and Bill Cosby in the television show, "I Spy," only we'd be stoned and making mischief.

Rather than drive straight toward New Mexico we decided to go to Milwaukee to see a friend; and from there we went to Chicago to see the sites where the rioting had taken place two weeks earlier. When we were leaving Chicago we were followed by a cop car and just as we got to the edge of town, we were stopped. The cop wanted to know who we were, why we two hippie punks had this high performance sports car, and if we were up to no good. After checking out our paperwork for the car, searching and harassing us, he said, "Get your heads out of your asses, get out of town and don't ever come back!"

Since we were in a Corvette we decided we would take Route 66, just like on the television show, Route 66, two guys traveling across America in a convertible Corvette. On the highway just outside of Chicago, we saw a hippie couple hitchhiking. We decided to check out the freaks. (That was what we called obvious counterculture drug compatriots.) When we stopped to talk to what was a very attractive hippie couple, they told us they had dropped acid and decided they wanted to go see some mountains, so they were hitchhiking out west, hopefully to the Rockies. We said, "Far out!" But since the 'Vette only had two seats we were sorry but we couldn't give them a ride.

"Born to Be Wild' by Steppenwolf had just come out, and it seemed that every radio station along our Route 66 journey was playing it, so it was like the theme song for our trip. We sang it at the top of our lungs whenever it came on and we were barreling down the highway. When we got just outside St. Louis, a car passed us blowing the horn. In it was the hippie couple we had seen outside Chicago. They had obviously hitched a ride. They signaled for us to pull over and we did. The guy driving them wasn't going all the way into St. Louis and because it was nightfall, we decided they could crowd in the 'Vette with us at least as far as the city. It was cramped, but fun any way, especially when with the top down and the Steppenwolf song came on, we all sang out into the summer night sky, "Born to be wild...!"

We dropped them off in a park in downtown St. Louis. They had long since come down off their acid high and were regretting the dumb idea of hitchhiking out for a Rocky Mountain high. They had no coats, just tie-dyed tee shirts, so I gave them one of our two blankets, and said farewell.

Bruce and I had a great trip. We decided we would drive over to Denver which was way out of the way; but how often would we have a chance to travel so free and at such high speed. We had thought that the car's owner would be paying for our gas, but when we checked the paperwork we discovered that the contract stated that only the first tank full was prepaid; the rest of the gas and oil was on us. So we used only regular grade gas, never checked the oil and we went twice as many miles as was required.

By the time we got to Las Cruses, the car was sputtering and smoking. When we got to the Air Force base we were hoping that the 'Vette would make it to the captain's quarters. When we got there, he was furious. He didn't like us and he hated the condition of his Corvette. He was so angry, he wouldn't even give us a ride to the highway and there was no bus headed west, so our only options were to go back 30 miles to El Paso, Texas or to try to thumb a ride west toward California. We decided to try to thumbing.

We stood out in the hot desert sun trying to hitch a westward ride. Yeah, sure; a white hippie and a black activist-looking guy had two chances for that happening: slim and none. None came up. The sun was blazing in a clear sky. A way off in the distance there was a tiny black speck of a cloud that took the whole day to make its way toward us. Late in the evening it was huge and directly overhead; and it dumped a horrendous rain storm on our heads. Luckily there was a small underpass which gave us a little shelter. Now if you've never spent a day and night on the desert, you may not know that, yes, it does rain sometimes, and it can get as cold as a witch's tit at night. We spent a cold, wet night there, sharing one blanket, because we had given mine to the hitchhiking hippie couple in St. Louis!

The next morning we decided to give up on trying to get a ride headed west, so we crossed to the other side of the road to head east back toward Texas. The first car that came by screeched to a halt and the driver said, "Need a ride? Hop in!" And we did. He said, "Where you headed?" We said, "We're trying to get to California." He said, "That's where we're headed." I said, "But you're headed east!" He said, "I know," and swung the car around in a squealing u-turn.

Ted (not his real name because I don't remember his name) explained that they had just passed us when we were on the westward side of the road and they decided to turn around and pick us up, but by the time they got back to where we were, we had crossed over headed east. But now we were in for a wild westward-ho ride!

It turned out that Ted, who was from eastern Canada, had an argument with his wife, stole her credit card, rented a car and was on a wild joyride across the U.S. He had pick up a 16-year-old boy in upstate New York and a 19 or 20-year-old chick in New Jersey and the three of them were having a joyous adventure driving to California.

As soon as they picked us up, Ted asked Bruce to drive. With Bruce, the young guy and I in the front seat, Ted got in the back seat with the chick so they could neck and pet. At one point we were driving on the highway alongside a train track and Bruce decide to race the train at 100 MPH. Well, of course we got pulled over by a highway patrol; but there was no speed limit. So after checking Ted's identification and ascertaining that the car was legally rented in his name, the cop let us go.

After a wild day's ride, we made it to Yuma, Arizona and Ted rented us all motel rooms (on his wife's credit card, of course.) In the middle of the night, he came to Bruce and my room to tell us that he had called home and his wife told him if he did not get back to Canada in two days, she was going to call the FBI and have him arrested. So he said he was leaving right then and leaving the young chick there.

Bruce and I got up and left at sunrise, taking a Greyhound Bus to San Diego. And from there we flew up to San Francisco. The trip had cost us more time and more money than if we had just flown direct from NY, but the wild rides and adventures had been worth it.

San Francisco was a Mecca of counter culture and hippydom. One area of the city in particular, Haight-Ashbury District (or "the Haight"), the neighborhood around the intersection of Haight and Ashbury Streets was populated by hippies (freaks) living in communes, eating vegetarian health foods, doing yoga, having free rock concerts and love-ins in Panhandle Park, and taking and smoking a lot of dope.

The City of San Francisco took a hands-off policy regarding policing the area, and marijuana and psychedelic drugs were abundantly available.

Hippies could be selling ounces of Marijuana on the street and a cop would come up to tell them, "Just move around the corner with your stuff, Man."
San Francisco became a destination to be visited by hippies and tourists from all over the country. The hippies would come to see what life could be like if they were free to create their own urban legal and social environment. What if free love, communal living, psychedelic music, tie-dyed cloth and paisley buildings were allowed to flourish? It would look like the Haight-Ashbury. Tour buses would cruise through the Haight full of straight visitors gawking out the windows pointing at the freaks. Hippies were good for the local economy.

The San Francisco Bay Area included the city, Oakland, Berkeley (with the famed University of California campus), Marin County and it extended down the peninsula to San Jose and Palo Alto (and Stanford University). The area was as progressive as any place in the country. The UC Berkeley campus was home to radically left, strongly anti-war students and faculty. Oakland would be the birthplace of the Black Panther Party. And San Francisco had a widely diverse, politically-aware, third world population that included almost equal shares of Blacks, Chicanos, Chinese, Japanese, Filipinos, gays and others.

There was an imaginary pipeline between San Francisco and New York. Progressive political ideas were being promulgated and promoted on both coasts; and, sometimes these ideas seemed to fly right over the heads of Middle America. Theoretical social and economic systems discussed at eastern universities might play out in California communes. Protest tactics developed at Berkeley might be utilized by students at Yale or Columbia. Black power organizing in Oakland and L.A. might be replicated in Harlem and NewArk.

And the pipeline between New York and San Francisco also transported drugs as well as political idealism. In those days college students could fly at half-price or cheaper using student discount cards readily available from the airline companies. (As a student, I could fly between New York and Richmond, VA for $23! Sometimes the NY to Cali fares would be as low as $59.) Also, the prices for marijuana and psychedelics in California were way, way cheaper than the prices on the East Coast, because most of the grass was grown in Mexico and the acid was manufactured in the Bay area.

The combination of cheap airfares and cheap drugs created ample opportunities for profitable businesses. The trade route was made safe because in those pre-hijacking days, airports were safe havens. Because only the rich, upper middle class people and students flew, airports and planes had little or no security or police presence. In contrast to these 21st century days of TSA screenings, high-tech heavy security, luggage x-rays and no-fly lists, back then, air travel was so unguarded and so safe.

I knew guys who made their living carrying suitcases of contraband from the West Coast to the East. They would say their biggest worry was travel through the city streets by car; because once they got to the airport, they could breathe a sigh of relief, having made it to the safe haven of those gateways to the friendly skies. They would regularly fly back and forth between NY and Frisco, sometimes with carry-on luggage filled with 50 pounds of weed, with no worry or cares about getting caught. In fact, the red-eye weekend midnight flights from Frisco to NY were notoriously filled with young, transporting freaks, partying on the planes.

(Of course, this trade route would be all but shut down with the advent of the political hijacking of airplanes and terrorism.)

The guys I knew who did that business were Ivy League students from Columbia. They were smart and entrepreneurial. Some were freaks, some straight. Later in life, one would go on to become a Broadway producer. One would go into import-export. Another would become a New York judge! Some were in it simply for the money and some had a political agenda. Some were social ideologues for whom ideas about creating a counterculture were not nihilistic, but experiential. They were all rebels with or without a cause.

Legal prohibitions can cause the rise of black markets. Black markets can be exploited for purely micro-economic profits; and black markets can be used for macro-economic systems. Drug-dealing hippies were sometimes conscious supporters of the development of a counter culture. Drug profits could be funneled into supporting political movements. At the international level in more modern times, revolutionaries, mafias, cartels, terrorist groups, and other underground movements have used drug profits to fund their agendas. The U.S. government has been accused of using drugs in its Counterintelligence Program (Cointelpro) and its Ollie North led Iran-Contra operation, among other scandalous enterprises.

Drugs have long been purported to have financed many entertainment enterprises, from music projects, movies, casinos, night clubs, speak-easies, tours and media companies. Entertainment has often been a loosely regulated industry, ripe for laundering ill-gotten gains.

Sometimes mafias, cartels and other macro criminal operations controlled large swaths of the music and entertainment fields. Sometimes these criminal elements were aggressive and sinister in their control and exploitation of artists. With large sums invested in payola in radio, control of major venues and night clubs, gangsters would often use strong-arm tactics to keep their investments profitable and to minimize competition.

Sometimes the illegal activities have been small-time and relatively benign. A rock band funding their first recording or tour with the profits from selling herb (grass) was not unheard of. A Grateful Dead-type psychedelic rock group might bring music and acid to its audiences for fun and profit. A black funk group might deal in drugs to finance their own consumption habits. Certain rap artists were known to have been street level dealers before finding fame and fortune in hip-hop.

The intersection of music, politics, drugs and economics created a countercultural vortex and its ripple effects have lasted for years. Supply, demand and third party intercessions; macroeconomic and grand conspiracy theories; festivals of music, massive multimedia multinationals, and massive social media trends reordering of the entertainment industry and society at large – it's all about sex, drugs and rock& roll, Man.

A life's journey can and will have lots of twists and turnings. There will be side roads, dead ends, tangents, circuitous routes, pit stops and direct straight-line paths between destinations. The challenge is to learn from and enjoy and be made better by each leg of your journey.

The one thing I would say about my life is "What a trip!"

The war on drugs has been an abject, trillion dollar failure. Hippies knew fifty years ago that marijuana was a relatively benign intoxicant, was not a gateway drug, had potential medicinal uses, and had no known overdose. It is probably not possible to outlaw stupidity. Some of the outcomes and repercussions of laws can't be determined at the point of their enacting. But there ought to be a statute of limitation on how long stupidity should be allowed to stand. If after 50 years a law or policy is ineffective or counterproductive, then it should automatically be revoked. If after 50 years of a war on drugs which was supposed to reduce both supply and demand, we find that use and availability are up and prices down; then that war should be declared lost. And instead of spending billions on police, interdiction and incarceration, we should tax the consumption of marijuana and make money on the deal. We should decriminalize drug possession, strongly advocate for reduced drug consumption, and treat addiction as the mental and medical problem that it is.

These facts are cited by The Drug Policy Alliance (DPA), the nation's leading organization promoting drug policies that are grounded in science, compassion, health and human rights:

Amount spent annually in the U.S. on the war on drugs: More than $51,000,000,000.

Number of people arrested in 2013 in the U.S. on nonviolent drug charges: 1.5 million

Number of people arrested for a marijuana law violation in 2013: 693,482

Number of those charged with marijuana law violations who were arrested for possession only: 609,423 (88 percent)

Number of Americans incarcerated in 2013 in federal, state and local prisons and jails: 2,220,300 or 1 in every 110 adults, the highest incarceration rate in the world.

Proportion of people incarcerated for a drug offense in state prison who are black or Latino, although these groups use and sell drugs at similar rates as whites: 61 percent

Number of states that allow the medical use of marijuana: 23 + District of Columbia   Number of states that have approved legally taxing and regulating marijuana: 4 (Alaska, Colorado, Oregon and Washington)

Estimated annual revenue that California would raise if it taxed and regulated the sale of marijuana: $1,400,000,000

Number of people killed in Mexico's drug war since 2006: 100,000+

Number of students who have lost federal financial aid eligibility because of a drug conviction: 200,000+

Number of people in the U.S. who died from a drug overdose in 2013: 43,982

Tax revenue that drug legalization would yield annually, if currently-illegal drugs were taxed at rates comparable to those on alcohol and tobacco: $46.7 billion.

The Centers for Disease Control and Prevention found that syringe access programs lower HIV incidence among people who inject drugs by: 80 percent

One-third of all AIDS cases in the U.S. have been caused by syringe sharing: 354,000 people

U.S. federal government support for syringe access programs: $0.00, thanks to a federal ban reinstated by Congress in 2011 that prohibits any federal assistance for them

Portugal decriminalized personal drug use over 12 years ago. Since then possession of small amounts of marijuana, cocaine or heroin is a misdemeanor on par with a parking ticket. Some experts are pleased with the results of this societal approach to the issue.

A fantastic, new book on the subject is available: *"Chasing the Scream: The First and Last Days of the War On Drugs"* by Johann Hari. Here's what a few reviewers say about the book:

"Johann Hari's book is the perfect antidote to the war on drugs, one of the most under-discussed moral injustices of our time. It combines rigorous research and deeply human storytelling. It will prompt urgently needed debate."
-         —Glen Greenwald, Pulitzer Prize winner

"Wonderful... I couldn't put it down."
-         —Noam Chomsky

"This book is as intoxicatingly thrilling as crack, without destroying your teeth. It will change the drug debate forever."
-         —Russell Brand

"In this energetic and thought-proving book, Hari harnesses the power of personal narrative to reveal the true causes and consequences of the war on drugs."
-         — David Nutt, former chief science advisor on drugs to the
British government

⌘⌘⌘

Chapter 4

The Army

In the fall of 1968 I received a draft notice. The draft system was patently unfair. It was administered and manipulated in ways that allowed rich, privileged kids not to be sent to war. College guys got deferments. Black and brown young men more often ended up on the front lines. I couldn't imagine a worse fate: conscripted to fight a controversial war that I and many of my generation were totally against.

I went home to Richmond to take my pre-induction physical examination. Though my blood pressure was low, it was not quite low enough to render me ineligible for service. Hoping to fail the final medical exam, I took high blood pressure medication to lower my pressure even more, during the weeks before I was to report for induction. The medication I took gave me terrible headaches and I was sure I would fail the second physical. When I went to the induction, they didn't even test me a second time.

When it came time to be sworn in, I refused the draft. My father worked for the IRS in the federal building where the draft board was housed. It didn't take long for him to know what I had done. He was warned that he and my mother, a teacher, could both lose their jobs. For the sake of the family, including my two younger brothers, my teary eyed parents convinced me to go back and go in to the army. From the very moment that I stepped forward to accept my fate, I was determined to get out.

I was shipped to Fort Benning, Georgia, for basic training. On the train I met Plunie Pleasants, a young black guy from my Richmond neighborhood. Plunie had been living in Baltimore when he was drafted. We hit it off immediately. While I was dour, political and serious, he was funny, upbeat and jovial. We had in common, however, a mutual revulsion for the army, and all things right-wing.

During my first week in the army, I went on a hunger strike. My plan was to further weaken myself so that I might have a physical breakdown, disqualifying me from service. But my fasting broke down abruptly on day six when roast chicken was served.

While my army stint would only last several weeks, it was a humorous tragedy a la Hogan's Heroes, Mash and Gomer Pyle U.S.M.C., all together. Plunie and I were placed in a company of 160 guys divided into four platoons. In the previous two basic training cycles, two young draftees had died and our drill sergeants were under investigation. They were advised that two undercover CID lieutenants would be planted in the unit to determine if the drill sergeants were excessively violent. From the very beginning, the sergeants surmised that it was Plunie and Plunky who were the two undercover lieutenants.

Plunie used humor to disarm people and get out of tight spots. I was direct and defiant. The more obvious my defiance, the more convinced the sergeants were that I was the undercover spy trying to provoke them into violent action; and they weren't going to take the bait. No matter what protests, antics or debates I initiated, they pretty much let slide. Crazy. There I was, a counterculture, subversive agitator trying to undermine authority and be disciplined, and they mistook me for a covert army officer. What an ironic joke!

Basic training was eight weeks of hazing, physical conditioning and mental toughening. Although the training was standardized and non-specific, it seemed, somehow, individually tailored, as well. If you were fat, you'd lose weight; if you were skinny you'd gain weight. If you were wild, you'd be tranquilized. If you were timid, they'd make you aggressive. At the end of the basic training pipeline you'd be a sharpshooting, fighting automaton ready to give your life for your unit and your country.

CID Captain Bob would visit every few days, paging me over the camp speakers, "Private Branch, report to CQ under order from CID." The drill sergeants would exchange knowing looks. The CID captain would often pick me up in his little convertible Ford Falcon and we would ride around base talking about drugs and hippies. This ruse often got me out of the more unpleasant basic training duties, with the exception of rifle training and bivouac, which were mandatory.

I had told everyone that I was going to refuse rifle training on the basis of being a conscientious objector, but Capt. Bob and others warned that I could be sent to the stockade for refusing that training. I changed my mind and decided to get the training because I believed that the black revolution was on

Army ID card

the verge of erupting, and the firearms training would serve me well.

On the first day of rifle training, we were told that we would use a BB rifle to shoot and hit a 50 cent coin tossed in the air. It sounded unlikely, but by shooting from the hip and not "aiming," but using a swivel motion and relying on instinct, we were able to hit the coin with remarkable frequency. The exercise demonstrated that while we can train our muscles and learn techniques, we are often, equally, if not more, efficient when we relax and use instincts to guide our actions. (These many years later, I have still found this to be true whether shooting basketballs, hitting tennis shots, or playing complex musical passages on the saxophone: to be most effective under pressure, train, practice, then relax and execute.) In just one week, I learned to shoot an M-16 and hit a target the size of a man at distances of up to 300 yards, and ultimately I earned a "Sharpshooter" rating.

Meanwhile, Plunie was doing all he could to fuel the suspicions about our covert assignments. He worked in the company Command Quarters office and would write fake notes to me like, "Branch, check on Sgt. Ross and file a report on his adherence to procedures. We may be able to bring charges." He would leave the notes where they could be easily discovered. We had them bamboozled. The clincher was when I requested a meeting with the base Chaplain, a Major, to get counseling as I was considering becoming a conscientious objector, a deserter or worse. But the major took the conversation in a different direction, acknowledging that "everybody knew" I was in the CID. Apparently they had "checked the records." And while he understood that I could not blow my cover, he implored me to go easy on the drill sergeants, because they were "good soldiers." Wow! How stupid. The army did not require brilliant, critical thinkers, just people good at following orders, no matter how unwise.

In week seven, most recruits got their first weekend passes, authorizing them to go anywhere within fifty miles of the post. I did not get my first pass until a week later. When I did, I went straight to the airport and bought a one-way ticket to New York[*].

I never went back to Fort Benning, GA. I never saw or heard from Captain Bob or anyone else there, except Plunie. 25 years later he suddenly showed up at my door in Richmond to catch up on old times and to buy my recordings. He shows up again every few years to do the same and I always enjoy seeing him.

It is one thing to have a philosophical overview of politics, war and peace, and conscious responsibilities, and quite another to apply those to one's practical experiences. Sometimes the episodes where theories intersect with living can be tragic, ironic, or downright comical. Sometimes we have to laugh to keep from crying; and sometimes laughter is the best medicine.

I returned to New York a different person. I had gained 20 pounds of muscle. My large Afro had been whacked down to a nearly bald scalp. I was startled by my own reflection in storefront windows. I stayed in Barbara's dorm room and roamed the campus incognito. I also began seeing a Scarsdale psychiatrist who determined that I was psychologically unfit to serve in the army. His file on my neuroses was extensive.

With my shrink's report in hand, I contacted the army medical staff at Fort Benning. I was told to get to Fort Dix in New Jersey and get a travel voucher to come back to Georgia, and if their tests confirmed my doctor's diagnosis, then I would be discharged. When I got to Fort Dix, they asked me how long I had been AWOL; and I told them 59 days. The processing officer said, "Then you don't need a travel voucher, you need a lawyer because you are going to the stockade!" I didn't know that anything more 30 days AWOL was a felonious offense.

During the Viet Nam war times, military stockades were brutal, as bad as or worse than the war zone. This was necessary in order to deter objectors, like me, from opting for prisons rather than Southeast Asia. When I got to the Fort Dix stockade I found the conditions to be like I imagined slavery to be, only with German sadists as overseers. Hard labor and physical mistreatment were the order of everyday. I was able to maintain a modicum of fortitude because I did yoga and the guards and other prisoners thought I was a weird guru. I was steadfast because I thought that once I served my time, I would then be kicked out of the army. Fellow prisoners, more knowledgeable and experienced than I, laughed. Most of them had been AWOL a lot longer. They told me that I would likely be sentenced to a few months in the stockade, and then be sent back to duty.

A funny thing happened on the way to my court martial. The announcement came that everyone who had been AWOL for six months or less would be released immediately and sent back to duty. That's because there were more than twice as many incarcerated "deserters" as the buildings could hold, and more and more AWOL's were coming in every day.

After 30 days in the Fort Dix stockade I was unexpectedly released and ordered to go back to duty. On the day I was released, I hitched a ride with two Puerto Ricans to New York City. I would be gone for three years, a month and five days...

---

*Viet Nam War Facts
War deaths between 1965 and 1974:
    Allied Military 282,000 (U.S. Military 58,220)
    Communist Military   444,000
    Viet Nam Civilian   587,000
    Total deaths: 1,313,000 (not counting Cambodians, Laotians and others in the region)

Black Casualties in Viet Nam (from Wikipedia)
Blacks were suffering disproportionately high casualty rates in Vietnam, and in 1965 alone they comprised almost one out of every four combat deaths. With the draft increasing due to the troop buildup in South Vietnam, the military significantly lowered its admission standards. In October 1966, Defense Secretary Robert McNamara initiated Project 100,000 which further lowered military standards for 100,000 additional draftees per year. McNamara claimed this program would provide valuable training, skills and opportunity to America's poor – a promise that was never carried out. Many black men who had previously been ineligible could now be drafted, along with many poor and racially intolerant white men from the southern states.[61][62] The number of U.S. military personnel in Vietnam jumped from 23,300 in 1965 to 465,600 by the end of 1967. Between October 1966 and June 1969, 246,000 soldiers were recruited through Project 100,000, of which 41% were black, while blacks only made up about 11% of the population of the US.[61]. Of the 27 million draft-age

men between 1964 and 1973, 40% were drafted into military service, and only 10% were actually sent to Vietnam. This group was made up almost entirely of either work-class or rural youth. College students who did not avoid the draft were generally sent to non-combat and service roles or made officers, while high school drop-outs and the working class were sent into combat roles. Blacks often made up a disproportionate 25% or more of combat units, while constituting only 12% of the military.[59][63]

Civil rights leaders including Martin Luther King Jr., Malcolm X, John Lewis, Muhammad Ali, and others, criticized the racial disparity in both casualties and representation in the entire military, prompting the Pentagon to order cutbacks in the number of African Americans in combat positions. Commander George L. Jackson said, "In response to this criticism, the Department of Defense took steps to readjust force levels in order to achieve an equitable proportion and employment of Negroes in Vietnam." The army instigated myriad reforms, addressed issues of discrimination and prejudice from the post exchanges to the lack of black officers, and introduced "Mandatory Watch And Action Committees" into each unit. The proportion of black casualties began to decrease, and by late 1967, black casualties had fallen to 13%, and were below 10% in 1970 to 1972.[61][64]/ Upon the war's completion, black casualties made up 12.5% of U.S. combat deaths, approximately equal to percentage of draft-eligible black men, though still slightly higher than the 10% who served in the military.[64]

Plunky plays at the Martin Luther King monument August 22, 2011

Chapter 5

San Francisco Juju

After I left the army, I went to San Francisco and changed my name. I was still Plunky, but not James Branch. I used a friend's ID and did not communicate directly with my family in Richmond. The FBI's search for me was sporadic but relentless. Agents would show up at my parents' house at odd hours or in the middle of the night, on holidays, birthdays, or after the deaths of family members. Family and neighbors were told they would be arrested for harboring a fugitive if I came around and was not turned in to the authorities. But I stayed on the west coast.

When Barbara graduated from Barnard, I went back to NY; and we drove her convertible VW bug across country and moved into an apartment in the Haight-Asbury district of San Francisco. Over the next few weeks and months, several of our friends also moved to Frisco: Kent, my Soul Syndicate bandmate; Bruce, my trip-mate; Paulette, Barbara's poetess friend; as well as future Chicago attorney, Arnim; future black newspaper publisher Alexis; future San Francisco Sassoon hair stylist Henry, and several others. Our apartment became a welcoming center/crash pad for all the friends and friends of friends who would be relocating to the Bay Area.

We became vegetarians. I did yoga religiously. Barbara got a job writing for the local newspaper. I would try to eke out a living playing music. To find work I went to private jam sessions and rock, jazz and soul clubs. On weekends I'd go over to the Berkeley campus where there would be loads of conga drummers and percussionists jamming. I played with jazz cats, beboppers, organ trios, R&B groups, Latin bands and avant-gardists.
Then I met South African emigrant musician, Ndikho Xaba.

I was introduced to Ndikho and his wife, Nomusa, by a mutual friend who knew Ndikho was putting together a group. After a few rehearsals we

Ndikho Xaba onstage.

quickly bonded and developed a mutual respect and professional admiration. Ndikho saw me as an energetic, young lion of a horn player with soul music experience and an affinity for jazz and the avant garde music of John Coltrane, Sun Ra, and Pharaoh Sanders, et al. I saw Ndikho as a musical mentor, political theorist, and a wild and crazy Zulu revolutionary. Together we were quite a formidable, searing hot, dual core of his group, Ndikho & the Natives.

Ndikho album cover

The members of the Natives were an eclectic crew of individuals with various international origins. In addition to Ndikho and me, there was Keita who was of West Indian descent on drums; Baba Duru who had studied percussion in India on tabla drums, congas and percussion; Lon Moshe (Ron Martin), from the Chicago new music scene on vibraphone; and Ken Shabala (Kent), now a Columbia University graduate and soul singer, on bass.

Ndikho gave us all South African names. I was called (S)Plunky Nkabinde. He said "Nkabinde," literally translated to "tall bull" and he gave me that name because I was lanky and a ladies' man. Ndikho would also bestow new names on Barbara, who became Thulani Nkabinde, and her poetess friend Paulette was renamed Ntozake Shange.

Ndikho & the Natives became recognized for our high energy, percussive, expressive performances. Ndikho used his music and his gigs as opportunities to expound on the political situation in South Africa, African culture and Pan-

Africanism. Our musical repertoire ranged from traditional Zulu songs to romantic, mellow originals; from township jive rhythms to wild screaming depictions of historical battles and the coming revolution.

In the context of that time in the Bay Area with its hippies, anti-war protests, Black Panthers, rock and roll, jazz fusion, and the avant garde jazz movements, Ndikho & the Natives occupied a unique niche. We were Afrocentric and creative. Our group inspired a small but influential collection of artists, fans and followers. We played in cultural centers, political rallies, night clubs, churches, schools, street fairs and even at the Berkeley Jazz Festival. Over the years Ndikho and I would also perform in Detroit, New York and numerous times in Washington, DC.

Ndikho was recruited to record the background music for an LP album by Cousin Wash, a folksy poet/storyteller. Originally I was not so keen on the idea because I thought the project would be too corny, non-commercial, apolitical and un-hip. But as it turned out, Cousin Wash's stories were quite humorous and historically valid and educational. And even more importantly, the project gave us some recording studio experience which led Ndikho to take the opportunity to record an album, Ndikho & the Natives.

I don't remember much about the actual recording session for our album. I do remember that we prepared the songs well before the session and that the songs were recorded live, without overdubs, in one take. I also remember that we were all generally quite pleased with the recording and the experience, though I was, and still am, a bit peeved about a squeak/flub on my soprano sax at the beginning of my solo in the song "Nomusa." In today's studio productions we would fix that "flaw" in one way or another, but back then, preserving the raw, real, "divine error" of the improvised performance was more important.

Ndikho could be described as a renaissance man. As a musician, he is an improvising pianist, percussionist, vocalist, and poet and he is a world-class songwriter, composer, arranger and band leader. Onstage he is an imposing and gifted performer who can be forceful, humorous, romantic, combative, theatrical and inspiring. Ndikho is also an artisan, crafting innovative musical instruments and jewelry out of art materials and found objects. Ndikho always seemed to take on the role of educator, using his music and performances to teach audiences about the history, politics and culture of South Africa.

It was this aspect of Ndikho as an artist-educator that had the most profound effect on me and my musical career. As a living embodiment of the use of African music as a cultural, educational, political and economic resource, he inspired me to incorporate this philosophy into my subsequent musical expressions. Even when I would later move toward more commercial music endeavors, I would still find ways to party with a purpose.

[After more than 30 years Ndikho would find his way back home to South Africa. In 2015 the Ndikho & the Natives album would be reissued in South Africa and Europe. A documentary about his life is in production. I hope that the film will capture some of the story of his and Nomusa's struggles as artists and revolutionaries, raising a family and eking out a living in the U.S., "belly of the beast." Here is the link to a video about the reissuing of the album: https://www.youtube.com/watch?v=xwJ62wauRbQ&feature=youtu.be]

After working with the Natives, my next significant gig was performing as a member of the music group for a theatrical production entitled "The Resurrection of the Dead" by playwright Marvin X. The production was an actual quasi-religious ritual with high energy drumming, music and dancing. During each performance one or more cast members would actually be renamed. The premise of the play was that black people were in a state of being dead: unaware of their true nature, their history, and their potential. Going through the ritual and taking a new name signified that participants were being reborn or resurrected to a new life.

Three of the members of Ndikho's group, Ken, Lon and I, were recruited as musicians for the play. We joined local musicians, pianist, Tony, and two percussionists, Mike and Dennis who got new names (Al-Hammel Rasul, Babatunde and Jalango) during the six-week run of the play. (Also in the cast was Victor, who would go on to become the lead singer with the Village People, the group that made the hit song "YMCA.")

When "The Resurrection of the Dead" ended its run, we, the six pit musicians, decided to form a group. We wanted a name that would reflect our commitment to African culture; so we called our group "Juju."

Juju is black magic, African spiritually, and the casting of spells. It is a Nigerian music genre that was polyrhythmic and mysterious. It's etymology encapsulated things we wanted to convey. Juju continued the mythological religiosity of Ndikho, the "Resurrection of the Dead," and the drumming cultures of Brazil, Haiti, Cuba and Africa.

Juju would have daily high-energy rehearsals that lasted for hours on end. We studied recordings of all things percussion. We would jam all day then go to other sessions and ceremonies at night. We were vegetarians and health food adherents. We were almost obsessed; and we became powerful.

We gigged around the Bay Area creating a stir and earned recognition for our energy and our fervor. When we appeared at a large anti-war rally at Kezar Stadium with our faces painted like African warriors our reputation as the premier representatives of African culture in the region was cemented. A group photo taken of us at that rally became an iconic image that would be used as the cover of our first album, Juju – A Message From Mozambique.

Juju's political activism was oriented towards Black Nationalism. We were very supportive of groups like the Black Panther Party in Oakland and United Soul in Los Angeles. But because the Bay Area was so culturally diverse, our constituencies and our personal relations led us to be involved with other ethnic groups as well.

An artists' collective, 3rd World Communications, was particularly noteworthy for its publishing and organizing activities among the many ethnic communities in San Francisco. Thulani, Ntozake and another writer, Jessica Hagedorn, would stretch their creative wings in that incubating collective. And I and Juju would use our music to build alliances and expand our worldview. Here was where I learned that the world was not simply black and white, but in fact made of many colors, shades and cultures. And I learned that we are much more alike than different, especially in terms of our aspirations and goals.

Here was where I experienced collective political, social and artistic activities reaping both personal and community benefits. This was an enlightening period that helped shape my view of a multicultural future, where our society could be seen not as a melting pot, but a quilt of many different fabrics and colors, stitched together with fibers and threads of commonly held objectives and respect for self and others. But obviously that nirvana was still a long way off and it would and will take a lot of organizing and struggling to get there. During this time the Soledad Brothers case and Angela Davis was prominent

Juju performing for Bay Area inmates - 1972

and controversial. (http://en.wikipedia.org/wiki/Angela_Davis) As members of the activist community, Juju and I were involved in the discussions and demonstrations in support of Professor Davis and the cause. Thulani covered the story for the newspaper and got the opportunity to interview and report on the key persons involved.

Personally I had the triple threat of being a fugitive, living in the center of the drug counterculture, and being politically active in revolutionary art and politics, all at the same time. With Juju, I even played music for inmates in Bay Area jails. It is perhaps miraculous that the FBI didn't arrest me, but maybe the sheer number of leftist activists, causes, and organizations in the Bay Area doing even more extreme things than I, gave me cover.

I was de facto leader of the Juju, but the group was truly a communal/democratic operation. My jobs with the band included musical director, manager, booking coordinator and marketing director. Oh yeah, and saxophonist. In a group composed of two percussionists, pianist, vibraphonist, bassist and a saxophonist, the sax player should be the leader. That's my opinion.

While we all wrote and helped to select the songs, Rasul, the keyboardist, was the principal composer. He wrote amazing music, with beautiful melodies encased in sensual or compelling chord changes, often in odd time signatures, like 11/4 or 7/4 or 5/4. He was self-taught and his unique approaches to composition were innovative and refreshing.

Lon Moshe, played with a wild and crazy, atonal approach to the vibraphone. He pounded and hammered away at the instrument making its beautiful chimes sound like an incongruent weapon. Ken Shabala, the bassist, used his R&B singer's ear to learn the bass and hold down the foundation of the music.

Babatunde and Jalango were the Afro-Caribbean percussion and African drumming purists. They studied and practiced the rhythms incessantly and they played with a ferocious, driving energy that propelled us into the future while remaining grounded on a solid traditional foundation.

Jalango's roommate, Bill, was one of the local authorities on Afro-Caribbean music and drumming and he wanted to join the group, but as leader I decided the six members we had were enough. It would prove to be a decision I still regret to this day. Bill Summers went on to join Herbie Hancock's Headhunters group; and later Bill would work with Quincy Jones in creating the music for the Alex Haley's "Roots," one of the most-watched television events ever. Whenever I see Bill, he never fails to remind me that I wouldn't let him join Juju.

My saxophone playing incorporated the two extremes of the basic blues scales, and the high energy screams and wailings of the avant garde players like Archie Shepp, John Coltrane and my idol, Pharaoh Sanders.

Juju's collective approach to our music was the liberal use of high energy to express our commitment to African principles. We blew, pounded, and stroked our respective instruments as if there would be no tomorrow, like we were on the battlefield, like our very life's work was wrapped up in this two to four hour session. We approached our performances as if they were actual religious rites, and then by pushing ourselves and the music to the limit, we would find new levels of consciousness or ecstasy. And often we did.

We were bridging traditional African music and the avant garde jazz, "new music" of the time: Sun Ra, Ornette Coleman, Albert Ayler, the Art Ensemble of Chicago, Phil Coran, Marzette Watts, and others. We called ours "new African music." The music was innovative and intoxicating, sincerely spiritual and impactful. The music mesmerized, informed and awakened people.

Our first album, A Message From Mozambique, contained six songs: 1. (Struggle) Home; 2. Soledad Brothers; 3. Freedom Fighter; 4. Make Your Own Revolution Now; 5. Father Is Back; and 6. Nairobi Chants. The titles of the songs and the genres show the range of topics and textures that were our inspirations. The fact that each member was credited with composing one song shows our egalitarianism; but, in fact, ours was collective approach to improvising and creating.

We recorded the album on a four-track, reel-to-reel tape recorder in a friend's living room. I acted as producer, directing the session. Later I would take the master tape to New York and work with Marzette Watts[*] in his studio to do the mixing, editing, and mastering of the album that we would release on the Strata-East label.

When A Message From Mozambique was released in 1973 we were trying to make a political statement with the title of the album. The anti-war movement was focused on the Viet Nam war, but I wanted to call attention to the fact that there was a war being waged in southern Africa as well. South Africa, Angola and Mozambique were places where battles were being waged over the issues of white supremacy; the cold war between the West and the Soviet Union, and Africans' struggle for self determination and control of natural resources. But in the U.S., there was not much news or advocacy about these struggles, even among the progressives. So that was why I chose that title for our LP.

There were also business and artistic reasons for our album release. Of course, Juju wanted to gain wider exposure for our music. We wanted to document what we were doing. We wanted to create tangible evidence of the dedicated work we had put into honing our crafts and our music. We wanted to have the feedback from the marketplace and critics to assess the validity of our theories and applications. We wanted more gigs and the possibility of touring. We wanted to impact the world.

Record albums are usually monuments that signify both endings and beginnings. They are the culmination of creative and production processes and the beginning of marketing, touring and a new cycle of career development. Our first album represented both for us.

But navigating the business and also inner politics of the group would prove to be both educational and challenging.

---

*Marzette Watts
From Wikipedia, the free encyclopedia
Marzette Watts (March 9, 1938, Montgomery, Alabama - March 2, 1998, Nashville) was an American jazz tenor and soprano saxophonist and sound engineer. He had a brief career in music and is revered for his 1966 self-titled free jazz release.
He attended Alabama State College, where he was a founding member of SNCC. He moved to New York, where he lived in a loft building on Cooper Square which also had as a tenant Leroi Jones (later Amiri Baraka). Watts studied under Don Cherry and played in his loft and around the city. Watts' loft attracted many established and up-and-coming musicians who would hang out there and play at parties, including Ornette Coleman, Cecil Taylor, Don Cherry, Archie Shepp, and Pharoah Sanders.
In 1965 he decided to devote himself to music more fully, and moved to Denmark for further study. He wrote film scores and did production work for his own films, eventually abandoning music to work in film and record production.
Watts moved back and forth between Europe and New York, teaching briefly at Wesleyan University. Late in his life he moved to Santa Cruz, California. He died of heart failure in 1998.
Listen to Marzette Watts: https://www.youtube.com/watch?v=nyob6s3E2qE

⌘⌘⌘

Chapter 6

BACK TO THE BIG APPLE

Life is a lot like jazz ... it's best when you improvise.
—George Gershwin

In July 1972 Juju came to New York to do a series of gigs and to relocate. After spending the night at Kent's parents' house in Brooklyn, we got up, went out to our van to go to our gig, and I was arrested by the FBI. After three years, a month and five days of being vigilant and careful and incognito, I would be caught at the same house on Brooklyn Avenue that was my last known address before being drafted. The FBI tactics of surveillance and threats to families and neighbors had worked. I was upset. I was disappointed. I was going to miss our gigs.

I was relieved. Even though I might be facing serious charges, I felt like it was going to be good to finally get the AWOL ordeal over and behind me. Even though I might have had to serve serious time in prison, the Viet Nam war was winding down and sentiments regarding those of us who had protested and resisted had ameliorated.

So I was taken back to the Fort Dix stockade in New Jersey to await my court martial. There was some irony at being right back at the same facility I had left so many months, miles and happenings ago. But the stockade was a lot more relaxed this time around. It was still jail, but without the arbitrary abuses. I was even allowed to have my saxophone in exchange for playing for chapel services on Sundays.

The highest ranking military lawyer in the state of New Jersey proposed to the army that because there were so many long term AWOL's and "deserters" to be tried, that in terms of costs and time, everyone would be better served if, instead of trials, we were all given the option of simply being discharged under less than honorable conditions. The army brain trust agreed. It was fine with me. No, it was great! Instead of facing long years in prison, I'd get to go free, immediately in exchange for accepting an Undesirable Discharge. Happiness is…

Plunky on flute circa 1974

Six weeks after being arrested I was back on the streets of NYC, a free man. My family, friends, Thulani and my Juju band mates were relieved and happy for me. All their letters, poems, prayers and work on my behalf had given me confidence that I could rely on their ongoing support, and I could get back to pursuing my music, poetry, and cultural agenda.

Juju was a New York new music group now. Our first album was released on Strata-East Records. We were in the main arena for jazz in the world. We were avant-garde artists and revolutionary agents for change. But we were always only one step from starving. We lived in the East Village (bohemia), or the Lower East Side (slum), depending on how romantic your vernacular, on St. Mark's Place. Thulani and I sub-let the apartment of Felipe Luciano, one of the Original Last Poets. Kent lived at his parents' house in Brooklyn. The rest of band lived in a storefront loft owned by, Ray, a friend of mine. Juju scraped by on the gig money we earned which only afforded us enough to subsist on a diet of pizza (we called it a 25-cent "slice for life,") and a $2 vegetable curry dinner from the Shah Bagh Indian restaurant whose owners befriended us as their first, real, regular customers.

My main pursuit in life was the hunt for gigs for the band. (That seems to have persisted for the next 50 years.) We worked at the places that supported our kind of music, including: the Spirit House in NewArk; The East and the Children's Museum in Brooklyn; Slugs in the Lower East Side; New York

University (NYU) in the Village; and in the lofts: Studio Rivbea and Joe Lee Wilson's 24 Bond Street in SoHo. Occasionally, I was able to book us uptown at Mikell's Club or at Columbia or City College of New York (CCNY).

Up until that time jazz had been mainly music of the nightclub. Nightclubs have always been small drinking establishments that featured musical entertainment. Whether rural juke joints, western saloons, Harlem bars, or highbrow hotel lounges, they are all basically places to have a drink and be entertained. In fact jazz is said to have been born in the bawdy houses of New Orleans around the turn of the 20th century, where pianists and small ensembles played music as the sonic background for drinking and prostitutes and their johns doing their things. Some say the word "jazz" comes from "jass" music which came from "jasm," a term for the sexual juices associated with where the music was first heard.

The etymology of the word "jazz" has other possible paths. Early 1900s New Orleans musician Jasbo Brown claimed the term came from his fans shouting "Play it, Jasbo, play Jas!" Others say back in that day musicians spoke of "jassing" the music while improvising which meant adding nuances and covering up one's mistakes.

As the music traveled up the Mississippi to the major cities along the way it became the popular music of the early decades of the last century. During the "Jazz Age" it was the music that people danced to and drank to; and during the era of the prohibition on alcohol consumption, jazz was the music of the speakeasies, underground, subversive though sometimes upscale, mafia-controlled nightclubs of New York in Harlem and other places. By the 1940s jazz clubs were legitimate, but still mainly night-time drinking places, and the music was a solid component of the record business and entertainment industry. Often white musicians received more financial benefits than the black innovators. One of the motivations of the development of bebop jazz with its highly complicated chord changes and complex syncopations was the idea of making it more difficult for white musicians to copy.

Some musicians began to rebel against the idea that the music was merely entertainment and they promoted the idea that jazz was high art to be valued as a cultural treasure. By the sixties as the avant-gardists explored new concepts of free jazz, atonality, high energy and international cross cultural connections and political statements of purpose that aligned with civil rights and even revolutionary concepts; they sought out and created new venues to present the new music because it was not always easy for the traditional nightclub audiences to digest its sounds and politics. The music was sometimes abrasive and often did not lend itself to creating background sounds for drinking. It was sometimes aggressive and challenging, intentionally making audiences uncomfortable with the status quo.

So some cultural activists and some musicians themselves developed alternative spaces to present the new music: galleries, loft spaces, storefronts, cultural centers and schools. In a gallery like Ornette Coleman's Artist House, the music could be perceived and appreciated as art. In lofts like Sam Rivers' Studio RivBea, or at Joe Lee Wilson's, both located on Bond Street in the SoHo district, patrons could lounge on pillows and beanbags and be up close and personally absorb the vibes of the musicians and feel the acoustic power of the music until the wee hours of the morning. At Marzette Watts' loft, high quality jam sessions explored the outer realms of music theory and improvisational artistry. At Reggie Workman's program at the Children's Museum of Brooklyn or on the Jazzmobile, musicians and audiences could experience jazz and new music in light and airy spaces or outdoors. At black cultural centers like Imamu Baraka's Spirit House in NewArk, NJ and at The East in Brooklyn, Black Nationalism and Afrocentric thought begat and supported the music of purveyors like Pharoah Sanders, the Last Poets, Mtume and Carlos Garnett, who played to audiences which were more like congregations for whom the music was a stimulus for transcendental experiences. In these revolutionary education centers, when the horns screamed, evoking African spirits, the audiences would scream back, exhorting the musicians and the music to higher heights of frenzied religiosity.

These were the places where we would find the music, study its effects, experience new ideas and perform. These were the types of places that represented the next level of my study of the music and its social and cultural impact. These were the places where I went on dates or went for worship or went for edification and entertainment.

These were the venues where Juju played, allowing us to purvey our ideas about the music and make our contribution to it. When we performed our high energy, ritualistic Afro-Cuban bata drum rhythms and Santeria chants with my wild screaming horn at The East, the dashiki and kente clad congregants would create frenetic calls-and-responses with us, and the darkened room would be transformed into a tribal cauldron in which I would be baptized and seared. There and in similar environs I soared into realms of musical ecstasy that would change me forever.

During those heady, artistic, low-income times, I was able to meet, hang out and jam with many of the purveyors of free jazz including Sam Rivers, Frank Lowe, Rashied Ali, Olu Dara, Sun Ra's horn men, the Last Poets, Imamu Baraka, Juma Santos, and so many more. And there were also momentous meetings, fortuitous encounters with saxophone giants that affected my philosophy and inspired me to stay the course of the career I had chosen. I had met Rashaan Roland Kirk and Sun Ra's saxophonist, John Gilmore in San Francisco and encountered them again in New York. They encouraged me to keep on blowing.

John Coltrane was an iconic saxophonist, idolized by a multitude of jazz lovers and musicians, including me. Embarrassingly, early on in my jazz appreciation I walked out on a Coltrane performance. In the summer of 1966, just after my freshman year, I attended my first music festival, the Newport Jazz Festival in Providence, Rhode Island, primarily to visit my girlfriend at the time and to see the Horace Silver Quintet. After spending all day listening to jazz and finally seeing Silver's penultimate group on the bill, I was not "ready" for the avant garde dissonance of the John Coltrane group that included his wife, Alice Coltrane, and saxophonist Pharaoh Sanders. I left in the middle of their set. And I never had the chance to see Coltrane perform live again. He died July 17, 1967.

Over the next few years I would become more than enamored, almost obsessed, with John Coltrane and his music. I was/am inspired by Trane's dedication to the horn, his enduring quest of perfecting his tone and to his pursuit of his spirituality through music.

Saxophonist Pharaoh Sanders stood next to John Coltrane onstage at that Newport Jazz Festival concert. And in the late 1960s and early '70s in San Francisco I would stand near Pharaoh by being as close to the foot of the stage as possible whenever he played. If Pharaoh played a week-long engagement at the Both/And Club on Divisidero Street in Frisco, I would be there every night. He came to recognize me as a devoted fan. Once, he had a gig in Frisco and I was there, and then two nights later he had a gig in Detroit and so did I (with Ndikho), so when he saw me in Detroit Pharoah was amazed. A week later, I saw him in New York as well. He could have easily thought that I was stalking him. But he came to know me and my group as purveyors of his style of music.

Eventually, Pharaoh gave me a gig on a recording date with him in New

York. I played shekere and flute on his Wisdom Through Music album released on the Impulse Record label. There were other musicians on that recording session that I would work with later, including Mtume, Norman Connors, Cecil McBee and Joe Bonner.

Ornette Coleman once referred to Pharaoh Sanders as one of the greatest tenor saxophonists in the world; high praise from Ornette, the world renowned alto saxophonist proponent of free jazz who had turned the music world on its ear with the release of his seminal 1959 album, The Shape of Jazz To Come. Ornette is known for his eccentricities, his outlandish formal fashion wear and his jazz and classical compositions and the musical theories and improvisational techniques he called "harmolodics." He is also one of the most important figures in the avant garde jazz movements of the 1950s and beyond.

Sometime in late 1972 we were invited to perform at Ornette's Artist House gallery, located at 131 Prince Street in the SoHo district in downtown Manhattan. When we did the gig at his place Ornette was there in a bright, colorful, paisley silk tuxedo videotaping us, and afterward he invited us upstairs to his loft. We talked for a while in his large living space with angular and curved walls, a billiard table, a suspended hammock, and loads of wild and crazy art. And then Ornette said he was going to North Africa for a few weeks to record with the master musicians of Jujouka, Morocco. He invited my group to stay at his place and asked me to run his gallery in his absence. Amazing! I don't know if he was just that crazy or if he had quickly assessed that we were sincere, good souls, or what; but we accepted the invitation and the responsibility. So our six member group moved in and stayed there along with alto saxophonist Julius Hemphill, who would later be a founding member of the World Saxophone Quartet that included David Murray, Hamiet Bluiett and Oliver Lake.

For a short while Juju moved up in the world, from starving artists, to living in a posh SoHo loft. For a few weeks, I was running Ornette's Artist House Gallery which was open, spacious and chic. It gave us a place to rehearse and perform, and surrounded us and our music with modern paintings and sculpture. The short stint as curator of a performance art space gave me a vision of what my artist life could be about and achieve. Ornette's world was centered on the "space" where free jazz and modern art merged with high brow European sensibilities. It was colorful, bright, stimulating, airy and extremely intellectual and while it tilted left, it bordered on being apolitical. And it had the support and financial backing of the moneyed class.

> *Jazz is the only music in which the same note can be played night after night but differently each time.*
> —Ornette Coleman

In July 1973 my group Juju performed at the Lincoln Center's Alice Tully hall in New York as a part of an alternative festival, the New York Musicians' Festival. We got a rave review in the New York Times.

NY Times July 2, 1973
Newport Jazz at Lincoln Center
Fledglings Test Wings at Tully
BY LES LEDBETTER

"Like a bright sun blinding drivers emerging from dark tunnels, there was a burst of musical energy on the Alice Tully Hall stage Saturday night that struck the audience so fast and so forcefully that some in the small crowd chose to leave quickly.

Juju, a two-year-old San Francisco septet dedicated to playing what its members call "new African music," was the most dazzling group to appear at the opening night of the Tully series of relatively unknown musicians being presented by the New York Musicians Five Borough Jazz Festival in cooperation with the Newport Jazz Festival in New York.

After a barely audible, gentle and seemingly standard ballad-like opening of several bars, Juju exploded in sound with squeaks, squeals, wail and thumps without warning and sustained this high level of musical energy for on unbelievable 20 minutes or more.

When the number, "Sunspot," was over, the echoes of the music still hung over the hall until drowned out by the loudly applauding and cheering audience that realized it had been present for an unusual and exciting musical event."

One of the reasons that we chose to migrate to New York was to work with Strata-East Records to release our first album. Strata-East was an important and innovative record company venture conceived as a collective/partnership of independent artists/producers. The company was directed by two jazz artists, Charles Tolliver and Stanley Cowell, who flipped the script of the usual record company model.

At that time the typical record company would own the copyrights to the recordings and give the artists a 10%-15% royalty from the sales of the records. At Strata-East the artists produced the recordings, retained ownership of the copyrights, and the company would get 15% of the sales revenue. It was a revolutionary arrangement that attracted several jazz artists who were interested in owning and promoting their music and creating change in the industry. Strata-East was a music business but it was making cultural and political statements as well.

Straight ahead jazz was the music of the vast majority of the musicians who came to be a part of the label's roster, which would include Clifford Jordon, Billy Harper, Pharaoh Sanders, Harold Vick, Charlie Rouse, Sonny Fortune, John Betsch Society, Brother Ah, Cecil McBee, Shirley Scott, Jane Cortez, Charles Tolliver's Music Inc Big Band, Stanley Cowell's Piano Choir, and more. These older, more mainstream jazz musicians were joined by what I would call some young lions. Gil Scott-Heron, Mtume and my group, Juju, would expand the scope of the music represented on the label to include African, Black Cultural nationalistic new music, R&B and spoken word.

Juju's two Strata-East releases, A Message from Mozambique (1973) and Chapter Two: Nia (1974), combined traditional African rhythms with odd time signatures, high energy keyboards and my wild screaming horn to create Afro-jazz avant garde music. Mtume's release, Alkebu-lan: Land of the Blacks, was a Black nationalistic exploration of music and a political call to action. Mtume would years later go on to perform with Miles Davis and find some fame producing hit R&B songs like "Juicy Fruit" and "You, Me & He" which were, to say the least, distinctly different from his Strata-East album release.

But the most impactful record released on the Strata-East label was Gil Scott-Heron and Brian Jackson's album, Winter In America (1974). Instead of acoustic jazz or avant garde the music on Winter In America was socially conscious R&B, spoken word and songs that coupled Gil's poetry and lyrics with Brian's music. They referred to the combination of blues, jazz and soul music as "bluesology," and they also incorporated some Caribbean rhythms, some free jazz and spoken interludes. On the album there were poignant songs about the black experience, but it was "The Bottle," an upbeat song about alcoholic abuse, that became a hit on Black radio and parties. And that changed things at Strata-East.

Before "The Bottle," Strata-East labored under the double whammy of swimming against the tide of the music industry, both musically and in business. The label's music was not commercial. The artists' producers were often much more focused on the music as art and culture as opposed to the marketability of the products. The music was progressive, esoteric, Afro-Centric, and even subversive, not necessarily the best qualities for commercial radio and market penetration.

The record business was geared toward hit records and radio airplay. Distribution was controlled by the major labels and radio was mostly influenced by sophisticated payola, pay-for-play schemes. Strata-East Records, which was set up to combat or at least circumvent these orientations and practices, struggled to get mainstream distribution and promotion. The label was surviving because of the artists' self-promotion and marketing, and the support of alternative radio, underground jazz press and progressive music lovers. The popularity of "The Bottle" created a level of demand that Strata-East was not prepared to handle. As the song got more and more airplay, customers, stores, record pools, deejays all wanted it. The albums were scarce, which made it even more valuable; and it became a rare phenomenon: a hit record from a small independent label. Everybody wanted it and they could only get it from this small, in some ways, obstinate record company, run by jazz musicians.

Within the company the commerciality of the record created debates about the viability and even the desirability of financial success for the label. Was the company going to represent revolutionary change in the record business or was it going to grow into an entity that was bought out by or brought into the industry? Distribution, business and merger offers were generated but the leadership of Strata-East was slow to react. Frustration ensued. Other cover versions of "The Bottle" were released by other artists who capitalized on the dearth of records and lack of follow-through. Gil Scott-Heron left the label and eventually signed a deal to become the first artist on Clive Davis' Arista Records label.

Lessons learned:

Put yourself where what you want to do is happening. Go there. Meet the people you need to meet.

Follow your dream, be prepared to take chances.

Be prepared or be ready to fall and get back up, encounter unexpected events and setbacks and move forward.

Perseverance furthers.

⌘⌘⌘

Chapter 7

ONENESS OF JUJU IN RVA & DC

New York was hard and cold. The music was great, but the city can wear you down.

(Thulani and I broke up. I fell out of love. I think I hurt her deeply. We had been together for five years, through Columbia riots and my drop out, through my fugitive years in Frisco and my stockade discharge, through thick and thin and back again. Through it all we had shared love, music and poetry, a hundred poems, as notes and letters and personal musings. We had grown up and graduated into adulthood. She and her friends were becoming renowned poets and writers. She got a job writing for the Village Voice, and would eventually get her PhD. She didn't need me, but she didn't know that at the time. She likely won't ever forgive me.)

In 1974, I decided to leave NYC and move back to Richmond, Virginia (RVA) and the band followed. It was a decision based on New York's high cost of living; and we were in need of space and time to take a breath of fresh air. I thought Richmond could be like a retreat, a creative environment, a little bit more like San Francisco; and the cost of living in Richmond was certainly lower than in Manhattan. The move was my idea and the group decided to go with me. I was the leader and they trusted my judgment. They had traveled across country in pursuit of our collective musical dreams, and they decided not to give them up yet. So our journey would take us south.

Juju and our new African music were very different than any other group or music in the Richmond area at that time. Our African garb, big Afros, our diet, our dialect and our cultural nationalism were all different, and somewhat controversial.

In some ways Juju was a band of vagabonds, traveling minstrels, itinerant bluesmen, neo-African griots telling the story of how our music could enlighten, inspire and lead us to the promised land of black unity and advancement. We were nationalistic purists living as black music prophets and would-be

Plunky in Chimborazo Park 1974

priests. But we were poor and the living wasn't easy.

I had my family and my Richmond friends. But Lon, Babatunde, Rasul and Jalango had no roots in Richmond. (Kent, the Brooklyn, NY native, did have an aunt who lived in Richmond. Who knew?) We would have to largely rely on my funding, support, largess and business savvy to advance the music and survive. But the guys were all young, healthy and socially adept; and in relatively short order they would acquire Richmond friends and girlfriends.

When Juju came to Richmond we initially stayed in the home of my oldest and best friend, Lew. His was a large 10 room house in Church Hill, the historically black neighborhood in the east end of the city. While it was technically in the ghetto, the house fronted Chimborazo Park, a beautiful 20 acre park directly across the street, the site of a historic civil war battlefield hospital.

I wanted to bring some of what I had experienced in New York and San

Album cover Chapter Two Nia   Oneness of Juju rehearsal 1975

Francisco to Richmond. Lew's house would be dubbed the Juju Raga Artist House. In many ways it was modeled after Ornette Coleman's Artist House in NY. We lived upstairs and converted the downstairs into Kahero Gallery (Kahero meaning "conceived at home"), the first black arts gallery in the state. It also doubled as a small performance space, complete with a church pew and large pillows on the floor for seating. Juju rehearsed there daily and we had weekly performances, "Sundays at Sunset," open to the public when we served herb tea, health food snacks and poetry along with the new jazz we played.

Actually the house was always open to the public. We almost never locked the door. People from the neighborhood would come in and use the gallery space for meditation and respite. Friends thought Lew and I were crazy but while we did have a few almost lost souls who became regulars, we never had any serious problems with the people or the open door policy. We were practicing what we preached and demonstrating the faith we had in good vibrations. It turned out that music, poetry, art and progressive political discussion did have positive effects on individuals and the community. The place became a focal point of Black political and cultural activity. And the people supported the place and our idealism.

In June, 1974, Juju recorded our second album, Juju/Chapter Two: Nia at Eastern Recording Studios in Richmond. The music was still Afrocentric, if not more so, and we also included black nationalistic poetry written and spoken by Ngoma Ya Uhuru, a high school friend who had spent time in New

Jersey with Amiri Baraka's Spirit House. The album cover featured liner notes and poetry by Thulani, and her brother, Collis Davis, designed the layout and developed the front cover photograph from a video he shot of us at NYU. (The project was completed a few months before Thulani and I broke up.)
The album was released on Strata-East and Juju Raga Artist House was listed as our official contact address.

Juju's high energy music, commitment and charisma were obvious. We were the local Virginia exponents of the progressive ideas being expressed nationally and internationally. We attracted a small, active group of artists, followers, fans and supporters. But the music was not well received or appreciated by a large portion of RVA music buying public.

In our theory, music and art was only as good as it functioned in service to the community. Yes, creative expressions should elevate and inspire and reach beyond the mundane, day-to-day experience. And yes, our music should pay homage to our African roots and the greatness of our history and culture. But we believed the music should be a practical resource for the community. It should be a political rallying point bringing the community together. The music should educate the people. The music could be a business generator, bringing money into the community that could be used for development. The music should be of, by and for the people. The music and art should be about black power. All power to the people!

We believed this and we lived it. Juju had sacrificed much and struggled to advance these ideals and the music. But the music and art could do all this and more, only if it got support from the people.

We were not in New York anymore. We were not in Frisco. Richmond, Virginia, was in the South. It was the capital of the old confederacy. Its people – black and white – were conservative by nature. Black music listeners' tastes tended towards blues, gospel, soul and funk, and related only peripherally to jazz and ethnic music. And Richmond was known to be a tough audience to please. So much so, that Richmond was often used as a test market for new soul songs and R&B artists, because record companies and promoters came to recognize that if it could sell in Richmond, it could be a hit anywhere.

I came to realize that in order for Juju to serve the people, we had to reach the people. In order to bring them along to where we were going, we'd have to first meet them where they were. So I became convinced that we should add some rhythm and blues elements to our music. This decision had required some soul searching. Commercial soul music could be seen as simply entertainment, often without political purpose. For some jazz and new music purists, soul music was not art, and not worthy of honor. But I saw R&B dif-

Lady Eka-ete 1974

ferently. I had been raised on it. I saw message music and artists like Curtis Mayfield, James Brown, Sly Stone, the O'Jays and Marvin Gaye as having the capacity to deliver heavy political communications to the people.

So, after much debate, Juju decided to add trap drums and a backbeat to the rhythms and even more electric sounds to the mix. And we decided to change the name of the group to Oneness of Juju; Oneness to signify the realization that all black music was from the same source, based on the same forces of creativity, and ultimately of use toward the same ends.

Jalango was the first to leave. He moved back home to San Francisco. We replaced him with Ronnie Toler, funk drummer who lived right around the corner from Lew's house. Then Ken(t) Shabalala moved back to Brooklyn to use his Columbia degree to make a living and a difference. He was replaced on electric bass by my younger brother Philip, who Ndikho would rename Muzi (meaning one who extends the family).

(In another family-extending, full-circle trip, for a time Adolphus "Peddie" Maples, a childhood friend, joined Juju. 30 years later in life, his son, Adolphus Jr., a deejay, rapper and producer, would marry my daughter, Kaila, and they would give me three of the of the most handsome, talented and brilliant grandsons ever! So, Kaila would marry a musician like her mother did.)

So, Juju was transitioning into Oneness of Juju by adding elements of R&B and including local musicians into the fold. But the most profound change came when we added a female vocalist, Jackie Holoman, who would take the name Lady Eka-Ete. I first saw her performing with her own group, Eboni, which consisted of only her with three conga drummer/percus-

Oneness of Juju onstage l. to r. Lon Moshe, Babatunde Lea, Plunky, Ndikho Xaba

sionists. I immediately knew she could fit in with what Oneness of Juju was developing.

Lady Eka-Ete had a regal African sense of bearing about herself and her voice had the mellowness of Roberta Flack. She softened and changed the sound of our group without lessening our sense of purpose, which was to impact our community with positive vibes about our blackness and our future.

Over the next decade we continued to develop our R&B credentials and building a following in Richmond by playing the local clubs, at first the smaller niche ones like Ovoutee's Club, Ebony Island Club, The Devils club, and later the Third Word Club and Lucky Strike Club. In 1979 we secured an ongoing engagement at Richmond's Blues Alley, a swank, fine-dining night club just a few blocks from City Hall, right in the heart of downtown. There, we performed for the mayor, other politicians and business bigwigs who were regulars among the capacity crowds that packed the place when we were there.

After the owner of Blues Alley was busted for cocaine possession, we continued to play other Richmond clubs from those days forward. We played the Richmond Jazz Society Club, Ellington's, Ivories, City Lights, Military Retirees Club, Armani's, The Canal Club, The Flood Zone and others. We

Oneness of Juju 1976: Plunky in front; back l. to r. Muzi, Ronnie Toler, Ras Mel Glover, Nat Lee, Jr

also worked with local promoters like Joe Carter, Steve Branch, Carroll Epps and the Great Hosea Fox to perform in concerts and other special events.

In 1974 I met Jimmy Gray, the Washington, DC jazz radio disk jockey, record collector and independent record promotion man, when he was the Strata-East marketing and distribution point person for the District of Columbia, Maryland, Virginia (DMV) area. The tremendous success of the hit song, "The Bottle" created a huge demand for the label's Gil Scott-Heron and Brian Jackson Winter In America album. Because Gil and Brian were based in DC, they made sure that Jimmy Gray had an abundant supply of their all too rare album. At one point when the record was at its hottest, Jimmy and I had LPs when nobody else did, and that gave us quite a bit of influence and leverage in the region's business. We made connections with distributors and one-stops all over the region, the nation and even abroad.

With the contacts we developed, the lessons learned, and the possibilities for success we witnessed, Jimmy and I decided that we would start our own label, Black Fire Records, to release my next records and others. In 1975 we released the Oneness of Juju African Rhythms LP as the first album on the Black Fire Records label. For me and the group's branding, the album represented a significant musical shift, with the addition of female vocals by Lady

Eka-Ete and the incorporation of rhythm and blues grooves to some of the songs. The personnel on the album included: Me, Al Hammel Rasul, Lon Moshe, Muzi, Babatunde Lea, Ronnie Toler, and Reggie Brisbane. Also featured on bass on one song was my young cousin Philip "Peewee" Ford (aka Paris Ford), who would later go on to play with BBQ Band, Rick James, Lonnie Liston Smith, Michael Urbaniak, and others. My brother, Muzi Nkabinde, did the front cover painting, as he would for most of the Black Fire albums (and later for my albums on N.A.M.E. Brand Records).

The album would have a profound effect on our career. Critics would proclaim the music on the album as charting a new hybrid genre, Afro-jazz funk, and it would eventually get critical notice and airplay in the Mid-Atlantic region and in Europe and Japan. Never underestimate the power of the juju in the funk.

The African Rhythms recording sessions at Bias Recording Studios in Northern Virginia were engineered by Millard "Jim" Watkins, who was the chief engineer for Howard University's WHUR-FM radio station, where Jimmy Gray was a part-time deejay. When Jimmy Gray introduced me to Jim Watkins it was hilarious because when we were kids, Jim Watkins and I were neighbors in Richmond. I knew him as the nerdiest boy I had ever met, but even as a child I knew that he was an electronics genius.

When African Rhythms was released, Jimmy Gray and Jim Watkins assured the album was featured on WHUR. The afternoon news show on the station was called "The Daily Drum" and for months, different tracks on our album became the theme songs for the daily news show. (Jim Watkins continued to be supportive over the next 40 years, getting us airplay and bookings for events for the radio and television stations he managed.)

With the popularity of our African Rhythms album we were able to book more gigs in Richmond and beyond. We hooked up with Charisma Productions, a DC-based booking agency and production company headed by Brute, a friend of Jimmy Gray. Charisma's artist roster included: Gil Scott-Heron, Roy Ayers, Hugh Masekela, Chuck Brown & the Soul Searchers, Norman Connors, Lonnie Liston Smith, Plunky & Oneness of Juju and local groups, Brute, Chocolate Rain and Father's Children.

Hooking up with Charisma Productions meant that we were often booked to do shows with one or more of the acts on the roster, performing at clubs, parks, concerts, special events and political rallies. Every year Charisma would produce Brute's Summer Soul Festival using all of our acts. The last two years

Space Jungle Luv album cover 1976

the festival was presented at Take-It-Easy Ranch in Calloway Maryland and it grew to a three day camp-in event with non-stop music involving 20–30 funk and soul acts. The festival was attended by tens of thousands of DC area music fans who camped out at what was really like a black Woodstock-type event.

Through Charisma Productions we got booked at several venues in DC including Ed Murphy's Supper Club. When Ed Murphy developed his Harambe House Hotel, we played for the grand opening. Over the years we would play at other DC clubs including: Takoma Station, Blues Alley, The Kilimanjaro, Zanzibar on the Wharf, all coming from the momentum generated by Charisma and their staff, Brute, Bob Young, Samantha, Smokey and the rest. Getting hooked up with Charisma meant getting better known and getting to know all those artists on the roster with whom I would interact intermittingly over the years. Occasionally I have even done gigs as a sideman with Norman Connors and fellow Richmond native, Lonnie Liston Smith.

Lady Eka-Ete onstage

In 1976 we released Space Jungle Luv*, our second album on Black Fire. The music continued to blend genres, with a smoother progressive sound that featured Lady Eka-Ete's soulfully sweet mesmerizing vocals. That album also introduced the addition of guitarist Melvin Glover to the group. Not only was his instrument and his playing valuable to us, but so were his compositional skills. His songs would broaden the range of our repertoire by adding celestial, harp-like tones and smoother jazz textures. (Later he would be a charter member of a local reggae group, the Awareness Art Ensemble, and come to be known as Ras Mel. Years later still, he would tour with Eddie Grant, and even more notably, spend years touring with Bob Marley's original band, The Wailers.) Also on this album we were blessed to have the phenomenal pianist from Pharoah Sanders' band, Joe Bonner, who played so skillfully and melodiously that he made us sound jazzy and free at the same time.

Space Jungle Luv is an odd combination of words but an apt description

Lori, Ras Mel, Kevin Davis, Plunky & Muzi

Asante

Plunky & Oneness of Juju

Plunky & Eka-Ete

of the music, the lifestyle and the philosophical perspectives of Oneness of Juju in the era when this album was originally produced.

During this period we used several other musicians in Oneness of Juju. Keyboardist Nat Lee joined the group and replaced Rasul when he went back to California. After Babatunde left, we used several different percussionists to replace him: Rafael Solano, Alfredo Mojica, Reggie Brisbane, the Ilu Drummers from DC; and, Dick Watkins, Peddie Maples, Kevin Davis and Oginga Joyner from Richmond. All of them were great, but none had the lasting impact as did Ghanaian master drummer, Okyerema Asante.

I met Okyerema Asante when he was playing percussion and talking drums with Hugh Masekela's group in 1975. When the rest of his group went back to Africa, Asante decided to stay in the U.S. Asante performed with a number of jazz stars, including the Jazz Crusaders, Lonnie Liston Smith and Hamiet Bluiett, among others. He joined my group, Oneness of Juju, because he said we were the funkiest Afro-jazz group he had seen. Asante's presence, his charismatic performance style, and his rhythms were an influence on our music. Together we helped create a DC Afro-funk rhythm style that was the precursor to go-go music.

Asante would go on to performed on Paul Simon's Graceland Tour that featured South African musicians Masekela, Miriam Makeba, and the Ladysmith Black Mambazo. Later, Asante would do world tours as a member of Fleetwood Mac, the powerhouse, legendary rock group. In between these high profile tours, Asante and I would continue to do Oneness of Juju

---

*Here's what I wrote about that album for the liner notes for a Japanese re-issue of the album 30 years after its initial release: 2007 Thoughts on a 1976 Recording: Space Jungle Luv "Space" represented freedom and a vast expanse of uncharted territory. "Jungle" is a reference to Africa as an original source of all earthly things. And "Luv" is stated as the overriding universal spiritual element flowing through the hearts of all mankind. Lofty sentiments indeed, but sentiments shared and inspired by the group's musical mentors and idols.

The music on this album makes obvious references to Miles Davis, Sun Ra, Pharaoh Sanders, Earth Wind & Fire, Charles Lloyd, Roland Kirk, Sarah Vaughn, John Coltrane, Fela Kuti and others. The songs are diverse in their textures, ranging from natural acoustic jazz instrumentation to electrified, effected, synthesized sound sources.

My friend, partner and co-producer of Space Jungle Luv, Jimmy "Black Fire"

gigs in the DMV area or abroad. We played in London at the Jazz Café, the JVC Jazz Festival, and then toured in France, going from Paris, to Montpelier and Marseille. Most proudly, we enjoyed several trips to Ghana to perform and do other business. Those trips were a trip!

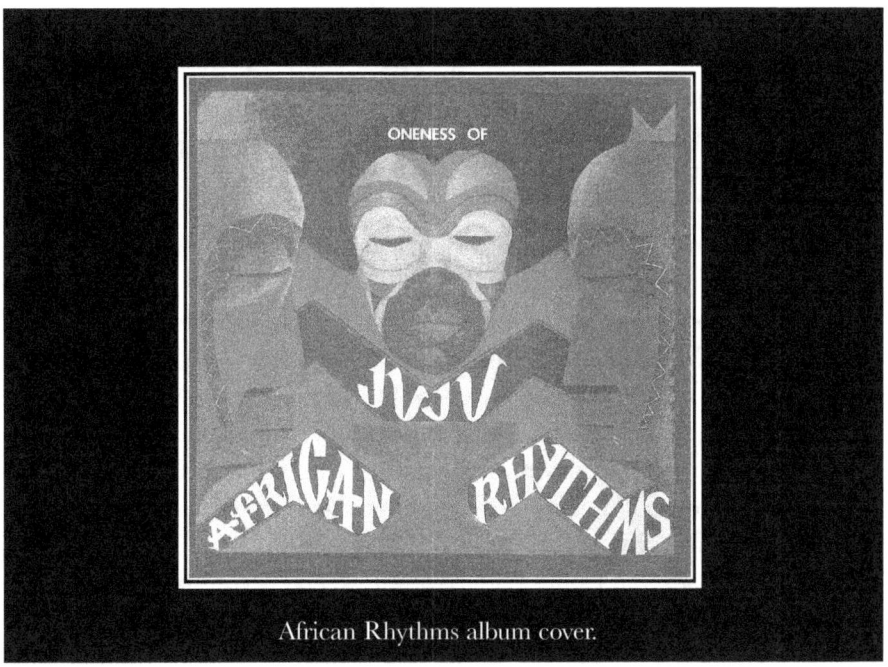

African Rhythms album cover.

Gray, and I worked at being spontaneous, coveting and exalting the creative sparks that fly when conditions are right for improvisation. While the most spiritual moments are rarely recorded, we were happy and pleased to capture what we did in these sessions. The members of Oneness of Juju along with our special guests, including Joe Bonner, were aware that we were a part of something special and magical.

30 years later, "River Luvrite" is still enchanting listeners, "Space Jungle Funk" is still as wild as a bubbling bitches' brew, and "Love's Messenger" is still delivering. It is amazing to me is that this music has stood the test of time and the production still sounds sonically current. That makes Space Jungle Luv a classic. But I am a bit biased. These songs are like my children and this record is like a snapshot of them when they were young and impetuous. They still bring me joy and I hope you enjoy them too.

—Plunky Branch, Producer and Leader of Oneness of Juju

⌘⌘⌘

Chapter 8

Family & Plunky & Oneness

In 1974 just before I moved back to Richmond, I met, or I should say, I re-met, my future wife, Cookie.

When Ron, a childhood friend from Richmond who was living in NY at the time, asked me if I wanted to ride down from NY to our hometown for the weekend, I originally declined. That is, until he said he was stopping in Philly to pick up his mother and sister. Then I jumped at the chance. Ron had talked about his sister, Cookie, and how fine she was. I had known her from a distance as his little sister before their family moved to Philly when I was about 11. Ron had come back to Richmond to go to high school, but I hadn't seen Cookie for 10 years or so, until Ron showed me her picture, which confirmed his little sister was no longer little and she was indeed fine!

The four of us drove down to Richmond with me and Ron in the front seats. They were going to visit Ron's grandmother, who happened to live just three blocks from my mother's house. At the end of the weekend, I volunteered to drive back and Cookie sat up front to keep me company. By the time we got to Philly, she and I were holding hands and making plans to stay in touch. And we did. We dated when she came to NY to see her brother. And later she would come just to see me.

After I moved back to Richmond I would go to DC weekly to conduct music business with my partner, Jimmy Gray, and to hunt for or perform gigs. Cookie and I found it convenient to meet in DC for our dates because it was halfway between Philly and Richmond.

Months later, I would convince her to give up her teaching job in Philly and move down to Richmond to live with me. And when she did, we first lived at Lew's Juju Raga Artist House, and then later in our own apartment.

Sometimes I made moves without considering the long range repercussions. Like when I moved back to Richmond, I really hadn't thought it would be permanent. I just realized that after being away and not being able to visit home for years, the place felt like the place to be. And in the park across the street from my mother's house, the same trees that had been there when I was kid were still there. Not similar trees, but the very same trees that we had used as goal line markers when playing football. The same trees that had ensnared my kites. And I realized metaphorically what it meant to have roots in a place. And Richmond was the place of my roots. Though New York might have been more fertile ground for my music career, and though I would later travel all over the world, I have lived in RVA ever since.

Similarly, it wasn't until I had gone up to Philly to pick up Cookie and all her things that I realized I was making a commitment far beyond just having a weekend guest. I realized I was going to have to marry her, because she was changing her life to come be with me.

So one day several months after she moved in, I said to her, "Come on, let's go down to city hall and get married. It's almost three o'clock, and I have a rehearsal at three-thirty; so we have to hurry!" We already had a marriage

Cookie in New York circa 1974

Cookie & the kids

license. We had let two previous ones expire. So she said okay.

We got Lew to go with us to be the best man and take pictures. I flagged down Muzi in his car as he passed City Hall on his way to rehearsal so he could be the witness. And in a few minutes the deed was done. And I made rehearsal on time. It was on July 16, 1975. That is significant because for the next decade, each year Cookie and I would not remember our anniversary date until it had passed. But we have stayed married for going on 40 years. I think we have survived because she is a steady, smart, beautiful, loyal partner and a wonderful mother to our two children, Kaila and Jamiah.

I marvel at Cookie's patience and her willingness to put up with me; my artiness, moodiness and quirkiness; my proclivities; and my endless traveling. But I often posited that my gigs and touring, my weekly trips to DC, my being away so much, has given us time to breathe and miss each other and have regular reunions.

Plunky & baby Jamiah   Kaila as a kid   Jamiah at 4

Having kids changes lots of things. One thing it meant for me was deciding not to go back and live in New York or any other big city that might have been more advantageous for my music career. Having lived in NYC and seen kids there, I knew that Richmond would be a better choice for raising my family. It was less hectic. I had extended family and support systems in place. Schools and neighborhoods would be more welcoming. And I felt it would be safer for Cookie and the kids when I was on the road.

Eventually Cookie, the kids and I would move into what had been Cookie's grandmother's house. So that was completing a circle: me having lived in NY and Fort Benning, Georgia, and California and in NY again, then ending up right back in Richmond, three blocks from where I grew up.

I kept a diary for 1976. It was an I-Ching calendar diary in which I wrote what I planned to accomplish for each week and made notations for what I did daily. At the end of the week I wrote summary comments, including noting any unexpected happenings. Reading the diary now gives me such a clear set of reminders of what I was doing that year.

I am impressed by how much we rehearsed, how often I went to DC, and how much time I spent hunting for gigs. Week after week, rehearsing almost daily; traveling to DC, Philly, Baltimore, NY, hunting for gigs; recording; and promoting the music to radio and press. It was a grind, but I didn't seem to mind. My diary also records my occasional frustration at how the gigs would go, or at not having gigs, or worst of all, when gigs were cancelled. But for the most part I seemed to have had boundless energy, enthusiasm and determination.

With the release of the "African Rhythms" and "Space Jungle Luv" albums and the gigs we played, we branded ourselves as Oneness of Juju. That was the promotional agenda: building name recognition for the group, promoting the records, getting gigs to promote the records, to get more gigs. We did gigs in Richmond at the Ebony Island Club, Lucky Strike Club, The Devils Club, Virginia Union University, and the University of Richmond. Gigs in DC at Ed Murphy's Supper Club and Howard University. Trips to radio stations in Philly and Norfolk and Baltimore. More trips to DC to work with Jimmy Gray. A gig at Morgan State College in Baltimore. A gig with the Pointer Sisters in Richmond. A gig at Constitution Hall in DC cancelled. On and on. That was the routine. The unchanging same, with something new happening all the time.

On June 1, 1976, my daughter, Kaila, was born. I had been on the road but got back in time to be in the delivery room for her caesarean-section birth. I fell in love with her in less than five seconds. She was like a beautiful chocolate doll baby, just like her mother, only cuter. Cookie's mother came down from Philly to help with the new baby. Two days later I had to go to DC to be a pallbearer at an uncle's funeral. And that day, while I was out of town, the gas and water were turned off at my house. What an embarrassing turn of events with my mother-in-law in town! But that was just a small anecdote in the life of a struggling artist, depicting the eking out a living and the wear and tear on the family. But we pushed on and survived the hard times.

One week in August 1976, we played two successive nights in Philly for a Black nationalist group; and both nights the cops came and shut the event down, arresting anyone who protested their brutal, racist behavior. The next day we drove to DC to do a recording session, but on the way, Muzi was arrested for reckless driving (or "driving while black" in Maryland in those days); so I cut the recording session short to drive back to Baltimore to bail him out. The next day we drove back up from Richmond to DC to perform at

Constitution Hall opening for Taj Mahal and another headliner. Then I stayed in DC for a nine hour recording session the next day at Bias Recording. The next week we played two playground gigs and a club date at an after hour's club in Richmond. Whew!

Managing the group was an ongoing work in progress. Rasul, Babatunde and Lon would eventually leave, so I would be the only original member of Juju left in the group. In the summer of 1976, Lady Eka-Ete announced that she would leave the group, and that had a profound effect on me and Oneness of Juju. Because Eka-Ete was the vocalist and her physical presence was endearing and commanding, she had become the "face" and the voice of Oneness of Juju. And I feared she was irreplaceable. Promoters and club owners would say "Where's that girl?" And people would ask if she was coming back. And the implication was that the group was less appealing without her.

Yes, I would eventually find other female vocalists, just as I would over time have to substitute and replace other musicians. But moving forward, I realized that I would be the only constant. I was who I could always depend on to be there. And I had to be careful about the people and images I used for branding the group, so that it would be less disruptive when there were the inevitable personnel changes.

So, I changed the name of the group to Plunky & Oneness of Juju, placing the branding emphasis on me and my name (like with Lonnie Liston Smith & the Cosmic Echoes, or Roy Ayers & Ubiquity, or Donald Byrd and the Blackbirds, or Sly & the Family Stone, etc.). This meant I could market the group for gigs and I could show up with whomever and whatever group configuration I happened to bring. So the band clearly became my group. (I also began to market Plunky & the Universal Jazz Quartet and I also did solo and duo performances.)

It was my band and I recruited the most talented young people I could find. Over the next 40 years I would perform, record or work with more than 100 Richmond musicians; some of whom would later go on to form their own groups or work with national artists. In a way, I consider my group to be an educational institution. Jazz great, Art Blakey, was known for being an innovative hard bop drummer and for discovering and boosting the careers of many young jazz stars, including Freddie Hubbard, Wayne Shorter, and Wynton Marsalis. I was like the Art Blakey of Richmond, in that so many talented local musicians have come through my group and then gone on to some measure of success.

Oneness of Juju 1988 at Dogwood Dell in RVA

I kept up a hectic schedule of gigs, sometimes three or four in a week, plus rehearsals, yoga, promotion of gigs, and going to the DC area to do recording sessions, gigs and promotion. Eventually, I found Virtania Tillery, who would be our vocalist for five years. She was attractive, sweet, and dedicated, with a fabulous voice, like Phyllis Hyman singing in a Baptist church. Virtania also worked in my office helping me with correspondence, media relations and graphic designing. She became our female caregiver, our glue and the star of our show. Virtania's nickname was Cookie (the same as my wife's); so for those years I had two Cookies helping my career move forward.

Versatility is one of the reasons Plunky & Oneness of Juju remained viable as a musical entity. We played jazz, African, avant garde, rhythm & blues and other genres. I worked to make that multiplicity of genres and the range in our repertoire a part of our brand; but sometimes our versatility caused some confusion in the marketplace. I remember one week I got a call from a black nationalist group in DC wanting to book us but they wanted to be sure we were still doing Afrocentric music; and I got call from a high school in Richmond that wanted us to play for their senior prom but only if we would

Oneness of Juju 1989 Plunky, Virtania Tillery, Muzi & Weldon Hil

assure them that we wouldn't play any African music. I did both gigs.

Our versatility allowed us to play a variety of types of gigs: jazz clubs and concerts; commercial music clubs and dances; new music at arts venues and festivals; and music history and appreciation concert lectures at universities and schools. I developed marketing systems and materials targeting all these types of gigs; and our efforts were largely successful. No one type of these gigs was bountiful enough to sustain us, but by using this multi-pronged approach I was able to keep the band working. Virtania served as my office manager and marketing assistant. She had a keen eye for graphic design and a flair for sensible, professional correspondence. Together we got pretty good at doing our marketing and management thing.

⌘⌘⌘

Muzi, Ronnie Cokes, Virtania & Plunky

Chapter 9

Black Fire!

In his autobiography, "Q," Quincy Jones drops more names of Hollywood music and cultural icons than the Carters (B. and Jay Z) have social media postings. Of course, in examining Quincy's career which intersected with Count Basie, Frank Sinatra, Ray Charles, Oprah, Steven Spielberg, Michael Jackson and encompassed Thriller, The Color Purple, Vibe Magazine, Roots, and so much more, it would be impossible to recount it all without dropping a multitude of iconic names. And Q didn't spare them…

At the opposite end of the spectrum there is a local musician in some small town who has only interacted with musical peers from his proximate area and he has "met" national artists only through recordings and other media. Or maybe he attended a show and waved or got an autograph. Undoubtedly, there are millions more of him than there are Quincy Jones'.

I am somewhere in between. I can drop the names of 20 or 30 well known musicians and entertainers I have encountered, worked with or been impacted by; and I will: Bobby Byrd, Pharaoh Sanders, Ornette Coleman, Gil Scott-Heron, Hugh Masekela, Mtume, Roy Ayers, Fela Kuti, Chuck Brown, Last Poets, World Saxophone Quartet, Rashid Ali, Sam Rivers, Asante, David Murray, John Gilmore, Brian Jackson, Bill Summers, Lonnie Liston Smith, Kevin Teasley, Najee, and others. I may be the Quincy Jones of my hometown. (Maybe, I will call my autobiography "P - The Q of RVA.")

A musician's life story catalogues various high points of achievement: gigs in special venues, hit records, tours to far-flung places, educational accomplishments, awards and other recognitions. Behind many of these events and successes are special people - collaborators, mentors, inspirers, benefactors, peers, celebrities, unknowns – some sought out and some met by chance; some valued immediately and others only in retrospect; some who were important before and others who became even more so later. I call these important encounters "momentous meetings." A momentous meeting is a fortuitous encounter of two people that is of monumental importance to at least one of them. A momentous meeting can affect one's philosophy, alter the course of a career or change a life.

As I look back on my career I realize I have had several momentous

Experience Unlimited album cover

meetings with important musicians who have had impact on music, entertainment and culture. And in some ways, it has been these hook ups that have placed me in situations that give validity to my own reputation, views and celebrity. I am guilty or elevated by association. I am "important" because I am a member of a relatively exclusive club of persons who have been in the presence of these specific great people, the exact collection of whom is likely exclusive to me.

"Black Fire!" was the rallying cry, persona and on-air moniker of 1970s Washington, DC radio personality, provocateur, Jimmy Gray. And Black Fire would be the name of Jimmy Gray's record promotion and distribution company, his music publishing company and the name of the independent, boutique record label he would establish with me.

Jimmy and I were more than business partners. He was a mentor to me and we were best friends. For years I made weekly commutes to DC and spent so much time in the District that people thought I lived there and was a local DC artist. In all those years, my DC trips began and ended at Jimmy's house

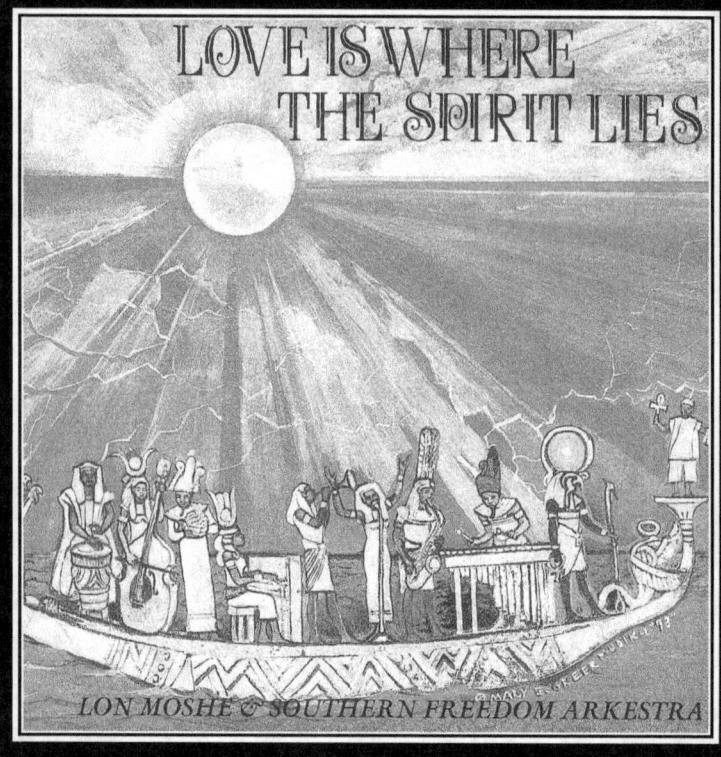

Lon Moshe album cover

on Douglas Street, NE. We didn't just do business; we had big fun, raucous, rip-roaring fun. We were crazy and wild, political and committed; and we were convinced that we could make a difference, not just in DC, but in the world. And into all hours of the night we talked music, listened to music, lived the music, made music and produced albums.

In addition to the albums by Oneness of Juju that he and I produced, Jimmy Gray recorded and produced music by several other artists and groups for Black Fire Records. He recorded Experience Unlimited (E.U.), Hamiet Bluiett, Byard Lancaster, Wayne Davis, Asante, Theater West, Lon Moshe, Southern Energy Ensemble, Baba Dontez, and Puzi Phillips & the Space Rangers, in addition to local poets and spoken word artists.

We did our recording at several studios in the DC area: Bias Recording in Virginia, Omega Recording in Maryland and later at Shannon Walton's Studio in Virginia. But in between, for several months we had afterhours access to Arrest Recording Studio located on the top floor of an eight story office building in downtown DC. We would go in after 9 or 10 PM and some-

Wayne Davis album cover

Southern Energy album cover

times record all night. I would come once, twice or even more times per week, driving 100 miles from Richmond. On at least one occasion the elevator was out of order and we had to make multiple trips up the stairs carrying equipment; but we got the session done. We had some great musicians coming through and we produced some great music. Jimmy Gray was the executive producer and the fly-by-the-seat-of-his-pants engineer and the master puppeteer pulling the strings.

An independent record promoter's job is to solicit radio airplay, press reviews, club play and anything else to boost sales for record releases and garner support for the artists of the various contracting record labels. Bridging his radio gigs with work as a record promoter for various jazz labels afforded Jimmy Gray the luxury of free, promo LPs which greatly enhanced his collection and also allowed him to curry favors among the radio hierarchy and deejays in the DC area. That bridging was also potentially a conflict of interest for a commercial radio station, so Jimmy began to use the mysterious, nameless persona called "Black Fire" on the air.

continued on page 90

Hamiet Bluiet album cover

Theater West album cover

DC native Jimmy Gray was a record collector and jazz musicologist. He was an on-air music programmer on WHUR-FM, the powerful and influential black radio station of Howard University and the Pacifica Network's WPFW-FM, the most progressive, news and music voice in DC, where Jimmy was known for his quirky blends of jazz, blues, R&B, avant garde, new music, poetry and sharp political rhetoric. Jimmy Gray was an icon and an iconoclast who knew his music and who used his extensive knowledge and vast collection of over 5,000 albums to his distinct advantage in establishing his credibility among those who loved, made and lived "the music." He also published a Black Fire Magazine, which was more like a monthly catalogue of the music he was marketing

Jimmy Gray, the record promoter, did work for several jazz labels, including Blue Note Records, Flying Dutchman and Impulse and he became the regional promotion person for Creed Taylor's CTI record label. Jimmy noted how those labels marketed and branded their companies by contracting and releasing the music of a stable of music artists, and developing their careers, having a signature sound, paying attention to the details and by utilizing high quality images for the artwork and photography of their album covers. Later Black Fire Records would use variations of all these branding techniques to create a market and a mystique around the label's music.

Independent record companies were the first niche marketers in the music business. They usually catered to a specific geographic area or a specific music genre. Early blues music labels, race record labels and even some country

Jimmy Gray at home

Black Fire Magazine cover

music labels fit this mold. By the late 1950s, a few black artists tried starting their own record labels to combat what they saw as prejudice and exploitation in some of the music industry's business practices. Sam Cooke, Lloyd Price and James Brown among others started their own R&B labels. In 1960, Berry Gordy incorporated Motown Records, which would go on to be one of the most successful, Black-owned record companies of all time.

The counterculture of the Sixties and Seventies was led by artists who often rebelled against the established corporate structure of the record industry. These artists and producers saw themselves as creating new pathways to self-determination, and artistic, and maybe financial, freedom.

Producers found that they could manufacture as few as 1,000 or even 500 records at a time. These short run pressings could be done for reasonably small investments of about $1.50-$2.00 per L.P. after the cost of studio time. The records could retail for $5.95 and be sold to distributors for about $3.00. In theory, a profit could be made; though, given the costs of marketing, profit could be hard to realize. And then there were also the lotto-long odds of getting a "hit" record, wherewith one might hit the jackpot and become a rich star or a mogul.

Most musicians came to see having an album as the validation or documentation of their music as art. Having a record release, whether by a major corporation or a tiny mom-and-pop label, was a necessary commercial venture by which an artist's career would be advanced. Even if a musician never made any money directly from the sales, their records were the only way to get radio airplay, publishing royalties, and to generate a larger fan base. Record albums were the principle way to promote one's artistic vision, one's political, spiritual and lifestyle views, and one's career. Records would be the advertisements for a musician's live performances and touring. Having an album created a certain cache of importance and status for artists. And if nothing else, musicians could merchandise their albums at their gigs and thereby increase their revenues.

Strata-East was the innovative independent jazz label and Jimmy Gray became the label's promotion man for DC and points south. [See Chapter 6 Big Apple Free Jazz.]

Jimmy was also a fan of the avant garde, new music, free jazz artists, such as Sun Ra, Ornette Coleman, Cecil Taylor, John Coltrane, Archie Shepp, Eric Dolphy, Albert Ayler, the AACM, the Art Ensemble of Chicago, Sunny Murray, Rashied Ali, Sam Rivers, and many others. In addition to listening to, collecting and promoting this music, Jimmy would later move into distributing the music of smaller independent labels to the radio stations, record stores and one-stops in the DC-Maryland-Virginia (DMV) area and beyond. Sun Ra was an avant garde jazz artist who inspired Jimmy Gray. Sun Ra used his compositions and Solar Myth Arkestra, a free jazz big band, to articulate his own cosmology, which promoted Egyptology and the ideas of music as a vehicle for space and time travel. Sun Ra's live performances were multimedia extravaganzas that included dancers, visual arts and poetic expressions and collective improvisations. Jimmy Gray loved Sun Ra's music, his eclecticism and his Blackness. But in addition, Sun Ra manufactured and sold his music on his own record label, Saturn records, and Jimmy loved collecting Sun Ra's music.

When Jimmy Gray died in 1996, he had a record collection of well over 6,000 albums and other recordings. Since I was Jimmy's partner, his family allowed me to buy the collection and the rights to the Black Fire business, copyrights and master recordings for a total of $50,000. I made a deal with a record collector to sell the record collection for the $50k.

When the record collector came to Jimmy's old house to buy the collection, Jimmy's son and my son, Jamiah, helped us sort through and load out the records. I explained to Jamiah that while the whole collection was valued at $50k, the 100 Sun Ra albums were worth $10,000 ($100 each). That was amazing because while Sun Ra was alive he could barely sell the albums at his concerts for $5, but they had gone up 2,000 percent in value after he died. Jamiah said to me, "Dad, that's how you're gonna be. Your records are gonna be worth a lot more when you die." Jamiah contemplated my legacy and his inheritance, then after a pause he said, "You gotta make more records!"

Here is my poem for Jimmy:

Black Fire
(for Jimmy Gray's Funeral)   10/1/96

a black fire burns at your core
spreading a warmth that radiates
through your love of our music
expressing itself through your words and deeds
low key and in the background
yet boisterous and smoothed with lots of reverb
your strength is in your voiced opinions
and in your ability to improvise on a theme
take an idea and run with it in your mouth
stop on a sixteenth note and spit it out
as a riff in a solo or a whimsical rhyming couplet
followed by a chuckle
to relieve the listener of the need to be serious
but you are always serious
serious i say
seer-ious as a soothsayer
a forward reacher just slightly ahead of this time
panasonic and panchromatic
like melodious chaos and multiple shades of ebony
you have vision
tunneled and expansive
you are a producer and a transducer

a resister and a transistor
a performer and a transformer
a defender and a transcender
a realist and a surrealist
blending colors to refracture images of the light in your eyes
your graying afro forms a halo to hold your apple jack cap
your chew stick is a symbol of quiet charisma
reminding you and others of your connection
to other times and unlimited dimensions
your fastings and your musical diet have made you wizened
beyond those ten years you are my senior
i'd like to think i'm smarter
but time and then again some little film clip of a digital sample of a
snippet of something that you said to me after i said it to you in the
first place comes back around to haunt me for not saying yeah you
predicted that it would come to pass   and that your name for it
would be the nommo that would cast just the right spell to blend the
juju and the blues to make the funk jazz juice that would serve as a
medicinal balm for the computer-induced viral complacency of a
new age
i should have said it before
well i'm saying it now in this poem
your ideas spark and enkindle with improvised whimsy
you are an inspiration
keep on burning
black fire!
   — Plunky

⌘⌘⌘

Chapter 10

Branches of the Arts

Black political power in Richmond rose during the 1960s as the percentage of blacks in the general population rose to over 50%. In 1970 the white majority city council annexed 23 square miles of the adjacent county that included a population of 50,000 people that was 90% white. The annexation was challenged in federal court; and finally in 1977 the 4th circuit ruled that the city's at-large voting system unfairly diluted the black community's political power. A nine-ward system was put in place with five of the wards having black majorities. In 1977, after local elections had been suspended for over five years, voters impaneled for the first time a black majority city council and Attorney Henry L. Marsh III was selected the city's first black mayor.

It was in this local political climate that our own efforts to advance black culture took root. I had kept up the commercial music promoting, and soliciting for gigs by doing mass mailings to schools, colleges and art venues. Then I started to explore getting arts grants to support our music and the neighborhood arts activities we were doing at Kahero Gallery. This diversification of my efforts would over time lead to me adding arts administrator, advocate, and grants writer to my job titles.

Most arts grants and are awarded to tax-exempt, non-profit organizations. In 1978 I founded Branches of the Arts, Inc., (BOTA) a tax-exempt, non-profit organization dedicated to the development of Black art as a cultural, educational and business resource for the community.

When I applied to corporations and foundations and was turned down, I would learn about their giving patterns and requirements and I would try again. Often the application procedures would take a year or more before funds would be received. I decided early on I would not let the length of time be a deterrent to applying and competing for funds. I theorized that no matter how long it took, we would still need the funds when they came. So I would persevere.

When I applied to the Virginia Commission for the Arts (VCA), the state arts support agency, and was turned down, I did some research and found that their funding almost always went to white organizations like the ballet compa-

Kwanza flyer 1984

nies, orchestras, galleries, and the Federated Arts Council (FAC), etc. I decided I would challenge the basis for the VCA's distribution of public funds, believing that the black community's organizations deserved to receive some of the tax revenues. We allied with a local activist attorney, Sa'ad El-Amin, and threatened to sue the state.

During that time we participated in debates over issues such as: the definition of art, cultural aesthetics, multiculturalism, the role of art in society, public and private funding for the arts, and the politics of the arts. My own

Federated Arts Council (FAC) News article
re: Plunky as Arts District Director

branches of the arts faces closing

Branches of the Arts has announced that its community arts center, located at 312 East Clay Street in downtown Richmond, will close unless additional funds can be raised. James E. Branch, Jr., executive director of the center, cited increased building maintenance costs as the primary cause of the art center's financial woes.

"When we opened the center, we considered the building and its operation as a work of community art. It was to be functional, committed and collective. And above all, it is to beautify the community. But it's been increasingly difficult to beautify when most of the corporation's energies have to be directed towards utilities, upkeep, telephone, insurance, alarm systems and on and on . . ." Branch was quoted as saying. "As a functioning work of art, the Center's greatest achievement might be demonstrating to the city that community art, a cultural center and the types of programming we have provided are viable and needed. We just hope that we aren't closed down and gone before that realization hits home. We need support now."

BOTA subleases office space, artists' studios and cooperates a printing shop at the center. The building's conference room-lounge is regularly used as a meeting place for art and civic groups, workshops and the advisory council.

The arts center operates with a paid staff of two persons. Executive Director James E. Branch, Jr., coordinates, schedules and implements projects for the art center. Additional responsibilities include developing, acquiring and maintaining a permanent art collection for the center, as well as appointing staff and volunteers to assist in the smooth operation of the art center. Branch also acts as public relations director for the center, formulating promotional campaigns, statements of public policy and press releases.

Administrative Assistant Jacqueline Holoman helps the director coordinate schedule and implement projects; and is also responsible for coordinating comprehensive exhibition schedules, mailing lists and registries of local minority artists.

Volunteers serve as building manager, curators of the galleries, and public relations specialists, while artists and other workshop instructors supplement their incomes by conducting classes for fees at the art center.

Regular seminar presentations on African-American music by the Oneness of Juju and other authorities at Kahero II make information available to the community that will help make the music more appreciated. These seminars have already been utilized in 15 Richmond public schools; and added to workshops conducted by visiting professionals will help cultivate better educated audiences for music and the arts.

Workshops and classes in dance, slimnastics, yoga, poetry, theater arts and disco dancing are conducted at the BOTA Center. These types of activities increase the participation in the creative process by attracting numbers of persons who might otherwise not have been moved to venture inside an art gallery.

Because accessible rehearsal sites can encourage better performances, the BOTA Center has created a basement rehearsal room that is available for rent by musicians for $5 - $10 per four hour session. In addition, Kahero II is used for rehearsals by several groups; i.e., Richmond Community Theater Guild, Touch of Glamour Models, Soweto Community Theater, Kuumba Dancers.

FAC article re Branches of the Arts Center closing

---

view was that the aesthetics of Black art were based on cultural identity, functionality and community support. I argued that these aesthetic criteria were just as valid as those ascribed to European art forms, and that tax funds used to support the arts should be more equitably distributed among groups who pay into the tax coffers. These challenges would eventually lead to changes at the state and local levels.

One of the biggest impediments to Black arts groups to get funding was the fact that most of them were not tax-exempt corporations, so BOTA functioned as a Black arts council, an umbrella group comprised of Black music, theater, dance groups, choirs and exhibitors. BOTA offered financial administration services, developmental support, and technical assistance to fledgling Black arts groups. One of our greatest successes was the creation of the Richmond Jazz Society (RJS) which was formed in my dining room. RJS is now 30 years old with over 600 members and still going strong.

BOTA eventually established an arts center in a former Black business school building in downtown Richmond's Jackson Ward neighborhood. Responding to the needs of the community, BOTA organized the Black Arts

5 north 6th

BOTA publicizes events and programs at the center through press releases, public service announcements on radio and television, posters, leaflets, and through member organizations of the advisory council. The corporation also utilizes its extensive mailing lists and nonprofit bulk mailing permit to reach hundreds of artists and art lovers directly.

BOTA plans to produce or co-produce a number of benefit concerts to raise money for the operation of the arts center. Concerts featuring Les Ballets Africans or nationally known jazz artists are being considered. VCU has pledged to utilize BOTA for public relations services in exchange for 10-15% of the receipts from its jazz concert series during the 1979-80 school year.

BOTA should be able to continue its working relationships with Richmond Public Schools, Virginia Union University, VCU and other educational institutions, by providing services to their student populations. In so doing the arts center may be considered as a "line item" in the budgets for future fiscal years.

"A black arts center can be an asset to Richmond's art community and to downtown tourist attractions," Branch said, "if we can get enough support to keep it alive."

The opening of the Branches of the Arts Center on Clay Street in June was an important event for both the arts community and the citizens of Richmond. During the past four months the Center provided programming in a wide range of art forms and a home for a number of Branches member groups. Under the strong leadership of James Branch, executive director, the Center worked to develop a broader awareness of community and black arts.

The Center has shown, along with its predecessor, Kahero I, and the studies done on Stonewall Jackson, the Broad Street Theaters and Blues Armory, the continued need and interest in a community arts center for the city of Richmond. The Branches Center has also demonstrated that hard work, strong leadership, massive in-kind contributions and real interest from the community are not enough to keep a center open. It takes dollars from both the public and private sector.

Branches of the Arts and the Federated Arts Council have been working with the City of Richmond to develop a comprehensive plan which will result in this badly needed center. The time is now. The facts are there. The citizens of Richmond, the arts community and the city need to take this important next step to ensure the continued growth of the arts in Richmond.

Kathy Dwyer
Executive Director, FAC

FAC article re: Branches of the Arts

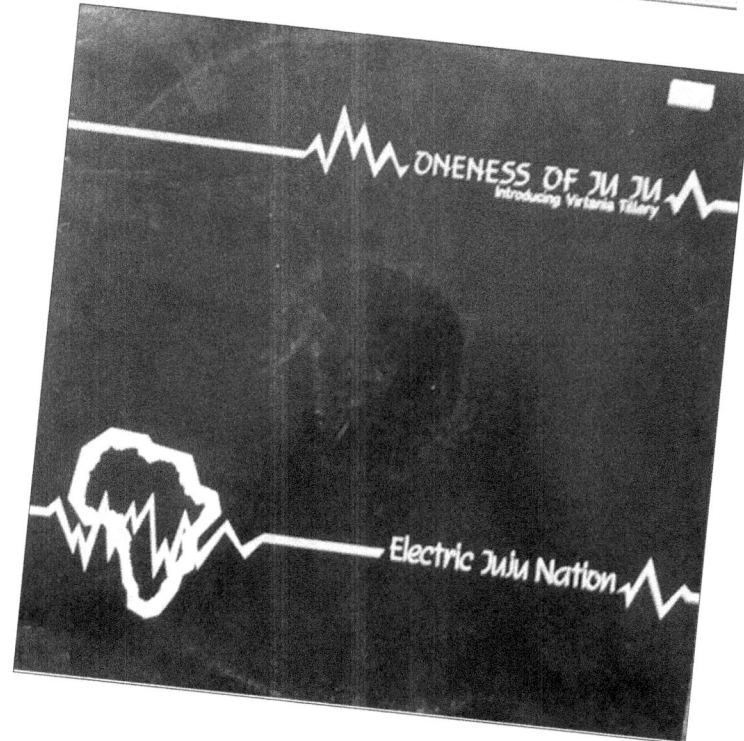

Advisory Council composed of representatives of music groups, dance companies, theater groups, visual artists, photographers, arts advocates and benefactors. The BOTA Black Arts Advisory Council served as a forum for the exploration of roles and opportunities for Black arts in the community and advocated for funding and support for Black arts initiatives.

But our cultural efforts and the black political power of the mayor and city council were not universally endorsed and accepted. The white corporate business community was wary of the black mayor and not quite sure how economic progress would be made. Indeed, some resisted the transition of power and worked against any black initiatives. Likewise, the established arts organizations were unsure how black culture and neighborhood arts could be incorporated in the landscape of programs and funding.

Our BOTA pressure and successes led to discussions with Kathy Dwyer, executive director of the Federated Arts Council (FAC). Kathy was not a native of Richmond and she was an astute political tactician. Her FAC board of directors was stocked with the who's who of the corporate community and her organization was well-heeled. Kathy understood the subtle potential power of the arts to build bridges across political and racial battle lines and she believed that getting factions to work together on arts projects could soften hardened positions that were often based on unfamiliarity and past differences.

Kathy and I talked about the political advantages of our two organizations, BOTA and FAC, working together to do big things in the city. We decided to create an alliance that would leave BOTA as a separate, independent entity and with me being hired as program director of the FAC. Kathy found in Mayor Marsh a partner who was willing to use arts and culture to show that cooperation could be beneficial to the community at large. The mayor shared the view that the arts could be the vehicle to bridge divides and bring folks together so they could learn to work together.

Kathy Dwyer became my mentor, and the two of us, working with the powers that be, were able to do some dynamic things. We created several popular programs, including an annual downtown arts festival called June Jubilee, which drew tens of thousands of attendees to downtown RVA. We were successful using the arts and planning initiatives as vehicles to bring Black political leaders together with region's corporate directors.

During that time I became a full-fledged arts administrator. I served on review panels for the VCA, the Mid-Atlantic Arts Foundation and the

National Endowment for the Arts (NEA). I was a consultant and site evaluator for the NEA and I served on their advisory panel creating a new interdisciplinary arts grant program. I was also quite active in local politics, working on community arts projects with Mayor Marsh and the other black city council members: Willie Dell, Walter Kenny, Claudette Black McDaniels and especially my district's representative, Henry "Chuck" Richardson. Later, I was also appointed to the Governor's Council on the Promotion of the Arts in Virginia by Governor Douglas Wilder, the first black governor in Virginia.

The arts administration gig was my day job while I continued to perform as a professional musician. I had come a long, long way from being the big Afro, dashiki-wearing, cultural nationalist activist to being a respected community arts leader.

In 1982, I was hired as the executive director of the Richmond Foundation for the Arts, an organization whose mission was establishing a district for the arts in downtown Richmond. The foundation acquired control of a five-story, 65,000 square foot historic building to be developed into the anchoring art center, in addition to two theaters and a few small shops. I and my staff operated the real estate, conducted fund-raising campaigns, and began to generate support for the project among the artists and the community.

But a funny thing called politics reared its fickle head on the way to establishment of the arts district. A new mayor was elected in June 1982 and because the arts district project had been so closely associated with the previous administration, the new mayor would not support the project. Without the support of the city government, the Richmond Arts District Foundation found it difficult to raise funds and eventually folded.

Disappointed with the whims of political shifts, I left the job of being a paid arts administrator, and decided that political rankling and posturing was not for me. But I kept working with BOTA and Richmond black arts groups like Soweto Stage Company, Ezibu Muntu African Dancers, Kuumba Dancers (children's group), choirs, non-governmental organizations, and individual musicians, poets, painters and photographers.

BOTA hired Delisa Saunders, a dynamic, young black college graduate, as our executive director and she guided the organization with outstanding competence and professionalism. We expanded our board of directors which was led by Attorney Charles Chambliss. We produced the annual BOTA Black

Arts Awards program to honor the best of the black community's arts. (That regal event was like our local Academy Awards.) We also produced the city's first Kwanzaa programs from 1976–1982 and brought in touring productions from the New York's Negro Ensemble Company. Working as an independent promoter and with Dr. Murray DePillars, Dean of the VCU School of the Arts and with the Richmond Jazz Society, we were over the years able to present in Richmond renown jazz artists, such as Jackie McLean, Sonny Fortune, Pharoah Sanders, Hugh Masekela, and Art Blakey.

I never stopped being a working musician committed to making a difference in the community in a direct way. Oh yeah, and I also worked as a substitute teacher in the public schools and as guest lecturer in colleges. So I remained quite active.

Plunky at Richmond Public School Legacy Breakfast

Plunky at school assembly program

⌘⌘⌘

Chapter 11

What a Trip – Africa and Beyond

1980 was significant for two reasons: Plunky & Oneness of Juju started working on our next album, and I took my first trip out of the country. We had released albums in 1973, '74, '75 and '76; so by 1980 it had been a longer than usual gap. The new album would be called "Make a Change" and it would be noteworthy, but it wouldn't be published until late 1981.

In September 1980, I went to Africa. Finally. I traveled there with my friend Garry, a New Yorker whom I had met 10 years earlier in San Francisco when he showed up at my door referred by a mutual friend. Garry and I became fast friends, and he remains, to this day, a close confidant, business partner and a favorite travel companion. Over the years we have shared many wild and crazy situations in West Africa, New York, Guatemala, Hawaii, DC and more. So many that we can't remember them all. Garry's own catalogue of zany and coincidence-filled experiences is so vast I have often said he should write a book. And my first trip abroad with him would fit right in to that tome.

We were leaving from NY, and ticketed through to Lagos, Nigeria, but we

Lagos street vendors

could only get a confirmation for the first leg of the trip to London, arriving at 7:00 AM Friday morning. Our plan had been to go into London and spend the day with friends there, and come back to the airport that night to catch the 11:00 PM flight to Lagos. When we arrived at Heathrow Airport in London there were hundreds of Africans at the Air Nigeria ticket counters wanting and waiting to take the one late night flight to Lagos. We learned that five of Air Nigeria's 22 planes were out of service so there were people in the airport who had been stranded for a few days waiting for the rescheduling of their canceled flights.

So instead of sightseeing in London, we spent that whole day at the airport maneuvering, jostling, and finagling to get our two boarding passes. Late that night when we were (miraculously) finally on board the plane looking through the cabin's window we could see a mob of Nigerians who had stormed through customs, running through the terminal toward the boarding area trying to get to the plane, as we taxied out toward the runway for takeoff. What a crazy start to a wild trip!

On the plane when dinner was served, I politely asked the Nigerian stewardess if I could get a vegetarian meal. She sucked her teeth, took my plate, and never served me anything else. I came to believe Nigerians are not the most hospitable, considerate people on the planet.

I was going to Nigeria to negotiate and consult on the development of a recording studio for Bala Miller, a musician from Kaduna, a city in northern Nigeria. Garry was going to conduct ongoing business with his friend, Esalinta, president of Ashland Oil of Nigeria. But even on a business trip, Nigeria is not the most welcoming place to visit.

When we landed at Lagos International airport Garry cautioned me, saying, "Stick close to me so I can get us through the customs and immigration process." But as soon as we got off the plane and I was walking behind Garry toward the terminal, a uniformed guy grabbed me and escorted me to an interrogation room. He said that I didn't have the necessary inoculation stamps in my passport and I would have to be quarantined unless I paid him $100. I paid it and when I caught up to Garry and related what happened he said "I told to you stick close by me!" And when I pointed out another "soldier" in the same kind of uniform, it turned out to be a custodial worker. I had been scammed by a Nigerian janitor before I even got in the country!

From the first glimpse I knew Africa was a different place than what I had fantasized and romanticized about for so many years. Lagos, Nigeria teems with black humanity in swelteringly hot weather with big leafed vegetation,

Garry White with his big smile

dirt, dust, and smells of waste. African art, images and symbols are everywhere. We took a cab to Ikeja, the area of the city near the airport, to a cheap hotel to get some rest. While we slept, the electrical power went off in the room. (Actually the power would go off in various parts of the city daily for hours at a time.) Garry woke up in a sweaty daze, went over to open the window and the air conditioner fell out and crashed down into the yard below, barely missing a maid doing the wash. He stumbled back to bed and when we, hearing a thunderous rain storm, woke up a couple of hours later, the room was flooded and there was a sopping mess.

The hotel manager wanted us to pay $1,000 and threatened to hold our passports until we did. Garry was able to negotiate him down to $400 and we got out of there.

Lagos is a city of millions, like an African NYC, only more congested, polluted, noisy and dangerous. There are a myriad of colors and musics. There is extreme poverty and not enough sanitation. The people are discourteous but I learned to not take that personally because they treated each other just as badly.

Esalinta lived on Victoria Island, the section of Lagos where the rich and

Bala Miller and Plunky

Plunky with Bala Miller's singers

Plunky with Bala Miller's horn players

Bala Miller album cover

privileged reside. And he was rich and privileged, earning a dollar a day for every a barrel of oil pumped by his company. And they pumped 50,000 barrels a day! That was more money than I could calculate. Esalinta had money, property and business interests in NY and London, and probably several other places. Garry, who had pursued an MBA at Columbia and had lots of experience in Africa, was Esalinta's procurer, U.S. business advisor, style consultant and running buddy.

Esalinta moved us into the big hotel on Victoria Island for the rest of the week. But even there and along the streets leading to Esalinta's offices and residence, the contrasting luxury of the rich juxtaposed against the poverty of the people living in corrugated metal shacks leaning against buildings with open sewage flowing along the gutters was disconcerting, to say the least. I was never able to reconcile the incongruity of the extremes of poverty and richness. It was capitalism at its worst. For a tiny number of elites to take so much at the expense and suffering of so many, was Nigerian callousness, glaringly personified. (And, I think, the exploitation and corruption by the Nigeria elite continue to this day.)

One night Garry and I went to a corporate sponsored banquet concert at the National Theater. They were honoring Pearl Bailey, but we went there to hear some juju music by Dele Obiodun and Chief Commander Ebenezer Obey. When the food buffet was opened, things got rowdy. (It seems that Nigerians never line up for anything, not at bus stops, ticket windows or food lines.) Only the first few people got served because they just took all the food, pouring it into purses and bags. When Pearl Bailey got on stage she lectured the audience about being discourteous to her and each other, and she was roundly booed.

We stayed at the event to hear the juju music and enjoyed it immensely, but by the time we left, it was past the 11:00 PM curfew and there were no taxis on the streets. So we bribed a bus driver to use a military bus to take us back to our hotel. We had to lie on the floor of the bus as we went through the army check points. I was scared as hell, but we laughed about it later.

On Friday we were to take a flight up north to Kaduna for my meeting with Bala Miller. When we got to the airport, we were directed to the hanger for the domestic flights and we found out the airline was still short of planes. There was a sea of humanity much more intense and densely packed than a week ago in the London airport. In this hangar there were people sleeping on the floor, cooking, tending goats and tending bundles of their belongings; temporarily "living there," waiting for flights. I called it the "temple of doom." Through this mass of humanity we had to navigate with our bags being carried on the heads of our baggage handlers to get to the ticket counter, only to be told to come back in an hour. We did.

At one point an airport security policeman came up behind us and started beating one of our baggage carrying boys about the head. When I protested, the cop said, "Master, this boy was trying to steal from you!" And I said, "No he is working for us!" In order to get the cop to stop using his Billy club, I gave him a few dollars. Later, I saw the cop and the bloodied boy splitting the money. Nigeria, land of scams!

We got our tickets to Kaduna. Two hours later there was an announcement over the airport P.A., "The plane to Kaduna is now boarding." That was all that was announced; no gate or plane number or anything. It was now pouring down rain and a mass of people poured out of the hangar, all just running across the airfield toward a plane 100 yards away; so Garry and I ran with them. I am a fast runner, so I was among the first to reach the plane only to be told "This is not the plane to Kaduna." So we took off running to the next plane, where we were told the same thing.

You have to imagine the spectacle of a mob of African people, some with bundles on their heads, women with babies tied on their backs, a few in business suits, several in Muslim robes, all running in a torrential downpour. I am laughing to myself, thinking, "This is why they call it a runway?" I am ahead of the pack, running beside a Muslim guy whose sandal had come off and he was kicking the shoe which skimmed along the inch high water. When we reached the third plane the whole mob just rushed up the stairs and packed into the seats and aisles of the plane. The steward said, "This is not the plane to Kaduna!" The passengers screamed back, "It is now!" And we flew to Kaduna.

Bala Miller is a big band leader and local celebrity in Northern Nigeria. I met with him to discuss the studio he wanted to build in the area with some governmental assistance. We put together some ideas, a catalogue of equipment needed, and a budget. That weekend I jammed with him and his big band at his open air night club. I enjoyed the music, his female dancers, and the enthusiastic response of the audience. My first experience in an African club setting was a rousing success.

One of the hitches to doing the business ventures we were attempting to do in Nigeria was the lack of international banking valuation for Nigeria currency (naira), meaning the naira was worthless outside Nigeria. So, one way to get some value for the money we earned in Nigeria was to pay for Air Nigeria plane tickets with naira and use the tickets or cash them in for dollars. This meant we could buy the tickets at 10 cents on the dollar, then either cash them in, or travel anywhere in the world cheaply.

The next week Garry and I flew to Banjul, the capital city of The Gambia. Garry had friends there and they were great hosts, putting us up in a quaint Scandinavian-style hotel right on the beach. The people, weather and water were warm and inviting. Once while we were socializing and recounting our experiences in Nigeria, one of our Gambian hosts said he used to live and do business in Lagos. He said he learned never try to fly domestically on a Friday (like Garry and I did when going to Kaduna), because that's when all the locals fly home to the countryside and the airport is a madhouse. And he asked, "Do they still do that thing at the airport where you have to bribe someone to tell you the gate and plane for your flight?" And I said, "Now you tell us!"

In the Gambia we had first class food, accommodations and music. It was a relaxing place to unwind from my first high-energy trip to Nigeria. The Gambia remains one of my favorite places in Africa.

Three months after we got back from Africa, I got a series of messages from my old college friend, Bruce, inviting me and Garry to come visit him in Guatemala, Central America. Bruce said there were some business prospects there, and since we could travel cheaply, Garry and I decided we would go on a working vacation and take his girlfriend, Delilah, and my wife, Cookie, along as a treat.

On the day of our trip, upon arriving at the airport in DC, Cookie discovered she had left her passport at home in Richmond. She would not make the trip but the other three of us did. We flew to Guatemala City, Guatemala, where Bruce met us at the airport. From there we took a lorry bus 80 miles to the southwestern highlands to a town called Panajachel – 5,000 feet up in the mountains and bordering the beautiful Lake Atitlan. From the town you can look across the lake to see two active volcano peaks side by side on the horizon. Bruce lived outside town in a rustic house in a dried up river bed. There was no electricity or plumbing but there were beautiful orchids and multi-colored birds all about. It was as an idyllic and isolated location as you can imagine.

We unwound there for a few days enjoying the area. Bruce told us he and his lady were planning to go into business exporting Guatemalan crafts and textiles. It seemed a hippy-ish cottage industry to me, but he thought it could be profitable.

Bruce entertained us and told us stories. He said there was political unrest in the countryside all around his place. By day, the military would come to him to talk about any peasant unrest in the area. And by night, the peasant guerillas would come through his property.

He also told us about a German architect who had come to do some building design work for one of the armies in the region. When it came time for him to collect his pay, the architect was taken by army jeep out into the bush where he was ushered into a warehouse full of cocaine. The army general told him he could only collect the $100,000 owed him by either arranging for them to buy German arms or by accepting a trunk of coke as payment. Since the

German had no contacts for German armaments, he came to Bruce to see if he could help arrange the sale of a load of cocaine.

We thought they were interesting stories and they gave Garry and Delilah and I lots to talk about when we got back to the states.

The weirdness of finding myself in the mountains in Guatemala and the beauty of the place never ceases to amaze my memory. 35 years later I re-read some postcards and letters I received from my Richmond roommate, Lew, when he was hitchhiking through Mexico and Central America during the time when I was living in San Francisco. In one of the Lew's letters he described the lake and the volcano peaks and the solemn beauty of a place called Panajachel. I am amazed that we all found ourselves in that same obscure place in Guatemala at different times.

The next time that I heard from Bruce, he was marketing crafts and textiles from Central and South America and Asia. I never did hear what happened to the trunk of coke.

Panajachel, Guatemala

⌘⌘⌘

CHAPTER 12
EVERY WAY BUT LOOSE

In the fall of 1981, we released the Plunky & Oneness of Juju Make A Change album. It would be musically noteworthy and lead to significant steps forward in terms of business and marketing. In fact, that album might be my most impactful ever.

My brother, Muzi, and I produced the LP which was recorded at Omega Recording Studios in Maryland. The personnel of the group and on the recording included Ras Mel Glover on guitar, Weldon Hill on piano, Kevin Davis on drums and both Lady Eka-Ete and Virtania Tillery on vocals. We worked on the songs and producing the album for over a year and a half. Muzi and I were committed to trying to have the album appeal to a wide music-loving public, so we incorporated reggae, funk, and what later would be called smooth jazz, in the mix. We felt the music on the album was special and the quality of its production values was quite evident. In the end, every cut got either radio airplay or club play, and the album garnered critical acclaim in local and regional press.

A review of the album written by C. A. Bustard appeared in the Richmond Times-Dispatch Newspaper at the time of its April, 1981 release:

"From a younger generation of Richmond jazz people comes another new disc, the third album by the Afro-funk-jazz collective Oneness of Juju, "Make A Change" (Black Fire BF-19811). Like the earlier issues, this one is a wide-ranging fusion effort, the new release differing from the first two mainly in terms of technical polish – it is beautifully engineered and mixed – and in the introduction of reggae to the Juju mix.

That occurs in the title track, which, along with the funk-oriented "Higher," ranks as the most substantial commercial matter on the disc. The balance of the album ranges from thunder-funk ("Every Way But Loose") to a synthesizer/guitar fantasia ("Runaway Bay") to a pair of evocative, semitropical romances (the instrumental "Loves Wonderland" and "Always Have To Say Goodbye," highlighting vocalist Virtania Tillery).

The group's leader, Plunky Nkabinde, proved his saxophonist's mettle in the "June Jubilee Jazz" show with a stunning John Coltrane tribute on solo tenor sax. Aside from a soaring but less ambitious soprano sax solo in "Loves Wonderland," however, he remains generally in the group on the disc.

The other solo highlights of "Change" come courtesy of guitarist Ras Mel Glover Jr. and keyboardist Weldon Hill in "Run Away Bay," a Glover composition. Otherwise, the disc is instrumentally paced by bassist Muzi Nkabinde, whose style might be described as funk with a light touch.
Chances are, the disc will be enjoyed more by dancers than sedentary listeners."

One song in particular, "Every Way But Loose," started to get played in clubs, as deejays discovered its appeal to dancers. The song was favored by gay cubs in DC and Philly because the beat was so current and the lyrics were intentionally filled with sexual and political innuendo.

EVERY WAY BUT LOOSE
(J. PLUNKY BRANCH)

We want to turn you on/ and turn you every way but loose
Turn you on/ with nothing but the truth
We want to turn you on/ make you shake your caboose
Turn you on/ and turn you every way but loose
Every way but loose (4x)
We want to turn it out/ with nothing but the truth
Turn it out/ and make you sweat out your juice
We want to turn it out/ get loose as a goose
Turn it out/ and turn you every way but loose
Every way but loose (4x)
Ain't nothing but the truth gon turn you loose (3x)
Ain't nothing but the truth gon turn you every way but loose

But our big break came when the song was played at the Paradise Garage, one of the hottest clubs in New York, by Larry Levan, one of the hottest deejays in the city. When he started playing the song nightly at the iconic gay club, it became an underground hit.

And we got a call from Buddha Records. They wanted to have Larry Levan do a remix of "Every Way But Loose" and release it as a 12" single on their Sutra Label. They also wanted to re-release the Make A Change album but re-title it Every Way But Loose.

After lengthy negotiations we agreed to terms. The single and the album would be released on Sutra Records and they would promote it nationally and internationally. The drawback for me was that they wanted to buy the album outright, meaning they would own the copyrights to the master tapes. In the end, they paid $15,000 plus 10% royalties on sales.

We got the benefit of their marketing, making our name and our music much more widely known. The "Every Way But Loose" single made it onto the Billboard Magazine Disco Top 80 chart and it also got up to #6 in London's Melody Maker Magazine's Soul chart. We got rave reviews in music magazines in the U.S., Europe and Japan. 40 years later, the song was used in a movie and a television show, and it would be included in "Grand Theft Auto," one of the most popular video games of all time. We eventually got bookings to perform in Europe and the song was reissued on several compilations. So the marketing worked. But it came at a price: I no longer owned the masters of the songs on that album. I can't say the trade-off wasn't worth it, but I have never again agreed to a deal that required me to give up ownership of my recordings or songs.

I did produce another album, Electric Juju Nation, that featured Virtania and the rest of Plunky & Oneness of Juju, but managers of Sutra Records did not accept it as the follow up album. We released it on my own N.A.M.E. Brand Records label in 1984 with very limited success. We got a deal to have it released in London on the Move Records label but that company went out of business right after we negotiated the deal.

Over the years I have written over 400 songs, some in collaboration with Muzi or my son, Jamiah. I love writing lyrics, which is an outgrowth of my love of poetry, and my desire to impart information and inspiration to my audiences.

MAKE A CHANGE (MUZI & PLUNKY NKABINDE)

Think about the tree of your family
Cause they had life so a dream could live
You are who you are
Cause that dream has grown thus far
Now it's up to you to see it through
Has it ever crossed your mind
Just why you're living in this space and time
Well I think that I know why
You are living so a dream won't die

Whose blood is flowing in your veins
Come on now it's time to use your brains
Things don't have to stay the same
It's on you to make a change
It's on you to make a change
It's on you to make a change
It's on you to make a change
It's on you to make a change

Well I tell you actually/ we are just one great big family
Different roots to the same tree/ many colored leaves now can't you see
Whose blood is flowing in your veins/ (your ancestors) come on now it's time to use your brains
Things don't have to stay the same/ it's on you to make a change

Electric Juju Nation LP

It's on you to make a change
It's on you to make a change
It's on you to make a change
It's on you to make a change

The eighties continued with the same hectic schedule and along similar diversified paths, centered on gigs at clubs, schools, festivals, etc., mostly con-

Local group's LP is No. 6 in England

Recording artists Oneness of Juju will be in concert June 28, 1982 at the Dogwood Dell starting at 8 p.m. This is their fifth appearance in the Arts in The Park Program sponsored by the Department of Recreation and Parks.

Oneness of Juju are Sutra recording artists who last week released their latest LP, "Everyway But Loose," nationally. The single "Everyway But Loose" is now number 6 on the Soul Charts in England. The group, one of the region's most popular

ensembles, recently performed at June Jubilee and the Michelob - Richmond Spotlight Summer Show Series. They are Two - time recipients of BOTA awards for their involvement in the community.

Plunky and the Onenee of Juju is the link between the music of Yesterday, Today and Tomorrow.

A dynamic group of multi - instrumentalists, songwriters, lecturers, record producers and teachers, Juju has recorded and released

THE RICHMOND AFRO - AMERICAN JUNE 26, 1982

five albums and two singles on their own Blackfire label. With their special magic, they have shared the stage with some of the brightest names in music Parliament - Funkadelic, Gil Scott Heron, The Pointer Sisters and Hugh Masakela, to name a few. And as a touring band for the Virginia Museum of Fine Art, the Oneness is called upon to teach, as well as perform. Now, The Oneness of JuJu has a new album and its title, Every Way But Loose, is indicative

of the music in the grooves.

The history and development of Plunky and the Oneness of Juju is an odyssey of performing, studying, challenge and truth.

Musical director, founder and leader, Plunky Nkabinde began his musical sojourn in the Richmond public school system under the tutalage of the venerable jazz violinist, Joe Kennedy. Though early studies were centrated on the tenor saxaphone, Plunky currently features flute and soprano sax, as well.

PAGE 17

Billboard Mag clipping & Afro-American article

centrated between RVA and DC. We opened shows for many of the national and international black artists who came to town, especially those who were artistic or cultural, and we played for and helped establish several community festivals and annual traditions, like Kwanzaa, June Jubilee and black groups performing for the Festival of Arts at Dogwood Dell in Byrd Park.

Plunky & Oneness of Juju played at the Hampton Jazz Festival and the first Richmond Jazz Festival. We played at the 1984 World's Fair in New Orleans and we started a local series of jazz performances at local Richmond

Pharoah flyer

THE RICHMOND AFRO - AMERICAN APRIL 18, 1981

Blazing a new trail

Oneness of JuJu develops new sound

By Jerry Turner
Staff Writer

The Richmond-based "African Rhythms" group, The Oneness Of JuJu has just "busted" a new jazz - funk - reggae album here called "Make A Change."

The new album on the Black Fire Records label was scheduled to hit the streets of Richmond, Washington and the Tidewater areas Wednesday, April 15.

According to James "Plunky" Branch, musical director and saxophonist with Oness of JuJu, "Make A Change" is a "statement" record package with "something for everybody."

"The album has percussions that people would identify as a JuJu sound but it's more related to straight R&B," Branch told an AFRO reporter on the day that a cut from the album was played on a local radio station.

Besides diversifying the tunes on the new album, Branch says the musical package is more commercial than their previous works.

"This one we look to sell a whole lot more because this one has more of a commercial sound than any of the others," he said.

The group's first four albums had combined sales of between 20 - and 25,000, not really a good showing. But Branch says he was encouraged by the fact that each new album sold more.

Branch has not made any sales projections for "Make a Change" but he believes the album has the ingredients to make it big, nationally.

The Richmond test market is "crucial" to the success of the album, according to Branch. Although nationally known artist like Stevie Wonder and Michael Jackson can "bust"an album nationwide, Branch says his roots and largest following are in Richmond.

Over an eight - year recording period, marketing luke - warm albums wuch as "Space Jungle Luv" and "African Rhythms," which have had some outstanding singles on them, Branch says he has built up a faithful following.

He has also left his previous straight jazz format to include funk, reggae and disco in the new album to keep up with the changing moods in the country. Branch said the politically - oriented reggae music is big now with both blacks and whites.

On the title cut, there is a "reggae feeling combined with a churchy, funky feeling," he said. "You could almost call it preaching," Branch said of the cut "Make A Change."

On the flip side of the album, "Every Way But Loose," the lead selection, may be the album's ticket to getting national air play.

Although it's a long dance tune, it starts with a bang and never lets up. It's possible to work up a seat on a cut like that. Branch said he was inspired to write the number after seeing and hearing his daughter practice a cheer, using the rhyme "get loose as a goose."

"Every Way But Loose" is a cut that will turn you on with nothing but the truth," Branch said.

For the music fans who like their fare a little softer, "Run Away Bay" and "Always Have To Say Good - bye" may be their type numbers, mellow with just a touch of disco.

Music fans who just want to listen will enjoy "Loves Wonderland." And to spice the stew, "Higher" will do just that with its mix of calypso and disco.

"I'm very excited about it," Branch said concerning the future of the album. He said the album had been in the making for two and a half years; and now the baby is born.

Branch says the album has an added potential of going national because of its "crossover" value — something for blacks and whites, 'something for everybody.'

"Good music that's the bottom line, that's where you start and where you end," Branch said.

James 'Plunky' Branch

Richmond Afro-American Newspaper review 1981

Philly flyer Harold Smith

playgrounds. We opened shows in Richmond for Donald Byrd, Angela Bofill, Gil Scott-Heron, Hugh Masekela, Melba Moore and Nigerian Juju master, King Sunny Ade.

Plunky & Oneness performed with the legendary Ray Charles in downtown Richmond at an outdoor Big Gig Concert that drew a record crowd of 30,000 people. (Well, it was a free show and it was Ray Charles!) That is still probably my largest single live concert audience.

We got lots of local press for our shows and recordings, and for my arts advocacy, so I became somewhat of a local celebrity and cultural thought

Backstage at the King Sunny Ade Concert: l to r. Muzi, Janine Bell, King Sunny Ade, Plunky, Jackie Peters and her son, Sidemnya

leader. And that press coverage helped to magnify my reputation and my credibility.

I also did a lot of lecturing at colleges, substitute teaching in the public schools, and artist-in-residences. I developed a seminar/lecture series tracing the history of black music from Africa, through the American slave period, on up through the blues, the jazz of the 20th century and ending with the black popular music of the day. I used the music to teach history and students loved it. It was a very popular series, especially in February for Black History Month programs. There were years when I would work 20 out of the 28 days of that month, and my school gigs put me in front of thousands of students.

The work in all these areas continued for the next two decades, but it required me to work tirelessly booking gigs, writing grants, promoting and marketing, traveling, keeping the books, paying taxes, keeping abreast of music industry trends and, did I say, trying to book gigs. Oh yeah, I also had to keep practicing my horns and I had to keep being a dad. Paying the mortgage on my family's residence required a miracle per month, and that miracle was that I was able to manufacture an income out of thin air, using creativity, diversification and discipline.

Plunky & Oneness of Juju at Dogwood Dell in RVA
l. to r. Plunky, Virtania Tillery, Rafael Solano, Muzi Branch & Marcus Macklin

My career was continuing to spiral upwards. I saw it as a daily/weekly/monthly grind punctuated by some occasional big gigs or momentous meetings. But over the long haul it was all going according to my plans. I was visualizing myself and the band doing great things in the future. Little did I know that my future would look just like that present. I would build long-term success brick by brick, gig by gig, song by song, and album by album, and every brick, gig, song, or album was just another single step forward. Whenever I had a setback or a down moment, before too long, the phone would ring with a gig or a business contact or the possibility of something really big or really cool happening and that possibility would motivate me to keep going. I might not ever have a mega-hit record or hit the lottery, but I could dream; and as I moved toward my dreams I would keep documenting the journey.

⌘⌘⌘

Chapter 13

AFRICAN VENTURES

The hoopla of the Every Way But Loose album sustained us from 1982 through 1984. After that, I saw the need to explore other business ventures. We kept Branches of the Arts, Inc. going as a program and service providing, tax exempt, nonprofit organization. We were very active doing gigs, particularly club dates in Richmond and DC, which enabled me to cover day to day living expenses. But I wouldn't release another album on my label, N.A.M.E. Brand Records, until 1988. In between, I was looking for opportunities to develop additional revenue streams. Asante had suggested that we diversify our business beyond our music. He thought Ghana wood products, like hand carved doors and sculptures might be profitable. So after some research, Garry and I arranged to go to Ghana for an international wood products trade fair and then on to Nigeria to see if we could do some business.

When I travel internationally I usually keep journals of all my activities and observations. Today they would be called blogs. The detailed logs of my thoughts and ventures are invaluable to my recall. Here are three journals of my business trips to West Africa.

April 6, 1985 (Headed to Ghana and Nigeria for timber and cosmetic businesses)

We made the plane! Whew! When you travel with Garry you know you'll be cutting it laser close! We actually got to JFK Airport at 10:00 PM for a 10:30 PM departure to Dakar, Senegal. Then we found out we'd be sharing the plane with a tour group of fine black young ladies called "Chocolate Singles!" As George Clinton would say, "Can y'all get to that!" I ate; then I slept all the way to Dakar, Senegal. Disembarked; reloaded for the next flight leg, to Abidjan, Ivory Coast. The scheduled wait time for the flight to Accra, Ghana was five hours. We had to wait six; but we arrived in Ghana only nine minutes late. African time.

The airport scene was the hardest part of the trip, not just in Accra, but everywhere: transit, customs, entry documents, disembarking forms, declara-

Elmina Castle, Cape Coast, Ghana

tion of money, visas, your passport please, jostling for/with luggage with the boys, customs, confusion, hands out: grasping, helping, hustling, begging, having fun, hands everywhere. Asante met us on time. On time! And we were off to the hotel. And so the journey began.

We had come to Accra to attend **GIFEX**, the Ghana International Furniture and Woodworking Exhibition trade show. Ghana has some of the finest mahogany, teak and other tropical hardwoods in West Africa and we wanted to see about developing some business, shipping wood products to the States. After **GIFEX**, we planned to go on to Nigeria to make a proposal to Garry's business man, Esalinta.

Accra, the capital of Ghana, has a beautiful landscape, British and typical West African buildings, roads, clothes, occupations and smells. The weather is hot year-round with a spring rainy season. The people are smart, conscientious and extremely cordial and they share a simple, relaxed lifestyle. But there are cultural shocks to navigate, like regular electricity blackouts for hours at a time, day or night. Sometimes the water is shut off too. I had to learn how to use one bucket of water in the mornings: first to brush your teeth, then bathe, and then use the rest for flushing. And there were no public phone booths; you had to go to one of very few Phone and Telex offices to use the phone. I was at first like the typical ugly American, complaining about how different things were compared to the U.S., but then realizing I was not in the Midwest, but West Africa, where the history and culture runs a lot deeper than anywhere else I might have been.

We would go to GIFEX at the conference center by day, meeting timber business contacts and hang out with Asante and friends and at clubs by night. One night we went to the Continental Hotel Casino and met Faisal Helwani, a legendary Lebanese/Ghanaian music promoter and manager, and we talked about music business prospects.

April 12, 1985 - Two hectic days

Garry wanted to go to Nigeria in time to attend Esalinta's brother's wedding in two days. We couldn't get a visa from the Nigerian Embassy in Accra, so we decided to go to Togo, the country just east of Ghana, to get the visas from the Nigeria embassy there. So we hired a car and driver to take us by road on a majestic, powerful, scenic drive across the countryside. Luckily the driver knew the road well enough to take it at 70, 75 sometimes 100 miles per hour, sometimes cautiously avoiding potholes by going onto left or right shoulders, all at maximum efficiency.

Along the way we had to go through three army checkpoints, the first one of which was all too thorough. The army guys made a big issue of some surplus cash they found on us, until the tension of the situation was broken when they discovered I was a musician. I played them a soprano sax solo version of Michael Jackson's "Billie Jean," and the soldiers danced around smiling. I gave the sergeant one of my albums and the currency violation was forgiven.

When we got to the border it was teeming with Friday crowds. After four more searches and document checks, we made it into Togo's capital city, Lome, still with our car and driver. We had intended to go back to Accra once we got the visas from the Nigerian embassy, but when we found out there was a plane from Lome to Lagos at 7:30 PM, we decided to stay in Lome and take that flight.

We had lunch at posh beach front hotel and then went to the airport. Although we had our tickets endorsed, we couldn't secure boarding passes or seats, so we missed the plane. We spent the night at the posh hotel, hung out with an old girlfriend of Garry's and went to a disco. The next morning we find out there is only one flight on Saturday to Lagos, at 5:00 PM on Air Nigeria, so we decide to go back to Accra to try to make an evening flight from there.

When we got to the border we were told that we could not re-enter Ghana because we had no visa. Even though we showed that we had just left the day before, and that we were flying out that night, so technically we were in transit, the border guy was a hard ass and refused us entry. Leaving the guy's border crossing office we were supposed to walk out and turn right (to stay in Togo), but instead Garry said, "Just turn left, keeping walking and don't look back!"

And we just stole our way back into Ghana, hired a driver at the border and raced back across the countryside at 90 miles per hour. We got back to Accra only to find there were no airline seats available going to Lagos that night, and we missed the wedding after all that. So, we hung out at GIFEX, went to its concert that night at the State House Concert Hall and heard some great music instead.

April 14, Sunday

Awoke at 6:30 AM, dressed, packed, went to the airport, checked in, went to have breakfast, returned to the airport, and we did not make the 12 noon flight. So we went back to GIFEX where we saw the best furniture and doors of the whole week!

We left the fair, went back to the airport by 2:30 PM to wait for the 5:30 flight. I stood at the counter the whole time. We had things arranged. It looked good, then bad. Then yes, then no. Then maybe. Then YES, we got boarding passes!

We made the flight and got to Lagos around 7:30 PM. After airport hassles, customs, waiting, and waiting some more, we finally left the airport at 11:15 PM. Five army checkpoints later, we got to the hotel, had late night snacks, cognacs, tea and went to bed at 2:00 AM.

We spent six days in Lagos waiting for Esalinta and working on Garry's proposals for his cosmetics business. I was a bit frustrated because Lagos is not my favorite place and this was not my deal.

It is worth noting that on most days throughout my travels, I do my yoga exercises and practice my horn. It keeps me focused, relaxed and feeling like I am in touch with my true purposes.

On April 20 we went back to Accra, and Ghana felt like home. We spent the next 10 days in Accra, doing business by day and going to clubs and me jamming by night. We took a road trip to Kumasi, Ghana, passing through several towns in between. We got wood business research done, and I ordered 10 doors to ship back to the U.S. as samples. Garry decided to work on the timber business with Asante and me, but Garry thought it would be more lucrative for us to deal with raw wood and logs by the boatload, rather than selling finished goods. But as we would learn over time, a bigger deal isn't always a better deal.

On May 1, I left Ghana to go back to the U.S. I was thankful to be leaving my African home for my real home, grateful to all who helped make this African experience a positive one.

The next trip to Africa came a little over a year later, from March 21 – April 3, 1986

From my journal I can recall this trip back to Ghana to conduct wood business and to Nigeria for Garry's cosmetic business. The journal helps me remember going through the usual Nigerian scenarios: a 12-hour flight and 2? hour airport customs hassles, intrigues, immigration problems, police arrests of associates, legal moves and countermoves, yoga and jamming with night club bands in Lagos.

Then we went on to Ghana in what was the rainy season for more business inquiries, yoga, horn playing and more meetings with lumber companies from Accra to Kumasi and Takoradi, a city along the coast to the west. I worked with Asabere, our major timber contact whose father is one of the biggest, longstanding timber transporters in Ghana. At one point we went out into the bush near Kumasi to see how the logs were cut and extracted. It is like pulling gigantic teeth from the landscape, only heavier by tons and tons. The lumber workers, wearing shorts, t-shirts and rubber thong sandals, toiled with hand-tools cutting four-foot diameter trees, and they had to run and dodge falling trees and logs rolling down slopes. They then used old caterpillar tractors to pull and load the logs onto overused hauling tractor trailers. It was extremely dangerous, hard labor. Third world workers and countries are usually underpaid for natural resources culled from the earth. Farmers, miners, and drillers are paid pennies for working outside in the elements, while Wall Street commodities brokers work in air conditioned offices making millions.

Ghanaian bank note

Dirt roads through Black people's lands
Lead to the World Bank
The ancient cycles are also today's realities
Continuing cruelties to indomitable spirits
We exist to prove we can endure
No, Africa must move forward with new vision

We traveled all around the country making timber contacts and looking for companies to supply bedposts or railroad ties or park benches or coffins or doors or round logs for export. Easter weekend we went from Accra to Takoradi three hours away, passing through Elmina, a small town near Cape Coast. Elmina is the site of a famous castle fort which was an infamous, major slave shipping port. I was quite moved by the experience of visiting the slave dungeon and exit door used centuries ago.

We spent Easter Sunday at the Elmina Hotel. Our rooms were right on the beach. With the sea roaring and waves crashing in the background, it was very meditative. A band played Ghanaian highlife music until 8:00 PM. After that we sat out on our porch facing the sea, listening to a pre-recorded Quiet Storm WBLS radio show, very loud on the stereo boom box, while watching and witnessing a real quiet storm in front of us. The soft winds, light rain and lightning made a surreal sound effect and light show provided by God. The setting and the good company helped to create an extraordinary experience, one we all will likely never forget.

Ghanaian phone card

After three more days of yoga, business, travel, shopping, music and more in Accra, I left to come back home to the States.

About a year after that, in February of 1987, I went back to Ghana and Nigeria to attend that year's GIFEX conference and to continue to pursue music and other opportunities. (I will share some of my experiences, writing in the present tense, because that is how I wrote in my journal.)

February 5, 1987

I landed at the Lagos airport and this time the entry ritual was a relative breeze. But my baggage didn't make the flight. Garry has a cosmetics and hair care products factory in Lagos now. Overall the city has changed for the better and Garry has settled in as a long term Nigerian resident businessman.

February 6

I hang out with Gboyega Adelaja, a musician friend who used to play with Asante and Hugh Masekela. Gboyega has a media company in Lagos, but he still plays music; and he invites Garry and me to a Friday night jam session at the Extended Jazz Family night club in downtown Lagos. When we arrive, the club is packed with a mixed crowd, including lots of ladies.

Fela Kuti, the legendary Afro-Beat pioneer and political activist musician, is on tenor sax. Gboyega is on keyboard. There are two guitarists, bassist, drummer, percussionist, a female vocalist and others, and they are playing American jazz standards.

Fela is not at his best on sax. He hadn't played very much in recent months as he had recently gotten out of jail, having been arrested and imprisoned for sedition and generally being a thorn in the side of the government that he calls corrupt. Around midnight I go up to jam with the band, first on a slow ballad; then on "Bye, Bye, Blackbird." Next, we play a blues, after which Fela starts another blues standard in C minor. I take a killer extended solo, climaxing with a long-held, circular-breathing fueled flurry of notes. I got a standing ovation. And Fela sucks his teeth and says to me, "Yeah, but at least I stuck my stick in some meat pie…" before he left to go home to his many wives.

Different soloists come to the stage, play and go. Remi Kabaka sat in on drums, followed by a Ghanaian drummer who sang and soloed with a cymbal on his head, and turned the joint out!! Late in the night, an old, blind, street musician was guided in and mesmerized the place playing solo tambourine and singing. He was funky and spiritual, throwing down and raising us all up to the highest heights. That night was one of my best live African musical experiences ever.

(Over the years later, Fela would make many acclaimed recordings, become an international star, be arrested numerous times, and he would die of AIDS. Fela was the subject of numerous articles, documentaries and an award-winning Broadway musical, "Fela!" He was a bold, crazy, innovative, committed, legendary black musician, one of my musical idols and thankfully, I had the opportunity to play with him that night.)

February 7

Garry and I go to Ghana for this year's GIFEX trade show. We are now well-known and more involved and we help with hosting an International Hardwood Producers Association (IHPA) delegation coming to Ghana for the first time. Garry, Asabere and I help show the white people around the trade show and around the country. There are 10 people including two wives in the delegation. And our little ex officio, ad hoc committee worked for three days to get them first class accommodations and service: the best airport entry, first class hotel and a brand new German limo bus with plush seats, carpeting, air conditioned and with stereo speakers over each seat with individually controlled volume.

Tuesday, February 10

We register the white folks at GIFEX where they get presentations from timber company reps. The Ghana commercial bank hosted them for a luncheon at a new Chinese restaurant where there was an orgy of food. We go to Tema, the shipping port area about 15 miles outside Accra, and meet the shipping company reps.

The next day we take the delegation to Kumasi. Our limousine bus makes the trip quite special as we glide past villages and stares and waves and smiles of the people. I have the bus stop at the village of Asante's wife's mother, and I give the old woman messages, money and a hug from her daughter in America. Very touching. She was the queen of the village that day, having hosted the delegation of VIP's.

Kumasi has over 50 mills and it is a bustling timber capitol. We tour several mills and the next day we take the bus back to Accra and GIFEX.

Friday, 13 February

We spend the morning at GIFEX, then in the afternoon we leave for Elmina. Once again the limo bus makes the drive through the countryside and up the coast a unique experience. At Elmina the beach is scenic, but the white people don't like the accommodations. I do. The white people annoy me. I walk the beach alone. Meditating and contemplating.

The next day we go off to Takoradi and spend the day visiting hardwood companies. That evening the Lebanese timber men hosted a beach party. I get in a moonlit swim. There is a bonfire. We share walks on the beach, a soprano sax–guitar duo and big fun. And food: barbeque chicken, shrimp kebobs and too many great things in abundance. Six of us spend the night on the beach; the others go to a Takoradi hotel.

The next morning I have a great experience on the beach. I take an undulating sea ride out to an island on a giant open canoe (actually a large hollowed-out log shaped like a boat), powered by chanting, rowing Africans. The waters are azure and though sharks had been caught earlier that morning, I jumped in and swam for a short while alongside the boat.

When the bus came back with the delegation, the Lebanese lumber men had a great lunch for us: curried shrimp, shrimp salad, shrimp cocktails, chick-

Ghanaian carved doors

Woody carved door　　　Ghana door maker

Ghanaian carved door on Plunky's house in Richmond, VA

Ghana village boys

Garry White with Ghana girls

Ghanaian fishermen

en and assorted Lebanese dishes. They went all out for us; but the white women turned up their noses and continued to piss me off. By 3:00 PM we take the long bus ride back to Accra.

On Monday, February 16, the white folks leave for Abidjan, Ivory Coast. Hooray! Months later, Garry and I would go to their IHPA conference in Hawaii, but that's another story.

I spend the rest of the day doing business at GIFEX.

On Tuesday we have a hectic day, shopping and getting our souvenirs cleared at the museum, documenting our artifacts as tourist art, not valuable antiquities/relics. Then we went to visit friends, a group of Black Hebrews, who operate an elementary-high school in Accra. The visit to the school was tremendously inspiring. The bright eyed, well-disciplined, uniformed students were awesome and endearing. The faculty and staff were dedicated and right on. Four students performed poetry for us that made me cry. I gave a brief solo sax performance and seminar and was overwhelmed when the students surrounded me clapping and chanting their approval. Later that day we left for Nigeria.

Wednesday, February 18, I spend the morning in Lagos doing yoga and organizing my notes and papers from GIFEX and Ghana. That evening I watched basketball on TV until falling asleep.

On Friday I leave for home. By 4:00 AM I am on my flight over the Atlantic writing in my journal.

Postscript:

We never did develop a timber or wood products trade business. What I got from these trips were the opportunity to go to Ghana multiple times, music contacts, gigs, a wealth of experiences and my own, unique, hand-carved, African teak, front door for my house in Richmond.

I did ship 10 carved doors back to the U.S. as samples, but I ended up selling half of them without making a large wholesale deal. The doors cost about $400 each (including shipping and finishing) and were sold for around $1,000, but we were not able to compete with the large manufacturers who were using Brazilian and Philippine mahogany which had a much lower shipping cost. At that time there were only two ships carrying freight between West Africa and the U.S. Only two boats per month! Those boats would leave West Africa and stop in Philadelphia, Norfolk, Savannah, and New Orleans. By contrast, there were hundreds of ships per month between Asia and the West Coast of the U.S. Africa's trading partners are mainly its European former colonizers. Historically, the main things imported into the U.S. from Africa were slaves.

Oh yeah, another thing I got from these journeys to Africa was material for my autobiography.

⌘⌘⌘

Chapter 14

The Nineties Albums

It is remarkable that I have kept so many artifacts documenting my career, but I have always believed I would be famous or, even if not, my experiences and observations would be of some importance. So I kept: boxes of tapes, notebooks full of poems, diaries, journals, hundreds of photos, letters, file cabinets filled to the brim, memories...

Records and albums of my music are some of the best collections of expressions because the music, lyrics and album covers allow for time travel, back and forward, in 3-D. An old recording is a set of memories played out loud...

By the late Eighties and Nineties I maintained my ongoing pattern of gigging, recording, touring, and teaching that would be my life. The wood business in Ghana didn't pan out, so my trips to Africa were curtailed for five years. I was writing songs and working with young Richmond area musicians and releasing albums to market my music, to stay relevant, and to document my ideas.

Production is about creatively capturing and presenting the music. Because I kept having new musical ideas and inspirations, I kept on going into studios and working on new songs. And because I continued to work with young people, their energy and creativity kept propelling me forward. The world, politics and culture kept moving forward too, so those things kept giving me reasons to comment and use music to promote ideas.

Production is also about technology, and I continued to like the science and engineering involved with replicating sound. I found new and different techniques and equipment that challenged me to learn new things and then push boundaries to create shortcuts and pathways to do more things with the music.

For me production is about perseverance. It's a recurring theme for me and my methodology, having the ability and discipline to spend hours and days concentrating on getting a job done, being motivated and focused enough

Plunky & Oneness: l. to r. Hannon Lane, Ronnie Cokes, Plunky, Lady Eka-Ete, Muzi

to sit there day after day, completing a large scale creative project by breaking it down into incremental segments and actually executing those steps. Producing an album, writing a book, making a movie or video is about being crazy enough, obsessed enough, to sit there all those hours at your desk or workstation, and doing it.

Production is also about the financing. In an environment of limited resources, production often hinged on having the money or backing to do projects. One of my principle tasks was to manage income streams and re-invest the money from gigs for the longer-term benefit of having a continuing flow of new album releases. I got investors, took out loans, wrote grants and apportioned gig fees to produce records. I was a committed, diehard indie musician before the genre was codified. He who paid the piper called the tunes, and owned the masters.

"People don't understand the kind of fight it takes to record what you want to record the way you want to record it." — Billie Holiday, 1915 – 1959

Over the years my experience showed that the records I produced would often achieve value over the long term. My albums would find an audience 10

Plunky & Oneness: l. to r. Kevin Teasley, Ronnie Cokes, Plunky, Carlton Blount, Muzi

or 20 years after I initially produced them.

My marketing strategy was based on being intensely local and also international at the same time. I avoided trying to service or market to the whole U.S. I couldn't afford that. Plus the major labels and big independent record companies had the U.S. market under almost total control by restricting competing distribution, payola to radio stations, and exclusive arrangements with television and other media. It was difficult to get any national media or market penetration, and without large sums of money it was nearly impossible.

So I concentrated on working in two very narrow niches. First I marketed in my own city and then expanding to DC and the Mid-Atlantic region only. And second I would reach out to specific cities and underground labels in Europe and Japan. But even this dual-pronged marketing strategy was geared for the long haul. Getting a "hit" record was about as likely as hitting the lottery, but as they say, you can't win if you don't play. Winning, for me, was building a body of work, a quantity that would build and sustain credibility over time.

In Europe, a long career could be a marketing asset. After producing good works and lasting for more than a generation, I could be considered an oldies act, or a venerated artist, or even an important historical figure in the development of black American music.

So I continued to produce record albums and CDs with all these things in mind, while teaching the history of black music, and courses in the business of music in schools. And I shared my theories and methodologies with the scores of younger musicians who work with me.

Here are my albums from that period:
Plunky - Tropical Chill (1988)
Plunky Branch - Spiritual Sounds Within My Soul (1993)
Plunky - The Oneness of Funk (1994)
Plunky & Oneness - I Can't Hold Back (1996)
Plunky & Oneness - Groove Tones (1998)

PLUNKY – TROPICAL CHILL (1988)

I released this Tropical Chill album under my name as a solo artist but it featured the Oneness musicians I was working with during that time: Muzi on bass, Ronnie Cokes on drums, Weldon Hill on piano, Hannon Lane on guitar, Miguel Pomier on percussion and Carlton Blount on vocals. This was the first album I produced after having gone to Africa three or four times and the songs reflected a mellow, warm vibe. "Kumasi Night Song," "Tropical Chill" and "When I'm Loving You," were original compositions and album included three cover songs: "Green Dolphin Street," Stevie Wonder's "Skeletons (on Sax)" and Sam Cooke's "A Change Gon Come."

PLUNKY – MOVE INTO THE LIGHT (1990)

Recorded in a home studio in Hopewell, Virginia, Move Into the Light was the beginning of working with Kevin Teasley on keyboards along with several other very young, creative musicians in the area. The songs were collaborations with Muzi, Kevin and Dwayne Calvin (the engineer) and the material ran my usual gamut of funk, smooth jazz and even a Luther Vandross ballad, "Here and Now." I also included a rap version of my own "African Rhythms."

PLUNKY - ONE WORLD ONE MUSIC (1992)

The One world One Music album featured the return of Lady Eka-Ete to the recording studio with us, along with a very young singer-songwriter, James Banks. The songs on the album reflected a world music influence with Asante adding his Ghanaian talking drums throughout. Muzi and I were still doing most of the writing, with me providing most of the lyrical content. We had the good fortune to include a song with Ghanaian acoustic guitarist, Tommy Ebo Ansah, which added to the authentic world music feel of the album.

"ONE WORLD ONE MUSIC" (Rap)
(J. Plunky Branch)

Well the music's in effect/ and anyhow/ it's time to move/so get down
Forget your inhibitions/ just diss'em/ there's no reason not to change
 your condition
Into something you can use to/ get into this groove/that's made to move you
Out on the dance floor/ up on the ceiling/ this beat will have you

rocking and reeling
From the top to the bottom from the bottom to the top now
Shake your booty and don't stop now
Dance to the rhythm dance to the rhythm dance
Dance to the rhythm dance to the rhythm dance
It's a new world music it's in the air/ one world music poly-rhythms everywhere
Jump at the chance jump up and dance/ jump at the chance jump up and dance
It's a hype world beat exotic and new/ it's the rhythms of the streets and the continent too
One world music/ accented on the one/ with a hundred melodies coming from the drum
And all saying the same thing: Let's have some fun/ Let's have some fun
One world one music/ One world one music
One world one people/ One world one people

—J. Plunky Branch

SPIRITUAL SOUNDS WITHIN MY SOUL (1993)

Spiritual Sounds Within My Soul was my first gospel album, most of which was recorded live in Coburn Chapel at Virginia Union University and featured Lady Eka-Ete (Jacqueline Lewis), Martina Taylor and Larry Everette on vocals, and Milton Marriott and Kevin Teasley on keyboards. During that time I was playing just about every Sunday at First Baptist Church of South Richmond. At the 11:00 AM service I would perform a featured solo with the choir, just before the sermon. Some members of the congregation said they would look forward to my solo feeling that it added to the spiritually of the service. For several years I performed there, mainly because my mother would be sitting out in the audience looking up at me with such pride and admiration. She used to say that people introduced her as "Plunky's mother" and she would playfully act like it annoyed her; but it was clear that she was quite proud of the fact that my celebrity gave her some notoriety. She was my biggest promoter and she never missed a chance to sell this CD to church members, even at funerals.

PLUNKY - THE ONENESS OF PHUNK (1994)

The Oneness of Phunk album, co-produced with Kevin Teasley, was the first of several that I recorded at Shannon Walton's recording studio in Woodbridge, Virginia. We got a great sound out of the small studio that Jimmy Gray also used for several Black Fire records. The songs on The Oneness of Funk LP continued to mix jazz and funk, as we looked for the right combination to strike a chord with the public and keep our creative juices flowing. We were playing gigs mainly in RVA and the DMV, and making folks move and groove was often the objective; finding art in the funk was the challenge.

PLUNKY & ONENESS - I CAN'T HOLD BACK (1996)
    Our gigs and the music continued to get funkier and funkier and I was very happy with the jazz funk on the I Can't Hold Back album. We did our first music video on the title song, produced with my dear friend and number one fan, Franklin Kersey. This was a collection of acid jazz featuring Kevin Teasley, Carl Lester, Ronnie Cokes, Muzi, Desiree Roots, Chris Beasley, and Rudy Faulkner. And I loved Muzi's cover art. I was fully invested in writing lyrics and rap/poetry and the liner notes to the album.

PLUNKY & ONENESS - GROOVE TONES (1998)
    For my 50th birthday I had a party/recording session with my band and the Jazz Poets Society at Alpha Audio Studios, a full service, large studio in Richmond. That session yielded most of the music on the Groove Tones album. This was the first session with two vocalists, Charlayne "Chyp" Page Green and Tonya Lazenby-Jackson,

who would be in the group for the next 15 years. This album included the song, "Just Know That I Love You," which was voted one of the top 50 soul songs of the year in both London and Finland. (I love the lyrics to that song.) And there is an instrumental, "Near the Castle at Elmina," which references an Easter Sunday I spent there in Ghana 10 years earlier. Groove Tones featured the creative consulting and graphic design of Patrick Mamou, a member of the Jazz Poets Society. I would continue to rely on his creative input for titles, marketing and motivating ideas.

"Masters Of The Universe"
(by J. Plunky Branch)
(Spoken word)

The distance between here and there is one thought. The time between somewhere and anywhere is the same. Places and things are collections of ideas. Mountains, molecules, molehills, Mars bars - just agreed on thoughts, the building vibrations of the universe.
Listen as Sun Ra meets G.C. somewhere over DC/ The Solar Myth Arkestra jams with the Funky-P, on a plain above music/ then breaking it down to make Space Jungle Luv music/ Like Jazzamatiky groove academy graduates in the [artists] house at primetime/ Like Digital hieroglyphics orbiting around talking heads in rhyme time/ meditating on a mantra with a backbeat/ This is the music of the new millennium and the street/ extra-sensory stimulations/ - the fuel for thought and good vibrations/ It's the way to travel out to the quasars/ in synchronicity with the superstars/ the mothership connected to outerspaceways incorporated/ forever and for days inundated/ with those vibes flowing through/ from them to me to you/ You can tune up on a higher plain of inner tonation/ and listen to a cold cocked trip hop station/ but in the FM band of gypsy angel acts/ Gabriel blows a tenor sax/ and you won't know what love is, Boy/ until you've had the blues and the contrasting shades of unlimited joy/
CHORUS: MASTERS OF THE UNIVERSE/ IN A DEEP SPACE RENDEZVOUS/ MAKING MUSIC FOR THE PLANET EARTH/ DEEP AS MIDNIGHT SKY BLUE
Inside is outside if you're on the other side. The upside is the downside if you're flipping in the middle/ It's a cosmic riddle/ You can dance if you want to change your state of mind/ and You can dance between worlds anytime you're willing to sweat and scream and jump up and don't come down - or get down and don't come up - for air/ The sounds of blacknuss will take you there/ Ask Rashaan between circular breaths/ free jazz mixed with some horny horns is so def
Switch to another wave station/ slide into hypno-transfiguration/ trance-dance over to tone poem number seven/ and look for insight eleven at 82 beats per minute and you'll find heaven/ Listen and love it or leave it alone/ and meet us at or near our home/ the rolling rock three steps from the sun/ - or pulsar 2010/ getting down on the one/ that we believe in/ Enough faith makes fear obsolete/ nonexistent and

Plunky & Oneness l. to r. Muzi, Charlayne Chyp Green, Tonya Lazenby-Jackson, Plunky, Chris Beasley, Ronnie Cokes, Asante

Franklin Kersey & Plunky

nowhere near dancing feet/ With a song in your heart you can be sub-atomic and macro-intergalactic; and if you sing and dance to the colors of the blues/ from the infrareds to ultra-violets you can find grooves/ in the music of the spheres/ in T. Monk go-go phunk & in the oneness of cried tears/

CHORUS: MASTERS OF THE UNIVERSE/ IN A DEEP SPACE RENDEZVOUS/ MAKING MUSIC FOR THE PLANET EARTH/ DEEP AS MIDNIGHT SKY BLUE

There are other worlds - only thoughts away from here. We go somewhere there and then all around/ on magic carpets like Trane's tapestries in sound/ We are moving into the light/ Moving to beats of music made like/ love, music like love, in love, as love, is love.

Tomorrow's forecast: cosmic showers returning as the tales of comets. Today's forecast: Sunny Ra Sunny Ade sunny and bright as we travel the inner-space-ways on Trane's sunship. Yesterdays' forecast: solar winds blowing us away to sites unseen and in ways foretold but not comprehended til now. Long range forecast: Enlightenment on the horizon - light years ahead, now here, then in the rearview mirror of your consciousness.

CHORUS: MASTERS OF THE UNIVERSE/ IN A DEEP SPACE RENDEZVOUS/ MAKING MUSIC FOR THE PLANET EARTH/ DEEP AS MIDNIGHT SKY BLUE

Harmolodic lives lived with cosmic karma are black around/ upper and lower Egypt out to lunar reflectors and back around/ to the twinkle in your grandfather's eye. These are the echoes of experiences from the zones of life/ that give deep meaning to the tones of life/ [being] downloaded from the mainframe/ to your gamebrain/ and on down to your booty - shake it and stir it up little darling, Stir it up in a fuzzy cup and don't feel shame/ 'cause your ancestors did the same/ And we can do it better if you listen and learn the rules of the game/ from the masters of the universe: First and second Johns Coltrane and Gilmore plus Pharoah/ Ornette Dolphy Ayler Shepp and Maceo/ They said We want the Plunk/ gotta have some Monk/ and the second stop is Jupiter, all out for Jupiter. Listen and learn from the silences between the groove/ The sun do move/ when you're standing on a balcony suspended over the stars/ and looking down you call out to Mars/ then jump into the scream/ naked as a native dancer on a moonbeam/ Diving down you reach up and out to beyond what you know/ to catch tomorrow's new world still moving on and on and on the go/ Listen to the sound of a pebble drop/ into a wishing well it goes plop/ The sound you hear when you drop into another dimension is ker-Plunk/ It's a fat, free sound and it's the funk! The funk, Plunky phunk...

CHORUS: MASTERS OF THE UNIVERSE/ IN A DEEP SPACE RENDEZVOUS/ MAKING MUSIC FOR THE PLANET EARTH/ DEEP AS MIDNIGHT SKY BLUE

—Plunky & Oneness - Groove Tones (1998)

Just Know That I Love You
(—J. Plunky Branch & Charlayne Chyp Green)

Sometimes we're in different places/when my travels keep me away
We're separated by open spaces / but I'm thinking of you night and day
I don't want you to miss me/ 'cause I don't want you to feel any pain
Just remember how you kiss me / until I come again

Chorus:
Just know that I love you/ just know that I care
Just know that I love you/ and wherever you are my love is there
Whenever you're longing to see me/ your consolation is I feel the same
I want to be there for you/ whenever you call my name
Don't you ever wonder/ or worry about our thing
You mean so much to me/ you're the reason why I sing

Chorus:
Just know that I love you/ just know that I care
Just know that I love you/ and wherever you are my love is there
No, I'm not there as I sing this/ and I know that you wish I were
I always want to be with you/ from January to December
We've got pictures and love songs/ and we've got all our memories
We've got love and our future together/ to fulfill new fantasies

Chorus:
Just know that I love you/ just know that I care
Just know that I love you/ and wherever you are my love is there

⌘⌘⌘

Chapter 15

JOURNEY OF A LIFETIME JOURNAL

[Now we get to the heart and soul of my book, the journals of my travels. A cautionary note: the journals are lengthy and detailed. They were originally written as stand-alone pieces to help me document my experiences, and to share them with others. When the journals were first made available, friends and associates often thanked me for letting them feel like they were traveling right along with me. Years later, re-reading the journals revives the feelings I had and allow me to look back on how the trips shaped my development and my worldview. As is often the case, the best stuff comes near the end of the journeys, because that's when you can look back and see how far you have traveled. I hope that you will wade through the many pages of days, miles and places and find some bits of wisdom, and life-thinking.]

In the spring of 1995, I went to Ghana, West Africa as a cultural specialist for United States Information Agency (USIA) for 15 days of performances and consultations. From there I traveled alone on an extended European train excursion from Rome through Zurich, Cologne, London, Paris and back. I called it my "journey of a lifetime," and this is the detailed journal I kept of my activities and thoughts on the trip.

April 6, 1995, Thursday afternoon
Well, here we go again! I'm on the plane headed for Africa - Accra, Ghana. My itinerary: from RVA to DC to Zurich, Switzerland; spend a day and a night there and then down to Accra, Ghana. I'll spend 15 days working in Ghana. Then my plan is to fly to Rome, buy a Eurorail pass, then take the train from Rome to Zurich to Cologne, Germany, then make my way to London, then to Paris and back to Rome for my flight home.

I have had a hectic last few days and a whirlwind final 24 hours getting ready to depart and as I sit here in the terminal waiting for take-off, I feel out-of-breath and a bit queasy. I had to run around to get a lot of things for Garry,

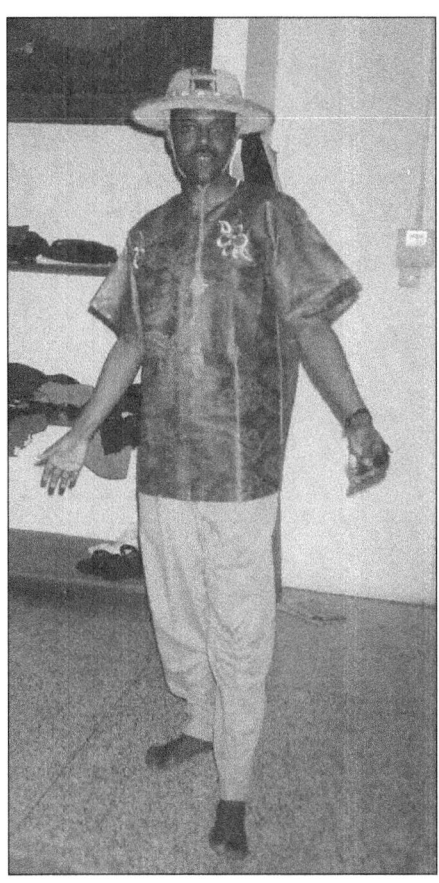

Plunky in Ghana hat

my host in Ghana (computer monitor, Gran Marnier, VCR, books, clothes) and I have been sending faxes, phoning and reaching out to everyone I know for international contacts. We had folks come over to my house last night for a bon voyage gathering. Stayed up most of the night to plan and pack. Woke up early to pack some more. I went rushing to the bank and to Radio Shack, then on to the airport; checked a bag and a big box through to Accra; checked one bag with me to Zurich; boarded this little commuter plane... and now we're taking off! Air travel is amazing! Up, up and higher still. And for the first time ever, I can see my neighborhood, the lakes, my block from the plane! Amazing. I mentally shout out to my son, "Hi, Jamiah! Bye-bye!"

A rediscovery (on the plane): A good meal, good wine and good music will put you high on top of the world. Then a coffee and an after dinner liqueur will make everything like wonderfulness. Another drink and remembrances of love-making and you're in heaven on high. Thank you, God. I'm on a mission. Going for the gold. Going for the goal. Everything coming together. The motto of this trip: "A culmination - A beginning."

[Later on the flight I woke up from napping, got up from my seat in a daze, and the next thing I knew I was being helped up from the floor. The stewardess was saying "Are you all right?" I said I was fine and the proceeded to walk up the aisle to find the bathroom. When I got to the door of the toilet, I was getting ready to go in and the next thing I knew, I was being helped up off the floor again. "Are you sure you're all right?" I said yes, but I wasn't really sure. I had fainted twice. I went in the toilet and came out much lighter.

When I got back to my seat a fellow passenger came over to me to say "I'm a doctor and I'm seated right over there, so if you need any assistance just let me know." And then a few moments later the pilot of the plane came to my seat to say "Mr. Branch, I am Captain Lovejoy, and I just want to be sure that you're going to be all right. I wanted to know if we're going to have to try and find somewhere to land this thing." I said "No let's just go on," especially since we were over the Atlantic Ocean at the time.]

> Morning comes much faster
> when you're rushing headlong
> into the east
>
> Catch the rising star
> It is the red sun
> peeking over the horizon
>
> The High Priest struts
> his chest swells with his importance
> But his real value is only
> as great as his humility, humanity and
> handsomeness of spirit

April 8, Saturday afternoon; after spending a day and the night in Zurich, Switzerland, visiting with my friend, Katherine Gogel; going to see David Murray in concert in Willisau, Switzerland, and making many phone calls and business contacts from Katherine's apartment, now I am on the plane, headed for Accra, Ghana.

High above the mountains we fly, I see them at first in the distance and then we are directly over the Alps, snowcapped, jagged, massive and impressive. Clouds suspended just-so give perspective and dimension. There is a spiritual quality to the mountains. They are expansive, and rise and fall much like an ocean of rocks - only much higher. The light is brightly reflected off the white snow. And, there is so much diversity in the mountain terrain: from all white glaciers to greens and browns of fertile valleys; from broad craters to intricate facets of multiple peaks.

The service, food and unlimited drinks on Swissair are all good. They make you feel like you are someone special going somewhere special and getting there on a special carrier. From my window seat on Swissair I saw a small private Lear jet streak by below us, headed in the opposite direction. From this plane I can phone to anyone anywhere on the planet who has a phone - mobile, cellular or home bound. [I called Jamiah at home in Richmond from the plane.] I want Jamiah to visit Scandinavia and Switzerland just to see their designs: buildings, clasps, greeting cards, etc. New perspectives will give him even greater ideas.

On the flight, we pass over the Mediterranean Sea, the Sahara Desert and over part of West Africa. Great sights, even from the air. After landing and going through customs in Accra, I notice that I just feel good in Ghana. Like I do in some other places, like Atlanta and DC. In Accra the people, the pace, the look of the place, the air, all give the locale its ambiance. Africa is one of my homes. Ghana certainly is.

10 April 95. After two days in Accra. The weather has been very hot 96-104° F. I have had to adjust to my new climate, time zone and surroundings. I have jumped right into the work and the music, on the day after my arrival. Asante and I have to rehearse a band of local Ghanaian musicians to be ready to do some shows. I am staying at the Poku House in the Tesano section of Accra, sharing the house with Garry White and his wife Veronica, who has recently moved to Accra from London.

Rehearsals have gone well these first two days. The musicians are good; they learn fast and we are funky together. As usual here in Ghana, the equipment is inferior. Asante has been sick with fever, and today he went to the doctor and did not practice with us. Because of the heat and the time zone changes, I have not been able to sleep sufficiently.

11 April 95

We did the first workshop at the National Theater today. We had an audience of about 40 people, many students from the University of Ghana at Legon. They were music students and they were attentive and asked interesting questions. The workshop was in a small outdoor amphitheater and it was so hot that I was completely drained afterwards. I came back to the house and took a hard nap. The Poku house in Tesano is the same place that I used to share with Garry when we used to come here in the 1980s.

I am suffering through my usual bout with diarrhea in Ghana. It is not as bad as on earlier trips, but I am still in discomfort. I hope that I am past the worst of it. I took the CVS Brand of Imodium AD for the first time tonight and I sure hope that will take care of it.

There seems to be lots I can do here. Asante wants me to get involved with cassette duplication and music distribution. But I'm not sure I have the money or the will to get involved that deeply. The market for the business does seem to be here. Okyerema is well-positioned in the music business here. He is well known and respected. I'm not sure if he could manage such a business here without administrative personnel and someone with computer skills.

Hotels are being built in Accra and there are already many foreign business people here, and more are on the way. The music scene will benefit from the increase in the number of venues and the increase in international exposure of the music through tourism.

Wednesday, 12 April

I am preparing to do the second workshop at the National Theater. I had a rough night with the diarrhea but I am a bit better today. It is hot as a midsummer mid-day and it is just 10:00 AM. We have moved the time of the performance back to 11:00 AM because the shade will cover the stage by then. The musicians, the Ghanaian officials and USIA all expect me to really make an impact here. I hope that I do not disappoint anyone. Apparently my music business experience and my knowledge can be of value to the music industry here.

Friday, 14 April, almost noon.

Last night we performed our opening night at the Bass Line Jazz Club after doing a workshop in the afternoon. It was a tiring day's work. The crowd at the club was enthusiastic and supportive.

After breakfast. I have my stomach back - a bit. "Cool in You," "Another Sad Love Song," etc. on the radio. I haven't slept much - reflecting on the show last night at the Bass Line Jazz Club, the show later tonight, my workshops next week, Kaila and Jamiah, etc. The future is now. I want to call home but I don't know if schools are out for Good Friday back in Richmond, VA. Everything here is closed for the holiday.

Ralph, the "house boy" here at the house in Tesano turned 29-years-old yesterday. He is a wonder - so diligent, thorough, knowledgeable, quiet, efficient and such a hard worker. I do not understand this unspoken system of "castes" here. Many of the workers in service positions are completely subservient, almost bowing down to their "employers." Is it training, tribal or tradition? The workers are very, very good at what they do. They are noble. Ralph is an inspiration.

"Heavy D" then "Don't Take It Personal" on the radio. I read Science of Mind for today - "Letting Go". I'm grooving.

Friday night/ Saturday morning 3:30 AM

Tonight Ghana Broadcasting Corporation (GBC) filmed the show at the Bass Line Jazz Club for TV. It was a major production: three cameras, lights, mics on everything, two mobile production trucks, etc. They did an interview of me before the show at sound check. I didn't get to see any of the video, but the GBC Director said it was great. I will get an edited VHS copy of the tape. The club was packed to the rafters. The people were into it. Our sound system was woefully inadequate. Asante and I worked as hard as slaves, sweated pounds, and we were beat but satisfied after it was over.

15 April, 8:00 AM

All in all, the music has been a very frustrating experience. The equipment is so poor, old and in disrepair; the musicians don't own their own instruments and they play on the equipment with not enough care. Loudness to the point of distortion is the rule - and it is not a pleasant sound. I want to hear more of the best groups here to make a more comprehensive assessment of the music situation in the country. There are probably some good musicians and bands and I pray that there are some who are getting a better sound than what I have heard so far.

My sleeping is broken into pieces. It is too hot and humid - fans are not enough, air conditioning too much. I need to wash more often in order to be comfortable but very often the water is not running and I have had to learn to bathe from a bucket. I'm good at it now, but it is a job.

When there is no water the toilets cannot be flushed. There are smells of water with sewage as you ride through some parts of the city. It stinks. Dust is a reality. Many of the streets have been paved and/or widened since I was here last in 1989, but there are still some roads that are unbelievably rutted, potted and not paved at all, making the ride over them bone, car and earth quaking and shattering.

The sun blazes but is sometimes forced to relent by clouds. Fortunately there is often a breeze. There are no shades at the windows in the living room where I sleep - curtains and light drapes, yes - but nothing to keep the sun from saying "get up" bright and early every morning.

Living is not as easy here as in Europe or America. Frustrating to turn the faucet one moment and get water and at the very next moment - no. Brushing your teeth with no water to rinse; then shitting in the commode, then bathing in the tub but out of a bucket, shaving from the bucket, then finally using what's left of the water to flush the toilet. Veronica is a hardy soul to have left London to live with Garry here. I don't think Cookie and Jamiah could do it. Oh, they could, but would they want to? For love and or money? I know Kaila wouldn't think of it. This trip is quite an experience. With all the frustrations, I must remember to look for the lessons and remember that goodness is at the back of it all.

Saturday, 15 April, 8:30 PM

Waiting for Asante and the car to pick me up and go to the Bass Line Jazz Club. Today was mellow, I got my stomach back and went back to the Regal Chinese Restaurant. Also visited Wayne and Denise Hemmings (Njambi's friends) who are both bigwigs in USAID. They live in a fully air conditioned, terrifically furnished and appointed house with all the trimmings. This is the way to go if you're going to live here - or anywhere in the world - A-1 classy. Theirs was the "baddest" set up I've ever seen in Ghana: trés chic.

Easter Sunday, 4:00 AM

The gig at the Bass Line is finally over, and I can't believe how poorly I think I was playing for all three nights, all the sets. This was quite a learning experience for me. But the people were pleased. A man wants to book me in Holland. Some thought I was great. Many expressed their sincere appreciation for the music and the show. I remember thinking at times on stage that I was "perpetrating" (impersonating). I learned that I had best never be anything but humble and grateful. Only by the grace of God... could I, with my equivalent of a high school music education, create a career of performing my own songs. The saxophone is quite an instrument; most of the time it is so easy-going, but when something is off by a milli-micron, it can be rough and unforgiving. How I could go from the virtuoso saxophonist I was at Benny's Jazz Club in Baltimore a few weeks ago, to sounding like the beginner saxophonist I was at the Bass Line jazz Club is enough to let me know that I'm certainly not "all that." Boy, do I appreciate my bandmates at home: Kevin, Muzi, Ronnie, Carl, Chris, Desiree, Carlton, Rudy, et al...

Sunday, 11:15 AM

So many lessons: People play to their own strengths. Example: if you are not strong rhythmically, you might like a lot of chord changes, so you could emphasize chords and melody, rather than improvising on the rhythms of the funk.

Went to bed at 4:30 AM and awoke at 8:00 AM because the air conditioner in the bedroom caught fire. And I had been lying there on a mattress on the floor in front of it half-awake because I was so cold I was imagining that I was a piece of meat in a freezer getting "freezer burns."

2:30 AM Sunday night/Monday morning. After the gig.

What a difference a day makes! What a difference equipment makes. I feel better. The Village Inn Jazz Club had a much better sound system and I am happier. Nick Robertson of USIS and I had a nice long conversation and he is cool. The gig was almost rained-out, but a few people came, the show went on and the vibes were cool. I netted $200 from the Bass Line. I gave Easter bonuses to the band totaling $50.

My experiencing so much joy performing at the Village Inn and my clarity of positive meditation feels like my own Easter Miracle - a resurrection of my spirits.

17 April, Monday night

We went to see Asante's mother-in-law in the small village of Aniyim. Then we went to see an old friend, George Osei (who is now called Gowad), in the town of Nkawkaw. After that it was on to Asante's mother's house in Koforidua to see his youngest son, Kwabena (Kubby), who looks just like Asante's elder son, Chief. It was a day spent on the road to Kumasi and coming back down the mountain from Aburi to Accra.

> I'm so thankful for love
> That it exists
> and you as love's agent
> are responsible for so much bliss

It's a wonderful thing
to be involved with love in any way
And it's great for me to know you
What else can I say

Thank you, Love
Thank you, Love
Thank you, Love

19 April, Wednesday, 8:15 AM

I'm up early today and ready for a personal business day. Yesterday I addressed the Ghana National Symphony. The workshop was on improvisation and jazz and it went extremely well. The musicians were interested and respectful. It was one of my best workshops ever. I wished it had been videotaped. We also went to the rehearsal of the John Teye School performers. They are quite good singers and instrumentalists: seven trumpeters, a bassist, two drummers, guitarist, two keyboardists, percussionist, et al. We performed a couple of songs for them and I brought some of them up to jam with us. Then we listened to them perform some of their songs and gave them pointers and suggestions. They and their headmaster seemed genuinely pleased and honored by our presence.

Garry, Veronica and I attended a very fine dinner party at the home of Wayne and Denise Hemmings, USAID directors. It was a high-class affair with all the trimmings: fine wine, lobster thermidor, roast chicken, zucchini, rice, flambé ice-cream dessert, and cognac. U.S. government Foreign Service workers live a different, but decent, middle-class lifestyle. They are treated well and they are a different kind of bureaucrat. Everybody at the dinner were all good Black people: friendly and intelligent.

19 April, 2:00 PM

We're at university of Ghana at Legon radio station waiting to be interviewed at 2:00 PM live on the air. It is a typical university station. The interviewer has just come in so we will begin shortly.

The radio interview went well but my little cassette recorder didn't work for some odd reason, so I didn't get it on tape. I go back to the USIS office and make calls to the world. Cookie's not home. Kevin's not around. But I did reach Chief at home, Goetz Buhler in Germany and Dennis Armstead in

England. The gigs for today and tomorrow have been canceled. We'll play Friday back at the Bass Line and Saturday back at the Village Inn.
Every song is you

20 April

A lazy day, but active at the same time. We drove Veronica to Achimota then we took the one-hour drive to Aburi where I buy carvings. The drive is scenic, bumpy and pleasant. The view from the mountain is spectacular. The carvers are skilled and I have a hard time deciding what to buy. We return to Accra and I go to the Art Center to shop for gifts and then go spend two beautiful hours at the beach. Later, we watch our Bass Line Club performance on TV. We looked and sounded pretty good on television.

21 April, Friday morning

Garry's computer is up and running. The monitor I brought him looks stunningly clear and colorful. I am reading a follow-up study guide to the Celestine Prophecy and it is reconfirming and enlightening. Marion, a friend of Garry's in Maryland sent him the book and it came in the mail today. The book explores and expounds on the nine insights.

The first insight is to be aware of coincidences. They happen a lot and they are meaningful. For example: Garry went to another town yesterday to see a man. When he got to the town he stopped a man walking along the road to inquire about the man he was there to see. The man walking happened to be that man Garry was to meet.

Another example: when I was preparing to come on this trip, I couldn't decide if I should plan to go to Europe to try to solicit business by meeting with new contacts. A few days before I left I got a call from Roy Ayers, who put me in contact with a young man in Germany, Goetz Buhler, who just so happened to be a fan of my earlier recordings and who is interested in meeting me to initiate handling my recordings in Europe.

The second insight deals with history and macro-consciousness. Movements and trends of thought and action which advance us to higher states of awareness and activity. Evolution. Blessings flow in new, exciting and sometimes unexpected ways: I go to the U.S. Embassy and they give me my per diem expense money $630 in cash, U.S. dollars. I am rich! I am so thankful to be able to do anything I want. Now more shopping for gifts.

The third insight is seeing the universe as energy, pure energy. One big ocean of vibrations coalescing into many forms. We are co-creators through our thoughts. Beauty raises our energy. That this Celestine Prophecy Guide book came to me during the second week of this trip here is nothing less than an ideal example of what the book teaches about coincidences and energy and attraction and encouragement.

3:00 AM Friday/Saturday morning

Tonight's gig at the Bass Line went super good: packed house, everyone having a fun time, music jamming, etc. I am a celebrity here this week, the talk of the town. Last week's show which was taped for TV will be shown tomorrow for one hour, and that will increase our prestige.
I am amazed at how my attitude and outlook has changed so profoundly in one week. I am upbeat.

A favorite song will take you to a higher plane. Masekela's "Marketplace Woman" had me up and dancing around, singing to the heavens and to the memories, at 3:00 in the morning, no less.

12 noon Saturday, 22 April
I had a rough morning sleep - diarrhea again. I was up to the bathroom every hour. I feel better now. I just have to make it through today and tonight and then to tomorrow night I'm off to Europe.

2:00 AM Sunday morning

Today was heavy - upset stomach, fatigue and no water in the house. No water for washing, brushing or flushing is a heavy thing. I took another bath from the bucket, and learned to appreciate turning on the faucet in the shower back home in Richmond and always having the water flow.
I was drained even before the gig tonight and now I have sweated a pound or two and used all the energy that I had left to make music on the stage one last time this time in Ghana.

10:30 AM Sunday

Early morning meeting with Prince, Garry's lobster partner. I am the "consultant," playing a role, using my common sense and listening and pretending to be important. Maybe I am important. My sense and sensibility just might have great value.

I have had great impact here in these last two weeks. I am a little amazed. Perhaps as I accept more, I will be able to spread my influence over a wider geographic area and among more people. I will have to stay on my path so that I will be strong and worthy of the responsibilities.

The Celestine Prophesy's fourth insight deals with the struggles for energy among people - the games people play, power plays, ego states, etc. The fifth insight is that people will experience transcendent states, the experience of inner connection with divine energy. Our life purpose may be simply to develop our own individual spirituality and in that way add to the overall consciousness of the planet.

The sixth insight is understanding the relationship of our parental lineage and behaviors to our own. Control dramas. The seventh insight is that we can evolve consciously, engaging the energy flow. Build energy, ask the right questions, follow intuitions not impulses.

Checked in for my flight at the airport at 8:00 PM and waited till 11:00 PM at the Aerostar Restaurant with Asante. Garry did not come to see me off. (Heavy!) I made the plane which departed an hour-and-a-half late. I was so tired, I slept most of the flight.

12:30 PM, 24 April, Rome

I'm on the train from Rome to Zurich! I took a train from the Rome Airport to the train station downtown; bought a Eurorail pass for $478 and made the 12:05 PM train to Zurich with two minutes to spare. My suitcase is too heavy and trying to rush with it after standing in lines for an hour, wore me out completely. Rome is charming and looks like the Italian village in Busch Gardens would look. The countryside is wonderfully green, lush and quaint, with farmhouse and villages.
International travel is eye-opening: we live in a cross-pollinated world, with Punjab Indians in turbans and Nike sneakers, Euro-girls in micro-mini skirts and headphones, et al. I will be amazed once I catch my breath and get comfortable.

Grassy plains with houses and towns atop over-looking hills; parallel roads on either side of a river; a magical looking village built like an ancient castle sitting on and in a rocky cliff that spills down into a river that acts like a moat; tunnels that move at high speeds over the train and are gone as quickly as they appear; a castle-like mansion overlooking a four-acre field yellow with flowers; finger-like trees line a road and then surround an old, small cottage; a major castle high on a hill - Italian style - with a fog-shrouded mountain in the background; more tunnels speeding by, sudden darkness and more sudden light; now a long tunnel (three minutes at high speed); good jazz taped in Accra on my headset, makes a great sound track for the movie being shown on my window - a train travelogue. We slow down to pass through a small city with nice houses with tall windows and doors and all small Italian cars for tiny streets – village-like.

Everywhere there are gardens, arches over doors and windows, shuttered windows, ivy-covered walls; this is Firenze, Italy. Then on up through more hills, towns and tunnels to Bologna. On through more flat farmlands, an occasional church steeple. Several houses in areas that would make you think of Grimm's fairy tales, or at least the illustrations that would be in the story books.

I never thought that I would like to visit Europe, but this train ride is idyllic. Oh, it's crowded (I'm standing while writing this), but the look of the peoples, the languages being spoken (Italian, French, German, Spanish and English) and above all, the look of the countryside is enchanting. Because I am traveling alone, I am basically in silent reflection - a meditative state - in a wonderland. I never knew Italy was so green with trees and grass. It is lush. Later, my book (Europe By Train) says, I am in for a treat: the railway from Milan to Zurich will take me through the Alps.

I would love to do this again with you. Of course, I would like to travel with Jamiah, but he would probably get bored after a short while. It is likely that I'll get to come back with my band, but we will probably travel by plane and vans. You would like this. We could be low key wanderers and share quality time. This we have to do.

Before I left Ghana, Garry tried to talk me out of taking these long train rides. But this may be a once-in-a-lifetime experience. My Eurorail pass gives me the option of various routes back to Rome - maybe down through the South of France and along the coast of the Mediterranean Sea to Nice and to Pisa. This could be quite a train trip!

6:30 PM

I have been going all day and now I am tired. I still have 3? hours to go.

It is evening and don't I want to rest my eyes because I don't want to miss any of the mountain views. We just passed spectacular gardens in this town. The mountains are shrouded in clouds or fog. I now have a seat in a six-passenger compartment. Earlier I had been sitting on a little pull-down seat in the aisle. We're in the mountains now in Southern Switzerland. We pass a large lake so scenic it is breath-taking: a beautiful lake with boats, mountains rising up all around bordering the lake and with super village scenes all along the base of the mountains, and even a pencil thin waterfall cascading down - too special! This is Lugano. This lake town was so beautiful I almost could not believe it. The fog on the mountains, the quiet calm left me gasping with every new view. It is almost dusk and we have stopped at the train station and I want the train to hurry up and push on right now so I can see more views, before dark.
It has actually been rainy and overcast all day long, but the gray has added to my mood.

Now it gets ridiculous - going up on the side of the mountain with distant vistas of snow-capped peaks across the way. We are still in the fog but it hugs low in some places and it glides high above, in others. All scenes are speckled with the precise, quaint Swiss architecture, old-new orderliness. You would love this. Now layers of fog - in bands across the strata of mountains. Too special!

At times I don't know which side of the train has the better view - rocky crags, multiple cascading mountains, snowcapped peaks with fog hugging the nooks and crannies like some alien but beautiful planet. I am twisting my neck from side-to-side trying to take as much in as my quivering stomach will allow and all the while kicking myself for not videotaping this most scenic journey. This ride has been surrounded by scenes of almost dream-like beauty. I want you here to see it for yourself, to have this experience. I am so blessed to have accepted today's journey and to have played it solo, without the distraction of an accompanying companion. Yet, I want you here with me.
Beauty can make you vibrate at a high level. And having experienced that level can open new thresholds for operating at generally higher vibrations on even normal days - for days. You remember the heights and know that they are always there - somewhere.

This is more mountain than I ever knew existed. Countless scenes drift by my windows. More churches, even more stunning waterfalls (it's spring so I guess some of the snows are melting), more villages, more bridges and trestles, more dimensional foregrounds, backgrounds, close-ups. I am dizzy, shaken and thankful that darkness has been slow in coming.

As twilight surrounds the train I feel like I can't take any more, but each time we exit a tunnel of darkness there is a burst of light and a scene of picturesque serenity and beauty. My stomach churns. Little tunnel openings, little huts of stone, grand vistas, tiny jewels of man-made light twinkling in the distance creating a mystical land of enchantment. Flumes channel some of the waterfalls which leap from one tier, down and disappear somewhere into the earth. Chimneys now spew smoke from evening fires. Night is coming to the Alps, giving me relief and release. I can close my eyes. Two hours to Zurich.

But no-o-o. Now there is snow right down to track-side. Snow in the town, not just in the higher elevated distance. And the colorful neon lights occasionally reflect in the white granulated crystals. A long tunnel lets me rest... Still more scenes, more beautiful in white, with frozen waterfalls, glaciers and Santa Claus villages in 3-D. I can't sleep and my meditation is a flood of pictures of Ghana music and mountains made of light and sound. And when I open my eyes the beauty still flows past my windows. How fortunate I am. The ice flows are waterfalls which are still frozen in time. I cannot fathom how such beauty could be so endless, and still be even more. I am still gasping at every turn, every tunnel exit, every new scene is a postcard as large as a picture window.

The next day, Tuesday, 25 April - 1:00 PM On the train - Germany

I am on my way to Cologne to meet Goetz Buhler of Soulciety Records. This is the most important meeting that I have on my schedule, but you never know when things will go even better than planned or expected.

When I arrived in Zurich last night, I called Katherine and thankfully, she was home waiting for my call. Katherine turns out to be very spiritually connected and centered. She once again takes charge of being the perfect hostess, giving me everything I need for comfort, business and rest. After she picks me up at the train station, we go out to eat spaghetti at an Italian restaurant. It happened to have been the holiday night of the "burning of the snowman" celebration, with marching bands in Swiss regalia as the background to our settings. Downtown, we walked past people dancing and having a wild time. Then we drove over to Moods, the jazz club to see if the manager, Pius

Knusel, was in, but he'd traveled for the holiday. We stayed there long enough to have a drink and to hear the last two songs of the quartet playing there.

It was late night by the time we got to Katherine's apartment. I took my first hot shower since I left there more than two weeks ago, had some juice and slept like I was at home. All too soon it was morning. Katherine went out for provisions for a light breakfast and for my lunch she would make for me to take on the train. While she was out I did my yoga.

We tried to rush through traffic jams to the train station and got there just in time to see the train pulling away down the track. Katherine decided to drive me to Basil, an hour away, to make the next train to Cologne. I am warmed by Katherine's giving nature and her testament to simply passing these blessings on to me as others have done for her previously. She says that she didn't like the idea of me "owing her one," but I feel I must repay her some way, someday. She even gave me coins and money in different currencies so I could use the phone and rent the pushcarts for my luggage at the stations in other countries. Having used her place for rest, telephone and sustenance, I am rejuvenated and I can push on with renewed strength and vigor. We talked of The Celestine Prophecy, plants, parks, beauty and destiny meetings, all quite casually, without romantic or sexual overtones.

Now all of a sudden the conductor checks my ticket and tells me I have a first class ticket. I am traveling first class for the rest of my journey! God is great! I move to a first class car of the train: more leg room, wider seats, velour seat covers, carpeting, wider windows. I'm more than cool.

This German train run passes through farmlands and villages and eventually travels along the length of a river. At regular five to ten kilometer intervals there are castles that sit high on hilltops overlooking the river and the villages below. Each castle has a church down below it. There are many towns and each one seems more special than the last.

These sights I am seeing make an incredible life experience. I am witnessing grand phenomena of nature and quaint narrow streets, and churches offering glory to God and castles implying military and government. Having this opportunity is awe-inspiring and I know this trip to Africa and Europe is like seeing the world, or more of it than ever. It is an experience of a lifetime. Traveling alone reminds me of Lew and his treks to Mexico and to Thailand. When you have seen enough of this world you can be ready to pass on to the next. I hope I am able to pass something like this on to others, light someone else's path, show someone the way - to higher vibrations.

Seeing so much beauty, knowing so much more exists, makes me so full of such joy that I could cry, sing, laugh, jump, rush, quake and more, all at the same time.

8:30 PM

Believe it or not, I'm already on a train headed for Ostende, Belgium, where I am to catch a ferry boat to England. I was in Cologne, Germany for exactly three hours. I met with Goetz Buhler and walked past the museum, its famous cathedral, the riverfront, etc. until it rained. We continued our discussions over dinner and by the time it was over I was aware that Goetz is a sensitive, conscious, positive, young music-loving entrepreneur. And I think we are friends.

9:30 PM

It is a rainy night in Belgium. The train rumbles on, deep into the dark, wet blackness. Little lights twinkle and are multiplied by the raindrops on the window. Towns with slick wet streets slide by. I am headed for the North Sea at midnight.

I've got to show my daughter, Kaila, more love. She may not know how much I do love her; so I have to demonstrate it more: More hugs, more talks, more being with her. She taught me what real love is the moment she was born. Now I've got to show her.

FOR KAILA
MY BABY MY BABY

You don't know how I love you
My Baby
I put no one nor anything above you
If you ask me about some things
I'd be guessing
But I know for positive sure
You are a heaven-sent Blessing
to me
I want you to see
that you can be any and every thing
you dream of
and even when you think you have
nothing at all
you can always call
on my love
'cause it's forever
and for ever more
you'll be my first love
and My Baby

—Dad

Kaila the little girl reader

Kaila the bride

Travel can give you new sights, sounds and images that can help you expand your meditations, visualizations and dreams. Just as there are other worlds outside and far away, there are other realms, inside and near to visit or pass through.

I am heading north through Belgium watching small towns speed by. A few days ago, I was heading north on the road from Accra to Kumasi, Ghana with small towns speeding by. How far away is that? Houses, roads, people - how different. How much the same - at midnight.

I can't believe how often I think of my keyboardist, Kevin "Teasmeister" Teasley. I see his face drifting through my thoughts. I met and played with a young keyboard player in Ghana, Richard Kojo Akwa-Harrison. He was tall, dark and handsome, but he reminded me of Kevin, even though Kevin is short and very pale. But writing Richard Kojo now reminds me of my long-lost, best friend, Lew Harrison. I guess writing the name - Akwa-Harrison - did it. The train was delayed two hours in Belgium, so I missed my connection for the last ferry boat to England at midnight. I made calls to the U.S. and slept in the train-ferry station.

26 April - 6:30 AM Wednesday.

After waiting five hours in the Ostende train station, I am now onboard a large ferry boat, crossing the strait of the North Sea to England. The sailing is supposed to take three hours. Sunrise was a nice orange orb timed beautifully to complete the romantic view just as we left the dock. The boat ride is smooth and not all that different from the train: the sound of the engine is almost identical but there is just a bit more pitch and roll. This boat is massive with four decks, large, comfortable seating for hundreds, two restaurants, a movie (even this early in the morning), a money changer, and enough space, nooks and stairwells to make finding your way back to your seat an adventure. I got up out on the uppermost deck just to feel some of the air and to get a poetic feel for this area. There are a few fishing boats out at sea to add atmosphere, but mostly the water looks empty, endless and cold. It looks like it will be a nice day.

Slept a very little bit on the boat. The trip took four hours. It is now 11:30 AM British time. I'm on the train headed to London town. I have been going for 20 hours straight since leaving Cologne, over 24 hours since Zurich. I am tired but in good spirits, listening to my Healing Suite for Lew duo tape.
The English countryside is similar to the rest of Europe: castles and towns, sheep and horses. I will rest my eyes and meditate.

5:30 PM

London is a hub of massive activity. It is a mega-metro area - the biggest in Europe. I'm still on a roll of mystical hook-ups. When I got here I came into Victoria Station, the big train station bustling with activity in the center of London. I think the money changer at the station gave me extra money in pounds by mistake. Then I'm making calls, trying to reach people. Among the calls, I try to reach one Michael Ali, a partner of Dennis Armstead. Dennis is my prime contact in London, but he was scheduled to leave for South Africa today so he referred me to his associate, Michael Ali, as a liaison person in London. I dial Michael's mobile phone number a couple of times, but for various reasons the calls don't go through. Then after I make a couple of other calls, I try Michael again. Not only does the call go through, when I reach him, he is in a car five minutes away, headed for Victoria Station to the very place where I'm standing. Amazing.

Then I go hook up a hotel room through the Thomas Cook agency. Michael and I take a cab to the Rushmore Hotel and it's the joint, the bomb, a great little Victorian style hotel. My room is right on the first floor and it has everything I need: shuttered windows, complimentary breakfast, phone, fax, pants presser, shower, cable TV with two remotes, etc. I go out for a walk and the neighborhood, called Earl's Court, is so hip that it overwhelms my senses. Down the block from my hotel is a busy street filled with hip people of all nationalities, little shops and a Pizza Hut, a Taco Bell, a McDonald's, Middle Eastern curry to go, Chinese food, a bakery, a deli, newsstands, clubs, a subway stop and a 7-Eleven. And everyone speaks English. I'm too gassed!

I get back to my room after having Chinese food for starters. I decide to fax Greg Boraman of Acid Jazz Records. I lay down for a minute then Dennis Armstead calls to say he will be here in London instead of traveling to South Africa, so we're getting together tonight at 6:30 or 7:00. I call Sean, Veronica's son, at his number, which was supposed to be disconnected, and I get him. Then my phone rings and it's Greg from Acid Jazz Records. He and the people at his office were excited to get my fax and he tells me they're having a slamming happening tonight at the Blue Note Club - a massive jam session being filmed for TV with a lot of acid jazz musicians and I'm invited. Wow! Very Celestine!

The night turned out to be another magical mystical music experience: After going to Dennis' for drinks and conversation, I took a mini-cab and got to the Blue Note Club around 9:00 PM. There was a long line of people already waiting to get in the club. I had my horns and my video camera bag over my shoulder so I just walked to the head of the line, past the security people and into the club. When I got inside I could hear the musicians warming up so I followed the sounds and found the basement of the building where the stage was set up. I was just in time for the sound check. The musicians asked me to check the horn mic, and after they heard me play, asked me who I was. When I told them, they said I just had to sit in with them for the jam.

After sound check I went upstairs to the second floor gallery which was serving as the musicians' waiting room and where they were videotaping interviews for Japanese television. The jam session was being promoted as a benefit for the victims of the earthquake in Kobe, Japan. I watched as Simon Bartholomew, guitarist with The Brand New Heavies, and another musician, sat on the sofa and answered questions from the cameraman. They came off as goofy as the guys in the Wayne's World movies. I was asked to do the next segment, and because I have a lot of experience at that sort of thing, when I was asked about my thoughts on acid jazz music and why I was willing to lend my talents to helping out the people in Japan, I expounded on my long number of years making this type of music and about how I always felt that music should be used for higher purposes, be they political, social or spiritual, and how the Japanese had always supported my music even though I had never been there, and on and on. When I finished my 10 minute speech, they all said "Wow!"

Then they asked me to do the interviewing of the next musician. He comes up and they tell him that they want him to be interviewed by Plunky. He says, "Plunky? Where are you from?" After I say I'm from Richmond, Virginia, he rushes over to hug me and says, "I'm Rob Gordon. I played bass with Gil Scott-Heron for 15 years. I used to come see you playing gigs in DC when I was coming up in the business!" During the interview he goes on to say that Plunky was one of the pioneers of jazz funk and a godfather of acid jazz. What an honor.

Later, in the jam session, I performed three of my songs with the band. It was quite a jam. The band, called Akimbo, was led by Simon, of the Brand New Heavies. I was given much respect and honor. The club was packed. The place went wild when I was on stage. And after my last number, which was "African Rhythms," the deejay when right into playing the album version of the same song. All in all it was a grooving and acid jamming night of revelry and fun.

At about 2:30 AM, I called the same mini-cab driver who had bought me to the club. He was a jazz lover and drove me back to my hotel through the late night streets of London with great music playing on his stereo system. I was on Cloud Nine.

The next day I meet Dennis Armstead downtown and I tagged along with him running his errands, making arrangements for a show for one of his artists, and sight-seeing from the double-decker buses. Then we make our way to another section of town, where we visit the Jazz Cafe Club, before going to a meeting at Ninja Tune Records. At the Ninja Tune I met face to face with the guys there, with whom I have been communicating for over a year by fax and phone. They have released a recording that uses a sample from my original version of "African Rhythms". We discuss music, the London scene, production and future projects and they even give me a check for 63 pounds ($100) for mechanical royalties. Dennis and I leave their offices which are in the Southwalk section of town, in a wharf area right beside the Thames River. We get almost all the way back to the tube station and I realize I left something back at Ninja tune. Dennis goes on his way and I go back to get my bag from Ninja Tune. Then I walk around the historic area, sit on the dock near the London Bridge and look out across the river for a relaxing evening rest. As I walk back toward the tube station, I passed through a church courtyard and decide to go in. It turns out to be William Shakespeare's parish church.

6:00 PM , 27 April (Thursday)

I am in Southwalk Cathedral for evening meditation: When we breathe, we breathe in love. We can project love, directing it where we will. It is an energy; a subtle, but very real force. We can project it when we play music, live or on tape, meditating as we play, to the audience, as receivers. The spiritual professionals: monks, priests, shamans, gurus, imams, etc., do their work for all mankind. They function as receiving and broadcasting antennae for mankind. They project positive energy to and for all, to and for the planet in word, deed, and thought vibrations, elevating our collective spiritual potential and threshold. Some artists function similarly, feeling and experiencing beauty, then documenting or reproducing some of the experience in their work, to elevate their audiences to new heights of awareness or emotional involvement with the moment.

7:00 AM, 28 April (Friday)

Meditation (music) allows one to operate or transcend to higher states of consciousness. Music, trance-dancing, drugs, etc. are inducers as well, but through meditation and prayer it is possible to achieve these higher states without outside stimulants. Concerts, parties, and clubs are mass gatherings for moving to higher states - music as inducer, musician as agent or catalyst or medium.

9:00 AM

This trip has helped me focus on our international world: global trade, cultural exchange, cross-pollination, media cross-fertilization, styles/artifacts, news, collage, war and peace.
I should use British funksters for that true international symbolism.

12 Noon

I'm back at the hotel (the Mayflower Hotel; I moved from the Rushmore Hotel across the street because I had only booked it for one night). This morning I took the tube to the Jaguar dealer to order parts for Cookie's car. When I got back here to the hotel, I called Greg Boraman at Acid Jazz who said that he wants me to come over to their offices to collect 200 pounds ($300) as payment for the other night at the club and to discuss future business. I am overwhelmed and so grateful for my good fortune. I am actively demonstrating the potential of visualizations, meditations, higher vibrations and faith. I know that I have a role to play in the international arena. I have known it for years. Now I must surge into that role.

I did go to Acid Jazz Records to meet with Greg Boraman. Then I roamed around the SoHo District visiting record shops, shopping and sightseeing. I went into one record shop, The Black Music Centre and asked if they imported records and when I told them who I was they were enthusiastic about my stopping in. One salesman told me a story about him dating a girl years ago who had wanted a copy of my "Every Way But Loose" LP. He said it took him months to get a hold of it. When he got it, he took it home and placed it at the bottom of his stairs and when up to shower and change clothes. He said he thought the gift of the record would be so special that the girl would marry him or at least he would really get over with her. Anyway, when he came bounding down the stairs to go on his date, he stepped on the record and broke it. When he finally was able to get another copy of the LP and took it to her, she listened to it and it wasn't the mix that she had wanted.

Saturday, 29 April, 1:00 PM

I am on the Eurostar, the new high speed train through the Chunnel, the tunnel under the English Channel, headed for Paris. The London train station for the Eurostar looks and feels like an airport. I am the only black person I see. This new train service is very expensive and today is Saturday, so I guess not many Blacks are traveling for non-business, at this rate. I've had a good morning, but I find that I am a bit nervous on days when I am to travel. I did my yoga (yesterday, too), had a continental breakfast; then when that was done, I took the tube (subway) out to the Jaguar dealership to pick up the parts for Cookie's car that I ordered yesterday. I rushed back to the hotel, packed, checked out and took a mini-cab to the train station.

The ride through London was quite pleasant. London is a fantastically stately and historic city. For classic architecture, it is one of the most rich and beautiful cities in the world. Parliament, the palace, Piccadilly Circus, all the bridges over the Thames, etc., were too nice.

Yesterday, I went back to the offices of Ninja Tune Records to cash the check for 63 pounds they had given me for mechanical royalties ($100). Then I went to Victoria Station to get my train tickets for today and then I went to Acid Jazz Records offices. There I picked up some of their CDs and 250 pounds ($375). [I kept receiving all this unexpected money on this trip.] They were very impressed with my jamming performance Wednesday night at the Blue Note Club. Eddie Piller, the president of the company, said it was the best jazz funk he'd heard in years. They were all excited about my presence there and that was a good feeling for me. They want me to come back and do some things with Akimbo, the band I jammed with at the club. The leader of the group is Simon Bartholomew, the guitarist with the Brand New Heavies. I want to do that as soon as possible, but I really want to bring my band over to London. We would kick A.

8:00 AM Sunday, 30 April

When I arrived in Paris yesterday afternoon, I spent time in and around the train station. Five or six hours of seeing the city. I had to take a cab from one train station to another and then I took an overnight train headed for

Rome. My train is now a day-tripper speeding through Italy down to Roma. It is cloudy and gray. The terrain is flat farmland then mountainous. Italian farmhouses, villages, villas and an occasional castle. Then some tunnels through mountains. I have spent the night in a couchette designed for six. I shared it with a married couple so I was not uncomfortable. He snored, but I had ear plugs that a young Swiss guy had given me on my flight over to Zurich from the U.S., so I meditated and got some much-needed rest. The Paris Lyons Station was crowded and had no comfortable waiting area, so I walked around the streets near the station for an hour or so. Then when it was time to board the train I had to walk a long ways to the right track with all my baggage and I had a rainy, sweaty time locating my designated train car. So I was happy that we closed the shades in the couchette and bedded down for the night around 10:30 PM. Now it's a rainy morning train ride out of Genoa, the largest port in Northern Italy. I still have five or six hour's ride to Roma. My seat mates have gotten off the train in Genoa, so I have the compartment to myself. As we speed down the track, the mountains with many houses built in are on my left and the Mediterranean Sea is on the right. It is all quite scenic and beautiful. I am anticipating a nice afternoon and evening in Rome. I'll be a tourist and do some sightseeing. Maybe I'll have pasta or pizza.

12 Noon

The train has just left the station at Pisa. This trip seems longer and longer, Roma farther away. I am still the only Black I've seen on the train, even though it is quite full now, having taken on more passengers at each station stop. My new Italian compartment mates are pleasant enough but ride along in silence; dozing or watching the mountains and the sea glide pass the windows.

I have ballads and jazz, Hugh Masekela and Loose Ends on my headphones. Two to three hours still to go to Roma. And I'll fly home tomorrow. That's an energizing thought.

I have been passing some of these minutes reading jazz magazines and I am struck by the recurring spiritual themes in the views of so many musicians. We musicians see things similarly, whether from Brazil, Britain or Bavaria.
I am not worried at all about finances. I've had such good fortune this trip; but not only that. I have renewed faith that I am on task, on purpose, on the right track. So I know I'll receive what I need.

Could we live
The two of us
In a cottage in the Italian countryside
With a small garden alongside a small road
  for our Fiat
Would trains speeding by
Filled with hopefuls headed to Roma or Naples
Unsettle us
And make us long for home
Or at least busier times.
Looking out the window
We see the world passing through
Tiny purple and yellow flowers
And reflections of our own faces
Is this enough
Or do we need:
A villa on the mountain
Equatorial heat
Something somewhere else?

11:25 PM Still Sunday (at the airport)

    Spent most of the afternoon in Rome train stations. It took a long time to make it from the station in the north end of Rome where we "landed" to the main station in the center of the city. There was no money-changing booth, no directions and no one spoke English in the North-end station. Finally figured things out with an American couple from West Virginia (Mr. and Ms. Tucker) and a young guy from Canada. We took the metro. I struggled with my bags, but made it. Once we got to the main station I helped the Tuckers find their way. (I had been there a week ago, so I knew where everything was.)

    They were very grateful for my assistance and bought me dinner. Meanwhile, all the inexpensive hotels in the area of the station were full because tomorrow (May Day) is a holiday in Rome. I couldn't quite get it together to go to another part of town, with my bags, and pay more and pay for cabs to and fro, so I just stayed there in the train station until 9:00 PM (about four hours), then took the train out to the airport. The hotels out here were 1) full and 2) four times more expensive. I suppose I should have spent the $100 to stay in a room but No-o-o... So here I sit, an all-nighter, waiting for morning and plane home. I didn't get to see much of Paris or Rome. Maybe some other time. Zurich, Cologne and especially London were great. I can't wait to get back to London to gig and promote my music thing there.

2:00 AM Monday

I awake in the airport lobby. It is almost empty and quiet. Two girls sleep on the floor, one older guy with his luggage on a cart, two other guys and three workers are the only ones in the whole place. Only five more hours to go till check-in at 7:00 AM. The plane leaves at 9:00 AM. Hopefully, I can get a couple of additional naps in to pass the time.

9:30 AM

I am on the plane headed for Milan. I did get a little more sleep, only waking once before getting up from my chair-bed at 6:00 AM. I washed, shaved and brushed in the men's room, checked in with United Air and waited to board this ship. A United Air lady, for whom I made space to sit in the airport waiting area, just happens to be my seat-mate on the plane. Another coincidence.

12:30 PM

At 10:00 AM we land in Milan. We laid over there until noon. Now we're back on board and in flight for eight hours, to arrive in Washington at 3:05 EDT. I'm on my way home but I'm too tired and numb to be excited.
10:00 AM EDT on the plane home.

Food was good. Wine was better. Star Trek: Generations, the on-board movie, had me in tears crying in the first 10 minutes - the similarities of my generational return - to Africa and back to home.
Wisdom from my seat mate: "The worst thing we can do is to hurt someone else intentionally; we are making our own memories today, and it is only bad if we don't learn from our mistakes and repeat them." This last part I have to share with Kaila.

I am learning so much and from so many sources: people I meet, magazines, movies, songs, mountains - almost everything we encounter can be a source of information, inspiration and direction along our path. We have to ask the questions - the answers will be presented.

This trip had allowed me to be at peace with my maturing. I can move toward middle age and be comfortable in my knowledge and experience. I can freely accept the benefits of my knowledge and experience. I can use everything I know, all my faculties, to reach my full potential. In seeking my highest role and demonstrating my fullest acceptance of abundance, I will be doing what I can best do to serve others, the planet, the universe, the creator.

In continuing to develop, I will move toward wisdom and the joys of maturing to old age. I can be an elder statesman as I move closer to becoming an ancestor for Jamiah's and Kaila's progeny.

EPILOGUE: JUNE, 1995

This was the journal I kept on my most recent journey of a lifetime. I have been back home a little over a month now. When I got back to Richmond, it took me about a week to rest and recover. Since that time I have received a contract offer for my next album from Goetz Buhler of Soulciety Records in Germany and a licensing deal for "African Rhythms" from Greg Boraman at Acid Jazz Records in London. This week I received my first letter from Garry in Ghana, who said that my visit was very positive and significant. I also received a copy of the evaluation report that Nick Robertson in Accra sent back to the Washington office of USIA.* In it he says that my consultancy was one of the best they ever had and my impact there was widespread and my leadership and artistic integrity was exemplary of what the agency's Cultural Specialist Program is all about.

My coincidences continue. My development continues. My journey continues.

JOURNEY OF A LIFETIME
(Song written in May after my return home)
You move me and groove me/ and that's all you need to know
To know that i want you with me/ wherever I go
You're sweet with me and we both know that's chill
You've got my heart forever and until
so come go with me/ and baby we will be
on the journey of a lifetime
i love you so/I want you to go
with me on the journey - journey of a lifetime
You give me the joys/ of living the good life
And you give me more/ every day and every night
So let's stay together and let's take our chances
Traveling life's road to love and romances
it's gonna be great/ together we will take
the journey of a lifetime
over mountains and valleys/ cross oceans and seas
on this journey of a lifetime

* See letter on page 182-185

Bridge: living large / we'll flow deep and wide
what's crucial is the mad love we have inside
we'll have the butter and love enough to share
and we'll share our love/ here there and everywhere
so stay with me/ and baby we will be
on the journey of a lifetime
together/ forever/ on the journey of a lifetime

Just so you know how saxy it will be/
I'm gonna blow my sax for you and me
Through thick and thin with me you have been
Now it's on your love that I know I can depend
Now that we're together let's go on and see
What this big old world has for you and me
we'll take a trip and it will be so hip on the journey of a lifetime/
to outer space and any other place
on this journey of a lifetime
if you are there/ then I'll go anywhere
on the journey of a lifetime
we'll take the train/ cars boats and planes
on this journey of a lifetime
I'm ready and waiting/ just
anticipating
this journey of a lifetime
let's make a date/ and baby don't be late
for the journey of a lifetime

---

*From: The U.S. Embassy, Accra, Ghana
To: The U.S. Information Agency, Washington, DC

Subject: Report On The Visit Of Cultural Specialist J. Plunky Branch, April, 1995
1. A complete winner - jazz maestro J. Plunky Branch proved to be one of our most successful and versatile cultural specialists so far. He arrived on a Saturday, went into a studio for rehearsals on a Sunday, and welded a group of Ghana's leading popular musicians into a tightly-organized, small jazz group. He adeptly blended the American musical experience with the African musical experience.
2. On his one-man tour of Ghana, saxophonist Branch (with the able assistance of Okyerema Asante, an internationally acclaimed percussionist), formed "the Accra Band," a quintet comprising a drummer, bassist, guitarist and keyboard man, as well

as percussionist Asante. His activities focused on working with this group, which was occasionally joined by legendary Ghanaian trumpeter, Mac Tontoh. While Ghana-based musicians are skilled professionals in a local context, they hadn't worked with a demanding instrumentalist and arranger like Branch. Asante's interest in bringing Branch to Ghana was to develop some of that facility and precision that characterizes professional musicians like Branch: the ability to work as both a soloist and a side man and to improvise skillfully on new chord progressions while keeping the arrangement in your head (if you aren't already a good reader).

3. The local quintet gave focus and continuity to Branch's program, but we wanted to offer him wider exposure: as teacher and musician. He gave several workshops at the national theatre for local musicians; these sessions were a fine opportunity for cross-cultural exchange. How much can one performer get across in a crowded workshop setting? Well. One veteran bassist, a member of the national symphony and GBC Orchestra as well as many of Ghana's famous high-life bands, told us that he initially attended out of curiosity and a sense of courtesy to fellow musicians, "but I never expected to learn as much as I did."

4. Plunky, who described himself as a contemporary jazz musician, gave a brief history of his background and the varied influences on his musical career, emphasizing the significance of his South African experience. Defining Black American music as a complete "cultural entity in a cultural world," he offered a thorough account of its evolution from its traditional African roots through the slavery/plantation kind of music and manner communication, up to contemporary jazz idioms. He mentioned the blues, brass band music, ragtime, cool jazz, rhythm and blues and other features which characterized various stages of the development of jazz. Underlying all these, he said, were typical African music forms.

5. Music students from the strike-bound University of Ghana found Branch's workshop as a complete lecture, taking notes and asking many questions about African-American music and jazz. The students also wanted to know more about Okyerema Asante's instruments, their origins, and their qualities of sound. A planned program at the music department of the university college of education at Winneba had to be canceled due to the university strike.

6. Most fascinating of all the workshops was the one organized for the John Teye school band, a locally well-known ensemble that shared the stage with the Rebirth Brass Band during their 1993 program in Ghana. Students played their own works for Plunky and were joined by him and the quintet. The workshop serendipitously took place on a school vacation day, and an enormous audience of students from schools throughout Accra drifted in from the nearby children's park.

7. There was a follow-up to this workshop after the John Teye School's Easter break. Once again, the pupils had the special privilege of listening to and learning from Plunky Branch. The discussions were mainly on music as a career. He stressed to the young people that music involved more than merely mounting a platform to perform. Highlighting such aspects as teaching and production, improvisation, the

thrust of his lecture-performances, was also touched on. Branch offered his critique of a couple of performances by students, and took questions and comments.

8. Another group on which J. Plunky branch made an impact was the national symphony orchestra. Although this ensemble features western classical instruments, it has been increasingly focusing on contemporary African symphonic and choral music, augmenting its strings, reeds and brasses with Ghanaian percussion instruments and voices as appropriate. Plunky has been doing that in his music too, so it was easy to find common ground.

9. Though Plunky's programs were centered in Accra, the nation's capital, GBC-TV arranged to film a performance of the quintet. This program was shown country-wide on the sole national television network, as a post-performance program. Plunky also had the honor of being interviewed on the radio station of Ghana's premier university, the University Of Ghana.

10. J. Plunky Branch can be termed a "natural cultural specialist" who delivered his goods without strain. He was irrepressible, making arrangements for individual meetings after his workshops, wandering around Accra at night to hear local music, and joining local musicians for a few numbers. This was not his first visit to Ghana; he has been working with Okyerema Asante since the mid-70s and was here on his own ticket as recently as 1989. We trust this will not be his last visit. It was a perfect combination of elements: a little consulting with the symphony, an unexpectedly large audience for a workshop, a TV program, and most importantly, a cohesive and well-rehearsed quintet of local performers. Okyerema Asante has hitherto agreed to take the stage in Ghana as a solo performer only: his years with Hugh Masekela, Paul Simon, and other luminaries have made him a very demanding band leader by local standards. In a couple of days, Plunky Branch had formed a group which met Asante's standards. That's more than musicianship - that's leadership, and that's what the cultural specialist program is about.

By Nicholas Robertson
Director
United States Information Service
Accra, Ghana

⌘⌘⌘

Chapter 16

ON TOUR IN EUROPE WITH BOBBY BYRD & SOULCIETY

For many years Bobby Byrd stood next to James Brown as a sidekick and collaborator of the Godfather of Soul. Byrd was a band leader, a Famous Flame and friend who wrote some of Brown's hit songs, including "Sex Machine" and "Soul Power."

James Brown was a musical inspiration for me and countless other musicians around the world. When I started my first band, the Soul Syndicate, at Columbia University in New York City in 1966, at least half of our repertoire was James Brown songs. Decades later, I am still likely to play a James Brown song or two in my shows and many of my original songs are stamped with his signature funky grooves.

In 1997, I did a tour in Europe with Bobby Byrd. Wow! Spending days on the tour bus, crisscrossing Germany, Austria and Switzerland hearing stories from Bobby Byrd and his wife, Vickie Anderson, about Mr. Brown was eye-opening. Playing onstage with Bobby plus getting intimate, behind-the-scenes insights about James Brown and the times they shared allowed me to personalize and validate my own relationship to the funk. The momentous meet-up placed me in the rarified air of being only two degrees of separation from godfather greatness. The passage of time gives it more significance to me.

Here is the detailed journal I kept while on that tour in 1997.
JOURNAL OF ANOTHER JOURNEY
A Gig in London and the Soul Society Tour
By J. PLUNKY BRANCH
PROLOGUE

I had always wanted to go on tour in Europe, performing music in night clubs, concert halls and festivals; playing before appreciative audiences and adoring fans. I always knew that it would happen; it was just a matter of when. After 25 years, it did. It was a long time coming, and while I worked for it and waited for it, I fantasized and visualized how touring there might be. Often times dreams are romanticized, idealized fantasies, barely resembling the mundane, ordinariness of the reality, when it comes. My journal documents the everydayness of my touring when it finally did come.

For six months, I had known that I would be going to London to play a club date with my group. Three weeks before leaving for that gig, I was offered the opportunity to do a month-long tour in Germany, Switzerland and Austria, working as a soloist with a concert package organized by Soulciety Records, the German record label that licenses my albums for distribution in Europe. It was to be a promotional tour, featuring some of the acts who record for the label, including Bobby Byrd, Lalomie Washburn, the Soul Society band and me.

I had been leisurely working on recording my next album, but when I got the call about the tour, I kicked my production efforts into high gear, trying to have master tapes for the completed album ready to take with me to Europe to be able to try to get a deal while overseas.

In the last days before leaving I was organizing, making travel and accommodations arrangements, and I was in the recording studio for countless hours, working feverishly to finish the album project. I was also gearing up to take lots of promotion materials with me so that I would have everything I would need to make contacts for future gigs and to promote myself and advance my career.

By the time I left, I was overworked, overloaded, over-extended and over-packed. But I was ready.

6:16 PM Thursday, 9 October, 1997   On the Plane.

We're off! On the 747, backing out of its parking space by the terminal. We're leaving on a jet plane - a non-stop flight: Washington Dulles to London Heathrow. This trip has been a long time coming and maybe a lifetime in the making. I am set to do a promotional appearance with my band at the Jazz Cafe in London, and then I go on as a guest soloist with a Soul Society concert package for a 30 day tour to cities in Germany, Switzerland and Austria. I got a total of two hours sleep in the days before leaving. Last night I was in the studio all night, and then this morning I had to assemble and pack all my things I would need for a five-week trip. Right now I am experiencing maximum fatigue and relief that I'm finally on my way.

6:05 AM London time.

A typically long flight, but not as boring as usual. I am traveling with my wife, Cookie, and three members of my band: Muzi, Kevin Teasley and Charlayne "Chyp" Page, and her boyfriend, Boyce. They were all pretty thrilled about this trip, and their excitement was making it more exciting for me, too. By the time we made the plane, I was so beat that I slept four hours of the six-and-a-half-hour flight over.

Friday night, midnight - 10 October. In bed.

When we got to London's Heathrow Airport, we made it through Immigration and Customs with minimal hassle, but there was no one there to meet us. This was an actualization of my worst fear because Dennis Armstead, who was the agent for this London gig, had made all the arrangements and he had assured me that the Jazz Cafe would be providing the ground transportation while we were in London, specifically and most importantly, our transport from the airport into town. This early in the morning there surely would be no one at the club to give me info, and Dennis Armstead had gone out of town the day before on tour with the Jazz Crusaders. I didn't even know the name of the hotel where we were supposed to stay, and, given that no one showed at the airport to pick us up, I could only hope that the hotel arrangements had actually been made.

I called Dennis' apartment and spoke to his wife who told me that we were booked at the Regents Park Hilton Hotel and that later I could contact Dennis' assistant, Michael Ali, who would take care of us in Dennis' absence. After waiting, and then checking out several alternatives, I made arrangements to take limo vans to get us all to the Regents Park Hilton Hotel in North London. There were six of us and we had our instruments and way too much luggage. The process of booking the vans and waiting and loading up took all of two hours before we could leave the airport. Then when we got to the hotel at 11:00 AM the rooms weren't ready. So we had a very frustrating and tiring morning.

London was bright, sunny and breezy. The air was very clear. Great for seeing the sights on the drive into town from the airport. Driving on the "wrong" side of the road is a trip, even when you're riding as a passenger. Our drivers seemed to delight in scaring us by maneuvering and zigzagging at hyper - speeds on the left side of the streets.

While waiting for our rooms to be readied, we got a call from Michael Ali saying that our rehearsal with the London musicians that I had thought was set for 5:00 PM, was in fact scheduled for 2:30 PM. So we would have just an hour to freshen up and be ready to be driven to the rehearsal studio.

Peter, the driver of the van, showed up at 2:00 PM, right on time to take us to "The Premises" rehearsal studio. When we got there, Andrew, the drummer, was already there and his drums were set up. While we were setting up, Tony Remy, the guitarist, arrived. We had a very decent rehearsal. From the first song we played it was clear that the music was going to be just fine. And as we went over more and more of the material, the songs began to take on a sparkle and funky grooviness. Both of the London musicians were just great: in the pocket, tasteful and really cool guys. The Premises studio space had a hip vibe as well, with several rehearsal rooms equipped with small P.A.'s and a trendy little cafe for food and refreshments.

After rehearsal Peter picked us up and we got a look at London in the early evening. Peter was a professional entertainment guide, procurer and chauffeur. He had hosted many stars, including Bobby Brown, Wyclef and the Fugees and many more. He gave us lots of hip info on the scene in London. Peter took us to get takeout food and we went back to the hotel.

It was nice having Cookie along on this trip. She's a very calming and steadying influence. She's a part of my private world. Most of the time when I'm on the road I am alone and to myself, working on the books, thinking about the music, writing music, or something, but definitely spending most of my time in solitude. Cookie gives me companionship. She wanted to go out on the town tonight but we stayed in and made love. Then, when we should have been dead tired from the travel and the day's activities, we were wide awake. She's reading a book as I write in mine at 1:00 AM.

Sunday 12 October, 9:00 AM. On the Tube headed to Earl's Court to check out another hotel.

Yesterday (Saturday), I rested in the hotel room, only going out to eat after doing my yoga exercises. It was a rainy, chilly day in London but everyone else, Chyp, Boyce, Kevin, Muzi and Cookie, went out shopping and sightseeing for the few hours we had before leaving to go to the Jazz Cafe club for sound check. At 3:00 PM, I rushed everyone out of the hotel in order to get to the club on time for the 4:00 PM sound check. But we got to the club to find a full house audience for a poetry reading and quiet music performance.

(Boring.) This was supposed to go on until 5:00 PM. So we went shopping in that neighborhood in the rain just to kill some time. My feet got wet and I was chilled through.

We got back to the club to find the poetry event running over time until 5:30 PM. We couldn't even use the dressing room yet. I was feeling like we were being dissed like some local band. Someone should have called the hotel to let us know that sound check would be delayed. When we finally got to take the stage and get set up, we had a good sound check until 7:30 PM. Then we went back to the hotel to get dressed, and then headed straight back to the club for the gig.

I thought the gig went extremely well. The crowd was sparse at the beginning, but grew to a near full house. And they seemed to really enjoy our performance. The audience was 95% white Europeans, young and very hip. They danced and responded verbally and clapped when I exhorted them to from the stage. When we ended our two-hour set we got an ovation and chants of "More, more, more..." but we could not oblige, because we had been told there was a definite curfew for us and we had already run overtime.

After the gig we were all in a super-upbeat mood. I went down to meet people who came to our merchandise table. There was a group of Danish people who all came by to say that we should come play in Denmark, and there were some German guys there who were asking me where I was going to play when I went on to Germany. When I pulled out the itinerary, they knew all about several of the clubs on the list and said that they would try to catch me sometime next month.

There was a 26 year old black guy there who said that his mother had bought my records in England twenty years ago and that since the age of nine he loved my stuff and that he had grown up listening to my songs. He told me that he had bought his ticket to the show when tickets first went on sale back in July. He even apologized for there being so few blacks in the audience. There were a couple of Black deejays who were there and who hung out in the dressing room after the show for way too long. They were fans who wanted autographs and they wanted to talk on and on, until we had to ask them to leave just so that we could have some privacy and eat our gourmet dinners.

Michael Ali came to collect the money from the club and to pay me but there were problems with the finances. Dennis Armstead had been paid half of the fee in advance and he was not around. He had paid an accountant to provide certain government tax forms so that the club would not have to withhold 20% of the fee in case taxes were owed. The accountant had sent a letter saying the form would be forthcoming but the club would not release the funds until the form was provided. So the funds would be held in escrow and we could not pay the London musicians who had expected to be paid in cash that night. This will all have to be sorted out on Monday.

Chyp and Boyce left the club around midnight. I introduced Kevin to two young, wild, fine chicks and he hung out with them. Cookie and I stayed at the club until about 1:15 AM; then went back to the hotel and crashed.

Sunday, 12 October - 6:10 PM. On the tube.

I got up bright and early and took the tube over to the Earl's Court section of the city to check out the Mayflower Hotel. I wanted to find a cheaper hotel for my group because our rooms at the Hilton were only booked for two nights and I was providing rooms for my crew for the rest of the time they would be in London. Muzi and Kevin were staying one more night and leaving on a 4:00 PM plane on Monday. Chyp and Boyce were staying an extra day and taking a flight at that same time on Tuesday. I booked the rooms at the Mayflower Hotel in the Earl's Court section of London and then went back across town to the Hilton, rounded up the troops. After breakfast we took three taxis over to the Mayflower and checked in there.

Then, even though I was dead tired, I went with the group sightseeing. We had a great time at Piccadilly Circus, the National Gallery, Trafalgar Square, Buckingham Palace, etc. That evening when we got back to the Earl's Court area we ate a big meal in a Chinese restaurant as a group. My chicken with black bean sauce and green peppers was super.

Tuesday, 14 October- On the plane flying to Germany

Cookie and I bought round trip tickets from London to Hamburg from a travel agency in Earl's Court near the hotel. We're flying on Lufthansa and it cost me an extra 65 pounds (around $105) for excess baggage for my tenor sax. Today we are blessed with nice weather for flying. No problems with customs exiting London. A quiet flight. I didn't even take the moments to be the least bit apprehensive about playing on the tour or rehearsing with the Soul Society band; I know it will be fine. Goetz Buhler, president of Soulciety Records, will meet us at the airport. I hope.

Wednesday, 15 October - 2:00 PM - On the tour bus.

Yesterday Goetz did meet us at the airport. He took us to check into a nice little Hamburg hotel (modern, angular designed room with purple, black and silver color scheme in our room; very comfortable) and then straight to the rehearsal with Bobby Byrd and the Soul Society band. The music was vintage James Brown: Bobby Byrd's classic songs, horn arrangements and rhythm licks. I had to work with the charts for the sax parts, sometimes writing out what was hummed out. My cold and a headache bothered me during the rehearsal but I made it through it. What was even tougher for me was some impressions and questions that struck me during this initial encounter with the band and Bobby Byrd.

I was a bit uncomfortable with the fact that these younger, German musicians were so "schooled" in this music. Everything was written down, not just for the horn parts but even for the drums and bass. Now of course this made it quicker and easier to remember and tighten up a large amount of material for a large group of musicians, but the rhythm section seemed stiff and not grooving. Also, it put me at a disadvantage because I am not a good sight reader and my forte is improvising and soloing.

I was also thinking about that fact that I was playing tight horn arrangements for these classic James Brown songs; songs and arrangements just like I had played 30 years ago in college with my group, The Soul Syndicate. This was like deja vu or coming full circle or maybe like going backwards. Had I come this far, worked so long and hard on doing my own music, been so committed to promoting music as a progressive social and political force, only to come back to playing background horn parts to old James Brown show music. Was this beneath my purpose in life?

Don't get me wrong; James Brown and his legendary music of the 50s, 60s and 70s represent the highest heights in terms of the impact of Black American music. James Brown may be the singular most important figure in the history of Black popular music. And I respect that to the fullest. I do a tribute to his music in my show with my band. But at that first rehearsal I questioned whether I would enjoy or feel proud to be playing in this type of show for my first European tour and for such a long gig at that.

Other more impactful questions had to do with Bobby Byrd, the man and the musician. Bobby Byrd performed, recorded and toured with James Brown for years. More importantly, Bobby Byrd wrote some of Brown's most enduring songs. Recently, Bobby Byrd had been ill with cancer and now after successful treatment, he is making his comeback with this 30-day tour with Soul Society instead of with his own family band and entourage. I was struck with Bobby's age and aging. He is probably 10 years my senior and he is still having to be at this rehearsal and doing this tour just like I am. Is this me and what I'll be doing 15 years from now? Is this what I want to be doing for the rest of my life? Is music and entertainment worthy of my talent and brain power? Should I be in political or religious or corporate or entrepreneurial endeavors in order to have impact on the world? Am I doing what I should be doing with my life? Are these simply the typical questions of a 50-year-old Black man facing a mid-life crisis or am I just tired and down because of my travels and a bad cold?

After the rehearsal, on the way back to the hotel, we stopped at a Turkish restaurant for takeout food. The food was plentiful and good.

In the morning we got up; I did my yoga, Cookie showered. We went out walking in Hamburg to change some money and to look for a black shirt for me to wear onstage. We checked out of the hotel and Goetz drove us across Hamburg back to the rehearsal site where everything and everyone was loaded onto the tour bus. The bus pulled off and we started out on The Tour.

The tour bus is top of the line and it is everything I have ever envisioned for my own tour bus: a double-decker with sleeping berths for 15 upstairs, four lounging areas with 16 seats downstairs, three video monitors, bathroom, refrigerator, microwave, cell phones, etc. Today it has all the creature comforts of home plus a smooth ride. I might get tired of it by the time this 30-day tour is over, but today it is as cool as cool whip.

The people on the tour are cool too. Bobby Byrd, the headliner and elder statesman of the tour; his wife, singer Vicki Anderson; her son, 38 year old keyboardist, Bart Anderson who serves as Bobby Byrd's musical director; and singer songwriter Lalomie Washburn, formerly with Chaka Khan and Ray Charles; and I, were the Black American guest stars.

The Soul Society band members are young, white Germans from Hamburg: Martin on bass, Sven on guitar, Klaus on keyboards, Claas on trumpet, Johnny on trombone, Tim and Jens (called Big John) on vocals plus the band's lead vocalist, an African-American sister, Sandra, and newcomer Stefan on drums. Also traveling with us are Jorn, the tour manager/booking agent; Martin, the sound engineer; and Detlef, the bus driver.

Thursday, October 16, 12 noon - On the bus

Last night we got to the Geiss 22 Club in Munster and set up for gig. The club was a small, stand-around type place near a college. The sound check went well and then we ate quiche-like casseroles and salads for dinner.

It was a full house for the show. Soul Society went on first and played three songs, then Lalomie Washburn sang five songs and finally Bobby Byrd came on to do his set. The whole show lasted 2? hours and it felt like it was a little long. The entire thing was funky though, with just a couple of spots that lagged a bit. It's quite a musical production with little or no choreography, but is too big for a stage as small as the one in this first club. We will be playing all clubs on this tour; hopefully some will have bigger stages.

We decided not to stay in Munster for the night. Instead, we rode the bus overnight, arriving in Berlin in the morning. On the bus I continued to wonder about the questions I had when I got to the rehearsal and saw Bobby Byrd conducting the band and tightening up the show. He was energetic and in great voice, but I wondered if this live performance thing is really what I want to be doing 10 years from now. Do I want to be leading a band of youngsters when I am old(er). Isn't that what I do now? Do I want my son, Jamiah to be in my band? Is old soul music enough? And I'm not sure I know what I mean by that, but it seems to me that my music with its jazzy progressive structures, chords and lyrics, has more substance and more weighty intentions.

I slept well in my bunk on the bus, considering it is a bunk on a bus. I only got up once to check on the driver, get something to drink and take a nighttime cold tablet. It's amazing that 15 people could fit so comfortably in such tight confines.

Berlin is a very cosmopolitan city.

Friday, 17 October, 10:15 AM
On the bus outside the venue in the next city.

Yesterday when we got to Berlin after riding all night, we checked into our hotel. Then Cookie and I walked around the immediate area, window shopping and then went to a Chinese restaurant for lunch. At 4:00 PM I walked from the hotel over to the Quasimodo Club for set up and sound check which took until 7:50 PM to complete. I went back to the hotel to get Cookie and our bags, because after the gig we would again travel overnight on the bus.

The Quasimodo was a really nice club with a reputation for presenting great music. The club has a large café upstairs on the first floor and the performance venue in the basement. The stage has professional lighting and the sound system was much more than adequate, with a 32-channel Yamaha board, tri-amped main speakers and six monitor mixes. The room is decorated with black furnishings and fittings bordered by solid mahogany.

The Quasimodo crowd loved the show, which was rhythmically tighter than the first night. I found myself a little more comfortable with the horn section parts. I also carved out more space in the show for my own featured solo work, which the band and the crowd seemed to appreciate.

Bobby Byrd is the star of the show. He comes on stage after 90 minutes of funk to do his 45-60 minute set and the crowd is hyped on those classic, super-funky grooves he wrote for James Brown. The show has a built-in first ending and encore, but even after that, the people screamed for more for 15 minutes. But the show was over for the night. We turned them over to Tim, our in-house deejay.

We loaded up the bus and left Berlin around 3:00 AM. We stayed up drinking, smoking and talking until the wee hours on the bus rolling along the autobahn.

I have concerns: money is going out more than anticipated; (excess baggage on the plane = 65 pounds, incidentals at the hotels, meals for me and Cookie, local phone calls in Berlin = 65 DM) and I am making less money than I thought I would. I am concerned about having no money when I get back home in the States. But then I know the universe will provide.

I am also feeling that it will be difficult to make the business contacts and advancements that I had hoped to develop on this trip. Oh, this tour will have its business and promotional benefits, but so far I have not been able to meet the club owners or promoters or radio and record people. I hope I'll do better networking as the tour goes on.

2:30 AM on the bus headed for the next stop.

Cookie is supposed to leave Europe to go back home on Sunday. I was worried today about getting her travel arrangements made and getting my own airline ticket changed. So she and I walked in the town of Krefeld, a quaint little place with few, if any, Black people. We went to the train station and then walked until we got to a travel agent who told us that the best thing for Cookie to do was what we had planned all along: to take a train back to Hamburg from Freiburg, where we would play tomorrow. Then we found out that the flight we booked her on from Hamburg would not get her back to London in time to make her flight from London to the U.S. So we also had to call British Airways to change her to a later flight on Sunday (at a cost of an additional $150). I also had to book my change of flight for November 16th at the end of my touring.

Once I got all that straight I felt better. We walked back through town, back to the venue, the Kulture-Frabrik, a club with two performance areas built in a former slaughterhouse-warehouse-dairy. The place was all concrete floors and tile; gray, damp, and cold, but clean. We hung out on the bus and in the big building, taking turns using the two showers/bathrooms. The weather was sunny and warmer than in recent days. But inside the building the temperature was as cool as Berlin. Still it was a leisurely day, we all spent "roughing it."

Lalomie has been in Germany recording and performing for four months and she did an earlier tour with Soul Society, playing at several of the same venues we are hitting on this tour. She told us about playing in several interesting venues, including one built in a large swimming pool with the stage at what was the deep end and the people seated at the shallow end and all around the edges. Another one she recalled was built in one side of a motor tunnel and had great acoustics and the other side of the tunnel was still in use.

The Kulture-Frabrik had a large room which could hold 1,200 and a smaller club which could hold 350 where we would play. I thought the gig that night went better than ever. The show was tighter and I got to do my rap and "Every Way but Loose" and everyone seemed to enjoy my songs and solos.
We ate a meal after the gig and I got phone calls through to Jamiah and others. I was "up" and stayed awake late. We're blazing down the autobahn on the tour bus, with the new Janet Jackson CD on the sound system. I'm really getting to know and like all the people on the tour. This ain't half bad. Indeed, I am enjoying this!
Sunday, 19 October, 1:00 PM - back on the bus.

Yesterday we played Freiburg, a hip, modern city in the southwest corner of Germany on the border of France and Switzerland. Before we got there we stopped at a highway rest stop that featured a Best Western Hotel, public showers and other creature comforts that reminded me of being in the U.S.

Our hotel in Freiburg was the InnerCity Hotel and it was new, modern and centrally located. My biggest concern headed into Freiburg was getting the train schedule information for Cookie's departure and getting her and her bags to the station and on the train. But the InnerCity Hotel was situated right in the transportation center of the city, which includes the train station, bus depot, cab stands, and airport transfer point. Super cool! In fact the InnerCity Hotel was literally right beside the train track that Cookie's train would leave on at 11:30 PM that night. Just getting that straight was a load off my mind. She would travel overnight, arrive in Hamburg at 8:30 AM and Goetz would meet her and get her to the airport for her flight at 12:25 PM.

Cookie and I enjoyed the sights walking around the area of the hotel. Then I went to sound check at the Jazzhaus Club. The venue was larger and more nicely appointed than any so far. It was another of the places in Germany with a rich recent history of presenting great jazz and R&B talent. The gig was packed with people. The stage was large and I played more tenor sax rather than alto at Bobby Byrd's suggestion. I played well and was again well received. I also did my song "I Can't Hold Back" with the band for the first time and I dedicated it to Cookie, who was there and had to leave right after that to make her train. Detlef, the bus driver went with her to the station while I stayed onstage to finish the gig.

After our performance, the Jazzhaus Club became a packed Saturday night dance hall like you'd find anywhere in the world. There were some fine children in there too, including two young, super pretty sisters from the Sudan. In the show, I'm taking more solos, doing two of my songs and being featured more. At this gig at the Jazzhaus, Jorn sold more of my CDs from the merchandise table than any of the others. So the promotion plan is working!

Yes, my promotion plan is in effect. But one of my concerns since being on this tour and seeing Bobby Byrd and Lalomie is, that being my age, maybe I should be further along my career path to make this undertaking worth the effort? Maybe I need to be younger in order take advantage of the long-term benefits of this type of promotional tour? Instead of this tour being my breakthrough step before stardom, it may be just one of several steps, one of several tours I will have to complete before I could warrant a full-fledged tour of my own, with my own group. Maybe I'll have to come back again and work with a Soul Society band like Lalomie has done, in order to build more name recognition and build up the audience for my music.

Also, I may have to add one or two straight-up funk songs to my latest album that I am working on, in order to fit more with what Soulciety is releasing and promoting.

Now it's 2:00 PM on the bus and we're headed to Switzerland. The terrain is getting a bit hillier and more interesting. The cars on the autobahn - Mercedes, Volvos and other Euro makes and models - go whizzing by at amazing speeds.

We cross the border and go on into beautiful Switzerland with its glorious mountains and fantastic views. We're jamming on the bus with the new Bootsy CD on the box.

Monday, 20 October, 1:15 PM - On the bus

Olten, Switzerland is a small, quaint city and the concert hall where we played on Sunday night was sparse and plain but it had super tech equipment and a very nice spread of refreshments. The show drew a large crowd, in part because it was the first show in the city in several weeks and also because Monday is a day off from work (holiday or something?).

The concert went as well as usual. We made a few changes in the show: Sandra sang a Chaka Khan song, Lalomie sang one less song, I did "I Can't Hold Back," and there were other fine tuning adjustments. I wore my black African outfit and it was a hit with the band.

After the gig we had a catered meal. I had a vegetarian rice dish with peas, pineapple, tomato, green peppers, artichoke and other fruits and veggies. It was delicious. The other dish on the menu was rice and veggies with chicken and rabbit.

The Hotel Europa where we were staying was an old building and only 50 meters away from the venue. The night before in Freiburg, Germany, the Inner City Hotel had great X-rated movies, but at the Hotel Europa in Olten there was only CNN. Actually, there was a hoochie-coochie bar with a live band and dancing girls in the hotel, but I went up to my room instead of going there.

I stayed up until 3:00 AM and I called Cookie, timing my call to reach her in my daughter Kaila's car, surprising Cookie and welcoming her back home in the states. Cookie had traveled by train from Freiburg to Hamburg where she was met by Goetz, who took her sightseeing and on to the airport to take a flight to London. She then made a connecting flight to Dulles Airport in Washington, DC where she was met by Kaila, who was driving her the 100 miles to Richmond when I called.

Soulciety Bobby Byrd on stage

After that I went to sleep and I woke up thinking about career moves, gigs for December back in the States, the long odds against record deals and touring deals, etc. I am not well-known enough to warrant those deals, but I do have something to say and I do have a great band and show, combining the best of jazz and soul. Now, the question is, is that enough?

Lalomie is quite a songwriter. She did several things for Chaka Khan ("I Am A Woman," "Midnight"). She is a super poet and she works her words into funky nommo vibes. She is a mellow spirit and is always positive, always sharing, always saying something kind and sweet.

We get to Basil, Switzerland to do a radio interview featuring Bobby Byrd and Lalomie. We have tonight and the next two nights off, so we'll go back to Munich, Germany to spend those days there, then move on to Vienna, Austria for Thursday nights gig at a casino.

Seen at a rest stop petrol station on the autobahn on an X-rated video - "Masturbation Guaranteed"

> 50 Year old Haiku:
> The seasons change
> for the 200th time
> round and round
> the learning goes
> —Plunky

9:00 PM Tuesday, 21 October - On the bus

I spent last night on the bus and essentially spent the day on the bus too. We parked the bus last night on the circus grounds in Munich, beside the railroad yard. Then we went to pick up Bobby, Vicki and Lalomie from the hotel where they stayed. We had lunch at a restaurant overlooking an outdoor public pool. The water in the pool was 86 degrees and people were swimming even though outside it was a cold, damp, windy 43 degrees. None of us went swimming though.

We went to a mall for an hour then left Munich and stopped at the first service area on the autobahn so some of us could shower, eat, etc. Then we set out for Austria, riding all evening.

I have gotten to know all the members of this traveling German troop and they are all really nice guys and ladies. Lalomie is a genuine good and positive spirit, a poetess; always willing and ready to add some "up-ness" to the mix, always with a kind word, always encouraging and sharing. Sandra, the vocalist with Soul Society, speaks fluent German and is likewise always ready to be helpful. She gets a lot of sleep by day after staying up late at night after the gigs, rarely getting up before 2:00 PM in the afternoons. Sven, the guitarist, is always ready with a joke, a crack and a smile. His brother, Tim, the deejay and singer is friendly and respectful. Martin the bass player is a music student in a Holland jazz program and an exceptional musician. Claus, the Keyboardist, is quiet and is into classical jazz and is mellow and introspective. Jens or Big John, as he is called, is a lot of fun and functions as one of the leaders of the band. He is the lead singer and he knows lots about the business, the tech and the instruments. He looks just like Skipper Bailey, a friend of mine back in DC. The other horn players are more stand-off-ish and weird. Johnny, the trombonist, is energetic on stage; whereas Claas, trumpet player, is quiet and very reserved. Stefan, the drummer, is new to the band and he is the weirdest one of all, but he is an excellent drummer. He is often off to himself and he is a reader and an intellectual. Jorn, the tour director and a booking agent is cool, business-like and also respectful.

Then there is Bobby Byrd, the elder statesman and star of the show; his wife and background singer, Vicki Anderson, the diva; and their son Bart Anderson, keyboardist and all around regular American guy. Detlef, the bus driver is nice, conscientious and doesn't speak much English. He is one heckuva driver though and he's cool.

10:00 PM we're in Vienna, Austria.

Being in Europe in so many different countries and watching CNN International and seeing so many environmental news stories, etc., has given me a more international view point. Actually, I have been contemplating things and issues on a global scale. Thinking globally makes local, personal, racial, and tribal concerns seem petty by comparison.

11:00 PM Wednesday, 22 October, in the hotel room.

We moved the bus and the crew to a new hotel on the other side of Vienna. The Hotel Pension Klimt is a lot nicer. Since we had the day off, Tim, Sven, Lalomie, Sandra, Jens and I decided to go sightseeing and to get something to eat in downtown Vienna. We took two trolleys and a subway ride to get to a most spectacular old city center.

We got off the subway at Stephansplatz station and exited into a fabulous area of Vienna where there were fantastic churches and narrow streets lined

Soulciety bus in the Alps

Vicki Anderson, Bart Anderson and Bobby Byrd on the tour bus

Soulciety tour bus

Sandra and Plunky on the tour bus

with wonderful buildings along a grand plaza. There were religious statues in the middle of a wide-bricked walkway bordered by commercial stores and shops. There were horse-drawn carriages carrying tourist couples and families. Quite a scene.

We walked to the end of the plaza, made a left turn and walked up the block toward this large and impressive building which blocked the way. When we got to the end of that block we could see another plaza in front of that building which was actually a gateway called the Virgin's Gate. To the right of that building is a wonderful, large 150-year-old coffeehouse, perhaps the oldest one in Europe. We all went in for coffee, tea, hot chocolate and pastries. After that we came out and passed through the Virgin's Gate building to come to and pass over a series of grand plazas and parks and malls bordered with some of the most magnificent and grandest old buildings I have ever seen. It was breathtaking architecture, very historic buildings, most with statues at the corners and edges of the rooftops. One of these buildings was the Parliament building from whose balcony Hitler gave an important speech in the 1930s.

In the park across from the Parliament building where Hitler once spoke, Lalomie and Soul Society gave a concert a couple of months ago. Lalomie spoke about being proud of the irony of being able to come and perform there

Vienna government buildings

Vienna historic area

where Hitler would not have liked to even acknowledge our presence or our worth. We continued our walk on to another commercial shopping street. I was so thoroughly impressed with Vienna's stock of grand old buildings. Vienna is a Grande Dame of a city. This is the city of Mozart and great music and arts. The coffeehouse we visited was one in which Schoenberg, the twelve tone composer, had long ago sipped his coffee and debated musical theory.

Earlier in the day on the bus ride across Vienna, Vicki told stories and anecdotes from experiences she and Bobby Byrd had had touring with James Brown, Maceo, Bootsy and those guys back in the days. Most of the stories were funny as all get-up and everybody on the bus was laughing and/or listening in awe of the history and inside info we were privy to and getting a glimpse of...

There were stories about James Brown getting into fights at gigs, usually over messing with some guy's woman, and his henchmen and bodyguards taking care of business protecting him and all of the members of his group. Many stories about performing in Africa, playing in stadiums for presidents

Soulciety Band dressing room with Bobby Bird, Vickie Anderson, Bart Anderson, Lalomie Washburn, Plunky and others

Soulciety dressing room with Lalomie, Sandra, Jens and Sven

Goetz Buhler and Plunky

Lalomie Washburn

and leaders. Crowds being beaten back. She told us about a time in Nigeria, a man brought a blind man past the barricades to the back of the stage, saying that the blind man wanted to see James Brown. An army soldier guarding the stage said "How can a blind man see James Brown," and then the soldier proceeded to beat the blind man and the man who brought him up there. Vicki said the soldier was beating the blind man unmercifully until she came out of the back stage area and glared at the soldier until he stopped the beating.

Then there was another time, also in Africa (Nigeria), and Bootsy was there with them. At the gig someone had given Bootsy some joints of marijuana, enough for the whole group but Bootsy was going to keep them all for himself. After the gig, Vicki, Bobby and Bootsy were in a car together being driven back to their hotel, but it was after curfew. The car was stopped by soldiers at a checkpoint and Bootsy hid the joints in his boot. The driver got into a loud argument with the soldiers and they ordered the driver out of the car. After more heated words, one of the soldiers yelled at the driver, "Let's have a look in the boot! Open the boot!" Bootsy almost had a shit fit because he thought for sure he was about to be busted. But they were referring to the trunk of the car as the "boot".

Vicki talked about going to Nigeria and arriving in Lagos, its capitol, just after the Biafra War and hearing the "pow pow pow" of gunfire outside their hotel grounds and being told that it was the firing squads executing leaders of the opposition. And the group had to perform the next day. She also talked about James Brown going to Boston to help quell the riots after the assassination of Dr. Martin Luther King, Jr.

These stories helped to remind me that music and performing can have meaningful social and political impact; and that this career path is worthy of my God-given talents and abilities. Earlier on this trip, at the beginning of tour, I wondered if I shouldn't be doing something "more" with my life, with my intelligence; something other than music as my life's work. Maybe work in politics or environmental business or with an educational company, do some religious work; do something more suitable for a mature man?

These stories about past tours reminded me of what I've known for the past 25 years: that being a performing musician does give me the opportunity to affect people's lives, to affect politics, and address current events and historical issues and future concerns. James Brown quells a riot or visits Nigeria

at the end of its civil war. Ghanaian Master Drummer Okyerema Asante goes to the Northern region of Ghana to ease tribal tensions at behest of the government. We go to schools to teach multi-culturalism, tolerance and history. These things do have great value; are socially meaningful; and no one could do them better than respected performing musicians.
5:30 PM Friday, 24 October - In the hotel room.

Yesterday and today have been low-key days off. After mid to late morning breakfasts, I showered, lounged about, then went to walk in downtown Vienna. I walked the length of the commercial shopping street in the central downtown area with Sandra and Claus. At the end of the walk we sat in a café and I talked on and on philosophically and passionately about my optimism for the future: computers, the internet, the youth and the next generation working together to solve environmental problems and create new paradigms, vistas and destinies. Good and right stomping out the illusions of evil and all things negative.

I told Sandra I needed to hear myself talk in order to figure out what I was thinking and to sort out whether my reasoning was sound. I am becoming a bit of a futurist, with definite, ambitious visions of positive predictions for worldwide society and a global culture.

11:00 AM Saturday, 25 October - On the bus, headed out of Vienna.

The gig last night was the best one yet. The venue was the old Baumgarten Casino, which has a large main room with a proscenium stage, high ceiling with ornate moldings, hardwood floor and adequate sound and lighting. The place was packed with young people ready to party. The band was kicking even though Martin, the bass player, Vicki and Bart all had flu symptoms. We went on stage around 1:00 AM and we were hot! After the gig I found out that the organization sponsoring the event was the Young Peoples' Socialist Party.

Earlier yesterday Lalomie had heard that her latest single was doing well in London and that her video was being shown on MTV and "The Box" there. So she was "up" and she was "on" for the gig!
8:45 PM Sunday Night, 26 October.

The World Series game on television. I had a great Sunday! A cozy, modern hotel room in the countryside with a vast green pasture with cows right outside my first floor picture window. I did a full hour of yoga and meditation, breakfast and then a day of cable TV channel surfing with my rented remote control unit and resting in bed.

Yesterday we rode from Vienna to Ubersee, Germany, four hours on the autobahn through beautiful, hilly and mountainous farmland. A beautiful, scenic ride.

The Roots Club is a tight little venue in the Bavarian countryside. It had a large enough stage, wooden interior, a balcony around the room, great lighting, special effects and adequate sound system. The crowd last night was a sell-out and they were exuberant. Our show was tighter rhythmically and even though there were some outright mistakes, this was a really good show. The audience was hyped and danced the whole 2? hours, having a really good time. After the set the club owners came to the dressing room and broke out bottles of champagne and all kinds of refreshments.

The last two gigs have been an interesting contrast. The Casino Baumgarten in Vienna is a club but it is more like a small concert hall in the city. The Roots Club was a small club in the country. The Vienna date was sponsored by the Socialist Party of Austria and the Roots club is in the most right-wing part of Germany.

I am spending more mental energy concerned about my bookings for December and even January, so I won't be totally broke when I get back home. Even though I haven't been as active in promotion and prospecting for new contacts here in Europe as I had hoped to be, this tour has been a real eye-opener with regards to my own status here in this part of the world, and in terms of giving me new perspectives on my show and producing music, both live shows and in the recording studio. I can see doing shows with my crew featuring my own band, plus Danja Mowf, the Jazz Poet Society, and others; producing shows with bigger, more elaborate production values.

8:00 AM Monday morning, 27 October

I woke up and looked out the window of my first floor hotel room to see that on the horizon, out beyond the flat pasture, stood some majestic mountains which had not been visible yesterday because of clouds and fog. The mountains were always there but the mist and rains had created a veil through which the beauty of the great mountains could not be seen.

If I had known beforehand that the mountains were there I could have and would have appreciated their presence even while they were shrouded in gray. Knowing the mountains are there would create an indelible impression in my mind, which would in fact color the view of the horizon in subtle shades of grays. Knowing your goals are out there, even when the clouds or fogs or mists obstruct your view, will allow you to keep on moving toward your dreams and seeing them and being inspired by them even in the bleakest weather - which, by the way, is never permanent.

By the time I wrote this, clouds had rolled in, once again covering the mountains, hiding them from the view from my window. But by then I had already had the vision. A little while later a light rain turned into snow just to prove that what we might perceive as gloom can produce seasonal beauty.

7:45 PM Monday evening, 27 October. Hotel room in Munich.

We rode the tour bus the short, one-hour distance to Munich. The bus needed some repairs. We were given the afternoon off for free time and were to meet back at the circus grounds railway yard where the bus was parked last week when we spent the night here in Munich. I opted to stay at the hotel sharing a single room with Bart. But this single is truly a tiny single, so I don't know if this was the best of ideas.

11:30 AM Tuesday, 28 October - On the bus.

Well, I made it through the night. After watching the taped delay showing of Game Seven of the World Series, I slept on the hotel room floor on cushions from the chairs. I slept fitfully. Bart gave me the comforter from his bed and he slept in his clothes. I don't want to impose on him like that again. I am concerned about my accommodations. And it is really getting on my nerves to be in this in-between status. Bobby, Vicki, Lalomie and Bart always have hotel rooms. The Soul Society band members always sleep on the bus and they agreed to that at the start of the tour. But I am supposed to have accommodations and I have decided to demand my rightful rooms.

I got up and had the complimentary continental breakfast. I am getting accustomed to that breakfast menu. Then the bus arrived to take us out of Munich and on the road to the next gig site: the Conrad Sohm Club in Dornbirn, Austria. It's a sunny, brisk day for the traveling. Clear and cold on the road.

On the bus ride Vicki told more stories of being on the road with her past musical employer: having to call him Mr. _____; having to be dressed up even on the tour bus, with the men wearing shirts and ties; and stories of him being quite a hard task master who tolerated no insubordination and no mistakes on stage. Vicki expressed her sentiments about her ex-employer in no uncertain terms: she didn't like him, thought he was evil and she had some fear of his powers. She even said that she thought that he had sold his soul to the devil or otherwise crossed over to the dark side, mentioning rituals involving boiling chicken bones in the back woods in the Deep South and an African shaman who traveled with the entourage.

Vicki also talked about this same famous black musician as having to have a woman every night. Every night! And told us about one night when she was the only woman around after a show and she was invited to his room. They found themselves alone and he fixed her a drink. Vicki didn't drink ordinarily but her boss man insisted that she have a drink with him. Well, she took one sip of what he offered her and immediately became violently ill. She said that she rushed straight into the bathroom and was throwing up what felt like her whole insides. The whole time he was saying "Don't be such a baby. Here, take another drink; it'll help settle your stomach."

She left and went to her room and as soon as she got to room and lay on her bed, she was immediately well and at peace. She was sure that he had spiked her drink with something and she was equally sure that it was God's answering her prayers that got her out of his room safely.

Another time she told us about was when they were on this entertainer's plane, flying through a violent storm en route to Cincinnati. She said that they had not realized that the weather was as bad as it turned out to be and actually they should not have even taken off on the trip. In this turbulent storm the bandleader called out to the pilot and asked how was the weather in Cincinnati and after a few moments the pilot spoke over the intercom saying that it was a rainstorm there as well.

At this point the fearless leader looked out the window pointed his finger to the heavens and proclaimed "I don't want a drop a rain to fall on me and my new suit when I get to Cincinnati!"

Well, Vicki said she was appalled at this remark obviously directed to God and she wished that God would retaliate for being spoken to with such irreverence. She prayed that God would do something to the man but not while they were in the air in that plane. In fact, she moved as far away from the man as she could.

When they landed in Cincinnati, the storm had slackened a great deal, and when the door to the plane was opened the star musician stood in the doorway and looked out into the last drizzle of the storm. Vicki said that she was cowering at the window looking out to see if he would be struck by lightning. She said that she was praying that when he walked out onto the runway that a big whoosh of rain would just come down and drench him in that precious sharkskin suit. But when he stepped off the plane, he walked out onto the tarmac, stretched out his arms and looked up at the sky and smiled triumphantly as not a drop of rain fell on him.

12 noon Wednesday, 29 October - Martinspark Hotel lobby.

This is definitely the nicest hotel of this tour and one of the nicest hotels and best designed hotels I've ever stayed in. A rounded two-story lobby and lounge areas; spacious, Euro-chic rooms; sauna solarium; fine restaurant, etc. We had a gourmet dinner here last night before the gig and it was fabulous! The Club, the Conrad Sohm, was set back off the road in a wooded, mountainous area beside a babbling creek on the outskirts of Dornbirn. It is not exceptionally large, but the venue has a great P.A. system with 32 track boards out front and for the monitor mix, super theater lighting and a full recording studio upstairs. The staff and management were very friendly and cordial and did everything in a first class way. The club has a continuous strong line-up of acts coming through. This week: Tuesday, Bobby Byrd; Thursday, Al DiMeola; Saturday, Billy Cobham, etc.

The Conrad Sohm Club owners went all-out for us. Light but full catering during the set up and sound check, then the gourmet dinner at the hotel. They pulled out Remy Martin and tequila, beer and wine before the gig, and after the hit, they brought out Italian champagne, more Remy Martin and all the beer we could drink and carry.

Big-time producer, Peter Wolfe, was in the house for the gig and he hung out in the dressing room, mainly talking to Lalomie. Apparently, they knew each other and did some gigs together way back when. Later some Austrian fans came in and rolled up a bunch of spliffs and the dressing room looked and smelled like a pad in Haight-Ashbury in 1970.

Because we played there on a Tuesday night, the crowd was light and definitely the smallest we've had on this tour. But we gave the full show, which continues to get tighter and tighter. The tape from the board mix was clean and sounded great.

This morning I got up and took a full sauna. Last night I talked to Cookie

on the phone for over half an hour, getting stuff off my computer at home. I'm gonna have a monstrous phone bill when I get home, but I have to contact people about gigs and on-going business.
4:45 PM - on the bus.

Great views as we go on the highway to and through the Alps. And just like on my train ride through the Alps two years ago, the views of the mountains just keep getting more and more beautiful, moment by moment. Snow on the tops, evergreens at the foots and along the sides of the roadway, and the sunset reflecting off the background facets, all add to special and spectacular effects.

12 noon Thursday, 30 October - in the hotel sauna room.

This hotel is just as nice as the one we had in Dornbirn, but this one is smaller and designed with more of a mountain lodge theme. Indeed, I woke up and looked outside to see that we are surrounded by mountains at close range. Vicki needs a laxative so I volunteered to go to the store. But the nearby stores had none. So I walked to find a drug store. I hiked off for about 2? miles only to find myself back at the hotel, having made a complete circle of the town. A very refreshing morning hike with picture postcard views of Austrian houses and mountains.

I slept well last night and for about 9? hours. I was relaxed and tired after having had a sauna yesterday and a toke of Bart's spliff after dinner last night. I am well-rested for the gig tonight. My favorite color is you. Take care of you for me.

Friday12 noon, 31 October - On the magic bus riding through the Alps.

Mountain peaks, valley creeks, walls of shear clouds, little houses, train tracks and trestles and too many postcard scenes to describe. The design of the bridges and tunnels were impressive and each time we came out of a tunnel, a new vista with light and shadow, clouds and sun, peaks and valleys and mountains' majesty. Austria is truly an amazing country for sightseeing.

Sometimes I'll take something that you've said and stash it away wrapped in velvet folds of memory to be taken out and savored at a time like right now. I do the same thing with certain prayer and meditations: tuck them away for safe keeping. Then I retrieve them from deep in the catacombs or from just below the surface of any old ordinary moment and use them to make a special time of thinking of you. Sometimes I don't even have to remember what

you said, I can just think about how you made me feel in a brief phone call over great distances. And that eases my missing you - like right now.
2:15 PM Friday, 31 October - same day. Same ride.

We stopped in the mountains for a scenic break. Then we came down and crossed the border into Switzerland.

12:30 PM Saturday, 1 November. Breakfast in the Salzhous Club in Winterthur, Switzerland.

This club is a nicely designed venue built in what was once a salt factory and warehouse. It is the largest venue we have played on this tour so far. The club celebrated its one year anniversary last night with free admission to a large party featuring our Soulciety show. We had over 1,000 people in the place and had a good show, good response and good vibes.
The club owners went all-out to see that we had everything the band needed to be comfortable and content. The afternoon catering was first-rate deli and abundant: rolls, deli trays, juices, Evian water, cases of beer, gin, vodka, coffee, tea - everything over flowing. We had dinner after the sound check at an Italian restaurant. (I had vegetarian ravioli.)

They served us champagne before we went onstage at 11:00 PM. After the hit, Italian champagne flowed like water, as did the Holland beer, brandy and Turkish hashish. A good time was had by all.

At the end of the night, I went to the hotel where Bobby, Vicki, Bart and Lalomie were staying. While Bobby and Vicki volunteered to move into Bart's room so that he and I could have their double room, I decided to sleep on the bus rather than displacing them. I listened to the cassette of the gig on the bus and went to my bunk around 4:00 AM. I slept quite well until 11:30 AM.
I am so impressed and thankful for the "niceness" and good-nature of everybody traveling on this tour. They're all genuinely friendly, caring, artistic and spiritual and humor-loving people.

Yesterday I had a bit of stress over Martin, the bass player and musical director, wanting us to have a horn rehearsal before sound check, in order to tighten up horn parts and to go over a new song. I was miffed because I needed my relaxing time, I didn't want to learn a new song and I didn't want to do any extra rehearsals, but after all is said and done, the rehearsal worked to make my parts noticeably tighter. So be it.

There is also some little stress with Lalomie and Vicki and their relationship with the band and show; this according to the band members. But I haven't really noticed it as being any big thing at all.

I do notice that it is disconcerting for me when the other Black Americans go off to hotels and I stay with the band for sound check or for meals and 90% of the conversation is in German. I am left out of the chit-chat and must introvert my personality. I am sometimes lonely in the group. Also, they all smoke and I don't. But this combination has had its benefits: I am getting more physically tolerant of smoke and I am getting even more time for contemplative reflection. I can also spend the time writing in this journal. I have even started two or three song lyrics. So everything has its upside.

Then, I took a break from writing in this journal and just finished doing some yoga stretches out on the club's dance floor with the house deejay providing the music and light show. Cool.

3:30 PM On the bus ride to Munich.

As we ride though the countryside, I notice several people walking the roads between the farms: mothers pushing strollers, joggers and bike riders. It is a clear day in Switzerland, perfect for walking, strolling, jogging or bus riding passing through.

Plot for a novel: traveling on a tour bus with people who are developed souls with heavy past lives, each having mastered some aspect of self and spiritual development, to be revealed and shared...

Boy! We just listened to a dynamite tape of last night's show. It was bad! That band was rocking!! Whoa! The whole show was good and the last set with Bobby Byrd was classic!!! This Soulciety show has real commercial potential. Bobby Byrd bringing his original R&B soul thing, Lalomie with her new soul music and her new-found audience for her songs, and the Soul Society band bringing their youthful exuberance and their European image to the stage, makes a super package. The show itself really moves; it has dynamics and it builds to a climax - all things you need for a theater-type show. This could be like "Beehive" or with just a little plot and dialogue, it could be developed into a full-scale musical.

2:00 AM Saturday night/Sunday morning.

We pulled into Munich around 7:00 PM and checked into the Hotel Senator. I had the double room rented for the band. I was hoping to stay in it alone but at the last minute Stefan, the drummer, came in to stay here. Boy, was I pissed-off and bummed-out. Not only did I want some privacy, Stefan was not my favorite member of the crew. He is both too weird and too much like me. He went out to dinner and I stayed in until he came back. We decided to go out to a jazz club to hear a jazz quintet. We took the subway and walked 10 blocks in the brisk autumn night air. It was quite refreshing and invigorating.

We got to the club and I enjoyed the group and the music immensely. It was avant-garde jazz - free and swinging. The musicians were quite good - European, arty and humorous. I was totally glad that Stefan had urged me to come. He and I had good conversations, mostly about the tour and the music we are making. I enjoyed his company, which is surprising because at one time I thought he might be gay and several times on this tour he has plucked my nerves with his detailed and meticulous sound checks, his wandering off alone and being away somewhere when the bus is ready to leave, and his aloof detachment. But I know he's just different from me, and a lot like me too. He is new to the group so he is kind of an outsider. He's a really good drummer. This is a good demonstration of the fact that I shouldn't be prejudiced against anyone. Everyone with whom I come in contact potentially has information, inspiration or something positive to share with me.

I'm sleepy, watching the Navy vs. Notre Dame football game.

12 noon Sunday, 2 November at Church.

I have come to a very large church for Sunday Mass. I have walked 2 miles to and through Old Munich. The bells of the church drew me in for rest for my weary bones and sore feet. The church has a ceiling at least 60-feet high and voices and sounds echo like Gregorian chants with massive reverberation added. Catholic Mass in German - strange - and even stranger with echo effects.

I walked through much of the major tourist section of Munich, through the main train station and through hundreds of people and I only saw one other Black person. Throughout this whole part of Europe (Germany, Switzerland and Austria), I see very few Black people; as few as there are whites in much of Africa. The global village is a virtual reality in cyber-space and in the minds of future thinkers.

Coincidence: When I walked through the main train station and exited out the main doors, I ran into Jens, who had taken the subway from the circus grounds where the tour bus was parked. He was headed to the hotel where I stayed to take a shower before going to the recording studio with Bobby Byrd. It was lucky that he ran into me so that I could give him the room key. On my walk back to the hotel I saw at least 15 other Black folks. But in my previous two times in Munich I had already come to the conclusion that there are more Blacks here than in most of the other places in Europe. Happy halleluiah, up in here!

I leave my watch set for the time zone where you are. I only check it to imagine what you're doing - like right now.

3:15 AM Monday night 3 - 4 November. On the bus for the night.

The gigs tonight and last night were interesting in that they were in larger venues and contrasting promotions. Last night (Sunday) we played the Strom 2000 Club in Munich which holds about 500-600 people. However the club owner-promoter had several problems publicizing the gig so we only got about 120 people. The sound and lights were good and the audience was fairly enthusiastic. After the gig, the bus was parked outside the hotel, instead of going back out to the dreary circus grounds rail yard where it usually stays in Munich. This was a lot better for the band people. Stefan and I slept in the band's hotel room.

The gig tonight (Monday) was in Zurich, Switzerland at the XTRA Limmathaus Club, which is a brand new venue that can accommodate up to 3,500 people. It just opened three days ago and tonight's show was only the 2nd event to be held there. It is a fantastic facility with brand new equipment, fixtures, decorations, backstage rooms, appliances, etc. It is designed like a theater, with a proscenium stage; but the audience stands, just like at all the other venues we have played.

The XTRA Limmathaus Club had a great light show that reminded me of the Fillmore West in San Francisco circa 1970 and state of the art sound equipment for the front house and monitor mixes. For the main system they had 32 track board, delays, noise gates, compressors, Eventide 3000 Harmonizer, and DAT and cassette decks.

Last night I did not have a good gig. I made lots of mistakes and really didn't get into it at all until the Bobby Byrd part of the show. But tonight, even though I had headache right up until show time, I had a really good gig, right from the first song through the end of the show. I played well and I danced and added lots to the proceedings.

Early this morning I got up and had breakfast at the hotel, even though I had just eaten late last night after the show. After breakfast I went out to get a newspaper at the main train station. Before I left the hotel, Lalomie asked me to pick her up some cigarettes and Bart said to let him know if I ran into an Afro shop. I knew that finding a black beauty supply shop was a long shot to say the least, but oddly enough, I did find a black beauty supply place in a really out-of-the-way spot in a little office building mall. I walked back to the hotel, got Bart and took him there.

On the ride from Munich to here (Zurich) we had a minor border incident at the Swiss border. I was asleep upstairs in my bunk when I was awakened and told that we all had to show our passports. So I got up, came downstairs and took my customary seat at the rear of the bus. There was a customs policeman on the front of the bus checking passports. Stefan decides to push the button, opening the back door and then he gets off the bus, just to stroll around and smoke a cigarette. The policeman got excited, put his hand on his gun and wanted to know what was going on. For a brief moment there was tension and a bit of confusion. The customs police did check each and every passport but eventually they let us go on. I got so mad at Stefan for doing such a stupid thing, that when it was all over and we were again rolling on down the road, I gave him a piece of my mind, and then I just went back to up to my bunk to sleep.

Anyway, the concert hall, XTRA was super slick. It was attached to a newly renovated hotel so that you could go from the backstage dressing room area, through a door and right up a flight of stairs to your hotel room. I let Martin and Tim sleep in the band's room and I slept on the bus. But the building was quite a complex: a 150-seat large restaurant/café and the venue had a couple of smaller club rooms as well. Quite an impressive facility. New, modern, state-of-the-art, top-of-the-line!

12:30 PM Wednesday afternoon on the bus.

Last night's venue was a smaller club in Konstenze, Germany. The club was built like the place was a rectangular pit. We were concerned about the audience we'd get out in the countryside on a Tuesday night. Sandra guessed we'd get two people, I said I hoped for 50. We got almost 100 college-age people who danced from the first note on until the end of the Bobby Byrd encore. Our show is funkier and tighter than ever. It's gotten to the point that the music will be funky, no matter what. Some of the musicians/performers might have a better or lesser night, but overall the show is going to be funky and tight as a piccolo snare drum. The show has a lot that can be improved upon, but it's quite a package. It's more like a review than a concert and it is continuously grooving enough to play in a dance club.

I continue to learn and gain lots of insights and I also have points of concerns. This is a magical mystery tour of dues-paying, learning and fun for all of us involved.

More German countryside. This southern region of Germany is like the bread basket of the country. Beautiful farmland and massive acreage of orchards and vineyards. We're listening to Lalomie's demo tape of songs she has worked on with Claus for her next CD while we are traveling on the bus to the next gig town where we'll play tonight. The tape was made from an eight-track demo, but the songs are awesome. It's going to be a great album and it should come out at the perfect time to follow up her current Soulciety release which is just breaking out now. Her current album is getting good reviews, dance club response and MTV play of her video. But these new songs are the Bomb! She will be ageless and timeless and a star when this new stuff comes out.

New views and vistas sail past the newly cleaned windows of the bus. I can see clearer now. Things and issues are becoming more and more completely or better understood with each passing moment. It is more of a process of unfolding. An issue will arise, then deeper levels of perception and understanding will be experienced. Lessons are revealed as moments pass and days come and go.

The ebbs and flows of vibrations with and between the people on this tour are interesting and instructive. But assessing my own thinking and feelings is to be aware of my own development.

> On Tour
> All the places I go
> And all the things I get to do and see
> Are just marks in the time
> Until I see you again

Today we took the bus on a ferry boat across a lake - a 20-minute ride on a bus on a boat. The weather continues to be good: today it is sunny and in the upper 50s, at least. On the highway, we did run into a minor traffic jam - our first one - on a two-lane highway in the countryside.

Today our ride should take about five hours to Regensberg. Then after tonight's gig we will travel overnight nine hours back to Hamburg, where the tour started, for a day off. We will then have eight more shows to do.
2:45 PM we ride and ride and still the German lands are beautiful.

It's nap time in my bunk. And I am finding more comfort there. It sleeps well. Much better than I thought it would when I was first introduced to it.
A McDonald's at a rest stop on the highway.

These have become a regular Godsend. McDonald's chicken wings are the closest thing to eating at home that I get. Though yesterday's dinner was for me a casserole of pasta, tomatoes, zucchini, and carrots, topped with two kinds of melted cheeses. The bomb! McDonald's is like home. Funny, I don't even eat at McDonald's at home, but here in Europe, Mickey D's is like home. Food and eating on this tour is no problem: every venue has afternoon deli tray catering and dinner before we go on or, if we prefer, after the gig, around 1:00 AM in the morning. There is continental breakfast every morning, so I get plenty to eat. I think I am gaining weight, big time. No playing tennis and no calisthenics on the whole tour may be taking its toll on my fitness.

I have this idea for postcards with pre-written verses or poems or messages - like greeting cards: Missing you, business trips, on tour, wish you were here themes. I think it's a winner of an idea.

2:45 AM Wednesday Night - back on the bus, traveling nine hours overnight to Hamburg.

The mood on the bus is super lively. Everyone has been drinking and smoking and there is an after-gig euphoria. But the elation is more than that: all of the German people in the tour group, and even Sandra and Lalomie, are headed "home" tonight. And we have tomorrow off. So everyone is super "up" waiting to get sleepy enough to go upstairs to our bunks. Then we all hope we can sleep straight through to Hamburg.
11:00 PM Thursday night, 6 November. Hotel room.

We made it to Hamburg. I slept on the bus until about 11 AM this morning and we got to Hamburg about 30 minutes later. We went directly to the Soulciety Records office and spoke to Goetz. Their office space was large, open, neat and sparsely furnished. Very efficient, modern, computer-outfitted and proper. The place was big enough to be a night club.

After that all the band people went to their respective homes and Bobby, Vicki, Bart and I checked in the same hotel we were in when we were here before. Very comfortable, clean, spacious, slick, purple decor and TV movies on pay TV. I got some takeout food to eat from the same Turkish restaurant as before, and chilled-out in my room all evening.

3:00 PM Friday, 7 November. On the bus in Hamburg.

Today Bobby, Vicki, Bart and I checked out of the hotel and went to the Soulciety office, where we made calls, sent faxes, email, took pictures, etc., until everyone gathered for the departure on the last leg of the tour. On the bus ride we watched a videotape of a tribute and telethon for Bobby Byrd that was shown of VH1 in Europe last year. It was cool, with Fred Wesley, PeeWee Ellis, Eddie Bo, Rad, and other Soulciety groups performing. All the performances were really good, but the highlight of the show was the singing of Bobby and Vicki's daughter, Colleen Anderson, who was in great voice and very emotionally inspiring. Bobby, Vicki and Bart had never seen the show before so they were quite moved by the tributes and the music done for Bobby.

7:00 AM Saturday, 8 November, On a plane at Hamburg airport, loading and readying for takeoff - to London to make a connection for the U.S.

My father died of a heart attack yesterday. It was just that sudden. I'm on the way home.

Yesterday our bus ride ended at the gig site, The Pumpe Club in Kiel, Germany around 5:00 or 6:00 PM. We unloaded, set up and started the two-hour sound check procedure. We were all hungry so we went up to the dressing room to check out the catering. I made a call to check my messages on my voicemail back home and had a message from my brother saying that my father had had a heart attack and that he was in the hospital. When I called my mother's house, my brother answered the phone and he let my mother tell me that my father had passed.

I was surprised but not shocked, even though my father was an active 73-year-old. He had gone to church two days ago and bingo last night, so he was not ill nor an invalid. He drove himself to the hospital for stress tests (treadmill, stairs, etc.) and had had a heart attack. My mother was called and she went to be with him and he died peacefully soon after she got there to talk to him and pray with him.

12:30 PM London time, Saturday afternoon. On the plane readying to leave for DC.

Last night when I found out that Daddy had died, I decided I would do the gig and then leave on the next makeable flight. We were in Kiel which is only two hours from Hamburg. I found out that we were to leave right after the gig, traveling along a route that would take us back past Hamburg. I would take a plane out from there.

Ideally, I would have liked to not have the people on the tour know about my personal grief. I would not have told anyone except Jorn, the tour director, and the bus driver, so that after the gig, there would not have to be this pall over everyone. They could go to sleep on the bus and I could be dropped off at the airport and they all could be told tomorrow in my absence.

But of course, it didn't work out that way. When I took Jorn out into the hallway outside the dressing room to tell him what had happened and that I would be leaving the tour, Lalomie came out to speak to him, and she overheard what I was saying to Jorn about my father. So Jorn and Lalomie knew before the gig. I told Jorn that I didn't want the group to know before the show and be sad on the stage. But Jens knew and Vicki knew and probably one or two others knew as well.

But the show did go on and it went quite well, indeed. We got a large Friday night crowd that danced and was very appreciative. I played well, probably because I was a little distracted. I was active onstage, though I did take a couple of breaks during the show, leaving the stage, once to tell Jorn to call Goetz in Hamburg on his cell phone to let him know what had happened.

Actually, I was deeply saddened to have to leave the tour before it was over and before the big gig in Hamburg on next Friday, when Goetz and his partner, Emu, would get to see the show, and it would be taped for television. The show was seriously strong and tight now and, without a doubt, I was an important component of it. I would be missed.

After the show, there was the pall I hadn't wanted hanging over the whole cast. One by one everyone came to share their condolences and I assured everyone that I was and would be fine. I talked to my mother on the phone and she was her usual angelic, super-positive self. And Cookie assured me that my mother was bubbly, full of energy and peace and was consoling everyone else. But Mama definitely wanted me back home, saying everything, including the funeral, would have to wait until I could get home.

My father and mother, Mr. & Mrs. James E. Sr and Beulah Branch

So I was going home on the first thing smoking, which was a 7:00 AM flight Hamburg to London with a 12:25 PM connection London to Washington, DC arriving at Dulles Airport at 4:00PM EST. It would be expensive (an additional $500). But my mother seemed pleased and impressed that I could be home by the next evening.

The Soul Society show people were deeply affected as they realized the gravity of the situation for me and how my leaving would be changing the dynamics of the show itself and the touring ensemble. I really regretted what my leaving would be doing to the show and the group. We had been so bonded together; so much like family. And I didn't like that it was I who was putting the group through these changes.

Lalomie gave me one of her big hugs and asked if I needed anything, including money. Bobby and Vicki slipped me $100. Sandra seemed to be already sure she would really miss me. I told her that I expected that I would be missed because, as is my usual practice in any ongoing relationship, I had made myself indispensable.

In this group, I had filled every gap and every role that I saw that I could fill without being too pushy or egotistical. I had been a listener, confidante, expert, humorist, talker, journal-keeper, bridge builder, over-viewer and articulator for the ensemble cast that we had become. I had no doubt that I would be missed.

Martin, the bassist, said out loud what several of them were thinking when he asked if I really had to go? Bobby voiced it in another way when he said he couldn't imagine doing the show without me. He and I really did relate well onstage. He looked to me for support aside from his mainstays, Vicki and Bart. Bobby said that I should do what I had to do at home, but if there was any way I could get back for the Hamburg show…

The round trip ticket Hamburg-London-Hamburg was actually cheaper than the one way business class ticket which was all that was available on the flight I was taking; so, of course, I bought the round-trip ticket. So if the money for the airfare for DC-London-DC could be found, I was definitely willing to come back to Germany for next weekend's gigs. So who knows? I'm starting on my second wine spritzer on this plane and with no sleep last night, so who knows, indeed…

> DAD
> What goals did you have?
> None more humble or majestic than those you achieved:
> self sufficiency
> providence
> self-control
> a slow ever-so-slow learning to exhale
> learning to let go and let God.
>
> The youngest son becomes the eldest son
> teaching his sons
> discipline is doing what you should
> even when you don't feel like it
> even when it's imposed by the strength of another's will
> discipline can be taught
> by living examples.
>
> Sometimes lessons aren't complete
> can't be completely understood
> until we've moved on to the next level

> the impact of a life can't be completely perceived
> until that life is completed
> yours is done now
> and we love you for it

3:00 PM EST - Still on the plane. One hour from landing in DC.

I've eaten twice, watched two movies and now I'm listening to a tape of Soul Society live at the XTRA in Zurich and thinking that the band is getting ready to play tonight back in Germany.

I started this story a month ago and along the way I wondered how it might end, never imagining anything like this for the finale. This month was so much of a learning experience, so much more so than I could ever write down. I met a lot of good musicians and bonded with a crew in Germany: Tim, Sven, Bobby, Vicki, Lalomie and the rest.

6:00 PM Thursday, 13 November - On a plane at Dulles Airport, British Airways Flight #216 to London.
This is not an epilogue. The story continues.

I am on my way back to Hamburg, Germany! Just to play this Friday and Saturday nights' gigs with the Soulciety All-Star show in Hamburg and beyond. This is one more wild development in a week to remember. I am going back to Germany because the other musicians on the tour put up money to pay for my ticket to take this flight to rejoin them for the last shows, particularly the one tomorrow night in Hamburg being taped for TV. So I guess that means that they liked me, or that they thought that I added something to the show, or both.

I was just at this same airport, Washington, DC's Dulles International, last Saturday. I landed here at 4:00PM and came through customs and pushed my luggage cart up the ramp to the departures entrance and my daughter Kaila's boyfriend, A.D., beeped his horn, right there right on time to pick me up and whisk me away to Richmond.

I was at my mom's house at 6:11 PM, just a little more than 24 hours after getting the news of my father's death. I had had little or no sleep, so after a brief visit with my mother and brother, I want home to Cookie and my bed. And what a great bed it was!

I spent most of the hours of Sunday and Monday at my mother's house. She needed no consoling. She was perpetually "up," smiling and constantly talking to the horde of endless visitors and callers. My mother is spiritually enlightened, religiously well-grounded and puts the most positive spin on anything that happens and on anyone she encounters. I expected her to react to my father's sudden death, or not to react to it, in just the way that she did. Others were more shocked and dismayed than she and our family. We were all fine and remained fine all through the mourning period and the funeral services.

We made the arrangements for the funeral to be held Tuesday at noon, after one hour of visitation beginning at 11:00 AM. The funeral services went as smooth as clockwork and as error free as my father would have wanted. I played my soprano sax with all the musical selections during the funeral. With so many relatives and church members there, it was like a regular Sunday service. Just before the eulogy, my brother, Muzi, read his remembrances and it was just a perfect piece of literature for the moment. I played an emotionally charged rendition of "Amazing Grace" and the pastor's eulogy was brief, just as my mother had requested. We went to the burial grounds for the internment and then back to the church for the repast.

I learned so much in these few days: that my father lived a life of sacrifice and saving, leaving my mother and family with an organized, comfortable estate; that he was well liked by relatives and friends; that he took care of my mother and they were compatible and complementary; that life is fragile and appearances do not indicate in what order people will die; that the life we live prepares us for what today and tomorrow brings; and that I am loved and respected by many old and new friends.

My father left my mother a few thousand dollars cash stashed in the house, several thousand in their checking account, several more in their savings account, a sizable amount in a retirement savings account in addition to their $125,000+ house. He had amassed all of this from scratch by working hard, scrimping, saving, sacrificing and by the shear strength of his will to do so. His life was a testament to setting goals, discipline, and fiscal conservatism.

Even though his death was sudden, two weeks before I left to go on tour in Europe, my father had come to me with all the information about his banking and retirement accounts, safe deposit box, cash in the house, etc. all written down. He said that he wanted me to type all that information into my computer so that I would have it when the time came. He also left instructions about what to do upon his death. I had then written out a last will and testa-

Soulciety venue Jazzhaus

Motel in snow

Lalomie finds her CD in a record store

Plunky in the snow

ment which he signed. Prior to that, my father had always resisted having a will or discussing anything to do with his estate planning, so he obviously felt that the time was appropriate for getting his affairs in order.

Before the beginning of this touring trip, I had been working on producing my next recording for release. One of my biggest concerns has been securing a record deal for this set of recordings. I have spent so much money, time and energy on this production and now that it is just about completed, I find that I don't like it. Maybe I have new views and opinions about what my next album should sound like and be about, now that I have been to Europe and I have seen what the market there is like. But whatever the reason for my disenchantment with the material is, this is a major disappointment.

I hope that the recording project can be fixed and brought up to standard so that I can find some measure of satisfaction with the music on the album. I will have to remix some of the songs, delete some, edit some others and add some new songs to the collection in order to make it right. I have already spent over $7,000 on it and I could easily spend another $5,000 re-working it. When and where will the funds come from, and should I actually go forward to complete the project, are major questions to be considered and answered.

6:30AM London time, Friday, 14 November.

Now we are landing in London and I have to decide whether to stay in the transit area of the airport or go into London for few hours before catching my 2:30 PM plane to Hamburg. Should I try to rest at the airport or continue my lack of sleep until I get to Germany?

2:30 PM London time on the next plane.

We're leaving and I am beat as can be. I did go into London. After we landed this morning, I took my horns to Terminal One, checked them in the Left Luggage area. I then took the underground tube for the 30-minute ride into downtown. I went to the part of town where there are lots of jewelry shops and traders and bought gold charms for Cookie and Kaila. Then I went walking through the Covent Gardens area before taking the tube back out to the airport to make this plane. Now I hope that I can get a little rest before arriving in Hamburg for tonight's gig.

4:00 PM in Claus' car, on the way to Lubek, Germany.

Goetz met me at airport in Hamburg and we had a pleasant talk on the way into the city. He took me to the Aston Suites Hotel which was "the bomb!": Euro-design, two-room suite with picture windows, microwave, mini-bar, and right across the street from a carnival with sparkling lights, rides and foods. The hotel was very posh and the setting was very romantic.

After I showered and freshened up, Goetz drove me to the club for sound check. Everyone was happy to see me and I got hugs and props from the band.

The show that night was hype and tight. Everybody put out their absolute best for the hometown Hamburg audience. The show was well received. The place was jamming from start to finish. Emu and Goetz were gassed and proud of the band and the show. Everyone was duly impressed.

1:00 PM Sunday, 16 November - Hamburg airport, waiting for my flight to London headed home.

After the show in Hamburg Friday night, we all went to the LaFonque Club for an afterhours drink and smoke. I had a good conversation with Emu about the show, his work at East West Records, Soulciety, marketing, etc. I felt like my comments were helpful to him in evaluating the potential impact we could have through Soulciety and I know that I gained insights from him concerning the importance of marketing in the scheme of our record industry efforts.

I got back to my hotel room stoned and exhausted. I had gotten up at 6AM in Richmond, VA, gone to the bank and other errands with my mother at 9AM, packed my bags and left for DC with Garry at 12 noon, had lunch at the airport hotel at 2PM, waited for my plane which left at 6:45 PM, took the seven-hour flight and landed at Heathrow Airport at 6:30 AM London time, killed time by going into downtown London until noon, flew out of London at 2:30 PM, landed in Hamburg at 5:00 PM, showered and went to sound check, and did the gig, playing hard from 11:00 PM to 1:45 AM and got to my room around 4:30 AM.

I slept from 5AM until 2PM on Saturday. AT 3PM we left for the gig in Lubek. Lalomie and I rode with Claus and the drive was less than one hour to go the 60 kilometers. The venue in Lubek was the central common area of a mini-mall, but it had a good size, permanent stage, more than adequate lighting and a very decent sound system.

As the musicians arrived and prepared for sound check, we were all into the realization that this would be the last gig of the tour. We were all ready for this gig. The audience filled the space and they were exuberant, appreciative and demonstrative. In fact, they were the best audience of the whole tour, without a doubt. They screamed and shouted, they danced and swayed from the first song and they gave abundant and long-sustained applause after each segment of the show.

After I did my "I Can't Hold Back" number, the applause went on and on even after I started to talk and began my intro of Lalomie. After Lalomie's four songs, they cheered so much that she had to come back for an encore. And of course for the Bobby Byrd set they just went off: jumping, waving arms en masse, screaming and at times peaking like they were having church!!!

We played like there was no tomorrow. We gave it our collective all. What a great way to end the tour, with such a tremendous show and fantastic audience!!

After the show we were all drained and drenched, with every stitch of clothing completely soaked through. We sat around, tired but happy, talking about this night, the tour and going home, while listening to the tape I had recorded with my little cassette recorder on the stage. After that, we all went to the Lubek McDonald's for our last supper. Lalomie and I rode back to Hamburg with Jens and I got to my hotel by 3:30 AM.

I watched some pay TV and went to sleep after requesting a wakeup call at 8:45 AM. I got up on time and had breakfast. Stefan came with his wife and two-year-old son to take me to the airport at 10:45 AM. Claus came to the airport to bring me tapes of the shows, and he and I had a good conversation about this business of music over coffee and tea.

Now I'm on my flight to London flying at 35,000 feet, having a glass of wine, headed back home and looking forward to life after the tour.

EPILOGUE

In the weeks after the tour I have maintained contact with the Soulciety crew via e mail and learned that almost everyone that was a part of the touring ensemble still feels that the tour was a supremely positive experience and a turning point in their lives. I realize that touring musicianship is like ambassadorship.

Financially, the tour cost Soulciety Records three times the amount that they had thought; the most they could lose in a worst case scenario.

My phone bill for calls from Europe totaled $1,600; more than I netted from the tour.

I have decided to finish working on my next album for release later this year.

I am working on going back to Europe to do another tour with my own group next fall.

I finished the following two song lyrics that I started writing on the tour:

BREAKTHROUGH

Fog between you and the mountain
doesn't mean the mountain isn't there
Clouds hiding your destination
don't mean you won't get to where
you know you're supposed to be
if it's your destiny/ then it will be

If seeing is believing/ keep seeing it in your mind
And no matter when you're leaving/ you'll get there right on time

Freewheeling/ cool running
moving in the light
Smooth sailing/ happy landings
everything's gonna be all right

You don't climb every mountain
Some you have to go through
But when you come out of the tunnel
A [bright] horizon's ahead of you

Problems/ can mean progress
Solve them/ and you're blessed/ you've passed a test

Freewheeling/ cool running
moving in illuminating light
Smooth sailing/ happy landings
everything's gonna be all right

Fog on the road to where you're going
doesn't mean where you're going isn't there
What's important is that you're knowing
your inner vision's not impaired

No matter how small the vehicle
your dreams are as big as you dare
No matter how dark the gloom is
the sun is shining somewhere

And it's headed your way/ This is the day
that's been made for you/ to make your breakthrough

Freewheeling/ cool running
moving in the light
Smooth sailing/ happy landings
everything being all right

TIME TRAVEL
He took you to the station/ led you by the hand
The track ran by the hotel/ on to a foreign land
You rode the train alone/ wondering about your fears
Were the streaks on the windows/ raindrops or your tears

Time travel/ moving through your mind
Time travel/ back and forth in time

He met you at the station/ every time you made the trip
He'd beg you to come to him/ when he kissed your lips
Back then things were simple/ for the young life always is
Remember when love was what you got/ now it's what you give

Time travel/ you come and you go
time travel/ moving to and fro
Time travel/ you come and you go
Where and when you stop/ you just don't know

He left you at the station/ you had to catch a plane
You bought a one-way ticket/ Only questions remain
Is love lost ever found/ Are those tears or rain
Will he meet you at the station/ if you ever come back again

Time travel/ moving to and fro
time travel/ where it stops you don't know

⌘⌘⌘

Chapter 17

2000's Records

I have written more than 1000 songs, most of them never recorded. The timing wasn't right or whatever. The songs that became the hits don't tell the whole story. Most songs disappear without a trace. You never know how people will take to them; what will strike a chord. If you did, you'd always do it. You'd record only hits. No one can do that.

— Willie Nelson

I agree with Willie Nelson: there are no rules, no sure-fire tricks and no guarantees to writing good songs and making hit records. If there were, somebody would be making hits every time they go into the studio. There are super-talented artists, with great producers, in the best studios, signed to the biggest record companies with fantastic promotion people with giant budgets, and they still might not make a hit song. The irony is that sometimes a quirky artist, or a garage band or a singer songwriter, can come up with the right sound and words that captures a massive number of imaginations and gets a smash hit, against all odds. Some of us indie artists live for moments like that.

I would love to create a song that serves as the soundtrack to special moments in the lives of people. A song that would convey love or a call to action or make tears have meaning for a million people. I want to make people sing, dance, jump, think, move, worship, organize, and get close to each other and their own inner cores. I want music to help people have fun on purpose or see the purpose to being here.

But with or without selling a ton of CDs or massive critical acclaim, most artists produce because they think they have valuable viewpoints to express. Like poets and painters and dancers, musicians want to give voice to their inner feelings, and put together sounds that pay homage to the things that inspire us all to greatness or to the most intimate we can be.

Here are the records I made in the 2000's:

Plunky & Oneness - Saxy Mellow Moments (2000)
Plunky & Oneness - Got to be Phunky (2001)
Oneness of Juju - African Rhythms 1970-1982 (2-CD Compilation) (2001)
J. Plunky Branch - Instrumental Praise (2002)
J. Plunky Branch - Solo Journey Between Dimensions (2002)
Plunky & Oneness - Got to Move Something (2002)
Plunky & Oneness - Forever In A Moment (2004)
Plunky - Cold Heat (2006) Plunky – Drive It (2008)
Plunky & Oneness – 2012 Collectors Box Set (5-CD Compilation) (2010)

PLUNKY & ONENESS - SAXY MELLOW MOMENTS (2000)

One of my most impactful albums, Saxy Mellow Moments, was the first in which I stuck to one smooth, romantic mood. I had finally realized that sometimes and in some situations people liked being able to put the CD album on and just be mellow and not have it make shifts in the genres, mood or aural setting. I learned that diversity and wide-ranging musical explorations are not always assets in marketing or customer satisfaction. Having a single, smooth groove repertoire worked to make this album suitable for play in a number of situations as background or mood setting music. And people liked it.

PLUNKY & ONENESS - GOT TO BE PHUNKY (2001)

I guess Got to Be Phunky was me reverting to the funk so I wouldn't be pigeon-holed by the smooth jazz of the previous release. This album was a collection of edgier and more rhythmic danceable grooves.

ONENESS OF JUJU - AFRICAN RHYTHMS 1970-1982 (2-CD COMPILATION) (2001)

This was our first compilation album, produced by London-based producer Quinton Scott and released by Strut Records. The 2-CD, 3-LP box set was a major production that included 25 songs plus photos and extensive liner notes from the Oneness of Juju's recordings from 1970–1982. Music collectors and critics praised the release. Jockey Slut magazine called it "some of the most exciting and experimental black music of the seventies and early eighties." Ministry Music magazine gushed, "...funkier than a pair of month-old bed socks... devastatingly hip!" International DJ Magazine said, "This is African music at its very finest."

Not only did the compilation garner great reviews in numerous publications, it also gave us a renewed promotional presence in Europe that led to tours in Britain and France. (See Appendix B. "Journals of International Tours")

J. PLUNKY BRANCH - INSTRUMENTAL PRAISE (2002)

My second gospel album featuring my solo sax ensemble, created by me overdubbing multiple tracks of tenor, alto and soprano saxes, accompanied by organist, Milton Marriott, Minister of Music at First Baptist Church of South Richmond.

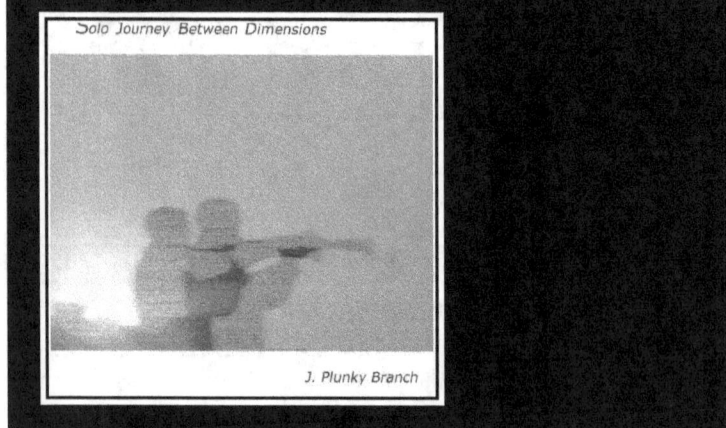

J. PLUNKY BRANCH - SOLO JOURNEY BETWEEN DIMENSIONS (2002)

My next door neighbor Joyce, a massage therapist, said she so enjoyed hearing me practice my horns that she wanted me to make a tape of my solo saxophones to use as background music for her sessions. The result of that suggestion is Solo Journey Between Dimensions, my new age music album featuring solo sax explorations. While saxophones are not usually the primary instruments in new age music, I know this album works because I have often used it as background music for my own yoga exercises, meditations and massages. Masseurs, yoga instructors and others have also confirmed that the album creates a soothing, probing and relaxing sonic backdrop for their meditation and therapeutic sessions. So my neighbor was right. (Thanks, Sister Joyce.)

PLUNKY & ONENESS - GOT TO MOVE SOMETHING (2002)

Got to Move Something is a double CD release. Disc 1 compiles studio recordings of jazz and funk songs; and Disc 2 is a live concert recorded at the National Black Arts Festival in Atlanta, GA. The studio CD contains several songs that we still use in our live shows 12 years later: "Funk U Up," "Everything Is Gonna Be Alright," "Up & Down," and the instrumental, "Play It Straight." There is also a song that I wrote that I love, "Will You Smile," though we never did do it in any live shows.

PLUNKY & ONENESS - FOREVER IN A MOMENT (2004)

A smooth jazz album with nine instrumentals and three vocal songs, Forever In A Moment is one of my personal favorites. I really liked the songs, the mood and the package.

PLUNKY - COLD HEAT (2006)

Cold Heat was one of my most important releases of the decade and maybe of my entire career. The single, "Drop," became a hit song when radio personality Michael Baisden played it on his nationally-syndicated radio show and continued to feature the song for 18 months. The song was co-produced by my son-in-law,

Adolphus "Danja Mowf" Maples, and it was the result of me asking him to create a track that could be a new, hip-hop version of my 1975 song "African Rhythms." "Drop" was a radio hit, and it was also played in clubs and became the music for line dancing and hand dancing in the region. The two videos I produced for the song got over 60,000 views on youtube.com.
https://www.youtube.com/watch?v=5BD10a-eAv4
https://www.youtube.com/watch?v=r7K3bcY9agU&feature=PlayList&p=5509E2593E74C40D&index=0&playnext=1
https://www.youtube.com/watch?v=RDTxELM6y_o&feature=PlayList&p=5509E2593E74C40D&index=11

The Cold Heat CD album is a 14-song collection of soul, R&B and jazz percolating over hip-hop beats. I wrote or co-wrote the songs and all the lyrics, then produced the recordings, soliciting the assistance of my longtime band mates: vocalists Tonya Lazenby-Jackson, Charlayne "Chyp" Page, Monica Jackson; bassists P. Muzi Branch and Ken Friend; keyboardists Howard Boisseau and Dovane Jefferson; guitarists John Jackson, Ras Mel Glover and Carl Lester El; and drummer Corey Burch; in addition to hip-hop producer A. Danja Mowf Maples.

I am a jazzman known for my multi-faceted musical interests and I have often ventured into the realm of funk to become the life of the party or to explore the politics of the times. Like the older musicians who've inspired me, including Carlos Santana, Maceo Parker, George Duke, George Clinton, Herbie Hancock, and so many others, I am like the ageless bluesmen who continue to play as long as they have something to say.

PLUNKY – DRIVE IT (2008)
This was the follow-up to the Cold Heat album but Drive It did not gain as much traction in the marketplace. But I liked the cover photo that made me look like i was the Terminator driving and steering with m sax

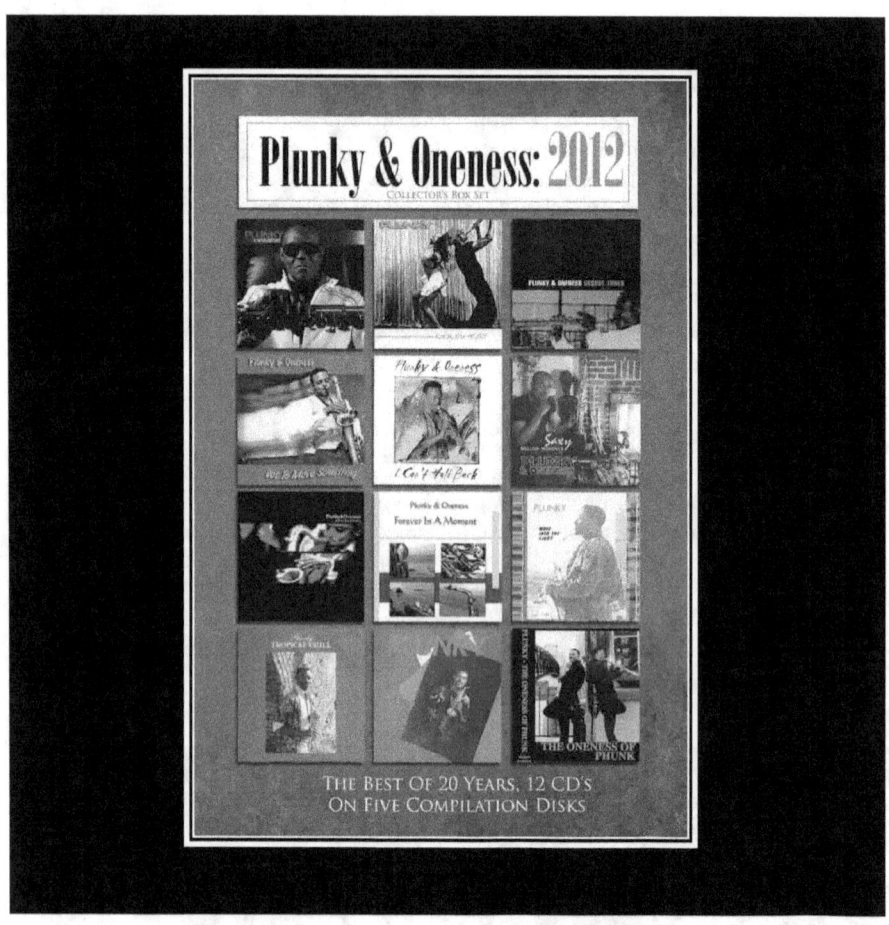

PLUNKY & ONENESS – 2012 COLLECTORS BOX SET (5-CD COMPILATION) (2010)

This 5-CD compilation was a very successful indie marketing venture. It was our most profitable sales item at our live gigs. People loved that they could get such a large cross-section of our music all in one package, at a bargain price. (We performed one set on the Capital Jazz Cruise and we sold $3,000 worth of that compilation.) The five CDs in the compilation were genre specific: a disc each for urban groove, love songs, smooth jazz, funk, Afro-world, plus a bonus disc of videos and data. And, the 2012 in the title referred to the fact that the songs were culled from 12 CDs over the past 20 years, but because it was released in 2010, it gave us three full years to market it while it appeared to be current. Because all the songs had been previously recorded and released, it didn't require a lot of costly studio time. I re-mastered the recordings and packaged the collection in a multi-disc DVD-type case. It was a great way to cap a decade of releases.

⌘⌘⌘

Chapter 18

UNDER THE RADAR CUBA TRIP

In 2001 I was contracted by my friend, Alvin Skipper Bailey, to go to Cuba with him to create and record the musical soundtrack for a film he was producing in conjunction with the humanitarian organization, Pastors for Peace, and the Cuban government. The film was to be about medical students from the U.S. coming to Cuba to be trained as doctors and returning to serve poor and underserved communities in the States. I brought my son, Jamiah, along with us for two trips to Cuba to assist with the music production and to videotape our experiences. After several weeks of work, the Cuban ministry terminated Skipper's film production over creative and political differences. So we decided to use the video footage that Jamiah had shot to produce a documentary film, Under The Radar – A Survey of Afro-Cuban Music.

UNDER THE RADAR
A SURVEY OF AFRO-CUBAN MUSIC

DVD NOW AVAILABLE

For more than 50 years the United States maintained an economic blockade against the Island of Cuba, restricting travel, investment and cultural exchange between Americans and their Caribbean neighbors just 90 miles south of Florida. Afro-Cuban music has inarguably been recognized as some of the most vibrant and influential rhythmic music in the world.

Under the Radar – A Survey of Afro-Cuban Music is a documentary that introduces viewers to the distinct music of Cuba and examines the enigmatic island's current music scene. The film documents the Cuban travels and recordings of its producer/director, jazz saxophonist, J. Plunky Branch, and his son, hip-hop producer, Jamiah "Fire" Branch; and highlights the musical interactions and collaborations of Afro-Cuban rumba, son, salsa, timba, rock, changui and hip-hop musicians and rappers.

Executive producer Alvin Bailey and the American musicians traveled to Cuba under the auspices of a number of U.S. universities and in collaboration with the humanitarian organization, Pastors For Peace, to carry out this project. They toured the cities of Havana, Guantanamo and Santiago de Cuba, to research and record a wide range of musicians. The result of their work is disseminated through this 85-minute educational DVD and a compilation music CD.

The film was screened at a number of film festivals, including Independent the Black Film Festival (Atlanta), Chicago Latino Cultural Film Festival, Reel HeArt International Film Festival (Toronto), Tulipanes Latino Art & Film Festival (Holland, MI), and, Tiburon Film Festival (California), winning critical acclaim and awards. The DVD was used by cultural organizations and by universities and schools for instructional purposes.
The following journals (this one and Chapter 19) detail the two trips to Cuba and the activities and interactions we experienced…

Journey to Produce Music in Cuba Journal
I decided to take the opportunity to travel to Cuba to conduct research in my professional field, Africa and African-American Music History. I spent several weeks making contacts, gathering information and developing plans to go the island and document the music there as it exists today and as it relates to the history of Black music in the Americas. I would take my digital recording studio equipment, video camera, other gadgets and my son, Jamiah, along with me for an 11-day excursion, research, production and performing junket that would be both memorable and rewarding. Here is my journal kept on my laptop during the trip. I share the information and observations with you in the hopes that you will benefit from my experiences, be piqued by my insights and enjoy the adventure…

Tuesday, 4/10/2001- 3:10am: On the train to New York.
An amazing beginning to a remarkable experience. We left Richmond

yesterday morning at the end of a two-week whirlwind of activity consisting of preparations for this trip to Cuba while continuing my ongoing activities of recording in my studio, doing gigs in schools and keeping up my personal relationships. Going to Cuba was not something that has always been on my life's itinerary. I had considered going to Cuba, but my schedule, my finances and the political pressures always combined to make the trip impractical.

Now, here I am on a train going to New York, where I'm planning to change to another train to Montreal, Canada, where I will spend most of one night and then take a plane to Havana tomorrow morning. I am traveling with my 19-year-old son, Jamiah, who has never been out of the country and never been on a plane. I suspect that this trip will change his life's view and be indelibly etched into his memory bank.

Tuesday, 4/10, 11:20 AM: On the train out of Albany New York

Though I hoped that once we were on the train out of New York, we would just have a straight shot to Montreal, we, in fact, had to change trains. Moving our considerable load of baggage is proving to be a demanding production unto itself. We have six parcels to transport: one fat brief case which includes the laptop, one shoulder-strapped saxophone case holding both the alto and the soprano saxes, one flight case for the Roland VS 1680 digital portable recording studio, a box of Sony Beta Cam video tapes, one overstuffed, over-weight clothes bag, and one oversized flight case containing microphones, wires, video camera, hard drives, batteries, tapes and all things technical. We have so much stuff that at every juncture I have to wonder if A) Jamiah and I will be able to handle it all; and, B) The authorities will let us board with it all. But so far so good.

I am so glad Jamiah is going with me. His going will be a giant step forward in his training in business, in his development as a man, and in his knowing the world as it exists. In addition to him being a videographer, a budding hip-hop beat-master and percussionist, Jamiah is important on this trip because I certainly could not be carrying all this stuff to Cuba without his being my chief baggage handler and roadie.

Thursday, 4/12 - 8:AM in my apartment room in Havana:
It has been an eventful 36 hours since I sat at this laptop to note what's going on. To re-count:
We did get into Canada without a hitch. The Canadian customs agents

Plunky in Havana, Cuba

boarded the train, checked documents, asked questions, but checked no baggage that I saw, and after an hour, the train moved on. When we got to Montreal, we took a cab out to a Best Western Motel right across from the airport.

I went to bed around 10:30 PM but awoke hourly, being concerned about over-sleeping, even though I had asked for a wake-up call at 3:40AM. I got up at 3:30, showered and we took the shuttle bus to the airport, arriving there at 4:20 AM to pick up our tickets. The travel agent didn't arrive until 5:30, but we got the tickets and boarded the plane without hassle.

It was a beautiful day for Jamiah's first plane ride: sunny and bright with just a few clouds to offer perspective and depth of field. After takeoff, he slept most of the way there. Our first glimpses of Havana from the air revealed that the city sprawls, empties into the sea and has the flatland topography of the typical coastal urban area.

We landed, went through customs and immigration with only a slight delay with a question raised about the box of Sony Beta Cam tapes. But when I said that I was a musician here to record, they immediately apologized and let us go into the main terminal and into Cuba.

Skipper was not there to meet us! Well, we were early. We had to wait about an hour for him to show up, but in his defense, he had been told that the plane would arrive at 11:45. We took a car and a cab into and across Havana to our apartment. The city had the look and feel of the tropical third world but with a cleanliness and bustle and energy that is refreshing. The people are a good-looking rainbow of shades.

Our apartment is at the edge of a part of town and is across the street from the water and a monument. The apartment is clean, nicely appointed, with two bedrooms and a maid. It will also cost twice as much as I had budgeted. We hire a car and driver for the duration of the stay and I shell out half the money I have with me and I will wait to speak with Skipper about what I have and how it will be apportioned until am to be reimbursed.

After dropping off our luggage, we head to the film institute to meet the director and film crew for Skipper's film, "Why." The film Institute training school is a government agency, which teaches students the art of filmmaking. We had lunch across the street from the film institute and discussed the film project with the director and assistant director.

After lunch we were joined by trombonist Craig Harris, one of the musicians in Cuba to do a recording with saxophonist David Murray for a French Canadian record label. Craig had arrived in Havana three days earlier and had already gotten a feel for the place and he had already been meeting some of the Cuban musicians who were going to participate in David Murray's session. And Craig had already been out to hear some of the tremendous music that goes on in this city.

We went back to the film institute where we watched some video about Bata drumming and the Santeria religion and we talked about the amazing quality and quantity of Cuban music and musicians. Craig is an engaging and smile-inducing conversationalist and we had an enjoyable afternoon hanging out.

At 5:00 PM we went back across the park to the Casa de la Musica for a club/concert by one of the most popular local bands playing salsa at its hottest. People started buying tickets at 4:00PM for the 5 o'clock show. When arrived at 5:15 the place was already crowded. The show opened with a Shango dancer who did fire eating, sword dancing and lifting a table with a girl seated on it with his teeth. Then the band ripped it up for two hours non-stop. Hot salsa, hot young bodies gyrating, in a hot, hot, hot happening! And

Skipper says this kind of thing goes on everyday around that time at places all over the country. Hot music in the afternoon. Then later, hot music in the night at these same clubs. Hot music and hot hips gyrating in African circles, fast, slow, up and down, round and round; mesmerizing…

Thursday, 4/12 - 9:00PM - Back at our Apartment

We got up and showered and got out of our place by 9:30AM. We rode around with Skipper and Carlos, our driver, to a couple of places trying to get things moving by prodding government officials along so that they would see our commitment to getting the music and ultimately the film produced.

According to Skipper there is a Cuban mentality that holds the belief that all meaningful things have to proceed in an orderly and prescribed way, and that way must pass through and be administered by the party bureaucrats. Bureaucrats by nature are not innovators or boat rockers and they guard their own turf and sense of importance. They tend to defer to other bureaucrats, particularly those of higher stature.

We were supposed to meet with a music producer who would be assigned to work with me and get me anything and anyone we would need in order to get my recordings done. We never did see that person today.

We did go see Salome, a Santeria priestess and local block representative in her neighborhood, which is deep in one of the barrios in Havana. We had to look for her place but we did find it, a small, one-bedroom, second-story walk up into folklorica. Her living room was a non-descript, dingy ghetto place that could be anywhere in the Third World; very sparsely furnished with a sofa, wooden chair and table and not much else. The whole apartment and terrace were as poor as any I have ever been in, but there was no revulsion but a certain invitingness about the place.

Salome is a very large woman; the type you describe by spreading your arms wide apart. She spoke very little English, and Skipper, who knew her, communicated as best he could, telling her we wanted to see her shrine to the Santeria spirits, that I wanted some information about her religion, and that we wanted a blessing concerning the project. She ushered us into her bedroom and showed us her shrine which was like a closet filled with a cornucopia of artifacts, whatnots, knick-knacks, beads, necklaces, figurines, feathers, hairs and whatevers… She spoke to us in Spanish about Yemaya, Shango, Obatala and Ogun. She said a prayer over Skipper and then one blessing for Jamiah and me. Jamiah videotaped the proceedings.

The rest of the afternoon was spent trying to make connections with people and discussing what we are trying to do. We took our meals at Skipper's apartment. He has a small place in the hood and he has a woman who takes care of his place and cooks for him. She fixed black beans and salads for lunch and later she fixed chicken for Jamiah.

At 5:00 PM we went back to the Casa de la Musica to hear another hot salsa band and to witness more of the hot dancing. The crowd today was different from yesterday, a little older and slightly more traditional somehow in their taste, but no less exuberant in their response to the music and the setting. The Casa de la Musica is a nightclub space by any other name. It has a great sound system, and the club boasts adequate professional stage lights and mirror balls for atmosphere throughout. It is a really nice place and would function anywhere in the world. Here in Cuba it is one of the places that make the national phenomenon of music an exhilarating release; music as the recreational highlight of the day; music as an emotional high; a reality here. It's like the whole city has a thank-God-it's-Friday party, every day.

And oh the women! Oh the bodies! And oh the shaking that goes on! Salsa Africanized at the hip! Rhythmic and counter-rhythmic sensuality in motion. The music, the dance, the energy – it's what changes day into evening in Havana.

Saturday morning, 4/14 - 9:30 AM – In bed at the Apartment

Yesterday was another experience in Havana. In the end it was an eye-opening, almost mind-blowing set of realizations that may have drastically changed my perspective of music in Cuba and what it can mean for the people here, but also the potential of this music to be a force in dynamic changes that may be underway in the world of music.

We had a long meeting with Dennis, a local musician whose band we had seen at the Casa de la Musica the evening before. Dennis has agreed to work on the music for Skipper's film and we were meeting with Dennis to discuss the specific arrangements for us to do some recording with him this week. Also at Skipper's was Marika, a young European music student from Holland who we met the evening before after Dennis' gig. Marika, who will serve as a translator for us, is blond, not hard to look at, adventuresome and is well traveled for her 26 years.

The meeting with Dennis is very productive. He has already written and arranged some music for the film and he is eager to work with us. We decide that we will record his band at a gig next Tuesday and, possibly again at another gig at the Casa de la Musica next Thursday. I suggest that we will record him doing some solo guitar and singing of the songs that he has composed for the film so that we will have more than one version of some of the songs for the film score and for the CD.

Over lunch we discuss many things, including finding other hip-hop, folkloric, salsa and rumba musicians to work with. Dennis and Marika will be very helpful with this because they really know the music scene in Havana. We also discuss some of the details of setting up to record in the clubs and other places. And we discussed the business and politics of what we are doing. Craig Harris came over with a couple of young guys and a good lunch was enjoyed by all. Food is expensive and a real concern for the working class people in Cuba; and sharing food is a real friendship builder here.

We decide that we should all go over to my place so that Dennis can see my recording equipment. On the way to my place I decide to have Denis go get his guitar so I could do some recording right then. We do just that, setting up the Roland VS1680 and we ended up recording three beautiful songs with Dennis singing and accompanying himself on acoustic guitar. I played some soprano sax on a couple of tracks and I think that Dennis was impressed with the music and the quality of the recording we made. The apartment is all marble, stone and plaster, so the acoustics have a nice, natural reverb; and although we had to contend with the sound of traffic passing by outside, we were able to record some beautiful and poignant music.

After the recording session we piled six of us (minus Jamiah) into Carlos' small car to take Dennis home for his band's rehearsal. We found the band all set up in a yard surrounded on three sides by the walls of two-story tenements. The whole group was in place: five horns, two keyboards, drummer, three percussionists, bass and soundman plus assorted roadies, friends and observers. The band consists of young players with good chops and obviously schooled in music. I listen to three songs and I am impressed with the intricacies of the horn arrangements, the attention to detail, the tightness of the rhythms and the professionalism found in this ghetto setting.

Just as Skipper and I were about to leave the rehearsal, Dennis indicates that he wants me to sit in with the band on tenor sax. So I am given the sax player's horn and we jam hard on the changes for "Autumn Leaves" in salsa and swing. We had a ball and everyone was all smiles as we left.

Later that night I went to hear Jose Luiz Cortez and his band at the Casa de la Musica. Fantastic! Stupendous! Marvelous! One of the best bands I have ever seen! Hot, spicy, energetic, super musicianship, super chops, super tight! I am just knocked out by the combination of musicianship and energy! Tightness and grooviness. These guys were terrible!

The cover charge was $15 as compared to $5, or even $2 that is sometimes the case. This band was worth the difference. Every musician was world class. Each one was a virtuoso of classical or jazz proportions, yet they played together in the context of this partying, grooving atmosphere. I am blown away.

I could live here! Between the music, the bodies, the energy, the climate. In a world where governments would exist only to provide for the distribution of goods and services equitably, for the general welfare of its own people and not have to be concerned with defense, I think Havana would be paradise for me. African and American. Music with rhythms and energy – moving the people. Tropical weather with perpetual breezes. People dancing at the close of the day and again at the close of the night. Who needs cable TV!

I woke up thinking about music here being a tremendous force for social change. Cuba may be the most musical place on the planet! It is certainly among the best places for hot music anywhere. It has an abundance of talent and its society has continued an African tradition of music being accorded a significant place in the culture. And Cuba's modern history has conspired to allow music to be a stress-reliever, a source of national pride, an ingrained part of the social dynamic and social life, and an economic generator. Music may be one of Cuba's chief exports and one of its great ambassadorial resources.

Easter Sunday morning, 10:AM – *Mi Casa*

I did go back to the Casa de la Musica to hear Manolito's band, another one of the best salsa bands in Cuba. They were as good as advertised, with strong rhythms, really interesting orchestral arrangements and a unique instrumentation, with a string section consisting of a cello and two violins added to the usual compliment of horn section, two keyboards, four percussionists and four lead singers.

Earlier in the day yesterday we learned that we would not be able to do the party and record the Santeria musicians at Salome's place, after all, because the drummers were going to do a gig in Martinique. I was disappointed because I was really looking forward to recording and being part of that happening. But Skipper said he had another possibility, so we had Carlos drive us to Guanabacoa, a deep Afro-Cuban ghetto, where he had a friend. Jamiah and Siul, our new, very fluent translator, was with us and we all enjoyed our drive across Havana to the other side of the docks, to a section of the city that had rough, barely paved roads, horses, pigs, and the appearance of a shanty town.

When we got to the compound of his friend, Skipper was greeted warmly by all, from the elders to the smallest children. We arranged to have a small party in order to record some music there that very evening. We left there to go looking for an extension cord and three-pronged adapter plug, and to go past David Murray's place to see if he and Craig would want to come hang out in the ghetto and see the happenings. Then we went back to my place to gather up the recording and video equipment and headed back out to the little recording session, a 30-minute drive away.

When we got there, we set up the recording studio in the yard, which was enclosed by the walls of the small apartments in the compound. It was almost a miniature rural setting that included a pig oinking, a pigeon coop, two small dogs, one dachshund and one mongrel with its left eye hanging out, assorted family members and children in a small yard that had a small creek running through the back. Jamiah and I placed five microphones in strategic places, got the video camera loaded and we were ready to roll. Skipper broke out the rum and soon our little recording session party was underway. They had two old conga drums, claves, a cowbell and five or six men doing unpolished chanting. Later a young boy brought his trumpet and another came in with a snare drum and a rusty cymbal, which he set up on an overturned bicycle frame.

The music was basic rumba. The rhythms had their moments of magic, but the singing was very unpolished and loose. I think that there was a lot of hesitation and uneasiness caused by the presence of all the equipment, which is more than understandable. There is what my friend, Kevin Teasley, calls "red light syndrome," where musicians of all levels of expertise go through some amounts of stress and tightening of the nerves when the recording light goes on and the engineer says, "tapes rolling!"

Carlos made another trip across town and brought back David and five other people in his entourage including two European women, one of whom is a photographer from Geneva traveling with David. They all came in and added an incongruent international and high tech flavor to the tiny informal yard party in the ghetto. A couple of times I joined in the music on my soprano sax; and a good time was had by all. After the recording session ended, we disassembled the equipment. Tables and chairs were set up and we all ate dinner and drank some homemade rum. Music on the little stereo included Kool & the Gang, Mariah Carey and Earth Wind & Fire; and after the meal when the salsa played, there was even some dancing and beginning lessons in doing the salsa.

David Murray asks me to do a cameo appearance on his recording session coming up next week. I am honored. He says that he would be a fool not to take advantage of my services since I'm here. I am a bit concerned because there would then be two parallel heavy schedules to fulfill and my priority has to be doing the recordings for Skipper's project. Working with David and the super musicians that he is assembling for his sessions would be really something!

Sunday night, 10:00 PM in my room.

This morning I stayed in until 12 noon when we dashed over the Skipper's place to pick him up to go to a cultural festivity on a special street in a downtown neighborhood. When we got there we found a city block that has been turned into a work of art by Salvadore, a renowned artist. His paintings covered every exterior wall like graffiti and his sculptures were everywhere along the tiny street. He had a shrine to the saint Ogun and an indoor gallery of his works as well. On Sundays on this block they have a rumba festival, and percussion and dancing groups come there to perform free for the people.

When we arrived, there were throngs of people jammed into the center of the street, which was really about the width of a wide alley. There was a covered shed under which the drummers and singers and dancers performed. The event was a neighborhood and an international affair, with people from Havana intermingled with people who were obviously tourist from anywhere. People were watching and listening to a rumba group drumming and chanting and the crowd was closer than shoulder-to-shoulder. What should have been aisles were jammed with bodies trying to get closer or to move through. Cameras, tape and video recorders were capturing much of the goings-on: polyrhythmic conga drums and *shekeres* with heavy chanting; people dancing or swaying or listening or looking at art and each other; a kaleidoscope of colors painted on everything; more people standing on the sculptures, on benches, on balconies of rainbow painted tenement buildings, all mixed together in the heat of the hottest day yet here in Havana. We videoed, took digital pictures and recorded audio on minidisk and still most of the stuff passed on out into the universe, uncaptured.

We sent Carlos, the driver, back to the apartment to pick up my horns so that I could play with the next group scheduled to perform. It was Rumba Morenga, an all-women's rumba group. They sang and played the drums, shakers, claves and bells and they excited the crowd with their energy. I did play my soprano with them, but I have to agree with Jamiah who thought it was not one of my better performances. The women sang with the microtones of African chants and I could not get in tune with them. But once again the crowd seemed to enjoy my playing and we grooved together in the moments that were ours.

After we left, we happened to see Hamiet Bluiett sitting on a porch. Amazing! He was in from New York to do the David Murray session and he was waiting for his ride to the rehearsal. We stopped the car and talked to him and his wife, and said we would see him later.

Monday, evening - 8:15 PM Back at my place.

Today I got up early (because I went to bed early last night) and did my yoga on the cold marble floor. We had an early meeting with the Vice President of the Music Association and though we got there early, we had to wait an hour or so before we actually got in to meet with him. Skipper, David Murray, Craig Harris, Siul (the translator) and I met with the Vice President and his assistant and discussed Skipper's project and how the film, the music and the musicians might be used as build support for ending the U.S. blockage and for better cultural relations between the two countries. We talked about what the music association could do for us this week, i.e., securing a studio or room to be used as a studio for recording and helping us contact musicians to be recorded this week. But we also talked about the prospects for long-term relationships and projects that could create ongoing work.

We concluded by agreeing that this proposed long-term, relationship-building program was worthwhile and should be pursued. We said that the next step was to put a proposal together so that the Vice President could carry it forward for approval by the appropriate ministry.

After that meeting I went back to pick up my horns and Jamiah to go to

David Murray's big band rehearsal for his recording sessions to start on tomorrow. Jamiah and I were among the first to arrive. The studio was old but well-equipped. The sessions would be recorded on two-inch analogue tape. The recording room is a large enough space to record the 18-piece big band and it is acoustically deadened so that it should be a really good recording. The musicians are some of the best in Havana. All of them have great chops and are great sight-readers.

David has been working on the compositions and the arrangements for quite a while and he has worked with two well-known Cuba composers for a week to incorporate the rhythms and feelings of Cuban music into his works. This big band sounds really good playing the charts. I did get to play soprano on one piece. I enjoyed being at the rehearsal and was impressed with the whole production, from top to bottom. I think the recording should be very successful.

Tuesday Morning – 7:30 AM in bed at mi casa.

Yesterday Jamiah said he was homesick. And I can dig it. Like Dorothy said, "There's no place like home!" As long as you are busy going from one thing to the next and you don't have time to think about it, wanting to be home is less of an issue. Oh yeah, you think about the people you love and those you work with. You mentally visit projects and habits you'd be doing if you were back in Kansas or Virginia or New York, but it doesn't turn into the pangs of pain until you have too many quiet moments strung together and your thoughts drift into the twilight zone of visualizing what you'd rather be doing and you remember where you'd rather be doing it. Home is wherever you'd really rather be right now and where you'd rather be for the long-term; and, as George Carlin would say, home is where you leave your stuff.

I don't know if Cuba would ever be my home. Though one night here, at the Casa de la Musica when I was in the heat of the Cortez band's set, and the music and the hips were pumping, I had the thought, "This is where I want to be, maybe forever!" But it's easy to want to be in the heat of a good, hot moment. Easy to forget about politics and loved ones who are somewhere else, until the quiet moments of reflection turn into prayers and the prayers turn into visions of heaven and peace. And those things are always centered where you have your love – home.

Wednesday morning in my bed at mi casa.

Yesterday was a day that we came here to have. After I did my yoga for the morning, I got Jamiah up and we went with Carlos to pick up Skipper to run a couple of errands and then we were ready to go to the film director's house located in a small seaside town 20 miles outside Havana. The drive was interesting in that I was our first highway trip since we got here.

The coastal town was sparsely populated with beachgoers and small shops and houses of various descriptions. The beach was the most dominant feature, with its azure water, palm trees, blue sky and wonderful Caribbean-flavored sights and sounds added to the general landscape. This beach town was the kind of place that you would describe as idyllic.

After going out to a wonderful little pizza restaurant that boasts a real Italian-style, brick pizza oven and fresh vegetables grown right there on the premises, we went to the beach for a swim: Jamiah, Skipper and I in the clear, warm waters of the Caribbean Ocean. Palm trees, bikinis, quaint shoreline houses and relaxing dreams of this being the life.

We drove back to Havana, and after dropping off Skipper and Jamiah and picking up my recording equipment, I went down to the Café Cantanta where Dennis & Swing would be performing at 11:00 PM. I worked with the house sound engineer and got my recording gear set up and ready in about an hour. Then I went back home to shower, rest for half an hour, dress, pick up Jamiah and leave for the gig.

On the way back to the club I stopped by the studio where David Murray's big band was recording to confirm that David, Craig, and Hamiet were going to come to the club and jam after their recording session ended around midnight.

This night was what we came to Cuba to do: capture some of the magic of the musicians from Cuba interacting with musicians from the U.S. and I had been a little apprehensive about it all day. I just hoped that all would go well technically and artistically. And it did!

In fact, the gig went exceptionally well. The club is located the basement of the national theater and it is quite nice, with an adequate stage, a dance floor, and really good sound and light systems. There was a tight first set with Dennis' band and halfway through it, David, Craig and Hamiet arrived from their recording session.

Then after the break Denis conducted his band and directed a jam session with all of the American horn players and Cuban musicians taking flight in an extended salsa-jazz version of "Autumn Leaves." We played it inside and out: David's big toned tenor sax, Bluiett's even bigger baritone sound, Craig's scatting trombone and my little soprano sax all soaring, dipping, swooping, screaming and singing together and then into a series of extended solos. It was quite a *descargas*, a mega-jam, a 30-minute freewheeling whirlwind of musical energy! And we got it all recorded in digital quality sound and video! It was a winner. It was a slam dunk night. And everybody had a great time. It was Black fire in Cuba!

Wednesday Afternoon - 2:30 PM

We did get a room in the Karl Marx Theater to use as our studio space for the rest of the week. Now we'll have to contact musicians to come and record. We don't have Carlos the driver and his car this morning so I don't know how much we'll get done today.

I did do some light yoga and listened to the recordings from last night. As I suspected, Dennis' band's first set was tighter and more "even" and made for a better recording than did the jamming second set, but all in all it was pretty decent. I took a cab to Hotel Cohiba to use the Internet for an hour. The Internet connection is painfully slow but I am thankful to have access to my email at all.

Wednesday night, 10:00 PM

When we arrived at the Karl Marx Theater, Rumba Morena, the all-female group who performed on Sunday at the artist's street festival, was already there waiting for us. The theater is undergoing renovation, so we entered through the first floor lobby which a construction zone. The room we will be using is a medium-sized, smooth stone hall with a wooden stage. It is dusty and in the process of being renovated too. The security man and the electrician are helpful in getting the small things that I need and after a short while I am ready to begin recording the women.

Most of theater's audio-visual equipment is in use in a production in the main concert hall, so they only have one microphone and microphone stand for me. I use chairs for microphone stands and large paintings as baffles to try and get some separation between the percussion and the vocals. The women are very effective in performing their songs and they are excited to listen back to the recordings after each take. We get a pretty good sound for the recording and I experiment with different techniques, effects and microphone placements. We were able to get five or six good songs recorded, including one percussion instrumental, five songs of percussion with vocals, and one song with percussion, and two tracks of me playing saxophones.

Marika came and said that she had contacted some of the rappers and they would be coming as well. A little while later, six rappers did show up and they listened to the last part of the women rumba group's session. Skipper spoke with the rappers about his project and its purposes and then I spoke to them about the recording process and artistic considerations and possibilities. They decided that they wanted to record with us.

We did get to record one rap song by a two-man group. They had music tracks on CDs that they brought with them so I was able to record the tracks directly into the VS1680 and they did their raps flawlessly, straight through, without a hitch, twice, non-stop. It went well. The other group didn't have their tracks CD with them, so we called it a day, packed up and left.

Thursday morning – 8:30 AM

The Zorro el Cuevo club is a small jazz place. Its size lends itself to more intimacy and closer involvement with the music. Last night the band was led by an older musician who used to be in the group, Irekere. The music was very engaging and quite varied. The instrumentation included the leader and a young cat on percussion, which included *bata* drums; plus three horns, drums, bass, keyboards and electric guitar. They played a number of styles and flowed from salsa to jazz to blues, to funk, to traditional folklorica, sometimes segueing between several genres in one arrangement. The young percussionist was great! After the set Marika introduced me to him (his name is Emiel Lazo) and we talked to him about coming to the theater to record on tomorrow or Friday.

Also I spoke with the keyboardist who invited me to sit in with his group tomorrow night at Zorro el Cuevo, he said that he would come by the theater to check out the recording session too. Ronald introduced me to Ellen, a friend of Skipper's who works for Pastors for Peace. Ellen was with U.S. Congressman Wynn from Prince Georges County, Maryland. I sat down with them and had a drink and a brief conversation with them. Ellen is into jazz and a long-time fan of the music. The congressman is here in Cuba on a brief fact-finding mission.

I am amazed at how many people are on the streets downtown late on a weeknight. So many clubs and restaurants open, so much music, so much nightlife. And Ronald confirms that it is always this way and I wonder if not having cable TV and so many other home entertainment options is one of the reasons that live music and hanging out is so popular in Havana?

Thursday Night/Friday morning, 2:23 AM, mi casa again.
"If musicians were kings, there would be no borders." That's my quote for today.
I did go to the Karl Marx Theater at 10:00 AM, right on schedule. When I got there, the women of Rumba Morena, the group we recorded yesterday, were already there, waiting for me. I left Jamiah in bed because once again he hung out until the wee hours, so I had to set up all by myself. Well, the electrician and the security man for the theater did help some, and so did the ladies. I spent the first hour letting the women listen to what they had recorded the day before, while I made dubs onto a minidisk. Then we shot some video of the women dancing to one of the pieces we had recorded.
Marika came and so did Emiel Lazo, the young conga drummer that I saw with the band at Zorro y Cuevo last night. I immediately set up to record him because the solo I saw him do at the club was so mean, I knew that any recording I could get of his playing would be a great piece of music for the film track. And indeed it was! Emiel recorded an eight-minute conga solo that was too terrible! And he is 17 years old! After that, we recorded him playing congas backing up the women doing a chant and we also recorded a piece with him and me on soprano sax.
While we were doing that, some of the rappers came in. The two-man rap group I recorded yesterday came in with the mother of one of them. I finished up working on what I was doing with the conga drummer. While the rappers were waiting for me to get with them, I was thinking that the mother had come to check out what we doing with her son, and maybe to make inquiries about the business we were conducting. Oh but no: it turns out that her son had told her about the project and she, the mother, had written a rap about the embargo last night and they had come hoping to record it today!
So the next thing we did was set up to record them doing that rap song. The process was that we used a track from a CD for groove and tempo and they rapped using that as their backup music. We intend to replace that with

music that Jamiah and others will produce back in the states. After I recorded the rappers, I recorded two tracks of the young conga drummer onto the song and when I get back home and put some other music with it I think it will be a hot rap song about the blockade.

"What's your name/ It's blockade/ You kill children everyday/ That's bullshit, Man/ Not my way!"

We recorded another rapper doing a piece about the revolution, and by that time, it was approaching 6:00 PM so we packed up to leave. It was a very interesting day of recording with the Rumba Moreno women interacting with Emiel, the 17-year-old conga virtuoso, and the rappers. I also videotaped an interview with the women and the conga drummer about the history of the music and rhythms in Cuba. And I even got footage of Emiel Lazo demonstrating the basic rumba rhythms on congas. It was a full day of producing in our theater hall; very gratifying artistically and also because I had the sense that we are accomplishing our mission.

After going to Skipper's to eat dinner, Jamiah and I took a cab back here to rest. Ronald called and said that he was coming over to introduce me to an older musician, Alfredo, a percussionist, who has been performing professionally with his family group, Papines, for 40 years. Their group is a four-piece percussion ensemble and they travel all over the world. Tonight they performed at a festival of Cuban percussion going on in Havana this week. My conversation with Alfredo was very stimulating and refreshing. He has performed with many great musicians over the years and his brother performed with Nat King Cole when he came to record in Cuba. Talking to Alfredo was a brief history lesson that I wish I had videotaped. It was Alfredo who said, "If musicians were kings, there would be no borders."

After Alfredo left, Ronald drove me to the Zorro y Cueva jazz café where I have been invited to jam with the group Bambaleo, led by keyboardist Lazaro Valdes. We picked up Marika on the way to the club and she wanted to go by and pick up Dennis. When we got to the club it was abuzz with musicians and patrons. A group playing straight-ahead jazz performed first and later Bambaleo went on. Lazaro Valdes is an innovative keyboardist and his group plays high-energy fusion. I did get to sit in on one number and although I didn't think my playing was so great, people including the club owner seemed quite impressed. I gave the club owner one of my CDs and he said that he'd play it on his weekly jazz show on the radio here in Havana.

Keeping this journal is a form of discipline. I am not so sure that it is not also a form of vanity to think that everything that I do is so great it should be documented on tape and in writing. But nevertheless, other musicians and people in general might benefit from learning of these experiences. And even though this late night note-taking takes time, energy and discipline, it may be easier to do it right now than to wait and try to do it when I get back home, because there, I will have so much work to do, catching up the my affairs there, plus organizing and producing what I have amassed here, and doing the ongoing gigging and record business that I must do to earn a living. So onward, upward, got to keep on keeping on. Unto to whom much is given, much is required; and I have been given so very much....

Friday night on my bed early – 11:30 PM

Today was the last full day of work for the week. Thank God it was Friday! And it was our last full day in Havana. I got up did a miniature yoga session and went to the Hotel Cohiba to retrieve my email. I was moving very lethargically this morning. My energy was low and my body just would not move out of first gear. I wondered if I might be sick, but it turned out to be nothing more than the residual effect of a couple of drinks and too much cigarette smoke and too much work and staying up late and not eating at the proper times to get the energy flowing this morning.

Skipper arrived after I set up but none of the rappers who were supposed to start at 11:00 AM got there before 12 noon, so Skipper and I had a chance to talk. We agreed that it seems like there is the potential of some really great things happening here, musically, politically, commercially and humanitarianly. But there is a tremendous amount of work that must be done if that potential is to be realized.

The rappers came in and we listened and made dubs of some of what was recorded yesterday. Telma, a female poet, came in and Skipper said that she was a strong rapper, so I eagerly pressed her to do a rap for us. The only sound track she had to rap over was something that already had her rapping on it, so I recorded her rapping to that for tempo and then had her do it again so that I had two tracks of her doubling herself. As with most of the other raps we have been recording, the intention is to take the rap recordings back to the States and put other beats and music on the tracks. But Telma's rap was something special. It was a poem/rap that was actually a kind of prayer to the

Orishas about her life, her love, her struggles and pain.

Then I asked if she could do the poem again set to a rumba beat and she said that she would try it. I cued up the rumba chant that the female group Rumba Morena had done with Emiel Lazo yesterday. When Telma heard the track she broke out into a broad smile and said she couldn't do it. But with a little coaxing she did and it turned out to be so bad! It was mad wild! Because here was a girl, doing a poem-prayer to the Orishas, over a rumba beat, and females chanting to the same Orishas. Too cold! Next I had Telma improvise a derivative poem over a track of Emiel on congas and my soprano sax and that came out great too!

Then we recorded another male rapper, Alexia, doing a poem about revolution. I thought his delivery was sometimes slightly off time but I also don't speak Spanish. I thought that his tracks that he brought in was a little distorted; but we are going to put new music to most of these raps anyway, so that was not a big thing.

When we were finishing up the rap things the two young saxophone players who were at the Zorro y Cuevo Jazz Café last night came in. But by 1:30 PM they were still the only musicians who had come, though we were expecting several others. We considered taking a break for lunch and coming back in an hour to see if any other instrumentalists would show up. Then I thought that I had better record something with just us three horns and if no one else showed up then I would just call it quits.

We spent about a half-hour working out some freewheeling musical ideas for a saxophone trio. The two young guys were good jazz students, with commendable experience and really nice tones on their axes. They looked like they were not sure if I wasn't a bit off my rocker with some of the things I was having them try; but in the end they began to hear and get a feel for what we would be doing. Jamiah came in, having walked from the apartment, so he could assist by starting and stopping the recording device.

We recorded three pieces. First we did an impressionistic piece consisting of the three saxes improvising over a set of chord changes that I charged the alto sax player to come up with. Next we did a slow blues that started out over blues chord changes and slowly evolved to a free state. And last we did a "salsa" piece with the tenor, alto and soprano saxes each holding a rhythmic part. This last piece was most interesting.

As we were listening back to the tracks, I heard the tenor saxophonist humming a bass line to the salsa sax piece while it was playing back so I asked him to let me record his voice singing the bass line for the track. It was fun sounding, so I got the three ladies from Rumba Morenga to do a three-part voice percussion track. While they were doing their thing, Emiel, the terrible young conga player, came in, so I asked him to "sing" a conga part with his voice on another track. Then I added a track by the rapper who did the revolution rap to the mix. And lastly I got poetess Telma to do her thing, which was the final touch.

It was salsa made from saxes and voices. As each layer had been added, the sound track sounded more and more like a Cuban paella or a gumbo, and each new performance was greeted by smiles and applause by all the young people there. It was a lot of fun and actually pretty incredible both in terms of how it all came together and how it sounded.

Skipper came in and I let him hear it and he was knocked out by what we had done. He said he thought Jimmy Gray (founder of Black Fire Records who died last year) was somewhere up there smiling down on us. Black Fire!

Skipper then assembled everyone and gave a wonderful little speech about the project and what we had accomplished in the three days we worked there. He also talked about being "cultural warriors" and thanked everyone for being supportive and giving so much of themselves. I spoke to the group, thanking them for their work, their creativity and praised their youthful spirits. I told them that I hoped that they had learned from the experience and that I hoped they would be inspired by history and also by the idea that together we artists can create new things and a new world.

We then adjourned and took taxis to Skipper's place for food and a house party. We ate, drank and made merry! Skipper's housekeeper, Maria, managed to get everyone fed. Rum flowed. Young horn players danced with Rumba Morenga ladies. Mike looked on and admired the sensuality of the dancers. And Siul, the translator, had fallen in love with the lead singer of Rumba Morenga and the two of them cooed and hugged and danced and kissed their way into the evening. That was a cute little development that made us all smile warmly.

Sunday morning, 5:30 AM, in Montreal, Canada, On the bus to St. Alban Vermont

The last day in Havana was a day spent waiting to leave. I had hoped to do some last minute sight-seeing and videotaping but it was not to be. Instead,

I spent the morning tying up loose ends, having my cell phone re-programmed, and packing my baggage.

Ronald took us to the airport and we checked-in and went through immigration with no hassles at all. Hamiet Bluiett and his wife were taking the same flight to Montreal and so we all sat together chit-chatting while waiting to board. The flight boarded and left 30 minutes early.

When we landed in Montreal we cleared customs in a breeze with absolutely no scrutiny or delays. Jamiah and I took a bus to the train station in downtown Montreal. I had hoped that we could check our bags and then maybe go out for a bit of nightlife in the city before waiting for this 5:30 AM bus, but by the time we got to the train station there were no personnel to check the bags. We spent the night in the train station. Jamiah rigged up a table to stretch out on and I did that nod-in-and-out-count-the-minutes kind of thing that drags on and on interminably through the night. Now I am on the bus to the final border crossing back to the USA wondering just how intense that might be. I have the documents, the regulations and the mental preparation to get through it; I just hope we aren't delayed. We'll see....
Sunday morning, 8:00 AM, in St Alban, Vermont, USA! On the train

Back in the USA! Customs at the border check was a breeze! Sure, when they found out that Jamiah and I had been to Cuba, we had to take all our baggage off the bus and we were taken back into the main interrogation room. They asked me what I did in Cuba and how long I was there. I told them I went for professional research in my field of the history of African and African-American music. They asked me if I consulted the state department before I traveled and I told them that I had. I showed them the copy of the regulations and where it stated that travel for that purpose was exempt from licensing restrictions. I showed them my letters from Johns Hopkins University, Hampton University, Richmond Public Schools and Richmond Jazz Society.

They then said they wanted to open one of our bags and they picked the clothes bag, which was the least sensitive of the six things we were carrying. The clothes bag had nothing but clothes in it. If they picked the VS1680 case and I would have to explain what the digital recording unit was. My brief case had loads of CD's, CD-ROMs, my laptop and miniature digital camera, etc. in it. And the big black box! Nothing illegal, but so many things to explain: blank computer hard drives, minidisks, mini DV tapes, a zillion wires and connectors, microphones, a microphone pre-amp, too many questionable gizmos. But no – they picked the clothes bag. We were in and out of there in 15 minutes! Back on the bus, 12 miles to the train, a 30-minute wait and finally, all aboard to DC and then home!

Sunday morning 11:00 AM on the train

I've lived long enough to see the changes that people and places go through. I've see warring enemies become favored trading friends. I've known bastions of segregation come to be led by able black elected officials. And I've seen enough gray winters give way to light green springs. Jamiah sleeps through most of the travel times, and although he misses the scenes flying by the train window, I envy his ability to sleep so readily. But I hope that this trip can be a part of his maturing process which will allow him to see and appreciate changes; to play through and pray through changes. Because surely changes always come.

I also wonder about Cuba. I wonder about any leader who is not preparing to lead his people towards some form of democratic expression of their will. I wonder when Havana will find its way out of the gray-brown winter of poverty to the spring of a brighter economy. I doubt that things have to be only "either" or else. Can't there be more tourism and development without greater corruption of officials and loss of cultural direction? Can the ideals of socialism be applied to a society without robbing individuals of their drive to compete and prosper? Can a roaring live music scene retain its vibrancy if 100-channel satellite television and home theater systems are available? Is Havana still Havana if shiny, new, and fuel-injected things replace dusty, old, quaint 1956 models?

On this trip I have had a re-confirmation of the fact that all people, every person, is special, has some great thing or talent or spirit about them. That we would do well to never underestimate what people can do, what one man or woman can contribute to your life upon meeting them. And I have been reminded of the utter joys and wonderment that can be revealed in the following of obscure paths, in the passing through open doors, the grabbing hold of opportunities to take risks.

The scenes projected on the screen of the train window go by at varying speeds, sometimes whizzing dizzily; sometimes in reverse, and sometimes creeping by, allowing the observance of details like one bud on one tree or a broken swing set in a backyard. But it is not the pace of the scenes that is rewarding to observe, but the fact that the scenes change and that there is both familiarity in the changes and at the same time a peculiarity and uniqueness to each scene. Unrelated to this fact is the fact that from the train window can be seen evidence of occasional derailments and despair, and even more evidence of repair and renewal.

Yes, I know I ramble on, but then so does this train, with its chatter and whistles and New England station stops and its southward heading, back toward Richmond and Cuba.

The Music

I return from Cuba with no clear outline of the music business or the politics of how it is administered there. I know that all contracts for recordings and tours for Cuban musicians are negotiated and executed through a central music institution which is a subsidiary of the Cultural ministry. It is evident that the Cuban education system produces a large number of outstanding musicians through its general schools and its numerous music conservatories. It is also a matter of governmental policy to promote and preserve Cuban culture and within that culture, music is valued highly.

The central government, through its cultural ministry, institutions and officials, controls and oversees aspects of the management of music and professional music groups. The music ministry said that there are 44 concert bands, marching bands and orchestras in Cuba. There are 11,000 individual musicians and 3,000 popular and folkloric groups.

The music conservatories used to teach only classical music theory, but now jazz, including big band and bop and the Cuba music are also studied. Because music is so prevalent and because it is seen as a potential vehicle for success and even international acclaim, the young musicians take their studies very seriously. Some achieve a high level of competence at relatively young ages. I saw that the salsa bands had lots of young players and I met several young players who were outstanding.

What I observed in Havana salsa bands was extraordinary musicianship combined with high energy driven by the rhythms and spirit of the drum, fused into showy entertainment, most often with the objective of making people dance. It is a potent concoction of art, spirit, entertainment and community.

Also the music was so very prominent and prolific and available. At the Havana music clubs there are live shows at 5:00 PM and also late shows at 11:00 PM, often with two groups. And this goes on almost every day in clubs all over the country! Then there are late night jam sessions at some of the jazz clubs. There are various festivals, street fairs and other special events. Added to this is the fact that groups that are successful are mandated to do a number of free shows for the community. Then there are rumba groups playing percussion and chanting traditional songs, folklorica, both at the professional and neighborhood levels. Music is in Havana and Havana is in the music.

I was utterly amazed at the amount of good music and great musicianship I heard. Of course, I was there to take in as much music as I could and I was there at a special time. Renown free-jazz saxophonist David Murray, from the U.S. but who lives in Paris, was in Havana to produce an all-star big band recording with baritone saxophonist and fellow World Saxophone Quartet member, Hamiet Bluiett and trombonist Craig Harris along with an array of world class Cuban musicians and composers. The rehearsals and recording sessions with this outstanding cast of players, writers and improvisers were incredible! And even after long days of rehearsals and recording, some of these musicians found time and energy to go out to an occasional late night jam in the clubs.

Also while I was in Havana, there was a several hundred thousand people gathering to hear Fidel Castro speak at an event commemorating the Cuban Revolution; a festival of traditional drummers and a 10th anniversary of a street festival area created by the artist Salvadore that had music ranging from the Cuban Concert band to rumba groups and salsa bands.

I talked with David Murray and the other jazz musicians in Cuba for his recording session and they all agreed that there a lot of terrific players in Cuba with "chops for days!" When I asked David, who travels all over the world playing in festivals and clubs in New York, Senegal, Paris, Japan, Turkey, California, etc., he compared Havana with New York. And I thought that was saying a lot, since New York is considered one of the great centers of music in the world!

Hamiet Bluiett said he was energized by the level of musicianship in Havana because "..all the cats can play, I mean really play and they can play to make people dance. It's a dance culture and it reminds me of when I was growing up and all the cats could play. All the music teachers in the Black schools could really play. But they couldn't get jobs with the symphony, so they taught and they also played in the R&B bands and you had to make people dance!"

Craig Harris said, "Man, some of these young cats can wail and they like to take things like "Giant Steps" at tempos way up here. But I had to slow them down, to let them feel my stuff, so they could feel the blues."

The Recordings

For my research and for the recording project I was involved with, I came equipped to record and document some of what I performed and witnessed. I brought in equipment that was compact and at the same time powerful. The centerpiece of recording gear was the Roland VS1680, a 16-track portable digital recording studio. My equipment list also included: a portable Sony MiniDisc recorder; a Canon GL-1 digital video camera; an Audio Technica AT822 stereo microphone; a DBX microphone pre-amp; an Audio Technical 4033 Microphone; several Shure Beta 58 microphones; various wires and connectors; 10 blank, 6.4 gigabyte hard drives for the VS1680; 20 blank minidisks; 25 mini DV tapes for the video camera; a miniature digital camera for snapshots; and a laptop computer. I was loaded for bear. I figured if I had to travel that far and if I was going to have a once-in-a-lifetime experience, I was going to capture it as well as I could.

None of the authorities in Cuba or the United States questioned me regarding my equipment when I entered or re-entered the respective countries. And, while I have no reason to believe that any of technology was banned or in any way illegal, I was surprised, because although the individual pieces were small, altogether it was a lot of luggage that my son and I had to manage. I doubt that this level of digital recording equipment often comes in private hands to be used in Cuba, if at all; though I suspect it may be used there more and more in the near future.

I used my minidisc recorder with a stereo microphone to make live recordings in nightclubs and at a street festival. I set up my Roland VS recording studio in a wide range of settings in Havana. I did a live recording of a 15-piece salsa band in a nightclub. I recorded a solo singer with guitar and sax in an apartment living room. And I recorded some neighborhood musicians at a backyard party in a ghetto with pigeons cooing, chickens clucking and a pig oinking in the background.

For the last three days in Havana I was given a large room with stone floor and plaster walls in the Karl Marx Theater to be my studio space. In that space I recorded a female rumba group doing vocals and percussion, three rap groups, a poet and a saxophone trio. In most instances, I used two or three SM58s for close miking; the Audio Technica 4033 with a pre-amp as the main microphone in the middle; and the stereo AT822 microphone for ambience and a wide stereo field. I got some great recordings with this set-up, even in the barrio yard party.

The cooperation we received from the ministries, institutions and the musicians themselves in Cuba was outstanding. Their support and the support of, by and for Pastors for Peace made the project possible. The music that I recorded was outstanding. It was Cuban and it was innovative in that I was able to get some of the younger musicians to experiment with the forms, and collaborate in new ways: poets with rumba singers, rappers with a percussionist, jazz saxophonists improvising with poetry and vocal percussion. And I was able to capture in digital quality sound recordings.

The Rumba

The rumba is an African-derived rhythm and the basic rhythm of Afro-Cuban music. The rumba is said to be the rhythm African slaves played to entertain themselves after work. The basic parts of the rumba are the clave and the parts played by two or three conga drums. There are different derivative rhythms that are types or parts of the rumba, including the *guaguanco*, the Columbia, etc.

Even more primal are the rhythms played on the *bata* drums. The bata drums are hourglass-shaped drums with a skin on either end. Ensembles consisting of two or three of these two-headed drums are central to the music of the Santeria religions. The sacred rhythms of the *bata* are directly descended from the rhythms played by the Yoruba in Nigeria. The Santeria religion is a hybrid, combining worship of certain African deities with some of the attributes Catholic saints. Bata drums are sometimes used in today's Cuban popular and jazz music, but the batas are not nearly as prevalent as the conga drums.

The Future

The future is bright with possibilities. The sheer number of fantastic young musicians in Cuba makes for wonderful prospects for great salsa and jazz on the island. If there are increased opportunities to record this music and export it to other parts of the world on records and by touring performers, then, indeed, Cuba will be a force in the world's music scene.

For me, as a musician, producer and record company owner, there are lots of possibilities as well. I might be able to go back to the island to produce more recordings. My equipment and my production skills could be valuable in such a process.

Certainly as a musician, I would enjoy returning to Cuba to play and perform, with my own group or as a soloist with groups there. Although I have to say that, while I was very well received, when I was there, I saw so many gifted and talented young musicians, I felt that the world might not need me to play at all.

And I haven't even been to Santiago and Guantanamo. Those regions of Cuba are said to have music that is even more African and more spiritual. Those areas have a higher concentration of Blacks because this is where Cuban and Haitian slaves, who escaped, took refuge. The religions and music there are supposed to be very deep like the roots of the culture itself. I may have to go back to Cuba soon to explore that culture more deeply.

When I got back to the States, the current issue of Vibe Magazine (April 2001) had an article on the Cuban rap music scene. EQ Magazine for the same month featured an article on the proliferation of the use of the studios-in-a-box like the Roland VS1680 in music recording projects.

⌘⌘⌘

Chapter 19

Under The Radar Journey to Cuba II

May 16, 2001- 7:15 PM; On a small plane traveling from Jamaica to Havana, Cuba

When I left Havana, Cuba, three weeks ago, I had no idea that I would be returning so soon. I wasn't even sure that I would ever get back there, though I certainly hoped that I would. But here I am on an airplane with my 19-year-old son, Jamiah, once again at my side. We are flying over the Caribbean headed back to Cuba, the largest island in this area and the center of the Afro-Cuban culture, the home of cigars, rum, Santeria-Yoruba religion and the hottest place on earth for Salsa and Rumba music.

Once again it has been a long day's travel to get here. We left Richmond, Virginia, at 7:00 PM yesterday headed to Washington, DC, where we spent the night at the office of my attorney friend, Franklin, before heading to the Baltimore-Washington International airport at 6:00 AM to take an Air Jamaica flight to Montego Bay, Jamaica. Because of the U.S.-imposed travel restrictions, U.S. citizens cannot travel directly to Cuba; so one has to go via a third country, usually Canada, Mexico, Venezuela, or Jamaica. Last time we went via Canada. This time I decided to forego the 15-hour train ride and pay the extra money to fly to Jamaica and then on to Cuba. But the trip has not been so short or simple, simply because we had a six hour layover in Montego Bay, Jamaica before taking this small, 37-seat propeller plane, and making a stop in Kingston Jamaica before continuing on to Havana. The arrival time in Havana is scheduled for 9:00 PM, so it has still been a 15-hour trip; more, counting yesterday's drive from Richmond to Baltimore.

Jamiah and I spent the morning at the Montego Bay airport getting conflicting directions as to the procedures and location of where to purchase our tickets to Havana. Instead of staying in the transit area of the airport, we went through Immigration and cleared customs so that we could go visit the downtown area of Montego Bay. Jamaica reminds me a little of West Africa but it is more like the Virgin Islands, with narrow roadways (and they drive on the left!), tropical vegetation, and shopping galore for tourists from the docked cruise ships.

Jamiah and I took a taxi to the downtown area to visit some shops and walk around a bit. Our main baggage has been checked through to Havana from Baltimore, but the smaller bags that we carried with us includes my two saxophones, my video camera bag and my briefcase with my laptop computer, and they are still quite heavy and unwieldy. I suddenly remembered that I have left all the blank videotapes for the camera at home, so I had to hunt around Montego Bay to find some mini DV cassettes for the video camera. After eating at a KFC, we took a cab back to the airport to wait the two hours before the boarding of our flight.

I napped in the waiting area and just at about the time for boarding I was approached by an old friend, Bill Brower, a freelance writer and jazz producer who lives in Washington, DC. I haven't seen him for a couple of years and it is interesting that I would run into him here in route to Cuba. Bill is an old acquaintance whom I originally met through Skipper Bailey, the man I am on my way to meet in Cuba! Bill is just coming back from a jazz festival on the island of St. Lucia. We caught up on old times and the things that we are now doing and I gave him a copy of my journal of the last trip I took to Cuba. I also gave him a copy of the CD of the music I recorded on that trip and I made him promise to get back to me when I return to the States. I am really interested in his opinion of both the journal and the music, since he often does articles in major jazz publications and liner notes for album releases. Bill tells me to give Skipper his regards and we both headed for our respective flights, both scheduled for 5:00 PM local time.

This trip to Cuba is already: fortuitous, odd, "a trip!," unexpected, mysterious, if not mystical, and it is an example of me living my life as if it is a jazz solo: scripted, planned for, but improvised and full of interesting and surprising twists and turns of events. Who'd have guessed that we would go back to Havana so soon after my first trip, after having not gone at all in all my 53 years? For 30 years I had had a desire to go to Cuba after studying and playing Afro-Cuban rumba rhythms and chants with my first African jazz group, Juju, in San Francisco back in 1972.

When I got back home from the first trip, I immediately produced rough mixes of the music I had recorded and I compiled a demo CD of 14 of the songs. The demo CD was enthusiastically received by all who heard it. Everybody was amazed at the diversity of the music, quality of the musicianship and the clarity of the recordings. After listening to the CD a few times, I began to hear the compilation as an album; a collection that was entertaining and enjoyable. And Skipper and I really began to contemplate the potential of recording more of these Cuban sounds and making them available to the international public.

Without conducting a formal marketing research analysis we decided that we would go with our instincts and invest the time and resources to go back to Cuba and record as much music as possible. My own schedule was such that the only window of time when I had a two-week stretch open on my calendar was now, the last two weeks in May. So I decided to cast my fate to the Caribbean winds and here I am on a plane right back to Cuba!

I am once again hauling my whole load of studio equipment, microphones, my video camera, saxophones, and Jamiah's MPC2000 sampling drum machine to Cuba. We have what amounts to a mobile recording production facility in two boxes. Now we will see if once again the technical equipment will function properly and if we will be fortunate enough to recruit the participation of a number of talented artists to make the trip and the experience worth it. Then we'll have to see if we can market what I produce. That, I don't know in advance, but I believe that I should go to Cuba and capture all that I can, while I can, and then sort out the politics, the business and the marketing of it after the fact. We'll have to wait and see if the strategy and the resulting products will be viable. I am keeping the faith.

Thursday, May 17, 7:15 AM in my bed, back at mi casa, Carlos' Apartment

Last night on the plane I had some anxious moments about the arrival of our baggage and equipment. I thought that I should have checked on our flight cases full of our high-tech gear before leaving Jamaica. But when we arrived at the airport in Havana at 9:45 PM, I was happy that all of our things had arrived with us. Going through Cuban immigration and customs this time, we had more questions about our business and our equipment to answer than we did on the previous trip. But we were granted entry with only a few minutes delay and without any real hassle.

Thursday, May 17, Midnight back in my bed again.

I got up this morning and did a full session of yoga stretches and meditation. My reading and my meditation reminded me that my focus should be on being thankful for this day and all that I have; I should smile so that I share my blessings, and that I should think of and visualize only those things I want to be manifested.

I took a cab over to the Hotel Cohiba to use the business center to go online and check my email. By the time I got back to the apartment, Skipper and Carlos had arrived. We spent the rest of the morning making plans, strategizing and mentally preparing for the agenda of this trip.

In the middle of the afternoon Skipper and I went across town to Festival Cuba Disco, a large music trade show that is going on this week. It culminates with an awards program, Cuba's version of the Grammy's. The trade show was impressive with its large assortment of booths, exhibits, vendors, and performances going on continuously. The exhibits ranged from high-tech, multi-screen video displays to artistically hand-carved conga drums; from the latest digital keyboards and recording equipment to record labels promoting their latest CD album releases. Musicians, music buyers, fans, ministers, producers and lots of fine young women were in attendance. Skipper and I spent the afternoon checking out the wares, networking, renewing musical acquaintances and recruiting performers to work with us.

Two days later, Saturday, May 19, 7:00 AM awakening in my bed.

One of the most amazing things about the last 24 hours is that I slept 10 hours! This almost never happens, because I usually function on six hours sleep or less; most times I wake up at the first sign of sunlight or any noise. Even the sound of birds tweeting in the morning is usually enough to set my mind in motion, thinking about what I have to do in the minutes, hours and days ahead. Then, I may as well get up and get at it because I'm not going back to sleep until the next night or at a rare power nap time.

But last night was different. I guess the fatigue from the travel and work and the warm humid weather all came down on me, and even though I had planned to go out last night and hear some music, I passed out around 9:00 PM. But then, I had worked all day, from 9:00 AM straight through until 7:15 PM, without so much as a break for lunch or even the bathroom. There was so much recording work to do and so little time in which to do it. So I made like a Nike and just did it!

Yesterday started like it should have. I woke up at 7:00 AM, did a series of Yoga sun exercises and woke Jamiah up at 8:00. We showered and took our studio equipment to the Karl Marx Theater by taxi at 9:00 AM. Once we were admitted, we set up the equipment: the Roland VS1680 digital recording studio, Jamiah's Akai MPC2000 sampling drum machine, five microphones, one mic pre-amp, five headphones, and all the wiring and connectors. The engineer for the theater set up a CD deck and wired up an amplifier and speakers for us to use as monitors.

At 10:00 AM the ladies of the all women group, Rumba Morena, began arriving. And a little bit later some of the rappers we recorded on the last trip came in too. We all listened to some of the demo CD I produced from the recordings we made last month. Everyone was eager to hear themselves and they were excited about what I had done with their songs while I was back in the States.

I gave a speech about the work we had done and the business prospects of what we came back to do. I asked if they wanted to continue with us by investing more of their work into this ongoing venture. They all decided that they did want to take this opportunity for us to record them, and promote the recordings, and we'd work out the business deals later.

We finally got started recording the Rumba Morena ladies around 11:30 AM. I wanted to do some innovative things with their basic rumba percussion with chanting format. I decided to record the percussion rhythm tracks first and then come back and overdub the voices and the *quinto*, or improvising solo conga drum, last.

I also decided to use some of Jamiah's drum machine sequences as click tracks and as a way to flavor the rumbas the ladies play. In addition to using some of Jamiah's hip-hop rhythms, we had the lead drummer of the group work with the machine to create the basic dance music pattern that she would be comfortable playing to. The MPC2000 is easy to use and has clean, bigger-than-life sounds and the lady percussionist smiled and giggled on hearing some of her patterns being played back on the machine.

The process was slow but effective. In four and a half hours we got only four songs done. But all of the songs were locked in with steady tempos, had innovative, modern remix possibilities and sounded good in terms of the recording quality.

Around 1:00 PM I sent the rappers out for lunch, while I continued to work with the women of Rumba Morena. When I finished recording the women we immediately went to work with the rappers. In fact even while I was working with the ladies, Jamiah started working on rhythms with the first of the rappers. The format for the rest of the afternoon was once I started recording one rap group, Jamiah would start working on the beats for the next group up. The tracks that Jamiah and the rappers came up with were banging and certainly good enough to motivate the rappers to do their thing with feeling, passion or grooviness.

We recorded The Profitas, the two-man group that recorded two songs with us last month, including one song about the blockade that was written by one's mother. We then recorded a long, eight-minute rap by Alexei and Next Guererro; and finally a smooth, groove rap by Michel, one of the guys who had come over to the apartment the day before.

We were supposed to finish in the Karl Marx Theater by 6:00 PM, but they let us extend our stay until 7:00. Even at that, I worked right up to the last minute. With Skipper and the workers at the theater getting antsy, we hurried out of the place by 7:15 PM. I didn't want to cause any trouble, but I also didn't want to come this far and invest this much time and money and not record as much as I could. One never knows how many opportunities will be coming, so I wanted to take advantage of that moment in time. We ended up getting four rumbas and four raps; a pretty good day's work. And I was bushed.

Jamiah had been really "on it", too and his work was great. Everyone was impressed with his skills. It seems that my lecturing the night before about this opportunity, his work ethic and my depending on him had paid off. I had also told him that we were investing a lot of resources to be here and that we couldn't afford to waste time and energy. I had made it clear that I needed his commitment and a disciplined effort.

We came back here to the apartment to eat. Skipper was miffed about how his film crew had missed an opportunity to do an important and provocative interview on film with Lucius Walker, the director of Pastors for Peace and one of the most important figures in Cuban-U.S. relations. Skipper and I talked at length about the Cuban mentality and his film project's fate being tied to resolving both internal and public opinion differences. Even though they have very similar goals and objectives for the film, Skipper and the Cuban film crew have different ideological and marketing perspectives. (Those differences would ultimately cause the Cubans to confiscate the footage and shut down the film project.)

I had every intention of resting a bit and then going out later to relax and hear some music. There was plenty going on in town, especially with the Cuba Disco awards going on. But, alas, I went to lie down on my bed and it was all over. I guess I needed the long rest that I took.

Saturday, 12 noon, back at the apartment.

After I wrote the last entry, I got up, did a little bit of yoga and took a walk down to the Hotel Cohiba to use the internet to check my email. It was a pleasant, 30-minute walk through the immediate neighborhood and along the

Malecon (the seawall) down to the hotel. Warm and spring-like, a beautiful azure sky over the deep aqua sea, which comes right up to the edge of Havana, the weather was almost idyllic. A few people were fishing from the wall but most were simply out for a morning stroll or out to take care of whatever business.

The people of Havana are good-looking. I don't know how else to put it. They are good-natured, handsome and always clean. Hygiene and neatness appear to be a national obsession. Everyone is always neat and clean. I don't care how poor they are supposed to be, they always have on clean clothes, pressed and neat as a pin. It may be only a tee-shirt and shorts, but they are always freshly washed.

And I still can't get over the women! They are generally so fine and often so sexy. They all have some variation of African butts. And as I noted in my last journal, they most often dress their butts in something tight – tight miniskirts, tight shorts, tights stretch pants, and many times the fabric is striped or patterned for emphasis. As a butt connoisseur, I have to say that the Cuban female's derriere is not as big and round and high seated as those in Ghana, West Africa. The Cuban bottom is low-slung and smaller but definitely round and attractive. And the girls and women know how to use them.

Saturday night/Sunday morning 3:00 AM, back from Jazz Café

Early in the afternoon I took a nap. When I woke up, Jamiah and members of a rap group were working on beats. I set up the rest of the studio equipment in the living room and got ready to record. During the course of the afternoon Skipper, Siul, our translator, Nayommi, who is a local contact, and the two housekeepers all came in. Food was prepared and everyone ate in shifts.

Jamiah and I spent the afternoon recording a song by Michel, the rapper. We recorded one of his numbers yesterday at the theater and I was impressed with his style. His delivery was smooth and suave and very self-assured. He and Jamiah created a very appropriate groove track for Michel's rap and it flowed in a very hip but unique way, breezy but with substance. The rap we recorded today took most of the afternoon but it was worth it. I even shot some video of him doing his thing in the living room and some shots outside with him messing around with Nayommi as the video chick.

After everyone left, Jamiah and I continued to work on beats and doing preliminary mixes on the songs we recorded over the last two days. I was surprised at how many hours we put in tweaking the sounds and making sure it was all saved. I was especially proud of Jamiah's stamina and commitment.

Later we both went out to nightclubs. For a moment Jamiah thought he might even hang out with me, but he decided he would go to a disco while I went to La Zorro y El Cuevo, a jazz cafe.

When I got to the jazz club, the manager happened to be at the door and recognized me. He greeted me by name and said "Saxy Mellow Moments!" I had given him a copy of my CD the last time I was in Havana and he said he would play it on his weekly jazz radio show. And he did. He said he played several cuts from the CD one Sunday night, beginning with "I Believe I Can Fly." On the air he asked people to phone in if they wanted to hear more. He got 12 calls in five minutes. He thought was a fantastic response and he wants me to come back to the club on Monday to jam with the band that will be playing that night.

Once in the club I saw Liodale and Martinez, the two saxophonists who recorded with me last month. They were performing at the club tonight. I also ran into Eliel, the young percussionist I recorded the last time as well. We all exchanged warm greetings and they seemed happy to see me. I spoke later with Don Pancho, a brilliant shekere player that I met and performed with at Skipper's house in Washington, DC, about two years ago. When the club manager introduced the band of the evening he also introduced me with kind words, saying that I was a great saxophonist, etc. So I really felt like I am getting to know the place and I am beginning to be known in this town.

Monday morning, 6:30 AM, in my bedroom easy chair

Yesterday had been another long day at the production facility in our living room. After getting up at 8:30 yesterday morning, I took a taxi down to the Hotel Cohiba to call home. I walked back along the Malecon toward the apartment. A black Cuban man out walking for his morning exercise joined me and we struck up a conversation in broken English and bits of Spanish.

When I got back to the apartment around 10:00 AM there were two rappers waiting in the living room. Baby, the housekeeper, had let them in. Jamiah was still asleep. I had to rouse him and get him to the drum machine. The two rappers, José Torres Salgado and Reniel Rodriguez, call themselves Union Latina. They spoke no English, so the communication was slow-going. I didn't even know who had sent them, though we got a call last night from a woman who had mentioned Nayommi and said something about rappers wanting to come over and I told her to tell them to be here at 10 AM. It turned out that these two guys were sent by Nayommi, who showed up about 30 minutes later.

After Jamiah worked on a beat for them, we recorded one rap song that came out pretty darn good. They had a loud style that went into a very rapid delivery. It was amazing how they could rap so fast and then duplicate it exactly a second time. We worked on a second piece with them. It was just a short song that they envisioned as an intro for their live shows. That song took us over two hours to complete.

While we worked with Union Latina, Skipper came in with Catherine Murphy, whom he describes as one of the most influential Americans in Cuba. She came to Havana to study for an advanced degree several years ago, when things in Cuba were economically at their roughest. Catherine had developed a plan for urban gardening in Havana and its widespread implementation was responsible for providing food for the people of Havana. Because of this, she is accorded great respect by the government and the grassroots people here.

Catherine was a very pleasant, small white woman with a ready smile. She enjoyed watching and discussing our production here in the apartment studio with the two machines, five headphone sets and wires running all over the place. She also served as our on the spot translator so we could get more done with the rappers. While we took a break for lunch, we talked about the music project and she had good insight into the music and the concerns of the musicians who might participate. Her husband is a classical guitarist and she knows lots of musicians and rappers, so she could be invaluable to us as we continue to expand our recording enterprises here.

We had hoped to go to the beach at 3:00 PM but around that time, Michel, the rapper we recorded yesterday and who was supposed to have arrived that morning at 10:00, called to say that he was finally on the way. We had to forego our trip. Michel arrived at 4:00 with two rapper friends, Alexia and Carlos. We went through the process of Jamiah working on beats for them and then recording the raps. The first guy's rap took two hours because he didn't have it totally together. He had to keep rewriting his words and there was a lot of stopping and starting to get the takes down. His style was kind of a sing-songy reggae-type delivery and because I could not understand what he was saying in Spanish, I couldn't fully appreciate or evaluate his work. I thought he was the weakest of all the rappers we recorded and because I was tired and disappointed about missing going to the beach, I thought that the session was not worth the time and energy it was taking.

We then worked on a rap with Michel and his other friend. It turned out much better. Michel is just bad! His style is so smooth, different, confident and distinctive. This second song we cut that afternoon made it all worth it.

Jamiah and I have decided that we could live here. If we spoke Spanish it would be a definite possibility. We really love the people and the sights and the music and the women and the food and the friendliness and the rappers and the dancers, et al. I don't know if everyone would find this place as endearing. Some might see the old buildings and old cars as shabby and shoddy. I have come to see them as quaint and charming. Some might see this economy as a result of the shortcomings of the communist system. I believe that any system is only as good as the people in it and its relationship to the world economy. Is Cuba a Third World country with an outmoded government? Or is it a potential First World country locked into a Third World position by a dominant neighbor? All I know is that if I could have a home internet hook-up and a satellite dish for sports and news here, I could make it my home, or at least one of my home bases. I don't need shiny new cars or strip malls or fancy shopping centers or fast food to be happy. My morning yoga meditation this morning revealed that I need to give my all to every task, to be the silence, and to give every person their due so that they can be all they can be also. I could do that in Cuba or anywhere really.

Tuesday morning, 8:15 AM; a late awakening.

Yesterday was a day of meetings and planning, listening to our recordings and learning more about the music, the machines and the artists. We actually didn't record anything. But we got some things accomplished.

After yesterday's yoga, I had to take my shower out of a bucket of warm water because the hot water heater in the apartment was out-of-order. Skipper came to our apartment to drop off a small stereo system with a CD player and cassette deck. This was a needed addition to our little studio setup. Now we can listen to the recordings through speakers without having to use headphones. We can also make cassette dubs of the music for the rappers and musicians so they can have copies of their respective works.

I went to the Hotel Cohiba for my internet session where I retrieved email and found out about the basketball playoffs, Tiger Woods winning in Germany and the news of the world. I shopped for some pastries, beer, water and juices. When I got back to our place two of the rappers from yesterday were here with blank cassettes in hand. I made copies of their rap songs for them and I also made tape copies of the music tracks without the vocal parts. This means that they can use the tracks as background to perform the raps at live gigs. They were very happy.

Later Skipper and Catherine came back from a series of meetings and Skipper got the good news that all four members of his film crew have been granted visas to go to the U.S. to complete the shooting of his film.

We had a long listening session and meeting with the group Free Hole Negres, one of the most creative and prolific rap groups here. Last month, we recorded Telma, one of their members. Now we were negotiating to do something with the whole group. We listened to a CD they recorded for an Italian producer and then listened to the things that I have recorded. They listened to a lot of Jamiah's beats and picked out some that they could really groove with and we decided to record them next Monday after we return from Santiago de Cuba. It should a great way to end our production schedule and I am excited because they are so talented and creative. In fact, I think they may be too creative and innovative and diverse and insightful and arty to be commercially successful. I hope I am wrong.

After they left, Jamiah continued to work on beats. Skipper and I talked about how diligently Jamiah is working. I think it's a combination of being out of his hood, without the usual distractions and that he is inspired by all these rappers using his beats and praising his work. He's learning and doing more. This is great for his confidence and his proficiency on the machine and it is great for his résumé. Skipper and I solidified our plans to travel tomorrow (today) to Santiago de Cuba.

After that, Jamiah and I took a cab to the Hotel Cohiba so I could once again check email and he could make a call to one of his friends in the States. When we got back to the apartment we had a meeting with Pablo Hererra, an old, but estranged, friend of Skipper's and Catherine's.

In the latest issue *Vibe magazine* Pablo was called "the only rap producer in Cuba." He had come to meet with us to check out what we have been doing and to offer his assistance or even some of his music if we should need it. He also listened to some of the things we have recorded with the rappers, most of whom are friends or clients of his. Most importantly, Pablo took the time to show Jamiah some things on the MPC2000 drum machine. The pointers were most appreciated. When Skipper came, Pablo left; so I guess their estrangement has not quite been reconciled.

Skipper and I went out to dinner. Afterward I went to La Zorro y El Cuevo jazz club to jam with the jazz musicians there. Once again, Liodale and Martinez, the two saxophonists, were playing and I sat in on one song. Boy, my chops are down. I haven't been playing my horns very much over these last several days and weeks. I must get some practice time in on my saxophones so that I will be able to get through my upcoming gigs when I get back to the States. I am a working musician and a producer and a businessman, etc. Unto whom much is given, much is required.

Tuesday afternoon, 3:00 PM

Our plan is to leave on an 8:00 PM flight to Santiago de Cuba de Cuba. We are supposed to be met by a cultural ministry person and then be hosted while we are there. Skipper has a friend, Eugene Geoffrey, who is in Santiago de Cuba. Geoffrey was educated at Harvard University and is a journalist, a radio deejay and an expert on the folkloric music in the area. He should be invaluable to us this week. Geoffrey said that he will get us access to as many of the best groups in the region as we want. It should be the bomb!

Skipper is scheduled to come back to Havana on Saturday and leave for the States on Sunday morning. Jamiah and I will stay in Santiago de Cuba until Sunday and take a 5:20 PM flight back to Havana. It should be interesting being in Cuba for a couple of days without Skipper around. I plan to record Denis and Swing at the Casa de la Musica late Sunday night, and then record the rap group, Free Hole Negres on Monday evening. Jamiah and I leave for Jamaica at 8:20 AM Tuesday and from there to the U.S. at 5:00 PM. A wild and full week lies ahead.

8:45 PM, On the plane to Santiago de Cuba

Air turbulence on board this old plane makes the flight a bit rough. (Skipper said it was the most turbulent one he's ever been on.) There is a delegation of Americans on board and they're having a loud and raucous time laughing and kidding around. Jamiah is trying to sleep.

Wednesday afternoon, 4:00 PM, Hotel Santiago de Cuba Business Center; waiting to use the internet in order to check my email.

It continues to be an interesting journey sometimes into a very different reality. Last night we got to Santiago de Cuba de Cuba and took a taxi to the Tropico Ville Hotel where arrangements for our stay had been made by the music institution in Havana and ICAP, the Cuban institution that coordinates international relations. These institutions have promised to provide everything we need to record the music in Santiago de Cuba.

It is interesting because the institutional cooperation seems to have come as result of the work we accomplished on the previous visit in Havana, largely without their help, even though their assistance had been promised. Last month the music ministry was supposed to have provided a place for us to record, a producer with access to all the musicians, and any equipment we might need. In fact, all they did was to let us use the Karl Marx Theater for the last three days of our stay. We used our own equipment. We never saw the producer. And all of the musicians we recorded, we contacted ourselves, through friends or by going to the clubs and concerts and recruiting musicians and rappers.

When we came back to Cuba with the demo CD of what we recorded, the institutions were surprised at what we had been able to accomplish; and they were astounded by the quality of the recordings. They had reservations about the inclusion of so much rap music in the project. But this time they pledged to be more supportive and make the best of the music in Santiago de Cuba available to us.

When we arrived at the hotel we thought it was great: nice exterior architecture, very large pool, guarded entranceway, etc. We said "Whoa." We had a letter from ICAP saying that our rooms would be discounted and it was true. Our reservations had been confirmed and our rate would be $21 per night including meals for a two-bedroom suite. We said "Whoa!" again.

(We are still traveling with so much stuff that it is a major production moving it all. Jamiah and I have eight things to manage including: two large flight cases of recording equipment, two suitcases of clothes, my saxophones, my brief case, the camera bag and the fold-up hand truck.) We found out that the room was a fourth floor walk-up and while it did have six beds and two air-conditioners, the refrigerator left a lot to be desired, the bathroom commode had no seat and didn't flush, it had no hot water and everything about the details were old and flawed. It was definitely not five stars. I told Skipper that it was a $21 room.

It was almost 1:00 AM by the time we got settled in. We went down to the poolside and ordered some fried chicken and chips. Then we turned in. I was beat. I slept until 8:00 this morning. A little later we took a cab downtown to the ICAP offices to meet with them and with the music institution director and his staff.

They are all committed to helping us get some music recorded. They assigned us a young lady, Ayler, who speaks some English and that is helpful to say the least. We met with about six or seven people at the music institution. They all said that they will do all they can to make our project successful. I think that they are sincere, but I am not sure about the quality of the music they will provide in terms of its commerciality or usefulness to what we are trying to do internationally. There are both cultural and generational differences.

The officials are around my age, and they do not have their ears open to rap and newer genres. But they have said that they will allow us the freedom to move and choose and experiment.

Ayler took us to the main concert hall in central Santiago de Cuba, Salon des Concertas. It is one of the oldest, if not *the* oldest in Latin America. It is small, with an all-wooden stage and "A" framed ceiling. It has two, nine-foot grand pianos and a large pipe organ. The hall was refurbished about five years ago and the acoustics seem reverberant but quite good. We should be able to get some really good sounding recording done in there. Videotaping could be interesting as well, depending on the music and lighting we get access to. It is wild to think of rappers coming in to perform in the hall, but we've done some pretty wild things on these trips so far, so I imagine that this will just be a continuation of our innovative, experimental journey.

Santiago de Cuba is very different from Havana. Mountains surround the city and its streets are narrow and hilly. Santiago de Cuba has French traditions in its history because many of the French colonialists came here from Haiti after the slave revolts on that Island. Santiago de Cuba seems more rural and its economy a little less inflated than Havana's. The people seem just as friendly so far. People here think that I look Cuban. But then people think I look Jamaican, Ghanaian, Nigerian, etc. I am a Black man. I am an American Black man who could be from anywhere on the planet where Blacks are found.

Thursday 4:00 PM, in a taxi driving to Guantanamo, 45 miles from Santiago de Cuba, Kool & the Gang's Greatest Hits on the car stereo: "It's ladies' Night," "Celebration," "Jungle Boogie," etc.

Yesterday after using the internet at the Hotel Santiago de Cuba, I went back to my hotel. A short time later, the director of the music institute came by to take Skipper and me to a meeting with all the music artists he had lined up for us to record during the rest of this week. So we went back downtown to the concert hall where they were waiting.

There were about dozen or so musicians representing their groups: one rap group, a saxophone quartet, a fusion group, a salsa group and a folkloric group. We discussed the project with them and I, as producer, gave them some information on the recording process and equipment that we would employ. I also talked about my desire to record at least two selections by each group: one documenting one of their own original compositions in the way that they would like to have it presented, and another done in a way that I would deem as innovative and collaborative. I asked them to be flexible and open to innovation and experimentation.

After that meeting, we went around the corner where a folkloric group of bata drummers and dancers were rehearsing. Though the building they were using was old and bare, like a small warehouse, it had a high ceiling, a large floor space and a stage. There was only one hanging lamp over to one side of the dance floor and because the sun had set by this time, the whole scene was very dimly-lit and shadowy. There was a Santeria altar set up on the floor to the right of the stage adding an air of religious authenticity to the place and the proceedings.

We talked with the director about allowing us to come in and videotape the group and asked if they would perform for us right then. They consented to do a number. The drummers struck up and one of the male dancers performed a jerky, spasmodic set of motions, intricate and detailed but energetic and mesmerizing. We agreed to come back and videotape them on Friday afternoon. I am booked to record two of the groups in the concert hall at that same time, but I figure that Jamiah and Skipper will have a great time with this bata group, because the drummers are good and the female dancers are great to look at and fun to watch. Jamiah will be very interested in this group, because he had just taken a bata-drumming lesson that day from a master drummer in Santiago de Cuba.

Friday Morning, 9:00 AM on the balcony of my room at the Hotel Guantanamo.

I am here in Guantanamo after a long day yesterday and I am just a bit behind in my journal keeping so the chronology may get a bit confusing. But I will continue where I left off writing.

After we left the bata group's rehearsal hall we went back to the hotel. In my meeting with the musicians at the concert hall, I made arrangements to go out that night to hear and record the fusion group at the Casa de la Musica club in Santiago de Cuba around 10:00 PM. (Every city in Cuba has a Casa de la Musica club that functions like the official nightclub for the town.)

The work tasks seem to flow into one another in a continuum; and I feel that I am always on the verge of being too tired. I decide that I will use the minidisk recorder and video camera and not take the big recording equipment to the club since I was to have an early start recording in the concert hall the next morning. I think left to my own devices, I would have opted to stay in and rest for more time, if not for the whole evening.

We took a cab back downtown. Jamiah, Skipper and I went to the club and this Casa de la Musica was quite nice with modern interior decorations, a great sound system and a music shop selling cassettes, CDs and other artifacts. Jamiah and Skipper left to go eat and go back to the Hotel, leaving me to do the recording and hang out with the musicians and one of the directors.

Actually the night went well. The group, Okan, was very interesting in that they performed a fusion of Afro-Cuba jazz and Salsa. But the most interesting thing about them was their personnel: four women and two men. The man who is the leader plays the stand-up electric bass and the other man sings and plays the *guido*, a grated, oblong gourd played by scraping it in rhythm. One woman played keyboard, another played the flute and one older woman, who had a voice like Sarah Vaughn and Lady Eka-Ete, sang lead. Most interesting for me was the sister who played percussion, playing both the timbales and conga parts at the same time, and doing them to the max. The group was actually quite entertaining. I recorded their first set and jammed with them on two numbers.

I left the club around 12:30 or 1:00, taking a cab with Luis, the assistant director of the music center. When I got back to the hotel, I found Skipper by the pool talking to his friend Eugene Geoffrey. Geoffrey had been talking to Skipper about going to Guantanamo and beyond, up into the eastern mountains in order to get to the real roots of Cuban music. I went to bed knowing that we had to get up early and start recording at 9:00 AM.

Jamiah and I were ready to go by 8:00 AM. The driver did not show up on time. Geoffrey's driver, who stayed the night in our room, was there, so he took us downtown with all our equipment. To move everything, it takes two vehicles each time we relocate. It is a major production.

We went to the concert hall and Jamiah and I set up the studio equipment. The rappers came in and we got things ready to start recording them. We decided to record two of their raps to the meringué music they had on a CD and another rap that they would do over one of Jamiah's beats. This group's raps were not that hot and doing the raps over their disco-meets-Latin music tracks made them seem even less happening. But they were some great-looking guys! They could be our N'Sync-type boy group. Two of the guys are identical twins and boy, are they handsome. The group performs in a Cabaret show four nights a week and their professionalism showed. They did their first rap over and over again to get it right. It took us a total of over three-and-a-half-hours to do the three rap songs. All in all they weren't bad. In fact they were very different from anything we've recorded so far.

The next group, a saxophone quartet, had been waiting for more than an hour before we got to them. While they warmed up, we reset the stage with the microphones and music stands for them. They had two compositions written by the leader of the group who played soprano sax. The tenor, alto and baritone players were all competent players and very good readers. The compositions were very structured etudes that included some jazz elements, but no improvisations. They too took a lot of time on the first number trying to make it just right. We even tried editing in passages that they replayed until it got to be a little ridiculous with the details the leader was trying to correct. The second number was played and recorded and because Skipper was back from making arrangements for us to go to Guantanamo and said we had to leave, that song only had one overdubbed section.

Just before they broke down their instruments, I had the sax quartet move to an uncluttered part of the stage so Jamiah shoot some video of me playing with them. They struck up one of their bluesy arrangements over which I began to improvise, and that number turned out to be hot! I wish we had gotten that on the digital studio machine, but the video should be very usable.

Before leaving Santiago de Cuba we stopped in at a house with Geoffrey where a meal of shrimp-fried rice, fish and salad had been prepared for us. Geoffrey lectured Jamiah on the effects of the U.S. blockade on the people of Cuba, particularly those here in the eastern region. He said that food is rationed with families receiving only four eggs per person per month and only so much flour, rice, and even cooking oil is in short supply. All while some farmers in the U.S. are producing surpluses of these foodstuffs.

It seems to me that people in general, but white men in particular, can be so wrongheaded and so stubborn. It seems to me that a blockade is a military and political strategy to punish or deprive one's enemy of the arms or technology they might need to make war. It seems that rarely, if ever, should a blockade be used to deprive a civilian population of food and medicines. It is not only inhumane, I think that it is politically wrongheaded to think that you could foster friendship among people who see your country as being responsible for starving their children or letting them suffer because they can't get medicines that you have readily available. But this is the wrongheaded policy the U.S. government has employed for 40 years against the people of Cuba, our neighbors, 90 miles to the south.

Friday night, 1:30 AM; my room at the Grand Hotel.

After the meal we took the hour and 15 minute drive from Santiago de Cuba to Guantanamo. The eastern Cuba countryside is interesting in its tropical greenery with the caballeros working and walking along the roadside. The poverty of the rural area is readily apparent. This is the part of Cuba that bears the brunt of the effects of the U.S. blockade.

This part of Cuba has the highest percentage of Blacks. It is the poorest part. And it is the area where the Cuban revolutions began. This is the area where runaway slaves would come and where French colonial slave owners fled when the slaves in Haiti revolted. Guantanamo is the area in which *son* music, and *changui* music developed, from which modern day salsa music evolved. So coming to this region was significant for us politically, socially, musically and historically. Not many Black Americans have come here to the blackest part of Cuba. Most probably don't know anything about it or even know where it is.

When we got to Guantanamo, we went to the regional cultural institution office where Eugene Geoffrey is a consultant. We were given a tour of the small offices out of which just about all of the arts and cultural activities in the region are coordinated. There are paintings and wall sculptures and some of the works are Afrocentric. We met with Carmen Lamoru, the director, who is a black woman. Geoffrey and Skipper began to explain to her the nature of our project, but after 10 minutes she received a phone call and left to attend a meeting.

We walked down the street to the Casa de la Musica of the town where some drummers and singers were performing outside. We shot some video of the group and after their performance we got them to perform a couple of songs for us again indoors. Jamiah met a little 20-year-old cutie, whose name was Yaumara (pronounced Jah-you-mara). Her name and his name were close enough and they bonded a bit even with the language barrier (but then they did have Geoffrey to translate and egg things on a bit). Jamiah and Yaumara arranged to meet later at the Hotel Guantanamo, where we would be staying for the night.

My laptop battery went dead so I had to stop writing until morning. It is now around 8:30 AM and I am up again with both mine and the computer's batteries recharged, both in amazingly little time considering how run-down we were last night. I am astounding myself with how much stamina and drive I have, often going and going for hours -on-end, barely taking the time to eat or go to the bathroom. I have been just that focused. Jamiah and I were up looking at MTV and talking until after 3:00 AM after the long day that we had yesterday; and I am back at the recharged laptop already this morning. It is Saturday morning and I'll pick up the narrative back where I left off:

Thursday evening around 6:00 PM.
    We went with Geoffrey and his driver to check in at the Hotel Guantanamo. It was a decent place with air-conditioned double rooms with balconies, color televisions with six stations, a pool and hot water for showers. We had made arrangements to meet with a folkloric group at 9:00 PM and a rap group at 10:00 PM so we didn't have a whole lot of time to rest and change before going out. Around 8:30 Yaumara and a girlfriend came and got Jamiah to go to a big outdoor concert that was happening across the street from the hotel. Then they were going to hang out at the disco at the hotel so Jamiah was set for the evening.
    Skipper, Geoffrey and I set out to the home of the leader of a changui music group. We went deep into the back barrios of Guantanamo for this experience. It was pitch dark and we walked along a short, uneven pathway to the house which was like a two-room hut with earthen brick walls, a tile floor, dusty old wooden furniture and one bare lightbulb hanging from the wooden ceiling. The group gathered in the living room where I would record them on minidisk and shoot some video in very low lighting.
    The instrumentation was acoustic guitar, bongos, two singers and a bass marimba (actually a large wooden box with metal blades constructed like a giant *kalimba*, or African thumb piano). The bongo player lit fire to some paper thrown down on the concrete portion of the floor over which he heated the heads of the drums, and in the dim lighting the procedure seemed all the more ritualistic. When they performed, the music sounded like salsa unplugged, very basic and raw, but at the same time the vocals were quite polished and the singers danced together with some choreographed steps.
    We recorded three changui songs until the batteries of the minidisk ran out. (Jamiah had used the minidisk recorder earlier in the day to record his second bata drum lesson back in Santiago de Cuba. We left the re-charger at

the hotel in Santiago de Cuba.) While we were recording the changui group, Carmen Lamoru, the director of the cultural offices, and one of her assistants came to witness the proceedings. I wished that I had had a set of headphones and more battery power so that they all could have heard the minidisk recording. I am sure that it will sound really good though.

The leader of the rap group we were supposed to record came by to say that he had decided not to allow us to record his music without first consulting with his German producer in Havana. We would have loved to have heard them perform their rap music over similar folkloric instrumentation because that surely would have been interesting. But we are getting so much good music that no one missed thing is worth fretting about. My attitude is that we represent an opportunity for any of the groups to be recorded at a quality level and the possibility for wider exposure. We don't have a lot of time for making convincing appeals. When we give the speech about Pastors for Peace, the film and the opportunity, the artists usually readily agree. In the case of this rapper, we didn't even have the time to do that. We let him go after he said he would make a call to Havana and try to get with us in the morning.

We spent another 30 minutes with me interviewing the leader of the changui group on video, with Geoffrey translating. Though the lighting was abysmally low, I think the interview was extremely effective and informative, covering the history of changui, son, salsa, rumba, Yoruba and Congolese roots.

From there the driver made two trips, taking Skipper, the two cultural administrators, Geoffrey and I to a small café restaurant in downtown Guantanamo. The town is a lot smaller than the cities we have been visiting. Its buildings are smaller, only one or two stories, and though the streets are wider and it has its little parks, Guantanamo is clearly rural and economically disadvantaged.

We had a dinner of spaghetti and sandwiches and then stayed at the restaurant talking until well after midnight. Geoffrey has the gift of gab and he is smart. We had lively conversations about art, music, politics, and connections with the history of this region. After dinner we drank rum and beer and I even tried my first Cuban cigar. I loved it! They said I looked like I was El Presidente. Now I know why Cuban cigars are considered the best in the world. The one I smoked was very mild and aromatic. Great!

We went back to the hotel and I went to find Jamiah at the disco. He entertained both ladies all through the night.

When we got up Friday morning, there was no water at the hotel so I couldn't take a much-needed shower. I had to go with just tooth brushing. We had a breakfast of grilled cheese sandwiches, coffee and juice, and then headed downtown to see a folkloric group performing a song and dance show at one of the performance halls. The leader of the changui group from the night before was the director and choreographer, and the lead singer from last night was the star singer of this production. We shot video of the performance, which included Spanish costumes, and elaborate dancing and singing over Cuban drumming. It was quite a show, with commercial potential in a world's fair or theme park sort of way. Very authentic.

After that show, we met again with the Carmen Lamoru, director of the cultural office for the region. Skipper said that he would like her to write a letter inviting me, Jamiah and a couple of members of my group to come back to Guantanamo for cultural exchange. He thought we might also include a health care worker and develop a proposal for a foundation to fund. The director was overjoyed at the prospects. Skipper's opinion was that Black Americans should be connected with this place. Even if it were only a few of us, it could still be quite educational to the people here. The musicians could give lectures and presentations on music and Jamiah could give instruction on the use of sampling drum machines in hip-hop music. The healthcare worker could share information on medical issues.

Guantanamo has a large Black population and it also has a widely diversified one as well. There are a lot of English-speaking people from Jamaica and other Islands. French-speaking people, including Haitians and Creoles, are also plentiful, in addition to the Spanish-speaking community. There are social clubs and institutional groups serving each of these populations.

The people is the area are really into American soul music, because the U.S. Guantanamo Naval Base broadcasts two radio stations that play current R&B and oldies soul music. It was so wild to hear soul music on the taxi radios and at gatherings in the neighborhoods. We even met the president of the local Soul Music Society. During our visit, Geoffrey would issue trivia question challenges about old soul songs. At any given moment he would break out into singing some old soul song. Skipper and I would join in for a street corner doo-wop session. Curtis Mayfield's "Keep On Pushing" became our unofficial theme song. The power of soul!

At 2:00 PM we hired a taxi to take us back to Santiago de Cuba. We were running late, feeling pressed because we were scheduled to start recording a group at 4:00 PM. We still had to move the equipment once we got back to Santiago de Cuba. We grabbed a quick bite to eat and started the drive back. On the way we had a flat tire, but the driver had a spare and the jack; and he got the tire changed in less than 15 minutes. We got back to Santiago de Cuba around 3:30, dashed to the Hotel to pick up all the gear and then we were off to record a rock-and-roll-influenced Latin band playing original songs.

The group was set up at a rooftop nightclub. We had to lug our stuff upstairs and set it up. I had to figure out how to approach the project. I decided to record the rhythm section first, and then overdub the vocals instead of simply recording the whole group live. It was more work for me that way, but in the end I got a better sound. It took me about four hours to record four songs.

During this time I sent Jamiah to video the rehearsal of the bata drummers and dancers. About three hours into my session with the Latin rock fusion group, Skipper came back with the bata drummers and their singers. He wanted me to record them. They had to wait awhile, however, and for a while things got a little tense. The rock group was concerned that it was getting too close to their show time to allow us to record the cultural group. The rock group needed to do a sound check and get the place ready for the doors to open at 9:30 PM. Skipper misunderstood and thought that there was some racism involved, but that proved not to be the case.

When I finally finished recording the rock group we did a quick three-microphone setup for the drummers and vocalists. In short order they played one of their traditional Yoruba chants. Once the chant got going, Skipper asked me to play my soprano sax with them. He directed the music while I wailed away, circular breathing on sax with bata drums and African vocals energetically going on in the foreground. It was a rousing end to the sessions. I was sweaty and exhausted from the long day's travel and recordings. We quickly packed up our things and got out of there, with the rock group's audience lined up on the stairway waiting for the doors to open for the night's concert.

I went back to the hotel to just breathe deeply and try to rest a bit. Luis, the assistant director of the music institute, had asked me to come to his club gig and jam with his band that night. Man, I didn't feel like doing anything, much less playing more music, but the club was literally right around the block from the hotel and I had promised him that I would. I tried to rest a little and looked at ESPN before going to the club.

All too soon it was 11:00 PM and time for me to leave for the club. I had dreaded it a bit, but when I got to the club it was actually all right. It was a long, narrow room with a bar that ran the length of the place. Facing the bar was a continuous curvy row of sofas where the patrons sat. The band was set up on a high platform above and behind the bar. The clientele was mostly white Cubans and European men with Cuban women. The band started by playing some mellow Cuban and Brazilian flavored light jazz instrumentals. Later two cabaret singers, a man and a woman, came onto the floor and they alternately worked the room using a microphone with a long cord. Soon it turned into a party with the band playing salsa and the singers urging people onto the dance floor.

I ended up playing on several songs and the people and I had a good time. I stayed until the set ended and Luis and I left the club and went around the corner to have a late night snack of fried chicken and French-fries. We then said good night and I went to my hotel room. Jamiah was awake. We watched television and talked until 3:00 in the morning.

I awoke around 8:00 AM and realized that I don't have to start recording today's groups until 2:00 PM and I was very happy about that. I got up around 9:00, taking a much needed shower and going out to find internet access and buying phone cards so we could make calls home.

When I got back to the hotel, Jamiah was awake and hungry. We went walking around, looking at paintings and sculptures at art galleries. We ate at a really nice restaurant that Jamiah found a couple of days ago. We had a shrimp and lobster paella and fresh shrimp fried in butter and garlic. Man oh man, that meal tasted as good as it sounds. It costed us $20 but it was well worth it! We topped it off by sharing my second Cuban cigar.

This afternoon we recorded Okan, the group with four ladies and two gentlemen that I jammed with a couple of nights ago at Casa de la Musica. I decided to go with recording the rhythm section first and then overdubbing the vocals. I recorded the keyboards, electric upright bass and percussionist with them using headphones. Then we recorded the flute, followed by the vocals. The recording process went slowly because the leader wanted to get everything perfect before proceeding to overdubbing. I finally forced the issue because we were running out of time before the next group was to be recorded. It took us three hours, but we did get two complete songs recorded. They were satisfied.

The last group to be recorded was Folkloyuma, a fantastic, long-established folkloric group consisting of about ten drummers and singers. They were dressed in uniform costumes, white with a blue floral pattern, and they were super bad! I got them set up really quickly and in one hour we recorded two long percussion and chant pieces. Skipper came up with the idea to have a jam session with this group along with the vocalist from the Yoruba group we recorded yesterday and me playing soprano sax. I thought that we wouldn't have time to do it but we did, and boy was it a terrific jam! Wild and crazy! Hot and super spicy! I played sax and then went to playing shekere. The singers were "sanging" and chanting and I went back to circular breathing and screaming on sax. It was a fitting ending to the day's recording.

Jamiah, in the meantime, had met some rappers who really wanted to be recorded. They had been waiting with hopes that we would have time to record them at the concert hall too. We ran out of time, but we agreed to try and record them tomorrow before we leave. I am also supposed to meet with the cultural director at 10 in the morning. We have a plane to catch at 5:00 PM. Tomorrow won't be an easy day.

Skipper left for Havana at 9:00 PM tonight. He'll go back to Baltimore tomorrow. Jamiah and I still have two more days' work ahead.

I went back to the club where Luis, the assistant director, was playing again. It was a mistake because I was too tired to enjoy myself. I came back here to type this until 2:00 AM. Jamiah hung out with his rapper friends until 3:00 or 4:00 in the morning.

Sunday evening 5:15 PM, On the small plane flying back to Havana.

It has been pleasurable but hot 90-degree day. In fact the weather in Santiago de Cuba was the hottest we have experienced in Cuba.

I got up around 8:00 AM, did a little yoga, took a shower and went out to make a call home to check on things there. When I got back to the hotel, I had breakfast, woke up Jamiah and went to meet with the director of the music center. His organization had been our host in Santiago de Cuba and I could tell that he was genuinely pleased with how our activities had gone. He and I shared pleasantries and positive delights about the work we had done. I felt that we had made music and made friends. I gave the director one of my

CDs and said that I hoped to return in September. And I do hope that I can.

I went back to the hotel and one of the rappers was in the lobby waiting for me. I should note that Cubans are not allowed to go up into the rooms of the hotels that cater to international travelers. Jamiah had lamented this fact whenever he wanted to bring some newfound friend up to the room. The Cuban government instituted this rule in order to cut down on prostitution and other criminal activity. But in our case, the rule hindered our friendship-making and limited our hospitality.

So I went up and Jamiah and I packed our things one more time, this time to check out of the hotel and go record with the rap group at the house of Linda, the leader of the Latin rock group we had recorded on Friday. By the time we came downstairs, the three members of the rap group we were to record today were in the lobby along with three members of the four-man rap group we recorded on the first day in Santiago de Cuba. They all helped bundle our stuff into and on top of a taxi. Four of us rode to the house. The rest walked.

Linda greeted us warmly and accommodated us wonderfully. She moved furniture around, got power plugs, let us use her stereo components and quieted her dog. Jamiah and I set up our gear yet again including five headphones so people could hear. After getting the equipment ready, Jamiah started working on selecting beats for the group we were recording today while I worked on making cassette dubs for the group we recorded a few days ago.

Jamiah had hung out last night with a couple of the members of the first group, the good-looking guys and set of twins. Jamiah went to the cabaret show that they are in. He said that it was interesting being backstage where 30 or 40 good-looking Cuba women were changing into skimpy, little costumes and going out onto a poolside stage to sing and dance.

Sunday night late, 1:00 AM, in our rented room in Havana.

The rappers we recorded today did two songs. The interesting thing was that if you listened to the two songs, you wouldn't know they were by the same group. One song was a down tempo reggae chant rap and the other was Run DMC meets the year 2000. Another interesting thing is that this group includes two look-alike brothers too. Their raps came out good and we were all pleased.

After making their cassette dubs, Jamiah went to eat with one of the twins and I did rough mixes and dubs of Linda's Latin rock group's three songs. I had asked the taxi driver who took us to Linda's to come back at 3:00 PM to take us to the airport. I did this because I figured we might be pressed for time, but mostly it was because his cab was air conditioned, which was a big asset in the draining heat and humidity.

The driver was on time and I had to breakdown and pack up the equipment without Jamiah's help. The plan was for me to pick him up at the restaurant. After getting Jamiah, I had the taxi take us around Santiago de Cuba to shoot some video shots of me with my sax. Then we went to the airport to take the flight back to Havana. At the Santiago de Cuba airport, I called Carlos and Ronald to arrange to be met at the airport in Havana and for a place to stay.

Ronald met us and we got a room right around the corner from where we usually stay in Havana. The house we're in tonight is right next door to the Mercedes Benz offices and I have a good vibe about the place. Ronald had forgotten about this rooming possibility until Jamiah requested to stay in this neighborhood, because Jamiah is familiar with the area and he has friends who live nearby. I like this place because it is clean and newly renovated. The owner, a little middle-aged man, and his family have done all the work on the place themselves and he says that they have been working on it for 20 years. This says to me: stability, perseverance, family structure, and responsibility. I think that it will be okay for us to stay here and I feel secure about leaving my things here anytime we have to go out.

Jamiah and I are really getting to be at home here in Havana. I asked him if he felt like we would be coming back and he said yes, but he'd like to bring a friend. I said, of course; it is a natural thing to want to bring somebody you know to some place to share the experiences you have. In fact, that's how I got here: Skipper has been coming for several years and he loves to bring friends along to introduce them to Cuba. It does take a little getting used to, but then, every place does. This place is well worth the investment and the learning curve. It is something I would recommend for any progressive, open-minded, politically aware person. I am sure that I would come again. As one of the rappers in Santiago de Cuba said as we were parting company, "One more new friend." And Cuba has made another new friend.

I know some of the streets and sights of Havana. They are a part of my territory now. When we go to the places we go, we are likely to be known and we are certainly comfortable and familiar enough with the city to find a groove and a good vibe.

Monday night, around midnight, on my bed in the rented room in Havana I just got in from recording Free Hole Negres. And it proved to be wild, long, creative, and worth it!

Today I got up around 9:00 AM, did a short yoga session, showered and had breakfast here at the house where we're staying. The breakfast was simple: bread with butter and cheese, fruit, fresh juices and Cuban coffee. Then I got Jamiah up. Once again he had stayed out late. At one point he brought two girls by here, but they didn't stay long, so he went back out again. The man who owns the house here was concerned with all the young people Jamiah was hanging with. He voiced concerns about someone robbing Jamiah or the police harassing him. But I told him that we had stayed in the area before and that Jamiah knew the guys that he was hanging out with. I also thanked the man for sharing his concerns with me. He also warned that there might be some who would take offense if Blacks tried to hang out with white chicks, but then that was not an issue for us.

After breakfast we took a cab around town to shoot some video of me with my sax at Havana tourist spots: the Plaza of the Revolution and the large cemetery know as Necropolis "Cristobal Colon."

We stopped by the Mondo Latino film offices and I picked up some old emails from Ronald, who said that he would talk to me later about arrangements for getting us to the airport tomorrow morning. After stopping by the Hotel Cohiba one last time, we left to go set up and record Free Hole Negres.

We recorded them at the house of Frank, one of their members whose father was a diplomat. It was a very nice place. Frank had cleared out his bedroom to make room for us. It was still very cramped quarters. One by one the members of the group showed up. We finally got started around 6:00 PM. It was a good session, but a little frustrating for me. Once again things took longer than they should have. Lester, the group's producer, started out trying to make the first track perfect before recording the vocals and we wasted a lot of time with that until I just had to take over and move things forward.

In the end we were able to record three songs with them. They were very pleased with their work and they hoped that I was satisfied as well. They were concerned because both Jamiah and I had such long faces throughout the long process. I explained that we were tired, hadn't eaten and had hoped that the session would run from 5:00 to around 9:00 at the latest. In fact we didn't get out of there until after 11:00 PM!

Jamiah was upset because he hadn't eaten and because he was supposed to meet his friends to hang out one more time. On the way back here I had the taxi driver let Jamiah out in front of the Rio Club to look for his two friends. When I got here to the room his two friends were outside waiting for him. After they helped me unload the equipment they went to look for Jamiah. I tried to get Ronald on the phone to make arrangements for the morning and he wasn't home. But a little while later Jamiah came back here with Ronald so everything is working just fine. It is now 1:00 AM. I will pack my clothes and get a little sleep before getting up at 5:30 AM to head for the airport.

There is no place like home!

I woke up at ten minutes to five in the morning; there was no chance that I would oversleep. We waited for Ronald until 6:20 AM and when he didn't come we took a taxi to the airport, arriving there at 6:55 AM for check-in. But the plane to Montego Bay, Jamaica was delayed an hour and forty-five minutes. We had to play the international version of the hurry-up-and-wait game.

We had a stopover in Kingston and another delay there. I slept so soundly on the plane that I thought that we were landing in Montego Bay when we were actually just taking off from Kingston. When we got to Montego Bay it was raining and already 1:30 PM. I decided to stay at the airport instead of going into the town. I had forgotten though that Montego Bay's clocks are set one hour earlier than my watch, so we actually had an extra hour before the plane to Baltimore. Our plane was supposed to leave at 5:00 PM, but it was 40 minutes late.

When we arrived at Baltimore-Washington International airport it was 9:35 and it seemed like it was exactly right on time! We went through immigration and even customs with not so much as a 3 minute delay. The customs inspector asked me a couple of questions about my traveling to Cuba. I showed him my copy of the regulations and my letters from Johns Hopkins University, Hampton University, Richmond Public Schools, the Richmond Jazz Society, etc., all stating that they knew of my travels to Cuba and that they were looking forward to my coming to lecture about my work there. And he said, "Okay, you can go."

And as simple as that we were back in the USA. And I was elated! Maybe things are getting better regarding travel to Cuba?

Now what lies ahead is my work listening to, cataloguing and mixing all the music we have recorded on this trip, then beginning the marketing process. And one day, letting the world hear the sounds of a new revolution.

Folkloyuma group, Santiago de Cuba

⌘⌘⌘

Chapter 20

2000 International Touring, Gigs & Trips

The name of our group always raised questions. What is Juju? What does Oneness of Juju mean? We had always intended the name to pay homage to our African roots. When I went to Nigeria to promote my records, people there would say, "Wow, this is great, an America group playing juju music!" But when they listened to the record, they would say, "This isn't juju music!" They thought we were perpetrating a fraud and trying to capitalize on their music.

Then when I went to Ghana with the group, the promoters there wouldn't even use the word "juju," because it was viewed as a term of black magic. So on the posters and on the radio they would advertise "Plunky & the Oneness of God." For another Ghanaian tribe the name, "Oneness of Juju" always elicited howls of laughter. And when I finally got someone to tell me why, they said it was because in their language "juju" meant the same thing as "do-do." They said our name was "...an amazing universal concept, the oneness of shit!"

So I dropped "juju" and changed the name of the group to Plunky & Oneness. Why have a name that was not a marketing asset here in the U.S. or in Africa? But Europeans had no such aversions to the name and throughout the years when we have toured in Europe we have most often been booked as Plunky & Oneness of Juju!

2001 Plunky & Oneness of Juju UK Tour

I had always wanted to do my own touring in Europe, especially since the tour I had done with Bobby Byrd and Soulciety in 1997. In 2001, Quinton Scott and Strut Records released a compilation of Oneness of Juju music and organized a tour of three cities in the United Kingdom: London, Leeds and Brighton. The tour was short and sweet; but I did get to take some members of the group to England, do some shows and promote the record. We had fun making music and new fans. I shot video and of course kept a journal of the experiences. (See Appendix B "Journal of the 2001 UK Tour")

2002 TRIP TO THE FRENCH RIVIERA FOR MIDEM

In 2002 I went to MIDEM, the largest international music conference, which takes place annually in Cannes on the French Riviera. I went to promote my recordings and to solicit gigs for Oneness of Juju; and while the trip was not demonstrably successful in meeting those objectives, it was quite enlightening and enjoyable. I went to the south of France in January! Tough work, if you can get it. (See Appendix B "Journey to MIDEM 2002 Journal")

2002 TRIP TO RIO

Two hectic weeks after the trip to MIDEM in France, I traveled to the carnival in Rio, Brazil. I went at the behest of Arnim Johnson, a friend from my days at Columbia University, who wanted to have me do the music for a film he was planning to produce in Brazil. The film was never made but what great music, what beautiful people and what an amazing spectacle the carnival was! (See Appendix B, "Journal of Two Weeks to Rio")

2004 OUR PARIS DEBUT

In 2004, we went to Paris to perform at the New Morning, a famous jazz club. The trip was coordinated by Reynald DesChamps, a French ex-patriot living in New York, whom I had met years earlier when he was a record distributor selling my releases in the Northeast and abroad. Working with his French partner, Samy Elbaz, they were able to book us at the club, get lots of press coverage, and arrange for the gig to be filmed and recorded for a "Live In Paris" DVD release. The gig went exceptionally well. The venue was sold out and the fans received us enthusiastically. Here's the way our publicist, Vanessa Carroll, described it:

Plunky & Oneness – Impressive In Their Paris Debut

Paris – Even before the concert began, there was electricity in the air. Monday, November 29, 2004, will long be remembered by members of Plunky & Oneness (of Juju) and their French fans as the date of the band's triumphant debut in Paris. The venue for the band's first Parisian concert was the New Morning, a place that has a history of presenting great jazz artists from Ella Fitzgerald and Dee Bridgewater to Chick Corea, Maceo Parker, Pharoah Sanders, Archie Shepp and too many others to name them all. And according to the promoters, the Monday night concert by Plunky & Oneness (of Juju) was up to the club's high standards.

There was a rush to get choice seats and stage-edge positions when the first 100 hundred patrons who had lined up outside were allowed inside the club 90 minutes before the opening song would be played. When the band did take the stage, a loud roar of approval was let loose as the by-then packed house got a glimpse of colorfully costumed band members with faces painted like African masks. After bandleader J. Plunky Branch joined the ensemble, intoned his opening statements and played an invocation on tenor sax, he launched the band into a 6/8 polyrhythm with his famous words, "These are African rhythms, passed down to us by the ancient spirits..." From that point on the magic of juju was in the house..

For the next two and a half hours the band and audience were joined in spirit celebrating the power of rhythm, energy and improvisation to create joy, peace and inspiration. The music was classic. The sound and lights were ideal. And the band performed wonderfully, reveling in the exhortations of the adoring crowd.

Plunky said, "I always thought it would be special to play in Paris with my band. It took me years to get to do it, but I always thought it would be great when it happened and I wasn't disappointed."

The band was as tight a tick. All night, fabulously funky drummer Corey Burch flailed away in perfect sync with Nigerian percussionist Chief Udoh Essyet. Original and longtime Oneness of Juju bassist Philip Muzi Branch anchored the ensemble and created the shifts from jazz to p-funk, sometimes while singing. Keyboardist Kevin Teasley added tonal colors and took several amazingly nimble solos. But it was the soulful voices that moved the listeners to higher heights. Divas Jacqueline "Lady Eka-Ete" Lewis and keyboardist Tonya Lazenby-Jackson sang alternately like jazz stylists, gospel singers and Funkateers, always invoking the blues and evoking oohs and aahs from the French music connoisseurs.

As director of the energies, bandmaster Plunky was a commanding presence and always fully in control. His saxophones soared, bringing back memories of John Coltrane. His words poked and prodded the intellect. And Plunky was a modern day funk conductor, in the mold of his idols: Fela Kuti, George Clinton and Prince.

The repertoire for the evening traced the history of Plunky & Oneness of Juju in song. Beginning with the 1974 composition "Nia" and proceeding through the 1976 "Space Jungle Funk" the stage was set for beloved vocalist Lady Eka-Ete to sing her classic, "River Luvrite," a song that has been reissued on several compilations since its release some 28 years ago. Her rendition of "Follow Me" was followed by stirring a cappella sax solo, which served as an intro to an intricate arrangement of Gershwin's "Summertime." Each break or transition would be punctuated by loud screams of approval and thunderous applause; and the volume of the audience's responses would only increase as the night wore on.

From the middle of the first of two 75-minute sets on, things got funkier and funkier. The party got more exuberant. The energy reached its zenith when Plunky & Oneness (of Juju) finally played their classic song, "African Rhythms," and Lady Eka-Ete sang the lyrics: "African rhythms make you clap your hands; African rhythms, they make you dance!"

Later Plunky would say, "One of the highlights of my performing career occurred last Monday, at the New Morning club in Paris with me and my band chanting, "Let the rhythms take you to the truth..." and the audience of 500 French people hollering back, "Mother Africa!" What a joyous musical high!"

At the end, even after two encores the audience was screaming for more. But mercifully Plunky released the crowd from the band's spell 'round midnight and sent

them out into the Parisian air floating on memories of a fantastic evening and anticipating Plunky & Oneness of Juju's return to the New Morning.

The whole thing was filmed for French television and a future DVD release. So hopefully the experience can be re-lived soon. In the meantime, the group's compilation double CD, African Rhythms Oneness of Juju 1970-1982, has been reissued by Black Fire Records and distributed all over Europe by Night and Day Distributors of Paris.

Online Review of the "Live In Paris" Double CD:
Plunky & Oneness Of Juju — Live In Paris . . . CD . . . $19.99 List Price: $22.98; Corner Shop, 2006 (2CD); Condition: New Copy.

One of the best recordings we've heard in years from saxophonist Plunky Branch – and one of the few to really capture the glory of his 70s classics with Oneness Of Juju! Given the billing of this set, it's clear that the older soul jazz spirit of Oneness is very strong in the conception of the set – and the live performance features many classics from the group's 70s albums on Black Fire, played here with a good live energy and a strong sense of soul that's way, *way* better than the smoother jazz Plunky has been putting down in recent studio sets. The lineup here is a small combo one – with Tonya Lazenby-Jackson on keyboards and vocals – working alongside Plunky's saxes, plus additional keyboards, bass, and lots of percussion. We'd even go so far as to say that the material here easily stands with the classic and all-too-small Oneness Of Juju catalog from the 70s – and the double-length 2CD set features 22 tracks that include "Up & Down," "Be About The Future," "Follow Me," "River Luvrite," "Space Jungle Luv," "Nia," "Sex Machine," "Kool/One World Music," "World Wide Party," and "Plastic (Is Easy To See Through)."

2006 OUR TOUR DE FRANCE

In 2006, we had our biggest tour of France organized by our French promotion team, Reynald DesChamps and Samy Elbaz. It was the occasion of the release of our "Live In Paris" DVD package, that included a video of our previous show at the New Morning and documentary film about my career. The touring group included Asante, Tonya, Muzi, and Corey Burch on drums and we were a small but tight working ensemble and we had several great performances in France. (See Appendix B, "Journal of Our Tour de France 2006")

2008 DRIVE IT TOUR IN FRANCE

This one-week tour with my band to Paris and Montpelier was gratifying and a result of our efforts to market ourselves in France. Our team had done

Paris drawings by unknown fan in the audience

a really great job of getting us in the press, clubs and on radio. Our music and performances lived up to the hype. (See Appendix B, "Journal of the DRIVE IT tour in France 2008")

2010 A WEEKEND IN PARIS & IVRY

We had a gig in Paris one night and the next night a gig promoted by Sheidia Badja of Soulflower Productions at Le Hanger club in Ivry, France. (See Appendix B, "Journal of a Weekend in Paris 2010")

SOME OF WHAT I LEARNED THIS TIME IN PARIS, 2010
BY J. PLUNKY BRANCH

1. For decades jazz and black musicians have found a haven in Europe, particularly in Paris and other major cities. Having had the opportunity to go perform in London, Paris and other places, I can confirm many of the typical attitudes and responses to the music that other musicians have written about and related over the years. Anecdotes I might share would surely echo what you have probably heard: that European audiences seem to appreciate jazz

Paris drawing by unknown fan in the audience

and black music more than some American ones, that some Black musicians can make a better living in Europe, that some Europeans know a lot more about the music and the musicians, that creative/avant-garde jazz is considered as high art, etc.

When asked why I think there is a greater appreciation for the music in Europe, I usually say that I think Europeans see the music as somewhat exotic because it comes from a faraway place like America or Africa, and it has a different energy and is more improvisational than their European classical music. I also say that when it comes to my own personal experience, in Europe, there is a greater appreciation of music and artists who endure or have some historical impact. I attribute this in part to the fact that Europeans respect things that are "classical" or that last more than a generation, because European culture is an older culture.

There has been a city located where Paris is for over 2,000 years. There are buildings in Europe that are older than the USA. Here in the States there is more of an emphasis on the newest, latest and youngest; whereas over there, there is also an appreciation of artists who have been around longer.

But this time in Paris I learned that some of the French simply love soul and funk music. They love the feel of it and the groove of it. They listen to it and study it and connect with the music's grit, its sophistication and its romanticism. Not just because it is exotic or classic but because the music moves them deeply.

Sheidia, the promoter, publicist and host for our gig at Le Hanger in Ivry, France, is Algerian-French. Like we call ourselves African Americans and others are called Black Africans, she and others from North Africa might call themselves White Africans, and in France they can suffer discrimination and bias. As a result, some of the North Africans from Algeria, Tunisia, and Morocco really relate to the plaintive call of Black American funk and soul music. Sheidia and her family explained that they have always loved funky soul music. The blues, the irony, the emotions and the messages in the music touch these fans in ways similar to Black Americans.

Samy, my agent in France, is a lover of soul music, funk and smooth jazz. He doesn't speak English but will often sing along with the R&B songs on his sound system. He tells me that he "knows" great music because it gives him goose pimples and touches him emotionally. Samy is very excitable, very French. Although his skin has a slightly darker hue and he looks Arabic, he is actually Jewish and his family hails from Tunisia and Algeria. Samy and Sheidia are prone to vehemently disagree about things, but both share a love of Black music and both compete to be supportive of me and my career.

So I learned that contrary to the way I might have seen things as a result of my American perspective, everything is not simply black-and-white. Some white people in France are not European, but North African. Some swarthy-colored, Arab-looking people are Jewish. Some French music lovers are a part of a broader international music loving family. And the music, the business and the enjoyment may cross cultural boundaries, but they do not entirely obliterate the history of differences between peoples. Not yet…

2. Most things are affected by the current international economic downturn; and music and entertainment are no exception. Whereas in the past, Europeans might have paid $200 per person for an evening's entertainment in an intimate jazz club for dinner, drinks and an up-close encounter with a well-known jazz artist; this is becoming rarer. Admission prices to see us at the New Morning jazz club in Paris were 24 Euros ($30) per person. At Le Hanger in Ivry, just outside Paris the admission price was only 10 Euros, but this was a

Paris drawing by unknown fan in the audience

special venue operated by the city government which underwrites the presentations there as cultural experiences for the citizenry. (Recently Maze Featuring Frankie Beverly was booked in Paris at a 1,500 seat venue with ticket prices at 60 euros ($75) and it was a tough sell. Rhianna was to appear in concert at a 6,000 seat venue at a 90 euro ticket price and it sold out in a flash!)

Booking performances in Europe for lesser known U.S. artists is contingent upon the performers having some name recognition and a potential fan base to warrant a promoter's investing the time, effort and money to bring the group over for gigs. Record sales, radio airplay, press coverage and all the other marketing and promotion indicators will help determine the viability of traveling to Europe to perform at festivals, concerts, special events and club dates. Two of the more important economic factors are the costs of air travel and accommodations. Airfare can be up to $1,000 per person and that would be in addition to ground transportation between hotels and venues and between cities. Under the best circumstances a festival or concert tour pro-

moter will pay for all these costs, in addition to a performance fee. However, these days, airfares are sometimes problematic.

As a bandleader, I have to consider doing what many of my jazz and R&B contemporaries have done, and that is to come alone and hire European sidemen for the gigs, thereby saving on airfares and even some hotel and food costs. If the musicians live there, you don't have to pay for them to fly, and they can stay and eat at home.

There are some trade-offs and you have to decide if the money saved is worth the advantages of having your own band members who know your music and the nuances of your show. I have on occasion used European sidemen on gigs in Europe and I have to say that the musicians were talented and well prepared and the shows went extremely well. But, over the long term, I am trying to build the camaraderie and cohesion that comes from a working band. A tight group performing in the organic synchronization that is built over time is like a fine tuned machine or a sports team whose members have a feel for and even anticipate what each other will do in various situations.

After the Friday night show at New Morning a guy came up to me to say how much he loved the show and he said, "I was passing by the club and heard you guys warming up at sound check and I said to myself those are not French guys playing funk like that. So I ran to get my girlfriend and I am so glad we came to your show!" So I guess there are some people who also can hear the difference.

3. Which brings me to another personal perspective on my own music and my performances in other countries: as a songwriter I spend a lot of time and put emphasis on my lyrics, trying to embed and impart multiple layers of meanings in my music. The messages in the songs are almost as important to me as the enjoyment that I hope the music and the live shows give to the audiences. But, now, as I play more international venues, I have to consider the fact that more of my audiences may not speak English! And therefore some of the nuances and subtexts in the lyrics and even in my stage comments may be lost for want of translation.

Of course, all is not lost. I know this because I can feel and hear the excitement and joy from my "foreign" audiences. And I also know this because I myself love lots of music and artists whose lyrics are not in English. I don't understand every word, but I love the music. And I mean I love a lot of music whose lyrics are not in English. Afro-Cuban music; Brazilian samba;

King Sunny Ade, Chief Ebenezer Obey, Dele Abiodun and other Juju musicians of Nigeria; and Youssou N'Dour, Baba Maal of Senegal all move my spirit, and I can't understand much of what their lyrics are saying. And for that matter, there are artists who perform in English that I can barely understand too. I don't understand certain reggae artists or Afro-beat pioneer Fela Kuti or even D'Angelo some of the time; but they still get me off! In many cases the rhythms are so strong that I can't sit still when the music is pumping. I am lifted up, even though I don't always understand the words.

So while I have to consider the languages of my audiences, my shows will still go on. It is a wonder that spoken word artists like Gil Scott-Heron or Jill Scott or the Last Poets or even hip-hop artists have lots of fans in France. But this might be confirmation that the artists and their music have the power to transcend the barriers of language and to create or utilize other levels of communication. Plunky & Oneness must too.

4. European gigs are not sure things. Because international touring can be exciting, fun, career-boosting, lucrative and artistically rewarding, we can sometimes be overly optimistic about the prospects for their success. The level of planning and detailed preparation and paperwork required can lead one to believe that everything is in order, paid for and assured. But it ain't necessarily so. Just because you book the gig, doesn't mean the work will be completed.

I know musicians who have gone on several different types of tours in Europe that didn't pan out the way they anticipated. From touring with gospel musicals to legendary reggae bands, friends of mine have shared the horrors of having gigs canceled or tours cut short and having to have funds wired to get them back home.

On our own recent trip to France, after booking the flights and making all the arrangements for hotels, ground transportation, instruments, interviews and food, the promoter for one of the two gigs threatened to cancel his show at the last minute. He had pre-paid the 50% deposit by bank wire and signed a contract, but because of low advance ticket sales and because the second gig was in close proximity and being marketed at half the price, he was prepared to sacrifice his deposit and cancel the gig. Changing the airline tickets would have cost me $300 each, so coming a day later was not a viable option. I was already absorbing the cost of an extra day of hotel for the group, so I made the decision to do the show at New Morning club for half price. I still sold

Plunky at Le Hanger

CD's which helped offset some of the loss, but the point is, for international gigging, you are much more at risk…

Other lessons I learned: where possible, pay the musicians in lump sums. They can do more with larger payments than with tiny, piecemeal, dribs and drabs that total the same amount. Pay agents, promoters and publicists at the end or only as revenues are received, not in total, out of the advance deposits on the assumption that all will go as planned. Having their pay contingent upon the success of the gigs makes these contracted professionals more likely to be more engaged through to the end of the tour.

5. Airline travel is more like futuristic space travel than old time bus trips. The security and safety concerns added to the economic and technological issues make airline travel complex and wondrous. International travel usually involves more international passengers thereby reminding us that we are planetary inhabitants, not just national ones. We earthlings are truly remarkable in our differences and our sameness. Air travel demonstrates our capacity for working with complex systems of air currents, computers, scheduling logistics,

weather patterns, metallurgy, psychology, germs, temperature extremes, stowage, baggage claims, food, clothing, identification, monitoring, belief systems, and hosts of other paradigms that must interact symbiotically thousands of time per flight.

I like traveling alone because sometimes I can be an almost invisible, silent observer. It can be a meditative, introspective experience. Companions, relatives and loved ones are cool, and when I am traveling by myself, I almost always spend much of the time wishing they could see this or that, or share some remarkable taste or sensation. But there is a secret pleasure in spending some short term periods of solitude, alternating between sitting in waiting areas and in high speed compartments.

I love being in faraway places making music and observing how we make life happen.

Getting there and back is half the fun

⌘⌘⌘

Chapter 21

Martini Kitchen & Bubble Bar – 2007

In my almost half-century of performing in a myriad of venues from classrooms to coliseums, from festivals to museums, from university campuses and churches to conferences and casinos, it is safe to say that the vast majority of my gigs have been in nightclubs. Most of the music I have played and witnessed has been in clubs. In New York, London, Paris, Ghana, Nigeria, Cuba, Rio, DC, Baltimore, New Orleans, San Francisco, and many small cities and towns, I have played clubs, big and small, public and private, swank and swampy, and every type in between. While I have elevated my career by diversifying the types of performances and types of venues, like most other musicians, my gigging and touring has been largely a long series of bar-hopping club dates punctuated by the occasional concert, wedding, festival or cruise.

Whether juke joints or country clubs, these are basically drinking establishments with entertainment. In jazz, blues or dance clubs, patrons get a chance to linger and listen while enjoying live music and their favorite beverage in the company of some like-minded connoisseurs. For the performers, clubs are where they hone their stage craft, test their music and interact with fans, and, oh yeah, make a living. From bawdy houses and stripper joints to lounges and cabarets to high-class emporia, nightclubs are where music is created, advanced, barely noticed or revered.

For me clubs have been my career's life blood. I have spent countless hours in route to, loading equipment into, setting up, playing for hours, breaking down, loading out in the wee hours of the night and traveling from one club to the next. Sometimes with hotel rooms or home stops in between. My touring with Bobby Byrd in Europe and my international gigs with my own groups consisted of fabulous club dates in fabled places. Here in the U.S., occasionally we did a one-night gig in New York at Mikell's or S.O.B.'s or at Ashford and Simpson's Sugar Bar. But by far most of my club experiences happened a lot closer to home. In Richmond at Ivory's, City Lights, Armani's,

Scandals, Ellington's, and in a revolving set of once-per-month dates at Lowell's in Roanoke, VA, Basin Street in Sterling, VA, House of Jazz in Virginia Beach, VA, The Talk of the Town in Durham, NC, McKenzie's in Baltimore, MD and Takoma Station or Blues Alley or Kilimanjaro or Zanzibar or Murph's or later, the Half-Note in DC.

But of all the hundreds of dates and places, my most impactful and rewarding club experiences happened five blocks from my house at the Martini Kitchen & Bubble Bar. It was a long-term club engagement beginning in 2008 and spanning almost six years, for three years of which time Plunky & Oneness performed most every weekend. What a great gig it was! During the peak period I was able to gross around $80,000 per year. That's certainly not pop star money, but it was A-okay for a local gig. It was a steady, reputation enhancing, regular gig that had an effect similar to me having my own club, like B.B. King in Memphis or Al Hirt in New Orleans. It provided an easy answer to the question, "Where can I hear some good live music in Richmond? Or where are you guys playing these days?"

The Martini Kitchen had an upscale décor with a long, well stocked bar, plush couches, arched windows, exposed brick, nice art work, a carpeted stage, a really good sound system, and lighting that set just the right moods. The food was more than decent and the drinks were expensive but ample. And the clientele was urban and adult. And it was five blocks from my house! Imagine, my last set ended at 1:30 AM and I could be home before 2:00! No long, sleepy highway drive in the middle of the night. No gas or tolls. No motel check-in. Just a two minute commute to my own bed.

Oh, the gig had its drawbacks: we had to play three, hour-long sets every night, there were rumors in the community of racial bias, and the Filipino club owner, Edgar Morales, was sometimes a pain to work with, but the Martini Kitchen was great place to hear live music, dance and socialize. I often touted the Martini Kitchen as an asset to the black community in Richmond. It was more than just a club; it was a nice enough place for black politicians, business persons and middle class adults to bring their friends and out-of-town guests. And it was a great place to watch and greet fine young people looking to party.

And it was a place for the musicians to perform, develop a fan base. Edgar had his critics, but one thing for sure: he was committed to presenting live music at his club. Unlike some other local club owners, who booked live bands when they first opened their nightspots and then switched to using mostly deejays to save money once they got consistent weekend crowds. The Martini Kitchen & Bubble Bar featured live music six nights per week for most of its eight years.

Many Richmonders think that Plunky & Oneness was responsible for the club's popularity, but in fact the club, which opened in 2005, was already hot when I started playing there in 2007 initially once per month. I hadn't agreed to a steady club gig in Richmond since the Blues Alley, Ellington's, Ivory's and City Lights 15 or 20 years earlier. I had opted to do fewer club dates and instead play more, larger events and concerts. But over time, Plunky & Oneness did more and more dates at the Martini Kitchen, and by 2008, our band was playing almost every Friday and Saturday night. And the party people would be up in there jamming; shoulder-to-shoulder, rump-to-rump, non-stop; with the band alternating sets with the deejay. Our songs and grooves flowed seamlessly together making medleys of dance music with positive messaging. Winter, spring, summer and fall, we'd be packing them in, the hottest show at the hottest club in town. It was the place to meet and greet and party and groove with the in-crowd and the black and beautiful adults from around the region.

After a while I grew to really love the gig. It was basically a dance club gig, but I made it my challenge to play hard-edged funk and go-go so people could party, and I concentrated on making the music as original and creative as possible so the audience could feel like they were experiencing something special. We did play cover tunes; Richmond dance audiences required it, but I used popular cover songs as intros and bridges to our original songs. I only played the big pop hits and covered well-known funk oldies, never obscure album songs. If I was going to play an obscure song, it might as well be one of my own originals.

As musical director, I programmed my sets of music like a deejay would do it if he had live musicians on his turntables, segueing songs and beats with similar tempos and keys, then shifting abruptly to different ones to boost the energy or change the mood as required to keep the music and momentum flowing. My personal technique of creating song flows and sequences is based not just on beats and tempos but also on the relevancy of titles, wordplay and associated artists, thus creating different potential levels of appreciation for

Plunky on stage with Eke Ete circa 1976

those who happen to "get it" at any given mix moment. For me, it's about using different rhythms, musical mind games, and party experiments to raise levels of consciousness and political awareness while we have fun. The funk can have that kind of power. As an African concept, music is complete when there are instruments, voices and dance. For me music is complete when there is a song, double meaning lyrics or titles (multiple levels of interpretation) and social impact. So in my musicology funk is an African and American music construct.

My band's music was not the only reason the Martini Kitchen became the place to be. The club featured good music by the best local bands all week long, decent food, classy décor, good drinks, good deejays, and the right location with adequate parking. But I have to admit that having Plunky & Oneness performing there regularly increased the status and reputation of the place because we had been around so long and had done so many previous higher profile engagements. Because I continued to work to get publicity in coordination with the club's advertising campaigns, we were constantly in the media. We continued to release CD albums and we produced music videos in the club featuring our audiences, and with me doing things like walking on a flaming bar in the video for my "Plunky on Fire" song. We would be showing the videos on the plasma screen above the stage while we were performing; and the deejay would segue his sets into and out of ours. The whole scene would be a myriad of sound and lights and music, and a crowd of folks on the dance floor right in front of the stage and the whole place would be rocking.

Because we were playing so consistently, the band and our shows got tighter and tighter and I often had the thought that if only I could have taken our Martini Kitchen show on the road, we could be international stars. If I could just get a tour in Europe with that band we would have been set for touring for the rest of my life!

My brother, Muzi, was still holding down the bass after all these years, keeping it simple and funky, plus adding vocals, and supporting me with musical ideas and career encouragement. He and I are a pair of brothers like so many other music siblings that anchor famous groups (i.e., Earth Wind & Fire, the Gap Band, the Whispers, the Heath Brothers, Nat and Cannonball Adderly, et al.), and I certainly couldn't have been as successful without his musical and moral support.

My son, Jamiah "Fire" Branch played electronic percussion using multiple drum machines which added poly-rhythms, hip-hop and go-go grooves and making the group a family affair.

Our lead female vocalist, Charlayne "Chyp" Page Green, one of my favorite singers in the whole world, worked with us for almost every gig at the club. She has a golden, soft, soulful voice and a fantastic musical ear for pitch, improvisation and melody memory. Joining her on vocals was our keyboardist, Tonya Lazenby-Jackson, a big voiced, R&B belter with perfect pitch and the ability to always find the perfect harmony, lead line or song quote or counter melody. They were sometimes joined by Monica Smith, Tonya's best friend, a great soprano singer who passed away in April, 2010, and was replaced by a younger soprano diva, Shonda Davis from North Carolina.

On guitar we started out using local rhythm master, Chris Beasley, who was replaced by Carl Lester El, Jr., one of the most proficient and versatile musicians I have ever met (equally dynamic on guitar, bass and drums). Eventually, we settled on Jose Pomier, a young, accomplished, college educated guitarist of Cuban decent. He plays lyrical Spanish guitar, straight ahead jazz, hard rock, and funky soul. Jose is the handsome and loyal cousin of Miguel Pomier, who played percussion with Plunky & Oneness of Juju 20 years earlier.

Jose Pomier

Muzi Branch

Monica Smith, Plunky and Tonya Lazenby-Jackson

Plunky & Oneness: back row l. to r. Derrick Simmons, Charlayne Chyp Green, Jamiah Fire Branch, Tonya Lazenby-Jackson, Jose Pomier; front row: Muzi and Plunky Branch

Carl Lester El, Jr

Derrick Simmons

The drummer for most of our years at the Martini Kitchen was Derrick Simmons, one of the best, most dynamic and funkiest drummers I have ever had. Derrick has his own group called Chicken Grease and I have often borrowed musicians from his group (Shonda, Brittany Hicks, J. L. Harris, Jeremy Evans and others) to gig with Oneness.

I served as promoter, conductor, master of ceremonies and leader singer/saxophonist in a show I would describe as like seeing Pharoah Sanders jamming with George Clinton and Jill Scott. I wanted the band to be like Kool & the Gang or Maze and I wanted to be a renowned local legend like Chuck Brown and a spiritual icon like Carlos Santana or John Coltrane. I wanted to have political impact if not change the world from my little platform.

But I know we weren't "all that." After all, it was just a funking gig and we had just a few functions. We were the jukebox in the joint. I used the stage as a soapbox to encourage people to use the ballot box (make choices) and hopefully caused somebody to think outside the box.

Each night at the end of the gig there are three relevant questions: Did they dance/have a good time? Did the music heads and/or ancestors smile? Did I give my all?

Postscript:

The Martini Kitchen & Bubble Bar gig didn't last forever. After three and a half years, the demographics of the clientele at the club began to change. The crowds were getting younger and they wanted a younger sound. Eventually, Plunky & Oneness were phased down to only one night per month. In 2014 the Martini Kitchen & Bubble Bar was shuttered due to delinquent taxes in excess of $50,000. After that, even though I had resented being cut back at the club, I did explore the prospect of opening a new club with Edgar as my partner, but alas it did not come to pass…

Links to Videos Shot at the Martini Kitchen & Bubble Bar:

https://www.youtube.com/watch?v=o7kkC1KjPmw

https://www.youtube.com/watch?v=zocxMlaHgfc

⌘⌘⌘

Chapter 22

40th Year Anniversary & Documentary

My Plunky & Oneness 40th Anniversary concert held on April 18, 2014 at the Hippodrome Theater in Richmond, RVA, my hometown, was memorable and spectacular. My current band members, Muzi, Jamiah, Charlayne "Chyp" Green, Derrick Simmons, Jose Pomier, J.L. Harris, Shonda Davis and Tonya Lazenby-Jackson, were joined by several local guest stars, musicians, and emcees, plus an audience of several hundred fans, family and friends in a restored historic theater making for an historic event. It was a reunion, a gala, concert and after-party all rolled into one commemorative occasion.

The proceedings were all recorded and documented, in high definition audio and video, by students and faculty of the Virginia State University Departments of Mass Communication and Music. Not only was the concert recorded, but we had also filmed the planning meetings, rehearsals, interviews and behind-the-scenes activities that took place in the weeks leading up to the event.

40 years is a long time to being doing anything, except growing and changing, evolving and getting better, and going with the flow… My last 45 years have been anything but boring because I have traveled, explored, took risks, loved, lost, profited, and kept re-inventing myself. I have been a musician, singer, songwriter, teacher, arts administrator, manager, producer, cultural ambassador, video editor, publicist, and promoter. In producing and promoting the 40th Anniversary show, I used some of all those skills and experiences to create a successful event.

In some ways reviewing my past 40 years in such detail was like a trip down memory lane that led to me writing this autobiography. It was also like planning my own obituary; though I am committed to doing it all again for my 50th anniversary!

The recap of my past four decades is mostly about the music. My latest album is called Never Too Late, meaning it's never too late to do good; it's never too late to be all you could have been; to be all you dream of; it's never too late to make a new start, to create a clean slate, to be great; it's never too

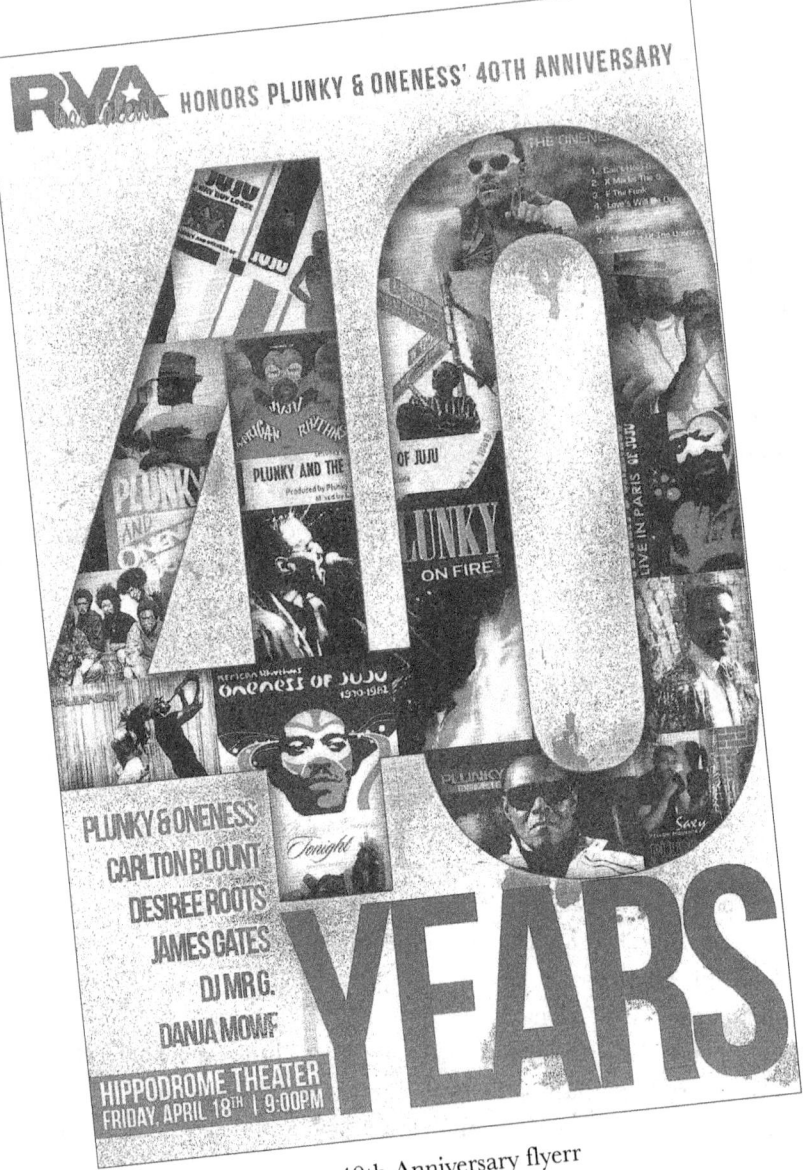

40th Anniversary flyerr

late for time travel. Producing the album and our 40th anniversary event was like time travel: using bits and samples and artifacts from my past to create a new day and new possibilities for the future.

The 40th anniversary show was presented at the Hippodrome Theater, a beautifully restored venue that historically was the place where black stars like Cab Calloway, Duke Ellington and James Brown performed way back in the day. My anniversary show was a complete sell-out and it was the talk of the town. I was quite honored by the way the community and dignitaries came out in support of my band and my career.

Here's the program and the flow of show:

The music records our history and tells the story of how we got here. "Nia" is a Swahili word meaning purpose, and it is the title song of our second album, Juju Chapter Two – Nia, released in 1974 on Strata-East Records. "Nia" is a modal song based on an African 6/8 rhythm. It sounds like something Pharaoh Sanders or McCoy Tyner would have recorded back then. I have been performing "Nia" for 40 years and it is a song that anchors me to my Juju roots, my Afrocentricity and my personal career history. It is always a fitting song for formal concerts and cultural performances.

For this anniversary concert, the song was particularly appropriate because "Nia" would segué from an extended African percussion solo performance by long-time collaborator, Ghanaian master drummer, Okyerema Asante. Because he has performed with world-renowned musicians such as Paul Simon, Fleetwood Mac, Hugh Masekela, Jazz Crusaders, Lonnie Liston Smith and many others, Asante brings gravitas, experience, cultural significance and his own individual musicality to any performance. Asante is visually engaging and audiences love him. "Nia" also benefitted from having accomplished jazz soloist, Dr. Weldon Hill, on piano. Dr. Hill, who performed with me 30 years ago, is currently an administrator at VSU. "Nia" never fails to ground me to my past and anchor me to my purposes, but having these two heavyweight guest stars certainly added significantly to the rendition on this special occasion.

The rest of the guest performers and emcees were all Richmond musicians and personalities who have impacted my career, and I, theirs. Larry Bland, who joined us to sing lead on my song "Everything's Gonna Be Alright," is a beloved gospel choir director who worked with me as an arts administrator and festival director when we were both at the local arts council 35 years ago. Desiree Roots, a musical stage actress and cabaret singer, was a student at

Virginia Union University when I taught there many years ago, was on next and she sang my song "Love's Will Be Done," which she recorded with us in 1994.

Then came soul singer Carlton Blount, who used to perform with us before moving on to sing lead with the Moments and doing radio commercials. Joining him was James Gates, a GRAMMY nominated saxophonist whom I taught in high school. They performed a reggae version of Marvin Gaye's "Let's Get It On."

The emcees were all local celebrities: comedian Micah Bam Bam White; radio and television personality Antoinette Essa; Chairman of VSU Dept. of Mass Communication, Dr. Ishmail Conway; actor J Ron Fleming; African culturist Janine Bell; and actress and granddame of musical theater, Marie Goodman Hunter. All were very professional and salutatory in their comments.

For the second set, we had the seats removed from the dance floor and turned the event into a party with a purpose. Our set list was as follows: "Tonight (Best You Ever Had)," the single from our latest CD, was followed by "Drop," my hit song from 2007. Then we did a medley of original songs over never-ending go-go beats: "Follow Me," "Never Too Late," "Hip Skip & A Jump," " Fire Me Up," "A Swing in Everything," and "Gotta Get Up." The reggae inspired "The Meaning of Life Is Love" segued into "Just Know That I Love You," which led into "Jump Wiggle Wiggle" which got the audience up and dancing the Wobble line dance. We ended the set with a long medley of funk songs and band intros. The audience and the band had a ball and a good time was had by all…

The Virginia State University video production planning committee for the event was led by grad student, Brandon Davis. He worked with a team of students supervised by faculty members of the Department of Mass Communications under the direction of Dr. Ishmail Conway, Chairman of the department. Brandon Davis completed work on Plunky: Never Too Late – The Documentary, the film about my life and the 40th anniversary event. It was working on the event and the documentary that inspired me to write my memoirs.

Link to the Trailer for the NEVER TOO LATE Documentary: https://docs.google.com/file/d/0BxaOmHx63ZJfVTNQRnFWeFFaUlk/edit

40th Anniversary flyerr

Chapter 23

Fire Music: The Last Albums

For me, the 2000s was a decade of meaningful projects: albums, documentary films, and touring. What made it possible for me to complete so much work was "T n T," technology and tenacity. Computers and software allowed me to record in my home studio and my ability to sit there working hour after hour, day after day, for weeks or months, allowed me to make up for any equipment or financial shortages and get the projects finished. Completing projects is always exhilarating, but the production processes are often grueling and draining. I thought each of the last three albums in that decade might be my last, especially 2012 Compilation Box Set that I released in 2010.

By 2011, I could have been finished recording albums, but for the insistence my son, Jamiah. Fire, as he prefers to be called, had come into his own as a hip-hop beat maker and producer. Doing an album together was actually his idea. And upon reflection, I agreed; because why not share my songwriting and techniques with him and at the same time encourage his? Plus, his talent and tracks inspired me. I thought working on albums with him might create a legacy, and also give him a business to build on. Producing albums with Fire confirmed that he has that "T n T" thing going too. He has an uncanny ability to work with tech and he can focus for hours and days and months on the minute details that make for refined, compelling projects.

The Plunky On Fire album released in 2012 was basically my songs and lyrics written and recorded over Fire's tracks; hence the name Plunky On Fire. Fire and I had been working together for years. He began shooting video for me when he was seven. He played electronic percussion with my band in 2001 when he was twenty. So producing the Plunky On Fire album was a logical next step in our continuing father-and-son working relationship. Though we had the assistance of the members of Plunky & Oneness, the project was largely a family affair, with my brother, Muzi, on bass, and my son-in-law, Adolphus "Danja Mowf" Maples, designing the album cover.

Here is the N.A.M.E. Brand Records press release about the album:

Jazz Saxophonist and His Hip-Hop Beat-Making Son Find Common Ground in R&B Music

J. Plunky Branch and his son, J. Fire Branch, have a meeting of the minds and grooves on their Plunky On Fire CD. The album is a collection of original R&B, soul, dance and jazz songs written, arranged and recorded by the duo. Fire produced the instrumental rhythm tracks for the songs which are quirky and mainstream at the same time; and the subject matter of Plunky's lyrics range from partying and sex to love and optimism. Theirs is creative, new music made to accompany what's going on in the club, on the dance floor, in the bedroom, in the arena and in political and personal advancement circles. Plunky On Fire has 14 songs with layers of rhythms, melodies and meanings which makes it a rewarding listening experience for a myriad of tastes.

For almost 40 years J. Plunky Branch has been expanding the boundaries of jazz and Afro-Funk, performing and recording with his groups: Juju, Oneness of Juju, and most recently, Plunky & Oneness. He has released 25 previous albums, performed consistently in his home Mid-Atlantic region of the U.S., toured in Europe and Africa, and made videos and film in Cuba and Brazil. J. Fire Branch has produced over 300 hip-hop instrumental songs, some of which have been used by several rap artists and by television shows such as BET's College Hill.

Eight years ago, Fire joined his father's group, Plunky & Oneness, performing live on electronic percussion and bringing a new hip-hop flavor to the band's funk jazz repertoire. Touring with the band, performing in concerts, at festivals and on jazz cruises broadened Fire's experience and his vision of his father's work. But this was not the first time the two had worked together. In 2001 they went to Cuba twice to work on a documentary film, "Under the Radar – A Survey of Afro-Cuban Music," with Fire as the videographer and Plunky as producer, writer and editor. Since that time, they have also produced 18 music videos.

Perhaps the very first time they did a gig together was for a school assembly program when Fire was in the first grade and they performed a duet of John Coltrane's version of "My Favorite Things" with Plunky on soprano sax and Fire on drums. Throughout his young years Fire played in the school band on sax and drums, even though reluctantly. He always had an uncanny creative ability working with art, video, melody and rhythms. Later Fire came to realize that following in Plunky's musical footsteps would be his career path.

They each have separate studios in their home where Plunky produces funk and jazz music and Fire does hip-hop and rap. A year ago Fire suggested that they should do a recording project together and the Plunky On Fire CD is the result of their months-long collaboration. Plunky says, "It wasn't always all smooth sailing. We're both pretty obstinate about what we like and we're both perfectionists in our own ways. Sometime we argued about some specific things, but we just really wanted the music and the production to be good. In the end I went mostly with his choices, and I am proud of the work we did."

2011 will be a year of taking their music and Plunky & Oneness on the road to

Jamiah Fire Branch

promote their collective musical endeavors. Already planned are dates in their home state of Virginia, Washington, DC, and New York and later in the year a festival tour in France. Fire says, "I hope all my dad's old friends and supporters will like this CD, and at the same time I have to hope we get a lot more new fans for this new soul music, too."

Plunky & Oneness continue to perform regularly in night clubs in the Virginia-DC-MD area, showcasing their live show and providing music for dancing and listening. But Plunky and Fire also foresee a lot more use of multi-media presentations and social media communications to share their creative expressions. Getting their music on screens – televisions, smart phones, computers, pads, movies – is their latest challenge and goal. Producing videos, blogs, documentaries and films is on tap for them in the near future. The release of Plunky On Fire is only their latest beginning.

Never Too Late

In 2014 we released our most recent album, Plunky & Oneness – Never Too Late. It is largely another collaboration between Fire and me, with huge musical contributions from our Oneness band mates.

For this project, Fire went back into my music archives and sampled pieces of some of my older recordings and then he sliced and diced the audio pieces and added new hip-hop beats to create historic-futuristic tracks. I wrote new lyrics and Charlayne Chyp Green helped me create new melodies and vocal

Jamiah's first gig: drumming with Plunky in kindergarten

Jamiah shooting video at a young age

parts. Muzi, José Pomier and J. L. Harris provided the bottom, middle rhythms and jazzy chords.

Here is an excerpt of the N.A.M.E. Brand Records press release about the record:

> Never Too Late, the new album by Afro-funk, jazz veteran, J. Plunky Branch, and his group Plunky & Oneness, bridges genres and generations. The ambitious 16-song collection includes neo-soul, nu-jazz, and hip-hop songs about love, wisdom and purposeful partying. With Never Too Late, Plunky & Oneness prove that eclecticism is no vice and variety can be its own reward.
>
> Produced by Plunky and his talented son, J. "Fire" Branch, Never Too Late is a collage of musical cross references and transmutations. The album begins with neo soul love songs, and it ends with go-go and funk. But, it is the meaningful message music in the middle that is the hip-hop jazz, heart and soul of the album. This is cutting edge stuff produced by Fire sampling Plunky's songs from the 1970s, 80s and 90s and dubbing in new live performances and looped beats. This is father and son using past and present techniques to create future music.
>
> NEVER TOO LATE album clips video:
> https://www.youtube.com/watch?v=3n4cv8e7eGc

- We released our version of John Legend's "Tonight (Best You Ever Had)" as a single. Tonight (Best You Ever had) video:
  https://www.youtube.com/watch?v=qz-RVzcqvuw&feature=youtu.be

Tonight (Best You Ever had) Live version video:
https://www.youtube.com/watch?v=NCyCJLyQRE0&feature=youtu.be

Then we followed up with a second single from the album. DC's DJ Dynamight produced five go-go remixes of the title song, "Never Too Late." I also produced several music videos of songs on the album in order to keep it active on social media and keep it on people's minds.

NEVER TOO LATE single video:
https://www.youtube.com/watch?v=boJkmqDdkGY&list=UUhE3D7aT9gh Uc16NdfWdxKw

⌘⌘⌘

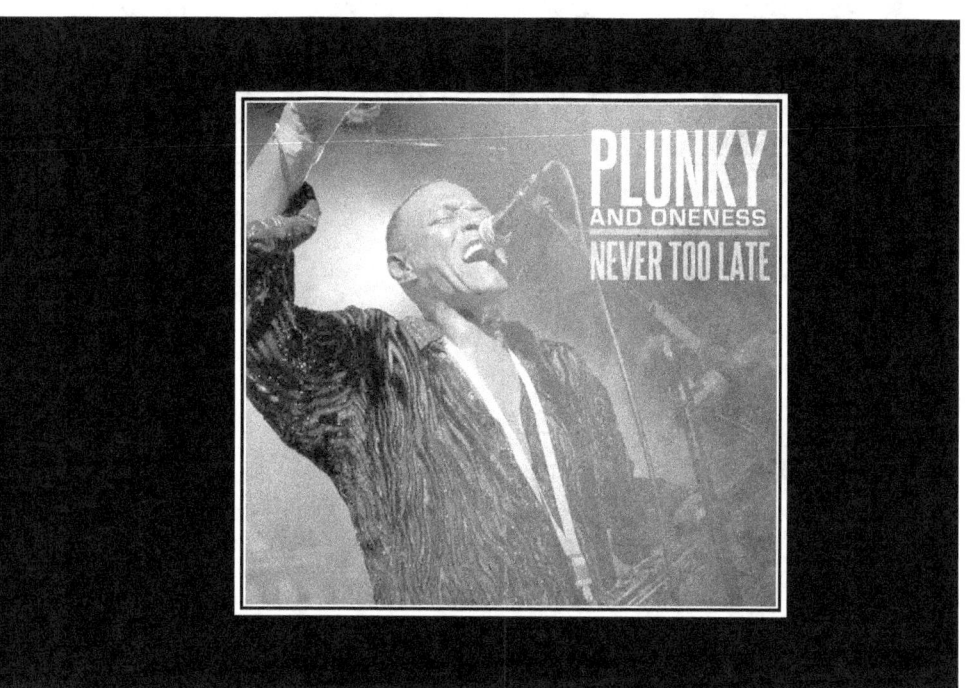

Remix jacket cover

Chapter 24

The Epilogue
Full Circles and Bright Moments

The seasons change/ for the 200th time/round and round/
the learning goes

– Plunky Haiku

By now, you know I have had several phases and re-invented versions of myself in terms of occupations and aspirations: student, chemist, dropout, musician, businessman, arts activist, producer, songwriter, filmmaker, teacher, international touring artist, and several other things that I care or dare not to mention. Some folks have been in more than one of these chapters, or they re-cycled back into my sphere at widely separated times. Family and friends, business associates and lovers (whom, the importance, and the number of which could be another book!), are interwoven in the fabric of my life in patterns of completed and incomplete concentric cycles revolving around me.

Obviously, my mother was there from the beginning and bridged just about every one of my evolutionary stages. She served as a guiding beacon to homeward landing. In April 2011, when she died at the age of 84, she completed the circle of her own life and a cycle in mine that began with the bond formed between us before I was born. In the months of her declining health, my brothers and I took care of her, and she taught us so many lessons about aging, faith, family, love and death. In her final days she became dependent upon us just as we had been so dependent of her in our earliest months.

Though he didn't approve of some of the career choices I made, and rarely was he very demonstrative with his support, my father was also there for me through all my cycles. My brothers were too. Muzi, my youngest brother, always looked up to me, as a kid, and later he completed his master's degree as a visual artist. He joined my band, co-wrote songs, painted my album cov-

Plunky and his mother

Plunky's wife with his mother

Plunky circa 1975

Fire, Plunky & Muzi

ers and became an arts administrator, all the while being on just about every gig and tour with Oneness. My other brother, Khari, as our road manager, business partner, promoter, and member of the boards of director for BOTA and RJS, was with us and keeps coming back for more.

Cookie, my wife, represents a circle that began when she, at seven years old, would stop past my back gate with her older brother, in route to their grandma's house three blocks away at 2218 Rosewood Avenue. (My grandmother lived on the next block at 2304 Rosewood.) My mother was Cookie's second grade teacher. Then 12 years later, when I was living in NYC and Cookie lived in Philly, we would re-meet; and later move back to Richmond, marry, have kids and live in what was once her grandma's house on Rosewood Avenue, where we still live today, just three blocks from my childhood home.

My daughter Kaila married Adolphus "Danja Mowf" Maples, Jr. I dated his mother once and hung out with his father in high school, and later his father would perform in my band, Oneness of Juju. My son-in-law is a musician, producer, deejay, rapper, graphic designer and computer whiz who has designed album covers, produced tracks and performed with me. In 2006 we co-wrote and produced my biggest hit record, "Drop." So Kaila married a musician like her mother did, and that musician's father played with me, Kaila's father. And Kaila's husband made a record with me, like his father did. Now I have grandsons. Full circles.

My son, Jamiah "Fire" Branch, represents a couple of my life cycles all by himself. He's my son, follows in too many of my footsteps, and surpasses my music and production skills. He still has to overcome his insecurities, be more disciplined and persevere, and then he will be a creative wonder. It is up to him to solidify my legacy by producing and establishing his own.

Drummer and saxophonist Ricky Cokes is son of Ronnie Cokes, who was the drummer with my group for over 10 years. He and Jamiah grew up together at our rehearsals and gigs and now Jamiah plays neo-soul and funk in Ricky's group, High Definition. Carl Lester's son, Corey, and Chyp's daughter, Kala, are both young, dynamic singer-songwriters. Corey is quite the performer, singing, dancing, rapping and doing it on his own and with his dad's band. José Pomier, who plays guitar with me now, is the young cousin of Miguel Pomier, my percussionist from 20 years ago. Even more recently Miguel's daughter, Kaila Valdez, has been singing with Plunky & Oneness. And yes, he named his daughter after my daughter, Kaila. All those are examples of talented next generational full circles.

Recently, In May, 2015, I was in DC on my way to the Howard Theater to see Nigerian Afro-Beat saxophonist, Lagbaja, when I ran into Jamal Gray, the son of my old partner, Jimmy Gray. I was overjoyed to see how Jamal had matured. And a few days later we exchanged emails wherein Jamal informed me that he considered himself to be the second generation of Black Fire and that his current creative endeavor was the seven-piece, hip-hop jazz group Nag Champa. Jamal is using sampling technology and infusing the group's music with Afro-beat, go-go, Latin and world music. I checked out a video of his group performing live and was quite impressed with their cutting-edge music. I told Jamal that Jamiah was doing related things, performing and producing with me, and Jamal wrote back, "…If I am not mistaken, the anniversary of 'African Rhythms' is coming up in 2016. I have been working on an idea for a project called Suns of Juju, which would show the bridge between the music you were making in that era with the sounds of today. To contextualize that, we could focus on the creative paths that both myself and Jamiah have taken and how we are working to extend the lineage."

That would be yet another major musical full circle…

Lew Harrison was my oldest friend. We met in 1949, when we were two years old. (Our parents were friends and may have been distant relatives.) In 1959, he would be the one who broke the news to me that my seventh grade girlfriend was unfaithful to me with two of my other classmates. In 1969, Lew would come and interact with me and my friends in San Francisco; then he went on to hitchhike around Mexico and Central America. In 1973, when I moved back to NYC, Lew was there becoming a theater set and lighting designer, working at the New Federal Theater and the Negro Ensemble Company which was managed by a classmate of mine from Columbia University. Lew would move back to Richmond and be there to house me and my band in his home in 1974. By 1977, he and I had turned his house into an art gallery. We started out together in Richmond; then we were together in San Francisco, in New York, and back in Richmond, fostering neighborhood arts programs.

In November of 1994, lying comatose in his hospital room, from a debilitating illness, Lew is not supposed to be able to hear his mother discussing with the doctor who should be called if Lew doesn't make it through the night. Lew's had been a long, painful decline. And his mother says, "Call Plunky, because I would rather get the call from him." I am at Lew's bedside on the other side of the room, literally thinking they shouldn't be having that conversation in Lew's presence; and I say to his mom, sister and the doctor, "You won't have to make that call. He has passed!" Holding his hand, I had watched Lew take his last breath. Precisely at a cycle completing moment.

Jackie Peters was the girl I met at the all-city band when I was in the eighth grade. She would be my tenth grade girlfriend and in the 11th grade I was briefly in her band, Jackie and the Citations. I recruited her to go to Barnard College while I was at Columbia and from there she went on to UCLA to study Ethnomusicology and African music, while I was in San Francisco actively practicing the same. Jackie went on to do consulting work with the National Endowment for the Arts (NEA) Folk Arts Program, as I did with the

NEA Inter-Arts Program; and she lived in DC during my Black Fire Records days. Over the years Jackie booked me for engagements at the National Black Arts Festival in Atlanta and other gigs. Jackie was engaged to Nigeria juju music superstar, King Sunny Adé, and she dated blues master, BB King, two of my musical idols.

Kent Parker was my best friend in my freshman year at Columbia. He was a member of my first band, the Soul Syndicate, and a member of both Ndikho & the Natives and Juju. We still remain close, even while separated by space and time. 40 years later he helped with the editing of this, my autobiography.

Arnim Johnson went to Columbia and we were great friends in the circle that included Thulani, Ntozake, and several others who would end up for a while in San Francisco. He would get his law degree from University of Chicago and re-settle there in his hometown. Arnim has often returned in my life (if he ever left), to connect me to doing an album with a Chicago poet; to be my legal consultant in musical issues and my fight with Sony Records. Later still he would recruit me to go to Brazil with him to research doing the music for a documentary film.

I met Ray at Columbia in 1967. Later he worked with Sly Stone, and he promoted Bob Marley concerts before the reggae legend was so widely known. It was Ray who gave Juju living quarters when we came to NYC and over the years Ray contributed funds to help me release two or three of my early albums. He became an off-Broadway theater producer and eventually helped to bring the award winning musical, "Fela!" to Broadway. Ray connected me with Cool Groove Press to publish this book.

I met Skipper Bailey in DC in the early seventies when we were involved with several business deals with mutual acquaintances. He is a jazz lover, arts supporter, filmmaker and political activist. Over the past 40 years we have re-connected many times working with Black Fire music events, political activities, art showings, performances, real estate deals, and music productions in New York. In 2001, we went to Cuba to produce our awarding winning documentary film, "Under the Radar – A Survey of Afro-Cuban Music." In

Jamiah Fire Branch on the jazz cruise

My daughter, Kaila, and son-in-law, Adolphus "Danja Mowf" Maples

Lew Harrison's photo
and funeral urn

Rahsaan Roland Kirk
saxaphone phenom

Three Amigos: Skipper Baily
Plunky and Garry White

2014, we worked on the political campaign of Ras Baraka who was running for mayor of Newark, NJ, 40 years after my band worked with his father, Imamu Baraka, at the Spirit House in NewArk. And Skipper and I plan to go back to Cuba to make "Under the Radar II," and complete that circle too. Skipper knows Craig Harris, David Murray, Ntozake Shange, Jimmy Gray, plus most of the people in this chapter, including: Lew, Arnim, Garry, Ray and my family.

Garry White and I have completed so many circles it is dizzying to try to recount them. Garry grew up in Brooklyn and went to college at Hampton Institute in VA. I grew up in Richmond and went to college in NY. But we met in San Francisco. Garry is an insightful musicologist and music lover who collects albums, podcasts, videos and movies of black music. He brags about his early beginnings as an appreciator of jazz, Latin, and funk music. He introduced me to King Sunny Adé's juju and other music of the world, and he has consistently exposed me to new neo-soul and progressive funk. He and I have traveled together internationally numerous times and enjoyed live music together in Africa, the islands, and all over the U.S., having been to more concerts, festivals and nightclubs than we can count. Garry knows and has dealt with so many of the musicians I have interacted with, like Roy Ayers, Hugh Masekela, manager Bob Young and promoter Dennis Armstead, but Garry met them all at different times and through different channels independent of me.

Recently, after knowing each other for over 40 years, Garry and I were having a conversation about music and he mentioned going to the Cheetah Club in NY when he was a teenager and seeing this "big, bad soul group, called the Soul Syndicate, who played funky James Brown stuff. They were on the bill with this group, Johnny Maestro and the Brooklyn Bridge!" At first I thought he was just trying to mess with me, but then I realized that he seriously didn't know that the Soul Syndicate was my band, way back then! We were both astounded by the fact that we had shared music together in the same room years before we ever met. We are still completing a circle that had begun even earlier than we knew.

Rahsaan Roland Kirk was a blind jazz saxophone genius who was renowned for playing two, three, or more horns at once. I met him in San

Francisco in 1971, and he tutored me on circular breathing, a breath control technique that allows a horn player to sustain held notes for remarkably long periods of time. It took me years to master the technique, but now I am an expert at circular breathing. Years later, after his passing, his wife would be an ex-officio member and advisor to the board of directors for the Richmond Jazz Society. That organization which started in my dining room in 1982, uses as its motto and greeting Rahsaan's signature phrase and song title, "Bright Moments!"

And I wish you,… Bright Moments!

⌘⌘⌘

Chapter 25

Lessons Learned / What Works for Me

Art is the result of the desire to share inspirations, and sharing is, itself, a social endeavor.   Plunky

Headline: Local Musician Makes Good: 27 albums, 400 songs, 40 videos, international touring, arts activism, community organizing, three documentary films…

It blows my mind when I think about my making music, and making it an effective business and cultural resource that affects people personally and a community positively. Making music that influences people, not just on my block, but even in cities halfway around the world, is amazing and awesome. Especially since I am an independent, local musician. And music is basically invisible. You can feel it, and it can touch you; but it is like creating something out of nothing. That I have had some modicum of commercial impact with my music is astounding, considering the millions of musicians and others competing for attention, and considering the geographical and governmental borders segmenting the planet's international marketplace. It is no small thing that a lone, small-town person or local group could make contacts, conduct business or do gigs with people in other countries, in other parts of the world. That we could do it, without the benefit of ongoing support of a multi-national corporation, but simply by using creativity, intellect, personal contacts, and a lot of gumption, is remarkable.

One thing I have learned is that you should strive to reach your goals and be willing to go to where there are opportunities and to where your dreams take you. This plays into the archetypical story of the odyssey to one's destiny, or journeying along one's career path.

Kevin Teasley, a former member of Plunky & Oneness in the 1990s, and local musician from Hopewell, VA, left central Virginia for Los Angeles, and against all odds, he found work in a major Hollywood studio, producing music and movie sound scores and performing with major pop music stars like the Jacksons and Jennifer Lopez. Exactly what he said he wanted to do before he left. Guitarist Ras Mel Glover left our group, went to Jamaica in the 1980s, and ended up doing world tours with the Wailers. Kevin & Ras Mel had the guts to pick up and, without any guarantees, go to where their dreams could unfold.

My journeys to Ghana, Nigeria, U.K., France, Germany, Cuba, Brazil and even to NY or California all involved a degree of overcoming apprehensions and obstacles and stepping out on faith. Following your dreams can be viewed as an adventure: sometimes exciting, sometimes mundane, but always worth the investment of time, energy, money and more, if your purpose and goals are set high enough. The idea is to be willing to do whatever and go wherever you have to, to pursue your grand vision of success.

Do all you can to stay healthy. Eat right, exercise regularly, get your rest and stay mentally active. Yoga, tennis and no red meat have worked for me. I have maintained a diet emphasizing fruits, vegetables, fish and fowl and I've have been doing yoga regularly, if not religiously, since my heady, hippie days in San Francisco in the late sixties. These days I am what I call a "chickentarian" and a tennis bum. I used to swim at every chance I could; I kept my swimming trunks, goggles and earplugs with me in my car, so if I was near a pool I could swim laps. It is great exercise, and it is solitary and meditative; but it was not competitive. I replaced swimming with tennis. Now I play tennis more times per week than I play sax. I recently bought a sweatshirt hoodie that says on the front, "I don't always play tennis...oh wait, yes I do." Though I have won several trophies for playing at my age, Tonya, my vocalist, said after coming to see my team play, "You guys aren't playing tennis; you are playing geezer-ball." But, that's okay. At my most recent annual physical examination my doctor said I am more fit at 68 years old than 90% of his patients in their forties. So I am blessed with good genes and I developed good habits and maintain a healthy lifestyle. You should too.

I believe success requires discipline, which I define as doing what you know you should, even when you don't feel like it. You have to have the discipline to do yoga, practice your craft, eat the right foods, and maintain your mental focus, even when you don't feel like it. You have to be willing to sacrifice some momentary pleasures in deference to your longer term goals.

Some forms of progress happen incrementally over time. The benefits of exercising or practicing are not all apparent on the day of the investment of the energy, but over time, things like endurance, muscle memory, increased skill, and ultimate readiness are manifested.

This incremental principle is also useful in tackling large projects like movie scripts or albums or documentaries or life: break them down to manageable pieces. Spike Lee says when he plans to write a 100 page script, the idea of having to do that much work might overwhelm him to the point of not getting started. But instead, he thinks of his task as writing three pages a day, just three pages each day, and in a little over a month the feature-length movie script is written. Just do today's work today. And if you work enough days, you will look up one day, and you will have accomplished all you imagined and more.

I have written more than 400 songs, and that sounds like a lot. But because I have been doing it for 40 years, it comes out to only 10 songs a year, or less than one song per month; which is really not that much. Of course, my creative bursts come in fits and starts. I might write six songs in one month and not write any in the next six months. But the point is, quantity can happen over time. Just do today's work today. Do that, day after day, for days. Don't fret when there are diversions or delays; just get back to your work flow as soon and as often as you can. Go for what you know.

To have success, develop your abilities in T, T & T: talent, technology and tenacity. First of all, if you have talent, work to enlarge it, inform it, nurture it and value it. Develop your craft through study, practice, performance and perseverance.

In the area of technology, learn computer skills to be used for production, marketing, business communication, and recordkeeping. Two areas in which computer expertise can be particularly useful are video production and social media communication. Because much of the marketplace can be accessed via screens, if you are adept at producing video content, and if you are skilled at communicating your views and disseminating your projects, you will be ahead of the game.

Tenacity is discipline almost to a fault. It is the ability or bullheadedness to stick to the work, even in the face of long odds, discouragement, fatigue or failure. It is the ability to work for hours on end, getting lost in the work; having to change course and then doing it some more. Tenacity is born of having the faith or the vanity to believe that you know what you should be doing, and doing it right now. And you don't stop...

Diversify. I diversified my activities and often reinvented myself and my brand focus. Not only did I explore and perform various genres of black music from jazz, R&B, African, soul, Cuban, gospel and reggae, I also pursued multiple markets, different audiences and various settings for my performances. I did commercial gigs in concert halls and nightclubs, arts gigs in museums and galleries, education gigs in schools and universities and international gigs in different countries.

However, too much diversity can be a drawback, especially if some of your particular gigs are in conflict with the images and brands of some of your other gigs. For example, it could be difficult to be seen as a unique and valuable artist for the museum crowd, if you are playing every night at the local juke joint; but it is not impossible if you are creative with your geographical boundaries and advertising metrics. It is also possible to navigate some apparent conflicts of interests, if you can articulate your theoretical and aesthetical justifications for the coexistence of opposing paradigms. The blues can be art, if you can give good aesthetical rationales for it. R&B can be educational or political, if the lyrics contain information and messages. Hip-hop can be cultural, if you can articulate the historical context.

I have at various times taken every gig I could get, and at other times I've been extremely selective (holding out for higher fees or higher profile engagements), depending on my marketing objectives for the particular time period. My bottom line advice is to take your music everywhere you can and book every gig that suits you, every gig that fits your current marketing plan. Be proud; know your history and your purpose. You'll discover that the trials and errors of booking and promoting can be educational, and the experiences enlightening. Every gig can be edifying.

Marketing and management are essential in the music business. Learn those skills or hire them. Running a band requires those skills plus: booking, promotion, bookkeeping, human resource development, counseling, logistics and more. Information is readily available online, in books, and in classes; however, experience may be the best teacher.

You can do much yourself. You can learn to be your own producer, manager, booking agent, legal representative and accountant in time; but you may be better served by hiring people with these skill sets, and learning from them as your consultants, partners or employees. Engaging nationally known producers, managers or booking agents may be difficult, as the most successful people in those fields are in high demand by those who already have thriving careers. You likely will have to have some substantial career accomplishments before you can attract and assemble a top-notch team. But a team you will need, even if, at first, that team is you and a very few close associates.

True story: One day back in the days when there were record stores, I found myself in Tower Records just browsing. Actually, I was aimlessly walking around in the store, literally wondering why I was there, when on the store's sound system, I heard a rap song that used the bassline from one of my records. I was at first stunned. Then I went to the sales counter and asked about the song and I was told it was the latest release by Big Pun, a rapper on the Sony Record label who had just died two weeks before. And I thought, "Wow! I'm gonna get paid!"

In fact that record did use an unauthorized sample of one of my sound recordings released several years earlier. Because the rapper had died suddenly, Sony's producers had rushed to get his record out in order to capitalize on the publicity surrounding the death of the artist. In their haste they had neglected to clear the sample with me, the publisher and owner of the copyright. I threatened to sue the company, and after a lengthy set of negotiations, I was able to receive a substantial settlement from the company. I handled all the copyright issues and negotiations myself. Later, others told me they might have gotten a bigger settlement, but at the time, most of the lawyers I consulted said I knew or understood the parameters of copyrights and royalties as well as, if not better than they. In any event, I knew the business well enough to go head-to-head with Sony's team of lawyers and get what I got, without having to pay a third to an attorney. The moral of the story is there are benefits to learning the business part of entertainment business.

Be open to change. Trends, musical tastes and styles change. Know this and be ready. If possible, anticipate change and be ahead of the curve. I have found that I am most often ahead of my time. My recordings have been rediscovered and achieved some level of critical acclaim years after they were originally released. My music and my views are often vindicated later. I used to say being ahead my time was just as bad as being behind the times. But when I said this to Tom Silverman, who, as president of Tommy Boy Records, has often been out front, pioneering styles before the masses arrived, he said, "No, being ahead of one's time was better, because then you get to be around to say I told you so."

Obviously, the best option is to be right on time, in sync with the current trends and flexible enough to be able to capitalize on pop culture shifts. Be aware of current events and what's going on in the news. Listen and learn about what's happening in other time zones and other countries. Artists are often the drivers of new trains of thought and they are sharers of what other artists are creating.

But having said all this about being on time, don't be afraid to march to your own beat, in your own time signature. Don't be afraid to create your own right time. Only you can be you, and if you're feeling something genuine, you have something important to share. Have a sense of purpose, and share it. Be real. People can often detect insincerity a mile away. If you care about people, they will most often care about you and what you have to say. Any time's the right time for realness.

It's less about where you've been, and more about what you've been doing. It ain't about where you're from; it's about where you're going.

Wherever you find yourself, go hard, be your best, right then and there. You don't have to know if what you do will be good; just know you'll do your best. Whether onstage in an arena in front of 10,000 or in a small club or classroom in front 10, do your best, every time out. That will become habit. Your muscles and your mind will remember that's how you roll, and people will too.

You never know when you'll find yourself back in someplace you've been before. Treat every place like you'll be back. A ghetto is a place where everybody wants to leave and nobody expects they will stay, so they don't take care of the place or each other. Don't ghettoize anyplace you stand; treat it and its people like you'd want yours to be treated. That way, if and when you find yourself back there, people will be glad to see you and treat you with respect.

Work with and within organizations to be more effective and to affect political action. Artists are often introspective loners. Even those who are celebrities and public figures sometimes hide behind personas. Work against your tendency to always create and work alone. Sometimes align yourself with groups and organizations of like-minded folks in order to be stronger advocates for progressive change. There is strength in numbers, in battle and in marketing.

Travel abroad. Often. There are different cultural perspectives out there to be experienced. You can see different views of your home country and different views of who you are when you are looking back at where you come from, when you are somewhere else. When you are abroad talking to people, reading their press, and seeing the effects of America's culture, you will see your country with a broader, more nuanced, point of view.

Record your songs, make videos, document your activities, and retain ownership of your masters. Have a website. Post your videos, photos, reviews, notices and opinions. Build a brand and a following.

Copyright your creations. Contact the Library of Congress Copyright Office. Understand there are two copyrights related to music: a copyright for the composition of the song and a separate copyright for each of the recordings of the song.

Learn about royalties and performance royalty organizations (e.g., BMI, ASCAP, SESAC) and the digital royalty collections organizations (i.e., soundexchange), recording contracts, licensing agreements, streaming revenues, video monetization and all the rest. Affiliate with a performing rights organization (ASCAP, BMI, or SESAC) as a writer and as a publisher. Understand the two basic types of royalties: payments from record companies as percentages of sales, and payments for performances of the song on radio, television, film, live, and other media venues.

In a music group or any collaborative project, first and foremost, define roles and relationships as early in the process as possible. That means decide who produces, publishes, manages, composes, and who owns what. Then get the agreement, release, or contract on paper, and signed by all parties. It is far easier to have these difficult conversations at the front end of a process than at the back end. Think of contracts as pre-nups. It can be tougher to come to settlement agreements after money has been made or after nasty break-ups.

Continue to study the music business. Take classes, attend conferences, consult with entertainment lawyers, intern with producers, read books and publications, etc. Educate yourself as much as possible. It's called show business because the show and talent is only half of it.

Understand a producer is the person who coordinates the creative, technical and business aspects of a project. That means he or she works with the talent, the engineering, and the financing. Unless working for hire, the producer (or executive producer) will often be the owner or part owner of the work.

Decide how your group/business will be organized: corporation, LLC, partnership or sole proprietorship. Many groups start out as partnerships, with the members sharing responsibilities and profits equally. In theory, this equitable sharing seems fair. But in practice, often people have different skills, temperaments, and aspirations. In most social and business settings, the different levels of work warrant different levels of compensation. In music groups, there can be differences in pay for the songwriters, road management, musical directing, booking, contract negotiation, bookkeeping, marketing, public relations, website development, etc. If this work is not equally divided or is contracted out to other service providers, or if the tasks are handled internally by one or a few members, then fair shares or compensation may be more difficult to work out.

Be sure to also develop agreements as to what happens upon dissolution of the group or when individuals leave.

After several years and after a number of situations, I decided that I would be a sole proprietor, leader and music director of my groups, and I would contract with my backing musicians for their professional services. At the end of the tax year I issue the musicians and technicians IRS 1099 tax forms and they pay their own taxes.

In 1955, when Richmond musician, Stu Gardner, played his regular weekend gig at a local black nightclub, he might not have thought he was doing anything extraordinary when he befriended a soldier and occasionally allowed that G.I. to jam with the band. But that G.I. was one William "Bill" Cosby, who, when he got his big show biz break, hired Stu Gardner as his long standing music director for Cosby's shows, including "The Cosby Show," "A Different World," and "Fat Albert."

Stu Gardner, in turn, would often hire Richmond musicians for studio work alongside well-known industry veterans, and I was fortunate enough to get a call from Stu to work on music cues for "The Cosby Show." We, the studio musicians, did not work directly with the cast, so I never did meet Bill Cosby and the other stars of the show. Rather, the TV producers would send the tape of each week's show to Stu, and he and his partner, Art Lisi, would write the short music clips that would be the background and transition music during and between scenes. Stu and Art would write out the parts for all the musicians and we would play the music while watching the scenes.

After a few sessions, I was allowed to improvise my own saxophone parts, so I would be in the control room with the engineers and producers while all the other musicians were out in the studio recording their parts. Then I would go out and record my sax solos over the tracks. It was a wonderful, résumé-enhancing gig that would give me confidence; perhaps too much confidence. I lost the gig when I once was in the control room and gave my opinion and criticism of Stu's funk. I was unceremoniously and discreetly fired on the spot. While it was short-lived, the experience and credit would serve me well for years to come. And I learned two valuable lessons: 1) be confident but not cocky; and 2) know your funk but also know who not to funk with...

Hold fast to your dreams, for without them life is like a broken winged bird that cannot fly. – Langston Hughes

And lastly, build your skills to such a high degree that you and your capabilities become your own credentials. Let your accomplishments be your diploma. Let your works be your testimony.

I do not have a college degree, yet I have taught in schools, lectured at major universities and served on panels with highly educated peers. When Dr. Odell Hobbs, chairman of the music department at Virginia Union University in Richmond, went on sabbatical for a year in Israel, he named me as his replacement to teach his courses, create and direct a jazz ensemble there, and to teach his History of African-American Music course at neighboring Virginia Commonwealth University. As the acting music department chair, I created an exhibition of magnificent African Art that VUU had in storage.

That one year on that job gave me fantastic additions to my résumé, but it came about because I had demonstrated that I could do the work, even though I had no framed sheepskin. My arts administration gigs also added to my credibility.

But not everyone can see your value, even when you do your best. The key is to not let others dissuade you from keeping on striving for the best.

True story: I had played at this club in Durham, NC, once a month for over a year, and we packed the place with adoring, dancing fans every time we were there. One night Asante and I were having friends come to the gig and I asked Sam, the owner of the club, to put three names on the guest list, and he refused. I was incredulous because we had been professional, never late, given good shows, and we had never asked for any complimentary admissions before. Asante was so mad, he refused to perform and stayed outside in the van the whole night. When I went on stage for the first set, in between every song I announced that this would be our last night playing at the club, ever. When I came off-stage, Sam met me in the center of the dance floor fussing and cussing that I didn't have the right to make that kind of announcement. I, of course, argued that as the artist, the stage was mine and whatever I presented was my choice as long as I wasn't breaking any laws, and his recourse was to not have me back again (which I had already proclaimed). In exasperation and with vehemence Sam said this classic line, "…you're just a f-cking musician!" To this day my band members and I still laugh about that moment, one of the few times I blew my cool in public.

Twenty years later, on February 4, 2015, I was honored to be named as one of the 2015 Strong Men & Women in Virginia History in a program sponsored by Dominion Power and the Library of Virginia, celebrating the Outstanding Achievements of African Americans in Virginia History.

Following is the link to my acceptance speech and performance: https://www.youtube.com/watch?v=PEKjv5YiabQ

Link to my project bio page:
http://www.lva.virginia.gov/public/smw/2015/honoree.htm?bio=branch

Here are my acceptance remarks from the dais that night:

>Thank you ladies and gentlemen.

Plunky standing by his 2015 Strong Men and Women in Virginia History display

Plunky with the Strong Men & Women 2015 honorees

As a person who studies history and who has documented the momentous events in my own life, this stands as the crowning achievement of my career. Words cannot fully express how proud I am to be standing here tonight. When I heard I was being recognized as a strong African-American in Virginia history, I was both honored and humbled. I had one of those "I'm not worthy" moments.

But after recently celebrating my 40th anniversary of performing, educating and being an arts activist in my beloved Virginia, I know that my accomplishments are not mine alone. My family, friends and my community are my supporters and my partners, without whom I would not be standing here. And they are certainly worthy. I want to dedicate this recognition to them, especially Cookie, Kaila, Khari, Jamiah, Muzi, the members of Oneness and the Richmond Jazz Society.

Mine is a "local boy makes good" story. A local musician makes good music and takes it to London, Paris, Havana, Rio, and also to Dinwiddie and Dogwood Dell. In some ways I represent local musicians everywhere. And certainly I represent the 101 local musicians who have played with me and allowed me to collaborate with them and have my name out front. I want to say to them, thank you. Thank you for being local and loyal to our art and for giving our location a sound and a vibe that is specific to us.

And I want to say to all the young people who are here and those young musicians and other creative people who will come after me: study, nurture your talent, use the technology of the computer and the internet, and persevere. Believe in yourself and your aspirations. Carry yourself as if your life and your dreams are important. They are.

Everybody do this for me right now. Turn to your neighbor and smile, a big, broad, toothy smile. If you are honest, you'll admit you feel better. Psychologists tell us it is nearly impossible not to be feel better when you smile. Even if the smile is fake, the feeling is real. The mind believes the smile means you should be happy.

COMMONWEALTH of VIRGINIA
Office of the Governor

Terence R. McAuliffe
Governor

February 6, 2015

Mr. James "Plunky" Branch
2218 Rosewood Avenue
Richmond, Virginia 23220

Dear Mr. Branch,

What an honor to be recognized by Strong Men and Women in Virginia History for your outstanding contributions to the arts. I am humbled and impressed by your achievements.

So glad I was able to share in this celebration with you. Congratulations!

Sincerely,

Terence R. McAuliffe

TRM/rfo

Patrick Henry Building • 1111 East Broad Street • Richmond, Virginia 23219
(804) 786-2211 • TTY (800) 828-1120
www.governor.virginia.gov

Governer's letter

So walk proudly and humbly toward your dreams. Get your swag on, even if you have to fake it. Carry yourself with pride, and you'll convince yourself and others you are worthy. Believe you can fly, and if your goals are set high enough, you will soar.

I ended my presentation with a soprano sax rendition of "I Believe I Can Fly" and got a standing ovation.

Not bad for just a "funking" local musician!

The End ....(for now)

Plunky portrait painting
⌘⌘⌘

APPENDICIES

A. Acknowledgements

Special Thanks, Honorable Mentions

Editing consultants: Gary Macbeth, Lisa Walker, Kent Rashid Parker, Jacqui Peters, Kathy Branch, Tej Hazarika, Danita Rountree.

Special Thanks:
Charles Chambliss, Garry White, Skipper Bailey, Ray Gaspard, Dr. Ishmail Conway, Adolphus "Danja Mowf" Maples, Reynald DesChamps, Samy Elbaz, Sheidia Badja, Ndikho Xaba, Okyerema Asante, Virtania Tillery, Jacqueline Lewis, Philip Paris Ford, Dr. Ed Peeks, Dr. Weldon Hill, Franklin Kersey, Kevin Teasley, Arnim Johnson, Nomusa Xaba, Roy Ayers, Quinton Scott, Goetz Buhler, Michael Baisden, Alexis Reeves, Dennis Armstead, Myrrh Cauthern, Tony Green, Janice Langley, Jane Cabarrus, Kathy Dwyer, Trudy Perry, Phyllis Demaurizi, Puffy Mitchell, Lew Harrison, Larry Bland, Marie Goodman Hunter, Jamal Branch, Ashiki Branch, Jerome Gray, Henry Marsh, Dr. Dwight Jones, B.J. Brown, Robert Payne, Janine Bell, Earl Wynn, Steve Branch, Edgar Rosales, the Estate of Jimmy Gray, Mother Popcorn, Dr. Odell Hobbs, Dr. John Jones, Milton Marriott, Rita Langhorne, Jay Lang, Antoinette Essa, Harold Brooks, Patrick Mamou, Millard Watkins, Tom Goldfogle, Juanita Newell, JJ Kane, Jerri Bass, Dennis Harvey, Ayana Conway, Patrice Hutchins, Faye Walker, Tom Silverman, J. Ron Fleming, Brandon Davis, Denny Williams, Frank Sheffield, Faunee, Peggy Baggett, Mary Dukes, Jeremiah Toles, Lee Curtis, Alonzo Bates, Grace Harrison, Cliff Hunt, Akhenaton, Shannon Walton, Victor Benshoff, Bob Yesback, Scott Harlan, Spade, Boyce Green, Bob Dawson, Rick Stanley, Katherine Mahmood, Wayne Clark, Nick Robertson, Shirley Yancy, DJ Dyn-A-Might, DJ Drake, Morris Baxter, Ornette Coleman, Willie Dell, , Steve Branch, Jerome Hughes, Mister G, George "Buster" Booth
    WHUR, WVST, WHOV, WEAA, WCLK, WCVE, WPFW, Radio One, Acid Jazz Records, Eddie Pillar, Giles Peterson, Ninja Tune Records, Strut Records, Sutra Records, Strata-East Records, P-Vine Records, Society Records, Instinct Records, Liaison Records, BK Music, Plan 9 Records,

Stones Throw Records, Sony Records, "Upper Room with Joe Kelley and Gi Dussault" Radio Show, Wheels of Distinction.

Family: Mr. and Mrs. James E. Branch Sr., Kathy Branch, P. Muzi Branch, G. Khari Branch, Jamiah Fire Branch, Kaila Branch

B. JOURNALS OF INTERNATIONAL TOURS

I. Plunky & Oneness of Juju's 2001 UK Tour Journal

Strut Records of London, England released a double CD album entitled Oneness of Juju African Rhythms 1970-1982. The album received extremely favorable reviews from music critics and music lovers. A major part of the marketing plan was a promotional tour for us in the U.K. to re-introduce the band and our live show to the audiences in Britain and to try to interest promoters in Europe to book a more extensive tour of engagements for the group for the next year.

Oneness of Juju was the name of my band from during the early years but for the last 15 years the group has been called Plunky & Oneness. For this tour, the group would consist of me (Plunky Branch) on saxophones; original members Muzi Branch on bass, Asante on percussion and Jackie "Lady Eka-Ete" Lewis as lead vocalist; plus Tonya Lazenby-Jackson on keyboards and my son, Jamiah "Fire" Branch, on electronic percussion. In addition, we would have Londoners, drummer Leo Taylor and guitarist Dave Okumo, as sidemen.

Thursday, October 25, 2001 Speeding down the British motorway from London to Brighton.

Well I said to myself that I wouldn't keep a journal of my travels and experiences on this trip, but I have succumbed to having too many thoughts and too much transit time. So journaling I am.

I like London. It is too big and too congested and too white and too British, but I really like the place. I love the architecture and the neighborhoods. The overcrowded megalopolis has found a way to maintain quaintness and comfort by sectionalizing and institutionalizing reservation and privacy. There are sections of this great city that beg to be walked and browsed and revisited.

It has been a few years since I was last in London and I don't know many of its sections by name. I just know now that I have returned to the city, I remember parts of it that I have walked in the past that I want to see and feel again.

I am here this time with my band, a reconstituted version of a latter-day Oneness of Juju, for a three-date tour consisting of club dates in Brighton, London and Leeds. It is a pretty exciting undertaking that has been a long time coming and just the first part of a long-term plan.

My goal is to headline major tours across Europe and Japan, performing in packed venues creating brand recognition for my band and impacting the entire music industry by creating and mentoring a whole new spectrum of music genres which demonstrate the powerful and positive effects of music and culture, then changing the pace, the health and welfare of the earth's population. I'm on a mission.

African Rhythms Compilation cover and stage backdrop image

In the meantime and along the way I am developing a music entertainment corporation to produce and market music, provide employment to family and friends, and educate Jamiah, my 19 year-old son, about music and entrepreneurship. And I am using my music and business undertakings as a long-term physical and fiscal focus for my own personal spiritual journey.

But while this is being billed as my group's first U.K. Tour, it is actually just a set of three club gigs in three different cities in Great Britain. We play Thursday night in Brighton, Friday in London and Saturday in Leeds.

We left from Washington, DC Dulles airport on Tuesday afternoon, flying on British Airways Flight #216. We left Richmond around 1:00 PM to make it to the airport early enough to get through the increased security. We parked our vehicles in the long-term parking area and spent the time before the flight having a good time in the airport. The flight itself was quite comfortable. The plane was only half full so it meant that each of us could have enough space to stretch out and rest. The food was pretty good and the drinks flowed and we arrived in London none the worst for the wear.

Our flight landed at Heathrow Airport right on time, 6:00 AM, but we had to wait for 20 minutes parked on the tarmac waiting to towed up to the loading area and for stairs to be hooked up to the 747 because the normal debarkation tube wouldn't work properly.

It took another hour to collect our baggage and clear immigration and customs. But when we got through it, Tinku, our tour manager, was right there waiting to load us and all of our luggage in a 15-passenger van and drive us into London. It was rush hour but by London standards the traffic wasn't too bad. It took about 90 minutes for us to drive to and across the city to the Ibis Hotel in Euston Station where we would spend the night.

It was around 10:30 AM before the hotel rooms were ready for us. Quinton Scott, the president of Strut Record Company, came to meet the group and he took me over to BBC Radio One to do a live interview on the morning show. The interview went extremely well. The deejay was friendly, knowledgeable, and into our music. He described Oneness of Juju as "one of the premier Afro-Funk groups of all time!"

On the air we talked about the group's history and the new Strut compilation album release and some personal tidbits. Between playing two or three songs from the compilation we talked about our tour dates, emphasizing the Friday night show at the Jazz Café in London. The deejay even had a phone-in contest giving away CDs and tickets to the Friday night show at the Jazz Café in London. The tickets sales had been going well in the weeks leading up to the show and we hoped this last-minute promotion on a popular radio morning radio show would push the interest and the ticket sales over the top.

After the interview we got back to the hotel in time to head straight to the studio that had been booked for our rehearsal. There we met Dave and Leo, the young musicians who would be the guitarist and drummer for the week. The rehearsal went reasonably well and by the end of the day we felt confident that the music would be more than all right for the shows. We also felt like it had been one long day since leaving Virginia 24 hours previously.

Later we went out to a Chinese restaurant for dinner and eventually got back to the Ibis Hotel around 10:00 PM to get ready for some rest. The band members seemed pretty excited about being in London and having the tour get underway. We were looking forward to the show in Brighton.

The next day, Thursday, we got up, had a continental breakfast in the hotel and loaded the van with the equipment and the baggage. It would be a tight fit with not a lot of luxurious space for lounging. Tinku was our driver. She is originally from Scotland and has lived in London for only one year and has only started driving around the city three months ago. Consequently she does not know all of the ins-and-outs of the crazy traffic patterns.

It took us about an hour to get to the outskirts of London and an extra hour to find the proper throughway to Brighton. Brighton is a coastal city right on the English Channel located about 75 miles south of London. It is a bit of a seaside resort city with lots of art galleries, open park spaces, pubs and a boardwalk which include major stately hotels and a small carnival amusement part. It is a lot less congested than London and many people commute to the big city from Brighton by train.

We arrived in Brighten around 5:00 PM and headed straight for the venue. Driving into the center of town, we saw a Strut poster advertising the tour plastered on a wall along with several others. And that was good to know that we were getting some street level promotion and it was neat seeing our logo and my stylized face on display in this far-off foreign city.

The Corn Exchange is the name of the performance space in an art center complex built in what was once a castle owned by the Prince of Wales. The castle had stables and an indoor riding area for the prince and that indoor riding area is now the Corn Exchange – a 1,000 person capacity performance space/nightclub with hardwood floors, a large black stage, theater lighting, excellent backstage facilities and dressing rooms.

We got the equipment set up and had a good sound check. During the set-up time we got our first glimpse of the big banner which would be our backdrop for the stages on this tour. Strut had prepared a really large, oversized version of the album cover artwork, the stylized painted-up picture of my face. We were excited when we saw it for the first time. Tonya said when it was hoisted into position high over the back of the stage, she was going to salute!

After sound check we went to check in the Travelodge Hotel. Then we went back to the venue to change clothes and prepare to do our first gig of the tour.

By the time the show started we had an audience of maybe one-third of the capacity of the house, but when we began the show everyone in the audience moved forward to stand directly in front of the stage. The sound system was really quite good and the engineer did a laudable job of making the music sound big, luscious and clear. The audience really got into the music and as the show progressed the response of the people was quite enthusiastic.

Everyone danced and appeared to have a great time. We ended the show by leaving Asante onstage doing a drum solo and then we all returned to the stage to do an encore.

Everyone was quite satisfied with the performance and merchandising sales went very well with people buying the new album, tee-shirts, posters and even some old 7-inch 45 rpm singles that I brought along from my own archives. We stayed backstage until about 1:00AM, then loaded the equipment out and went back to the hotel. Tinku and Jamiah went out and got take-out fast food for everyone. And we got to bed late.

The next morning we got up and went back to the venue to pick up a box of the t-shirts and the big banners of the logos for Strut and the backdrop of my big painted up face. There we got a scare when we couldn't find the banners. After looking backstage and phoning the stagehands, we called back to London to discover that Quinton had taken them along with him.

Plunky on tenor with Tonya

Before driving back to London, we took a few moments to drive along the boardwalk and take some photos and of the group on the beach of the English Channel. The waves were impressively large that day. It was windy and very chilly by the sea but Tonya decided to take off her shoes and wade a bit in the English Channel. That lasted about 15 seconds.

We stopped in town and got some KFC for lunch, then got on the road to London.

General notes about this tour: Most of our ground transportation took place in a rented blue standard shift 15-passenger van that carried us, our baggage and our equipment. It was cramped but not altogether uncomfortable. On the highway the van was fine and maneuverable, but in London with its perpetually congested, stop-and-go traffic, the big blue van was cumbersome and tough to drive, especially for Tinku, a small-but-feisty, young Scottish lady.

Also our accommodations were all double occupancy. There were six of us traveling together, which should have been fine, with the two ladies, Tonya and Jackie, rooming together; Muzi paired with Asante and my son, Jamiah, and I. But because Asante snores loudly, Muzi demanded to be my roommate and that forced Jamiah, the man with the least seniority, to have to room with Asante. Most of the time Jamiah would seek alternative accommodations. When we were in London Jamiah would stay at Tinku's apartment, because her roommate was away on tour and that left an empty bed for Jamiah.

When we arrived in London it was 4:00 PM so we went directly to the Jazz Café to set up for sound check. While we loaded in, the ladies went to the Ibis Hotel to check us in.

The Jazz Café is one of the premier jazz clubs in London. It is a trendy 435 person venue with a great sound system, decent lighting, a balcony restaurant, tasty food, three bars, comfortable dressing rooms, and an experienced staff. The club boasts live music seven nights a week and even some matinee activities. The music is diverse and includes jazz, soul, fusion, world music, funk and some of London's best deejays.

The list of artists who play the Jazz Café reads like a who's who of jazz and acid jazz luminaries. The club has been the site that boosted or rejuvenated the careers of many jazzers from the U.S., including Roy Ayers, Lonnie Liston Smith, Terry Callier, Gil Scott-Heron, Maceo Parker and Jon Lucien. The Jazz Café books African music and funk and Latin and Blues and the audience includes old aficionados and new young fans, people who come to listen, those who come to dance and some who just want to be in one of London's hippest night spots

The management of the Jazz Café includes promoters, booking agents and artistic directors who work with other club owners, music critics and festival directors all across Europe and in the U.S. and Japan. In fact, the Jazz Café books larger venues in England and soon the club will have outlets in New York and other major cities. Obviously, to say that the Jazz Café gig was important to us would be a gross understatement!

I was never worried about our performance at the Jazz Café. Everything pointed to a good gig. We played in Brighton the night before in what would amount to a dress rehearsal. At the Jazz Café we took our time and worked with the house sound technician and got a really thorough sound check, after which the sidemen, Leo and Dave, were a lot more comfortable with the repertoire and grooving with us. I felt that the music would be tight. During the sound check we got the word from the club manager that the gig was sold out, so that made us and Tinku and Quinton feel real good about things.

After the sound check we had a delicious dinner at the club and then retired to the dressing room to get ready for the big gig. We decided that I would paint my face like the African style of my face on the album cover and the stage backdrop banner. In the end, Muzi, Jamiah and even Asante went along with wearing the full make-up job as well. Alexis, the photographer for Straight No Chaser magazine, took posed shots of us in the dressing room and then it was time for us to take the stage.

I describe Friday night's gig at the Jazz café in London with a three-word review – "A major triumph!" It really was a phenomenal, complete success – a complete sellout, shoulder to shoulder pumped up crowd, all really into us and the music.

Bravo and Hooray!!!

II. Journey to MIDEM 2002 Journal
January 2002

I had lied to myself or I just didn't really know that I would be this excited about going to Cannes, France, to attend MIDEM, the world's largest international music conference. But by the time I arrived at the Palais Des Festivals conference center in Cannes to register I was really hyped up.

For the last several days before leaving for the conference I spent endless hours in my studio recording and mixing new songs and materials to take to MIDEM. I produced a nine-song CD of jazz-funk saxophone music, a compilation of hip-hop tracks featuring rappers, and I duplicated numerous CD-Rs of various music and video discs. I also copied press materials and collected artifacts to disseminate at the conference to promote my music and my companies.

But when asked if I was excited about going to France, I had told friends that I was fairly unmoved and only moderately eager to go. "Oh, I've done so many things like this over the years, that this will be just another conference." Or so I thought.

But MIDEM at Cannes is all that and a bag of goodies!

For several days I turned my downstairs studio and office into a factory manufacturing CD-Rs, doing recording sessions and mixing music from dawn to sundown and into the nights. I even impressed myself with my discipline, sitting there at the console even though my muscles would tense up and ache.

I kept working even longer than I customarily would as the deadline approached for my departure to France for MIDEM, the international music conference.

My British Airways flight was scheduled to depart from Dulles International Airport in Washington, DC at 6:15 PM on Saturday, January 19th, and by Thursday of that week it looked as if I would have to work in my studio and at my computers all night on Friday just to be able to leave by noon on Saturday to arrive at the airport 100 miles away at least three hours before flight time. Then on Friday came the winter weather advisory and a forecast of snow for Saturday with the heaviest accumulation predicted for the DC area. On Saturday morning when the snow started I decided that even though the weather might be bad enough to delay or even cancel my flight, I would leave my house in Richmond early enough to give myself more time to drive through the snowstorm to get to the airport.

I was traveling with my wife, Cookie. Her trip was my Christmas gift to her and she had been looking forward to it with more anticipation than I.

We did leave early on Saturday. It was snowing hard the whole way there, but we arrived without much delay and soon after we got to the airport it stopped snowing. Despite my anxiety about flight delays, our plane left on time. And we even landed in London a few minutes early. Then we waited for and made the flight from London to Nice, France. During the flights I nodded in and out of sleep, trying to catch up on the rest I had forsaken over the past few days. When I caught glimpses of the French Riviera as we approached the Nice airport, I began to feel the special allure of the region.

We entered the country without any scrutiny from customs and went straight to a *bureau de change* to exchange some dollars for Euros, the new currency for most of Europe. On the plane Cookie and I met Kimberly, a young, black vocalist from California also going to her first MIDEM conference. And at the change window we all met Andy Hussakowsky, a music businessman who claimed to have been associated with Billy Ocean, Buddha Records and several successful music projects over the years. Andy was friendly and talkative and he asked the right sort of questions as he probed for business opportunities.

We took a large bus from the Nice airport to the city of Cannes. The ride was scenic and pleasant. The weather was sunny and comfortable.

When we arrived at the center of Cannes we took a cab to our hotel, which was 15 minutes away. I was concerned about the expense of taking cabs each day between our hotel and the Palais de Festivals where MIDEM takes place. The taxi costs $25 each way. $50 per day for taxis would have made renting a car a viable option. But we found out that there was free shuttle bus service between the hotels and the Palais for MIDEM.

Our hotel was small, clean and fine enough considering we would not be spending a lot of time lounging around there. When we finally got in the room and stretched out across the bed my body felt like it was a relaxed accordion: happy it was not being squeezed for the moment. I could have easily lain there for the rest of the afternoon, but I decided to get up right away and go back downtown to the Palais to register for MIDEM so that I would not have to do that in the morning. MIDEM had actually begun the day before on Saturday.

We took a cab back to the center of Cannes and I went through the registration process and paid my $970 to enter the conference. During the hours that I was inside the conference hall Cookie would spend her time sightseeing and shopping, visiting the cafes, hotels and boutiques. I hoped that she wouldn't be bored or feel neglected over the course of the week.

The number of exhibitors and the layout of the booths and the high-tech displays and the quality of the music and the level of business being conducted make MIDEM impressive and potentially overwhelming. The lights, the colors, the intermingling sounds and the 5,000 attendees combined to bombard the senses. But I felt like the guy in the Circuit City Christmas ad when he gets to the door of the store and then goes running into the aisles leaping and screaming with excitement. I was certainly anything but nonchalant about this conference.

I had read an article in *Billboard Magazine* with the information from about 25 executives who would be attending MIDEM, giving their most memorable deals they had made at previous MIDEMs, what they were hoping to do this year and their advice to first time attendees. They said things like: make appointments before arriving, wear comfortable shoes, don't make any appointments before 11:00 AM, don't drink before 12 noon, try to get at least three hours sleep each night, try to keep focusing on what you what to accomplish, etc. All of their advice was good and right on point for what I encountered.

There was so much going on that one could easily get swept up into the whirlwind of activities and possibilities and forget what the objectives for the week are. I wanted to make licensing deals for my record catalogue in other parts of the world. I also wanted to make deals for my son's rap tracks, my new age music recordings and the Cuban music that I recorded last year. And I wanted to make some contacts for touring and promoting my band's recordings. MIDEM offers the playing field for all this and so much more.

I had the materials and the information but I did not have enough prior commitments or appointments. Quinton Scott of Strut Records of London was supposed to be at the conference and I had planned for him to be my guide and introduce me to a number of his formidable contacts from all over Europe and Australia. But at the last minute his father took ill and Quinton decided not to attend. So I was on my own, having invested a fair amount of money and time to be here and hoping that it would be worth it.

On Sunday afternoon by the time I finished registering, I had missed a conference session on doing business in Japan, but I was in time to make the 5:00 PM session entitled "Maximizing International Exposure for Latin Artists." At this meeting I got a sense of what is going on with Latin music and I gained a greater appreciation of the diversity within this genre. I also feel that there is a market for the Cuban music and specifically the Cuban hip-hop that I have produced. I introduced myself to a couple of the panelists and gave them copies of our Cuban Rap CD.

After that session, I met Cookie outside the Palais and we went to grab a bite to eat at the Upside Down Café across the street from the conference center and then went back to the hotel for some much needed rest. I slept soundly.

The next day, Monday, I got up at 9:00 AM and had a continental breakfast of croissants, juice and tea and then took the 20-minute shuttle bus ride to MIDEM. The ride along the Riviera was as scenic as the postcards you might have seen. Azure waters, sail boats, and the pearly white houses and buildings dotting the coastline with the mountains in the distance. When I got to the conference center I dove right into the whirlwind of activity, passing through the throngs of people and the numerous booths and the kaleidoscope of colorful high tech displays.

I had previously scheduled an appointment with a representative of P-Vine Records, the Japanese company that has licensed several of my early albums. I want to interest them in licensing some of my recent releases and I have recorded some new jazz funk that I want them to consider. Mie Toyama is the director of export sales for the company and I am giving her the sample CDs I have brought for Ken Tsukamoto, the A&R person with whom I have been communicating for the past several months. Mie and I had a cordial meeting for 15 or 20 minutes and then we moved on.

I went to several booths and met a couple of interested contacts. One was Kevin Muto with a company called Star Search, Inc. who was interested in licensing and distributing rap, dance and jazz products for South Korea. The other was Laura Salvaneshi with a company called Halidon, which is interested in licensing Afro-funk material. I was heartened by both those meetings and optimistic that they might like the music that I left with them. I went to use the internet to retrieve and send email correspondence and I wore myself out lugging around the MIDEM bag and my briefcase heavy with my press kits, printed material, CDs and my video camera.

Periodically at appointed times I would meet Cookie outside the front door to coordinate schedules. We met at 1:30 PM and went across the street to another sidewalk café for lunch. The weather was sunny and in the mid-50s and pleasant enough for us to eat outside and watch the stream of people flow past.

At 2:30 PM I dashed back into the conference to attend a session on "Packaging Hip-hop for a Global Economy." I shot some video of this session so that I could share the information with the rap crews in the States, but the session was not only about how the American rappers can be packaged for other markets, but also about how European rappers can be shared in other countries in Europe or brought to the U.S.

Then it was back to the internet café area for more emailing, followed by more booth exploring and videoing the conference. It was all very physically demanding: so much walking, lugging bags and meeting people.

I ran into Dan, a music business friend of a friend in the states. It was purely a chance meeting in front of the Germany music industry pavilion, where at 6:00 PM they were dispensing free Beck's Beer, so a crowd had gathered for drinking and schmoozing.

Dan was friendly and gregarious and he introduced me to his friend who was with a German publishing company. Dan said to me "You're at MIDEM; that means you're no longer an artist, you're a businessman in the center of where the music business happens."

After leaving that meeting, I met Cookie and we went to the Hotel Martinez, one of the three ritzy hotels that serve as the official/unofficial nightlife music and meeting places of MIDEM. We hung out in the bar lounge area where U.K. deejays were spinning records and a French radio station was broadcasting live. After a couple of drinks, I decided I would have a cigar. When I went to the bar to buy one, a young brother approached me and said "you don't have to buy one of those, I have some of these little ones if you'd like to have one."

He had a box of tiny, cigarette-size Cohiba's and gave me a couple of them and we struck up a conversation. His name was Bryant Spry from the Philadelphia Alliance of Music, his production company producing hip-hop artists. He had come to MIDEM looking for a label deal. He, his wife, Cookie and I shared conversation and experiences. I gave him one of the CDs of Jamiah's hip-hop tracks and Bryant said that he would listen to it to see if he could use Jamiah as a producer of tracks for some of his artists. We said that we would meet the next day at noon or communicate when we got back to the States.

Cookie and I took the shuttle bus back to the hotel around 10:00 PM, tired enough not to feel guilty at all for leaving early. MIDEM was wearing me out. I was as tired as a musician after a long gig. Being a businessman here is physically demanding. I am carrying too much stuff around. My muscles ached. I crashed and once again slept nine hours.

Tuesday morning felt like there was a routine to the MIDEM week. I got up around 9:15 amazed that I was sleeping as much and as well as I was. Breakfast delivered to the room was the same. The bus ride to the Palais was just as scenic as the days before even though it was overcast but not gloomy.

I took a more systematic approach to covering the main floor of the exhibition hall. By now I was familiar with the layout, which at first had seemed like a changing indecipherable labyrinth of international displays or some sort of futuristic high tech bazaar in Turkey or Ghana or Star Wars. But after a few days, I knew my way around the place and I could go directly to the coat-check stand, the internet café, the various food and drink concessions, the public phones and some of the stands of the various international record companies and product manufacturers were now landmarks for my wanderings.

I worked one half of the floor, walking up and down the aisles systematically, instead of being distracted and zigzagging to and from each successively more colorful display. I was more disciplined and made myself finish each aisle and not cross over toward the sound of Brazilian or New Age music to the left or to the large meeting area for German record companies in the middle of the row to aisles over to the right. In this way I was able to cover the one whole side of the first floor in the morning with the intention of covering the second side in the afternoon. I was beginning to feel like I might be able to wrap up the whole thing a day early and maybe do some more sightseeing or leave for Paris sooner than I had planned.

I was also a bit more efficient with managing the weight of the materials I was carrying. I brought my briefcase full of stuff as usual but I also brought the MIDEM bag. I would load the MIDEM bag with just enough stuff to make a presentation or two and leave the heavy-assed briefcase at the coat check, then I would periodically come back to the check stand and reload the smaller bag, thereby carrying a lot lighter load.

I met Bryant at the internet café and he said that he liked Jamiah's tracks. He said that he would think about how he might involve Jamiah for a few days and we would communicate when we got back to the States.

I met Cookie at the usual 1:30 time and we went walking to find the train station to get information about the trains to Paris. We walked through a different part of the main part of Cannes, exploring some tiny little alleyways lined with small shops and venders. It started to drizzle but that didn't make Cookie speed up at all nor did it make her pass up the chance to browse in several of the little stores. We did get to the train station and found out that our options for trains to Paris on Thursday were limited because the trains were almost sold out. So we brought two second-class tickets on the 10:00 AM Thursday train for a total of 150 Euros.

I left Cookie to do more of her shopping and I dashed back to the Palais to make a conference session, "Jazz – A Music Without Boundaries; A Business With Many."

At that session I saw Kim, the vocalist we met on the plane, and her friend Michael, a sax player from L.A. We shared notes on what we were learning at our first MIDEM and voiced our continued optimism about the benefits we would gain from being at the conference.

I made a call to make an appointment for the next day with Dan Baxter of Jazz Fm Records of London but since he was leaving in the morning I agreed to meet him outside the Palais 30 minutes before closing. I met Dan and Cookie outside. I gave Dan my CDs and we spoke about the possibilities for making a deal. I hope that we can do something with my smooth jazz stuff. After that, Cookie and I went for drinks at the Carlton Hotel and went back to our hotel soon after that to get some rest.

On Wednesday morning I woke up at 7:30 and did a little yoga. Then I used the directory of the companies attending MIDEM to plan which ones I would try to see on what would be my last day working the conference. I loaded up my briefcase full of CDs and press packets and then took the shuttle bus to the Palais.

When I got to the conference site, I made a phone call to Serge Kolpa, the producer of a summer world music festival in Cannes. I was supposed to see him in the morning but he could not see me until later in the day, so I spent the morning hours walking from place to place trying to see people and delivering packets. Kim had told me that Aosis, a Japanese record company, was releasing adult contemporary music and might be interested in my smooth jazz, so I dropped a packet at their stand. I also tried to see several of the European distributors for Strut Records. The few that I managed to find were very warm and friendly once I introduced myself as the leader of Oneness of Juju. They had all done well with the Strut Records' "African Rhythms."

I met with the A&R guy for AVEX, another Japanese company. I let him hear samples of our music and he said it was not for them. I did my best not to let anything get me down. I was determined to use this MIDEM experience as a learning step. And I was definitely learning about marketing music internationally.

I saw that producing music in niche genres and targeting specific international markets is probably the way to go for a tiny company like mine. I need color brochures and better printed materials in order to compete. I also need to have my music productions be better suited, more focused and more commercial in whatever genre I am doing. I learned that rap is cool but it is tough to market abroad unless it is well-known and getting lots of press in the U.S.

Neo-soul and new R&B are good genres for some markets (U.K., Japan, Germany), but so is jazz. Dance and electronica seems to "rule" and every country seems to sell it, though I don't know what makes it "good." I may not have heard the best of it though.

At MIDEM, there were many more companies selling their music and trying to license their products than there were companies trying to buy product or license music from others. There is a glut of music in the world. How to survive and prosper in that environment is the ongoing challenge.

By the end of the day I was beat again. But I worked the conference until the very end.

I met Cookie outside at 5:30 and she was a little disappointed that I wanted to go back in for one last meeting. But I did. I met with Johnny at the Aosis Records stand. The company is releasing music for adults over 25-years-old. Johnny explained the concept as being smooth music with a little more rhythm, more edge than the smooth jazz format.

He listened to some of the songs that I thought would fit that vein and he said that one or two came close to what he had in mind. He liked my saxophone style and said that the company might ask me to record some tracks or even some specific songs for them. I told him I was open to doing that and left a couple of CDs with him.

Upon further reflection, I should have let him hear some songs from some of my CDs recorded in the 1990s, instead of my most recent productions. But I can send him those as a follow-up to our meeting.

And then I was done at MIDEM. Finished. Because our train to Paris was to leave at 10:00 AM there would not be time to come back the next morning.

I won't know if I will term my experience a success until later. In terms of business, that won't be determined until I follow-up with the contacts that I made and see if any deals can be consummated and/or new deals can be initiated. In terms of my personal development, I won't know if this was a success until I digest the experience and decide how I will incorporate the information I have gathered into my ongoing plans.

At this point, I don't know what I am going to do. At the end of this week, at my lowest point in terms of fatigue, I really didn't know what I wanted to do or what I will do in the future. I was feeling like I didn't want to be a performing musician and I didn't want to be a music businessman either. It seemed that producing was what I most wanted to do. I like the technical, the creative and the business blend that makes up the producer's world. I like the fact that much of the work can be done in private.

What I don't like about music is that a piece of it might not appeal to everyone. I hate it when it is rejected. I hate it when it is not good. A good producer has to deal with that. A good producer has to produce good music.

I woke up in the middle of the night with a revelation. When one exhales and empties the lungs they are ready to be filled again with life sustaining air from the universe. When one is drained with fatigue, a rest is restorative. It is as if energy is poured into an empty vessel, like water into an empty vase.

Then the vase is ready to sustain a beautiful flower. The vase may not be aware from whence cometh the flower. The forces of nature that made it possible for the flower to grow, the hands that cut it, the eye and appreciation for beauty that impels the floral arranger to place the single rose or the bouquet of petals in the vase; these things may not be in the consciousness of the receptacle but when they all come together they make a beautiful picture. And they create synergy to inspire when a viewer or an audience beholds them.

My revelation was far simpler but just as profound. I simply became aware of the importance of knowing whom I am making music for; whom I am selling to. I suddenly understood the basic concept behind market research: know thy customer. And the better you know whom you are targeting, the better you can serve that audience.

My profound revelation was that I serve/play for an urban contemporary adult audience. It is fairly obvious but the fact had escaped my ability to recognize it and name it. I play for dances, concerts, festivals, receptions – all patronized by adults 30-60 years old. I have stated to others before that I no longer play for the college students and the undergraduate campus activities that used to be my bread and butter. Now I am booked by the *alumni* chapters of the sororities and fraternities for their dances and balls. When I look out into the audiences at my concerts I see the faces of people around my own age. I am aware that many of the festivals that I play, I have been playing annually for years. I have been amazed when someone comes up to me and says that their mother used to bring them to my shows or listen to my records when they were young. But I still didn't get it!

When I play and make music, in my mind's eye I am trying to please or impress or motivate, Garry, Vanessa, B. J. Brown, Skipper, Ray, Pharoah, Jimmy Smith, Billy, Franklin and my audiences, which are for the most part my contemporaries, Adults!

The information and evidence was right there, as close as my face in the mirror. As "right there" for me as playing a solo with my eyes open for a change instead of with them closed tightly. But I wasn't seeing it.

And this is important because creativity can be enhanced or at least channeled when the creator is armed with knowledge or awareness of his audience. Serving one's public can be a two-way mirroring process. Market research can be important not just to know who you are selling to and how to better reach them but also to be able create a better product for them. In other words, knowing your end user can help not just after the product has been created but also help the creation of new and improved products.

In the case of my music, I suddenly felt that armed with the revelation of who my audience is, I can compose, produce and even perform better for them. My music can be improved! I can be motivated to go on with renewed vigor because my objectives will be new again.

And certainly having a better picture of my audiences will help me sell to them better, help me make better marketing materials, graphics, choose better media outlets, better public relations activities. All because I know my public better. Hell, I will be able to say what kind of music I play: Adult Urban Contemporary. And the category can include all of the musics that I do – jazz, funk, African, Cuban, Brazilian, soul, Nubian age, dance - because adults do listen to all of it.

Teenagers can have a much narrower musical diet: hip-hop, neo-soul and dance. That's because younger people have a smaller range of activities: they go to school and party at clubs; they date and entertain themselves.

Adults on the other hand work for a living, provide for families, read, contemplate issues, try to relax, engage in politics, worship, mature, and they have many more past experiences for which music has played a vital part. For both groups music is extremely important. But their musics can be very different and play different roles.

All this is fairly obvious. But the thoughts crystallized for me overnight when the universe was refilling my tank. Maybe Dan was right when he said to me at MIDEM that now I am no longer just a musician, now I am a music businessperson. Now I was ready to go on to Paris!

Onward and upward. Ain't life grand!

On Thursday morning we got up early to get ready to leave. I had packed the major portion of my artifacts and technical gear before going to bed so I didn't have a whole lot to do in the morning. I had awakened at 4:45 AM and transcribed my thoughts into my laptop and then laid back down to rest some. We had a hasty continental breakfast, checked out of the hotel and took a cab to the train station.

The five-hour train ride to from Cannes to Paris was scenic and smooth. The high-speed train was sleek and efficient. Cookie and I were unlucky enough to have had the seats on the car that faced to the rear and faced another couple, so none of us could really stretch out our legs in front of us.

When we left Cannes, for the first hour we could look out the window and see the Mediterranean Sea with its blue waters and quaint coastal towns' architecture. Very pleasant indeed. Peaceful and restful enough for me to get a couple of hours of sleep.

When we got to Paris we had the mild inconvenience of maneuvering with all our baggage, which was far in excess of the amount reasonable people would want to have along. But we found a taxi right outside the train station and took it directly to the cheap hotel that David Murray had booked for us. La Palma Hotel was off the beaten path in an old section in the Eastern end of Paris just off Gambetta Circle. The best things about the place were the price of the rooms and its surrounding neighborhood, which had lots of small shops, restaurants, a taxi stand, a metro station and a McDonald's right across the street. The hotel was clean and it was a place for us to dispose of our baggage!

I called David on the phone and I told him that Cookie and I were going to do some sight-seeing. We took the metro to the Eifel Tower and acted like regular tourists, snapping pictures, shooting video and buying little trinkets for souvenirs. The tower is quite a marvelous monument to the city of Paris. When you approach it from the east your view of the structure is framed by the buildings housing the National Theater and the Museum of Cinema. In the evening when the tower is lit up it is a spectacular scene and supports Paris's moniker, "The City of Lights."

Cookie and I walked between the buildings, down the grand stairway and out past the large fountains that form the plaza that leads over to the 950-foot structure. We decided to take the elevator up to the observation deck at the top for a wonderful view of Paris at night. We also decided to eat at the restaurant on the first level and we enjoyed our gourmet dinner of French onion soup, crab-stuffed tomato, stewed leg of duck and roast breast of chicken and, of course, a French wine while looking out over the night lights of the city.

After our dinner we took a taxi to the home of David Murray, the renowned avant-garde jazz saxophonist. The taxi driver took forever to find the little street where David lives and Cookie was frustrated because neither the driver nor I would ask for directions. Although it was after 10:30 at night when we arrived, David was gracious and helpful.

I was there to impress upon him and his wife, Valerie, who does his booking that I was serious about performing and succeeding in France and in

Europe in general. Just the fact that I had come to France to MIDEM and had come to Paris to see them was indicative of my commitment. So I didn't have to stay long. We listened to some music, discussed our recording plans, reminisced about being in Cuba last spring and talked about our sons.

David said that smooth jazz was not a viable musical option in France for me but he liked the idea of Oneness of Juju performing with African-style face paint. He suggested that we might ask Archie Shepp to perform with the band in Paris. And because Archie has been a long-time idol of mine, and a legendary saxophonist who lives in Paris, I thought that was a stupendous idea! Even if it never happens, the idea was inspiring and expansive.

After a short while David walked us back to the hotel, which was only five minutes from his place. We had a pleasant rambling conversation on the way back and I felt like we bonded at a new level of friendship.

Friday turned out to be the best day of the whole week! I woke up at 9:15 AM, a little later than I had planned, but we got out by 11:00 AM and took a taxi to the RPM Productions office. There I had a meeting set up with Samy and Chico, the two principals of the company. They a distribute records, promote gigs and publish a magazine called "Funk U."

It turned out that both Samy and Chico are big fans of funk music and they were really into my music as well, being aware of the Strut Records compilation "African Rhythms 1970-1982." As we talked about it Chico would hum the refrain, "African Rhythms..."

Cookie & Plunky

They were enthusiastic about meeting me and they were happy about the prospects of distributing my "Got to Be Phunky" CD. This was a great prospect because I don't have a distributor for that CD even in the U.S. I have mainly used it as a merchandising item for sale at my shows. I was very uplifted to find that these guys might be a vehicle to get my funk music promoted here in France.

At the RPM Productions office I looked at pictures they had of Chico with a whole bunch of black music stars including James Brown, Bootsie, Larry Graham, Larry Blackmon, Stevie Wonder, Africa Bambataa, Buddy Miles, Gil Scott Heron, Maceo Parker, Prince and others. RPM Productions is the European distributor for Jeff Lober Fusion, which means the company has an openness to contemporary jazz too. We listened to tracks from our respective CDs and smiled a lot.

Then we went to a neighborhood café and had coffee and continued our smiles and conversations. We were joined by Hugo, a friend of Samy's, who is a fan of the music and a tour guide in Paris. Hugo volunteered to take Cookie and I around Paris and give us a ride to wherever we wanted to go. So away we went.

Our drive around Paris was a perfect way to see the City. We went to all the most famous sites, stopping to take pictures and sometimes videos, with me playing my soprano sax. Parisians seemed not all perturbed by my playing near their monuments and I was having a ball.

Hugo took us to a wholesale jeweler friend of his and we bought 18K gold charms as gifts for Cookie, Kaila and Shamelle. Then Hugo dropped us off at a large department store so Cookie could do some more shopping and I dragged along behind her or found someplace to sit and wait.

We took the metro back to the hotel, happy about our good fortune of having a tour guide for a friend. We went out walking in the neighborhood and had a large Chinese dinner. Then we came back to the room to rest up and to get ready to go out to a nightclub with Samy and Hugo late that night.

Samy and Hugo came by the hotel to pick us up to go out to a nightclub. Hugo brought along his copy of the original African Rhythms LP that he wanted me to sign. I thought it was amazing that he would have one of the first edition copies of the album. There were only about 2,000 of them manufactured back in 1975, so to me it is always a wild thing to find someone who has one of them. And the fact that Hugo has one all the way over here in Paris, France knocks me out! It is either a small world or the small number of like-minded people naturally gravitate to the same places and things and are then able to hook up.

The Champs-d'Elysee is the most famous street in Paris and one of the Grandest Boulevards in the entire world. At night it is all lit up in neon and bright illumination and full of smiling crowds of revelers and tourists. The Monkey Club is a Disco club just off the Champs-D'Elysee and it is close enough to the center of the action that it is important to the Paris nightlife scene. When we got to the club, Samy got us in past the velvet rope and we immediately went to the downstairs main dancing area.

The music was pumping and young people were on the dance floor. For the most part the music was soul and funk from the U.S. and the youth on the floor were Europeans. James Brown, One Way, Jill Scott, Patrice Rushen meet young, French teens on the dance floor. I am amazed at the universality of the scene and the sounds. It could have been a club in almost any city in the world. The same music, the same dances and same energy. I noted that some songs just always seem to boost the energy of the dance floor: any James Brown funk, Michael Jackson's "Billy Jean," and a host of others where the mix of the sounds and the vocals and the beat all come together perfectly to make the moment electrically charged and full of happy energy. I long to make such songs. Perhaps I will. Perhaps I have.

Samy introduced me to the Club owner who greeted me warmly. We all had a drink at our table and toasted the night. A few minutes later the club owner came over to talk to me through the din of the music. He told me that he had one of my records, the "Space Jungle Luv" album and of course, that blew my mind again! He also told me that the club had only been opened for about two years and that business was good. He lamented that house music was too easy and not real like the funk and soul music that he liked his deejay's to feature. He also said that all the funk musicians were welcomed in his club.

Samy said that the Monkey Club was a place where I could do a showcase performance. I wondered what kind of showcase I would do? A solo sax tracks date? A funkateer, painted face sax singer? Would that type of show make me a relative of a Marcel Marceau-type French mime? Or a sad black clown? Would I be more than an intrusion and an imposition on the dance night of French teens? And yet bringing a whole band into a disco presents an array of technical and logistical issues and problems that far surpass the worth of a one-set showcase there.

I left the club feeling really good about Paris and the prospects of during some performing and music business in France in general. Hugo and Samy drove us back to our hotel and I talked to Samy about the "Got to Be Phunky" release and the logistics of manufacturing vinyl. He was committed to trying to promote a club date for the band and asked me to send the contract technical rider and the fees via email.

I went to bed with a sense of accomplishment and closure to the week. We got four hours of sleep and woke up to continental breakfast in the room. At 11:00 AM we took a cab to the airport. Our 2:00 PM flight to London departed 45 minutes late. In London we made the connecting flight to Washington, DC with only a minute or two to spare. And we arrived back home in the U.S. right on schedule, happy to be back in the land of big cars, our own cellphone territory, unlimited internet access, juicy chicken and Black English.

When I try to talk about what I learned from this week it all sounds so obvious and full of platitudes. I learned that music is specific to place and time. Not all music works everywhere all the time. The world is big but full of small markets. Music is vast and varied but it can be approached as an array of niches. Songs can take an overview or the overview can be extracted from the minutest detail or the most specific individual experience or perspective.

Dance music, music that people can dance to, rules! Because people love to dance and they want to live the good life as depicted by American culture. Black American music is the hippest shit on the planet!

Soulful jazzy world music may be happening in London, while new age music is sold all over Europe at bargain prices. Germany is into techno-electronica while Japan is moving towards a smoother adult sound. The U.S. is spewing neo-soul and teen super stars while France is finding a rebirth of the Funk. But nobody has more than a clue of where it will all go. We can spot trends but not know how long they will last or how far they will spread.

There are so many factors that impact the music: politics, fashion, world events, superstars, hype, economy, creativity, spirit, media, everything. Music affects all these things as well, so the system is completely interactive and dynamically interdependent.

The production of music involves so many aspects it is almost impossible for one person or one crew or even one mega-multi-national corporation to know it all. Different tonalities and equalization settings for all the different situations where music is used: The hot club dance floor and the quiet meditation room; the giant stadium rock show and the small rural church; the Japanese airline headphone and the surround sound home theater.... So many situations, so much music, so many markets... Ain't Life Grand!

III. JOURNAL OF TWO WEEKS TO RIO

4:00 PM, Saturday, February 9, 2002, on the train from Baltimore to New York on the way to take a plane to Rio de Janeiro for Carnival, the ultimate

Mardi Gras!

Wow! What a two-week stint it was after I returned from Paris! I got back to the States on Sunday and I spent the week unpacking, getting organized, communicating with people I had met on my trip, trying to follow-up on business deals in Europe and Japan. I rehearsed my band for the first time in several weeks to prepare for a gig on Saturday in Atlantic City, New Jersey, at Trump Taj Mahal.

The gig was for the Deltas Sorority Alumni Chapter of South Jersey. It was a fund-raising Ball that we had played the previous year. After the one last year, I had sworn that I would never play it again, because the load-in and load-out was so ridiculously difficult. But the event itself was a classy, formal affair for an older Black crowd who really partied and enjoyed the band and the casinos at Atlantic City have a special allure for family and friends. So I let the lady from the Deltas talk me into doing the gig for her once again. And for weeks, my mother, my wife, my daughter and my sister-in-law had been looking forward to traveling with the band so they could get to gamble while we did the gig.

This year the logistics for the travel and accommodations and the load-in were a lot less strenuous. The band sounded good. I had bought a new mixing board for the sound system just the day before we left and it worked flawlessly. We had required the sponsors to have the hotel provide people to help with the equipment and they complied. The motel where we stayed was only six miles from the casino and it was a straight shot to it (unlike the year before when we stayed at a place that was 30 miles away and not easy to find). So the gig was quite pleasant and even traveling back home on Sunday had the feel of a family reunion outing.

I had found out that week my daughter, Kaila, was pregnant with her first child and my first grandchild. Yes, I am going to be granddad. Not an old one though. Life truly does keep on keeping on.

In the second week back from Paris I was scheduled to perform at schools in Danville, Virginia, on Wednesday and Thursday and then on Friday leave for New York from where I would depart for Brazil on Saturday.

On Monday of that week, I worked in my office conducting the usual correspondences, paying bills and getting things organized for my departure. I received the 500 copies of my latest CD, "Solo Journey Between Dimensions." I had Tonya log in the fax numbers for all of the city's public schools so that I could send out the information to them about our annual concert-lectures at Virginia Union University for elementary and secondary students.

On Tuesday, I had a doctor's appointment for a check-up scheduled for 3:15 PM, so I worked diligently in the morning hours because we were leaving that night for Danville so we would already be there for the 9:00 AM school concert on Wednesday morning. I was feeling a little scrunched for time since I would be leaving for Brazil as soon as I got back from the two days in Danville.

But when I went to see the doctor things got a little crazy. I told him I had been having chest pains that I thought was acid reflux or heartburn. This has been going on for at least a couple of years. When I have the attacks they feel like I am dying of a heart attack: I have intense pain in the center of my chest, I feel nauseous, I break out in a sweat, I have numbness in my left arm and I am not a happy camper. Usually, the symptoms go away fairly quickly if I take an antacid. Consequently, I keep bottles of Tums in the kitchen, in the bedroom and in my car so they will be nearby and handy.

When I described all this to the doctor he was cool. I told him that I am very active. I play tennis three or four times a week. I do yoga four times a week. I haven't eaten red meat for 30 years. I drink very seldom and have only an occasional cigar. My blood pressure is low. But my father died as a result of heart attack during a stress test on a treadmill. I told him I had just come back from France, then Atlantic City and I was going to Danville that night and coming back and going to Brazil on Saturday.

He was cool with all that until I told him that I was concerned because my heartburn was sometimes triggered by physical exertion like swimming or playing tennis or even during sex. This got his attention! I said if there is a normal correlation between physical exertion and heartburn, then I would be greatly relieved. But he said there was not a widespread association with acid reflux and sexual activity.

So he immediately called a cardiologist friend of his and asked him to see me immediately. And so at 4:00 PM I was going to see a heart specialist. And then because I was scheduled to travel to Rio, as a precaution the specialist scheduled me for a cardiac cauterization on Friday morning. And he put me on several medications until then. He even prescribed nitroglycerine in case I had an attack before Friday.

The cauterization would involve running a small tube in through a vein in my groin up to my heart and then shooting in some iodine in and around the heart so pictures could be taken. These pictures would then be able to show any blocked arteries and any abnormal activities of or pressures within the heart.

I left the second doctor's office more than a little concerned. Not so much about my heart but about the schedule for the rest of the week. I am not saying I was unconcerned about my heart, but I really felt that with my diet and level of activity and my lifestyle, my heart was not likely damaged. Still there was the chance. The doctors, my family and friends were all taking the possibility very seriously. And I still had to get through the week and go through the procedure and still try to make it to Rio for carnival.

I went home to pack my things, then went to pick up a rental van and drove it back to load up the equipment and the band members. Muzi was not making this trip so we would be doing the gig without a bass player but we would have Tonya on keyboards and vocals, Chris on guitar, Lester "Heavy" Kenny on drums, Asante on percussion and Jamiah on electronic percussion. I drove the van and Asante drove his own car. We got to the hotel in Danville by 11:45 PM.

The next two mornings we performed at a high school and a middle school in Danville. The kids loved the shows and they learned from my lectures. At the last school the young girls really cheered loudly for Jamiah when I introduced him. He had a sheepish little smile at all the adoring attention and I had a proud father's smile at his recognition. The gigs went well with Tonya and Chris covering for the missing bass parts, Tonya singing with her big, soulful voice and Asante and Heavy laying down some serious polyrhythms.

We got back to Richmond on Thursday afternoon. After unloading the van and taking it back to the rental office I came home to work at my desk.

My procedure at the hospital was scheduled for 1:00 PM on Friday afternoon but I had to report for pre-screening at 11:00 AM. So on Friday morning I got up at 6:00 AM to do deskwork and mailings so that I could keep the business moving right along. I got my royalties statement from Quinton Scott of Strut Records and I also answered an email form Ken Tsakamoto of P-Vine Records in Japan. I went deliver a check to Virginia Union University to pay for the rental of the hall for the March concerts for the public school students. And I mailed off several packages of CDs at the post office.

I came back home at 10:30 and had Jamiah drive me to the hospital. I was admitted and then had blood tests and x-rays done. After that I was taken to the cardiac unit where I undressed, put on one the customary open-backed gowns and was prepped for the procedure. The nurses were pleasant, professional and purposeful as they wheeled me into the room where the doctor would do his thing. They shaved some hair from around my groin area where the insertion would be made and swabbed me down with an antiseptic.

Dr. Abramson is a large, dark Black man with a bit of a New York-island accent. He explained everything that he would be doing and he proceeded to do it. First he numbed the area with a needle of lydocaine. Then he made and incision into the vein and inserted a small tube up through the vein toward my heart. I felt the prick of the needle when they numbed the area and I supposed it worked because I didn't feel the tube going in at all. However I did feel the intense pressure as the doctor pressed down on my abdomen and worked the tube upward.

After a few short minutes he said, "You're going to feel some warmth spread all over your body." And I did. It was weird to feel a hot liquid filling my torso. But the sensation quickly subsided. Soon after that Dr. Abramson said "All clear on the left side. You have no blockages in any of your veins on that side and that's very good. We'll check the other side now."

The other side was clear also. I do not have any heart disease. Hooray!

The procedure was over in less than an hour and it was 3:00 PM when I got back to the prep room. But I had to stay in bed there and rest for three hours. I was discharged at 6:30 and got home at 7:00 PM to rest, eat and pack. I had been told to take it easy for 24 hours: nothing strenuous, no lifting, and no baths. Everyone was concerned that I would be traveling this next day, but I was sure that I would be making the trip. Carnival in Rio. I wasn't planning to miss it!

On the plane from New York to Rio De Janeiro.

One of the things about writing a journal or recounting one's experiences is the pauses that are left out. Those times where nothing happens but the thinking. The boring moments when time just passes. The hours whiled away watching or waiting for them to pass. Like when I wrote about going to the hospital for the procedure yesterday, what I didn't convey was the hour that I had to wait lying on the gurney before the procedure could commence. Or the thoughts and the clock watching for the three hours resting after the heart testing was over.

Then there were the hours of traveling: driving from Richmond to DC, the hours waiting at the train station and the three hours waiting at Kennedy Airport after checking in and before boarding this plane. Some of the most interminable hours are spent on international flights. This one from New York to Rio is over 10 hours long.

But somehow I am able to get past all these hours with little discomfort or boredom. Perhaps it is because my time is most often spent in motion, full of activity, multi-tasking, doing too many things at once, so that when I am forced to spend one or more hours doing nothing but waiting and thinking, I rather enjoy the passage of time in slow-motion. I feel that this kind of passive activity is meditation on the move, with eyes open. These are the times that I get to appreciate the beauty of nothingness. I think boredom is a blessing! I usually have so much to do, so many people to stay in touch with, so many visualizations to detail, so much I'd like to create and so little time to do it all, that when I get to just be still and be bored I am as happy as when I am running around full tilt. So a 24 hour trip driving from Richmond to DC, train ride to New York, with hours of waiting and capped by a 10 hour flight to Rio – a piece of cake, a joyride.

Everyone says that Carnival will be a ball. And I am sure it will be a wild party and a grand time. But I am not full of anticipation. I am taking it as it comes. I want to make it a working trip since I am going to do research for doing the music for Arnim's documentary film. I want to try to insure that he gets some critical planning done for the film and that I get some samples of music and scenes that I can use for the film if it in fact ever gets done. But even if his film is not done, I want to gather video and audio artifacts that may have some value as I continue to develop my own documentation of my own experiences and create more music and video for entertainment and enlightenment.

So I intend to shoot video and record sounds on this trip. While wife and friends may be concerned about me getting into too much wildness, I know that capturing events through the lens of a camera makes one more of a witness than a participant. Listening to audio while aware of capturing it through a microphone makes one too objective to get fully caught up in the spirit inherent in the sound-filled moment. But I am prepared to sacrifice my own full participation in the spirit of the moments in order to work on Arnim's project and to be able to bring something of the experience back to my own audience, family and friends. So I will be part-journalist, part-producer, part-composer, part-consultant and part samba partier. But I am not sure how much partying I will do as an older man with a hole in his groin, heartburn issues and instructions from lots of people to take it easy and not get into any trouble!

It's pretty amazing to me that I have been asked to work on the music for two films about Cuba and Brazil by two old friends, Skipper and Arnim. They have known me for 25 and 35 years respectively and they are both progressive thinkers who have been involved with me and my progressive music-making. They have both traveled to their respective countries of interest many times and have become enamored with the culture and societies of Cuba and Brazil.

In studying the history of these two countries I have found that similarities abound. They both have cultures profoundly affected by the African slave trade, slave labor and African music and religion. Both countries are known for their hot weather, beaches, and beautiful women, but mostly for their rumba and samba musics. They would have to be regarded as two of the top ten places on the planet for Black music. They represent grand examples of the influence of African music and culture in the Diaspora. Both countries have large black populations, which make up the lowest economic classes of the societies. Both governments, one socialist and one capitalist, proclaim their commitment to the abolition of racism, indeed claiming racism doesn't exist in their countries, but racial discrimination is rampant and readily apparent, if benign and subtle in its application.

Monday morning sunrise at Iracy's apartment.

My writing is totally inadequate to begin to describe Carnival in Rio. The main parades in the Sambadrome are so elaborate that they make the Rose Bowl parade seem like a small rural walk for a county fair. The whole production for Carnival is like the Super Bowl times sixteen. I really believe there is nothing like this on earth! I don't feel bad about my inability to convey the grandness of scale through the written word because even watching it on television or on video you only get a small percentage of the grandeur.

The samba schools or groups represent neighborhoods or sections of Rio. They each produce a parade based on a theme consisting of floats, dancers, drummers and celebrities totaling four- to six-thousand participants, each dressed in the most elaborate costumes made with beads, feathers, bangles, lame, hoops skirts, and all things shiny and gaudy. The schools compete for the championship title of the Best Samba School for the year.

I went to sleep last night watching the second of the eight schools on television. I woke up at sunrise to watch the parade of Beja Flor, one of the grand schools. They had at least 5,000 marchers. The theme of their presentation had something to do with the development of life beginning with gigantic prehistoric dinosaurs and progressed through floats and hundreds of marchers depicting minotaurs, the renaissance and Leonardo daVinci, airplanes, King Kong, space travel and Black angels in heaven. Just remember that I cannot do the costuming, the pageantry, grandeur, the scale any justice. It is something that you have to see to understand or at least grasp the monumental amount of human effort, creativity and resources that goes into something of this magnitude.

The pageantry is based on the power of the samba drumming and dancing and is spiced by the beauty and allure of sexy bodies gyrating in various states of adored and bejeweled nudity. Some of the most beautiful mulatto women who look like they have stepped out of the pages of Playboy magazine dance topless atop floats with blazing smiles and gyrating hips and breasts.

People come from all over the world to this celebration that makes the New Orleans Mardi Gras look like a large backyard party by comparison. I woke up to watch the Beja Flor finale on television and to watch the sunrise through the window of hilltop apartment of Iracy, Arnim's friend. The sunrise was a glowing orange breaking through the mountains in the distance beyond the bay and over the neighborhood apartment buildings.

Between the sunrise and Carnival on television I feel exhausted already. But yesterday's activities may have had something to do with that also.

Upon arrival at the airport I went through immigrations and Arnim was there to meet me at the airport. We took a cab here to Iracy's apartment and after eating lunch and showering we went out into the streets for my first inperson look at Rio. We took a bus to the beach at Copacabana and walked the length of the beach to Ipanema beach. Then we walked through some of the nearby neighborhood and caught a little of the revelry happening in the throngs on the streets before taking a taxi back to the apartment to watch the carnival on television around 9:00 PM. We had intended to go down to the Sambadrome around midnight after resting. But when I woke up at midnight I just watched some more of the carnival and laid back down for more rest. I guess the travel from Richmond to DC to New York to Rio made for a long wearisome day, so my body, which had also gone through an invasive procedure at the hospital the day before that, needed some rest.

All that energy, all that money, all that dancing, all those hoop skirts twirling and all based on the samba. This is what the samba tradition has evolved to: a super bowl of samba school competitions in Rio and in Salvadore in Bahia with tens of thousands of participants and millions of revelers watching and joining in. Watching it even on television makes my mouth drop open constantly. If is not the scale of gaudiness or the grandness of the production, it is the beauty and sexiness of the women or the power of the rhythms. It is 500 old, black women in giant hoop skirts twirling in sync and marching in front of giant bedazzling float carrying the stunningly beautiful "Mulatto of Year" dancing topless at the top. Carnival is something one is blessed to see once in a lifetime or many times if you can afford to come, or every year if you live here.

The amount of money invested in this experience is staggering. 5,000 costumes costing at least $200 each, floats costing thousands, the man hours of construction, sewing, rehearsing; it is human effort on the grandest scale and it happens every year! It takes months to plan and execute. For the poor from the neighborhoods it is the focus of life for at least two to three months of the year.

Samba is a way of life that has evolved from the African rhythms of the slaves in Brazil who were based in the north of Brazil in Bahia. The music's melody, chord structure and words are infectious. It is light and airy. The tunes float above the rhythms and the little guitar figures and light percussion. There are moving chord changes that are sophisticated but not complex, but at the same time more elaborate than at first perceived. It is a happy sounding music made for dancing and introspection at the same time.

It is interesting that the Europeans were so against promoting the samba as the music that people would associate with Brazil, and yet the music has become the most prominent feature of Brazilian culture known around the world. Brazilians will tell you that there is no racism here "because everyone knows their place." It is as if, because no one is trying to rise above their place, then there is no active oppression being exercised to keep them in their place. There is little or no upward mobility in this society. The station or class into which one is born, is the level where one will remain for life. Unless you hit the lottery or become a football star, a black person or a person in the lower class has no way to graduate or educate himself up and out.

I am not an American patriot. I have too much knowledge and memory of what was and is done to black people in the U.S. to be a champion of that government. But in visiting some of the other cultures in the Americas I have come to see that the white man and the government in the U.S. have certain attributes that are laudable. The rule of law and the stated desire to rise to the highest of human ideals describe a set of goals that can be challenged when not attained. The recognition of higher ideals allows for challenges in judicial courts and in the courts of public opinion and these challenges can and do inspire social change.

6:30 PM Monday evening, back at Iracy's Apartment.

We, Arnim and I, went out sightseeing this morning. We walked down the long hill of the cobblestone street from Iracy's apartment at 9:30 AM to get a breakfast of fruit juices. We took the bus to the cable car train up to the Cristo Redentor, the large statue of Jesus Christ that overlooks Rio de Janeiro. It is Rio's most widely recognized landmark which sits at the top of Corcovado Mountain. The little train goes up the mountain through what remains of the Atlantic coast tropical forest and it is a quaint little ride. We took video from the mountaintop and I had Arnim take several shots of me playing my soprano sax and attracting the usual positive attention that brings from onlookers.

After descending the mountain we took a taxi over to another mountain to take two cable cars to the top of those two peaks for more pictures. I took a helicopter ride around the Cristo Redentor statue and over Copacabana beach. Though it was only seven minutes, that flight was spectacular and afforded me the opportunity to shoot some great video footage of Rio.

After those two outings, we ate a lunch of fried shrimp with rice and then we came back here to the apartment to rest up for tonight's trip to the carnival.

Tuesday morning after awaking at the apartment.

Last night was the second night of carnival. The official parades of carnival happen over two nights in the Sambadrome, a 75,000-seat concrete corridor with super lights and sound that makes it seem like half time at the super bowl or the Rosebowl parade times 20 or 50. To say that the samba schools go all-out doesn't begin to convey the level of production and pageantry and energy that 4,000 or 5,000 parading dancers embody.

While it started out as a pre-Lenten, religious celebration like Mardi Gras, carnival in Rio has evolved into something of a modern day cultural big-business, offering the most fantastic reason for tourism in the world. The Sambadrome is filled with revelers and tourists who pay from $50 to $2,000 per ticket sit in the open-air narrow stadium, while some watch the festivities from air-conditioned corporate sky boxes that start at $10,000. Carnival also happens in a number of free outdoor parades, concerts and parties in several neighborhoods and in all the major cities all over Brazil. Carnival is a massive party; maybe the biggest blow-out in the entire world.

Since the events in the Sambadrome are actually a competition between the 16 top ranking samba schools in the Rio area, each presentation is so elaborate as to be overboard. The presentations all have Brazilian historical or cultural themes, but they may be phantasmagorical, allegorical or related only by mythological reference to actual events. These are rallying excuses to party and get wild. The tradition of carnival and the energy of samba are enough to inspire an out-pouring of energy that reaches almost superhuman proportions.

Carnival and the samba have been going on for years and years and they have become the centerpiece of Brazilian culture. It is interesting and central to Arnim's film that the music is Black African derived and yet Brazilians ignore the influence of their African culture except in the myths of history and the fact of the lower class of workers who are the descendants of slaves.

Arnim and I rested from 3:00 to 6:00 PM and when we got up from our naps we socialized with Iracy, her daughter Marissa and an older neighborhood woman friend of theirs. We had a pleasant time listening to music over bread, butter, cheese, tea, juice and Portuguese conversations. I honored a request to play a saxophone solo for them and they enjoyed the horn playing and watching some of the video Arnim and I had shot during the day.

Then Arnim and I hit the street. We walked for an hour and a half to get to the first area where there was a live band performing in a public park. The band was interesting because they played funky rock music with rap and they were quite good, innovative and very entertaining. We watched them for their three first songs and then moved on to walk over to and along the main avenue where the main samba parades used to take before the Sambadrome was built. On the way to that avenue we passed through another large park in front of the National Theater filled with revelers witnessing a performance by a full big band and fronted by an older female singer doing old favorite Brazilian songs and inspiring the crowd to dance and sing along. It was not a madhouse but it was a raucous family-filled scene with parents and kids and teenagers and elders full of smiles and energy. The food vendors and artifact sellers were doing a brisk business and I was assured that at 9:45 the evening was still quite young.

Walking from the plaza up the main avenue for several blocks we passed through strolling throngs who were meandering equally in both directions. We were headed in the direction of the Sambadrome but most people seemed not to be in a hurry to go anywhere. We encountered wave after wave of families strolling, bands of costumed transvestites in sequins or dressed as Arabian genies, a few groups of samba drummers and lots of kids and teenagers walking and gawking or resting in place. There were a hundred vendors selling water, beer and sodas from Styrofoam chest full of ice. I shot video as we passed through the crowds just to capture a sense of the diversity, the colors and the Sunday-stroll mood.

When we got to the end of that street we decided to a take a bus toward the Sambadrome. On the bus, the street was showing more traffic and activity and I was finally feeling like we were making progress toward the center of the Carnival universe. I was surprised that the bus and the rest of the traffic were able to make their way steadily closer to the stadium. As we got closer and closer the crowds got thicker and soon we were seeing the floats and the thousands of participants of the samba school that would next be entering the arena to perform and compete. About 10 blocks from the Sambadrome we decided to get off the bus and walk so I could shoot more video and be in the crowd, which consisted of thousands of walkers, watchers, vendors selling drinks and foods, and costumed dancers getting ready or having finished doing their samba. I was again struck by the elaborate decorations and the sheer weight of the costumes. How could they walk wearing all that stuff in all this heat, much less be able to dance the samba and march for 90 minutes in a cast of 5,000? The floats were as ornate and complicated as any you have ever seen. They had gigantic figurines, moving parts, lights, platforms to hold dancers and models and enough sparkles, sequins and shining metals and materials to glow in the dark and burst into glowing flowing stars when hit by the glare of the hundreds spotlights in the Sambadrome.

There are throngs, mobs, gobs of people all milling about or standing with a view of the Sambadrome. The stadium is packed as this year's competition is a complete sell-out. We watch the Magueira School line up, get ready and then finally proceed into the parade stadium to tremendous applause both inside and outside the giant venue. They are a crowd and neighborhood favorite. After the samba school's continuous entering the stadium and with everyone chanting their samba song for the carnival for 60 minutes, the whole place was on a high.

Arnim and I decided to walk around to the other side of the Sambadrome to see if we could possibly get a scalped ticket or bribe a security person to let us in. In order to get there we had to retrace our steps and go back about eight blocks and then come back three of those blocks and turn left. It was another long trek through the crowds but it was all great fun.

But it did wear me out. By 12:30 AM I had to sit down and take a break. I was getting a migraine headache and I was not going to be a happy camper for much longer. I rested for about 30 minutes at one of the temporary beer gardens. I drank a bottle of water and closed my eyes for a while, then we trudged onward around and up and down through the pleasant mob. At about 1:30 AM we were able to buy scalped tickets for about $70 for the both of us.

Our section was at the end of the very last part of the Sambadrome. But I was in the main stadium for the spectacle of this world's parade championship. I kept shooting video of the grand proceedings and I enjoyed being in the crowd and watching them dance and samba and cheer their favorites. One samba school finished at 4:00 AM and after that I had to give it up and head for home. We took a cab and I was in bed, head still aching, by 4:30 in the morning.

The sun and the conversations came blaring in the porch sunroom and awakened us by 10:00 AM. I could have used more sleep, to be sure, but it was Iracy's birthday and she was having family and friends over for a celebration barbeque cookout and Arnim and I were expected to be guests and we couldn't very well be laying around dozing as the guests began arriving. So we just got up and flowed into the day around the apartment. We listened to and talked music and samba culture all day. It is amazing that the carnival competition has some of the same types of rivalries and year-to-year successes and near-misses as sporting contests.

Wednesday Morning 7:00 AM witnessing another sunrise from the window of the Apartment.

It is another glorious day in Rio. The sunrise from here is beautiful and prayer-inspiring. The mountains and the bay out beyond the neighboring hills and the art deco apartment buildings make a scene that one would put on a postcard or try to stay here forever to witness all the time. This is one of the reasons why Rio is considered one of the most beautiful cities in the world. I am just beginning to partake in the city's offerings but I can see how friends of mine have considered moving here and why Tina Turner, Billy Paul and many other celebrities have homes here. And I can understand why Arnim spends as much time here as is financially and socially possible. I have been blessed to experience these few days as a *carioke*, a citizen of Rio.

We awaken to witness the sunrise, the glorious orange glow from behind the mountain in the distance beyond the bay. Iracy and her daughters and one son-in-law have all slept in the bedroom and Arnim and I have stayed on the guest porch with the picture windows running the length of the little triangular shaped room. The view from this third floor apartment is nothing less than spectacular and every morning Iracy awakens us to watch the sunrise. When the orange glow sparkles a peek above one of the crests we ooh and ahh and then we give a light applause.

We have a breakfast of bread, butter and coffee. Then Arnim and I spend an hour discussing and working on his movie ideas. We are getting a lot of his thoughts fleshed-out and combined with the wealth of video I am assuming Arnim has to be pleased with the return on his investment. I am a great consultant and I am a producer by trade and my methodology is always to get something, on paper, on tape, to do it straight away and have something to show for it. That's what works for me. Often the preliminary artifacts that I gather or demo tapes I work on become a part of some finished product, so I have learned to treat all my activities and productions as if they may be released.

IV. Plunky & Oneness of Juju Tour de France March 2006

In November 2004 our group, Plunky & Oneness of Juju, played in Paris for the first time. Now, 18 months later, a DVD called "Live In Pairs" is being released and we are going on a mini- tour of France to promote it and to push for more touring in the coming months.

Sunday, March 19, 2006; on the plane at the Richmond Airport.

We are finally on the plane, finally ready for takeoff, finally on our way to Paris! If we can judge by the dues-paying, the number of delays and planning readjustments that we have had to endure to get to this point, and if you truly get what you pay for, then this tour should be nothing short of "da bomb!"

For example, just today, my luggage was overweight and even after trying to re-pack and redistribute the "tonnage" I still had to pay $25 extra. Then our flight from Richmond to Newark was delayed, jeopardizing our making the connecting flight to Paris. But I am confident we will make it. We have to. We've been through too much not to have things go well!

I have been anticipating this trip, this return engagement in Paris, for the past 18 months. In November 2004 we had a triumphant premier at the New Morning, a jazz and progressive music venue in Paris. It had been a sold-out, earth-shaking gig which was filmed for television and a DVD release and could launch a new phase of my career in France. We were supposed to go back a few months later in March of 2005. Then it was postponed until May. Then we were supposed to play at some festivals in July, but those dates were cancelled when the promoters balked at paying the plane fares during the high price season. In November of 2005, my French connections opted to invest in a large concert by the funk group, Brass Construction, instead of booking us.

Each of these delays was disappointing. Over time they had a cumulative effect, eroding my confidence and my energy. I had for many years thought that if I and the group could perform overseas the way we do at my gigs in the states, we could be a smash hit in Europe. And because my past European club dates have, in fact, gone so very well, they have in some ways spoiled me, making me want to devote all my efforts to touring abroad. It is a case of like the old song says, "How you gonna keep'em down on the farm, after they've seen Paree?" Touring in France and the major music cities on the continent became my focus and my goal.

So in December 2005, we confirmed the booking of this date, March 21, 2006, at the New Morning and added weekend dates in Marseilles and Montpellier in the South of France.

The plane takes off.

Then two-and-a-half weeks ago my French connections, Reynald, Samy and Daniel, called me to say they wanted to postpone this three-date mini-tour until May or June because of poor advance ticket sales, poor winter weather and several unfavorable business conditions. One of the main reasons for doing this tour was to support and promote the release of a "Live In Paris" DVD of our last concert at the New Morning and now the manufacturing of the DVDs may not be completed on time.

Upon hearing about yet another postponement, I was livid, disturbed and disappointed again. The band members were knocked for a loop. And the Frenchmen couldn't understand why I was so upset. They said, "The tour is not cancelled, it is only postponed!"

I had to explain to them that each person in the group has other jobs, gigs, families and other things to do besides being on call for me. Changing plans repeatedly or at the last minute undermines their confidence in the business and my ability to get this tour done. I was offended and the band was hurt that their personal plans would be adversely affected.

There were supposed to be seven of us in the group: Muzi, the bassist, is also the director of the arts and culture program at a major university hospital here in Richmond. Tonya, our vocalist/keyboardist, performs with three groups and gigs at least four or five times per week. Drummer, Corey, works a job and performs with gospel and soul groups and at a church in North Carolina on Sundays. Master percussionist Asante has just returned from Ghana where he is building a school for music studies. Kevin, pianist, works at a major studio in Los Angeles producing music for artists, movies, television and commercials. Lead vocalist Monica, works with Tonya's group and another touring band. So everyone has other things to do and plans and careers of their own.

After a couple of days of wrangling with management and the promoters in France and struggling with budgetary and personnel adjustments, we decided to do the tour anyway; but with a 50% reduction in the budget and cutting Kevin and Monica from the touring group. It was tough.

But all that is behind us now as we land at Newark Airport to transfer to our flight to Paris. Flying into a major city at night, you get the picture of an amazing light show on the ground: arteries of lights, sparkling jewels decorating the darkness on earth; awesome arrays of light decorating the night; sparkling colors like pre-arranged patterns of manmade stars. Car lights snaking in slow motion, like glowing blood cells moving through arteries. I enjoyed a futuristic "wow" moment seeing the light show as we approach our landing sight. This is like Sun Ra's Outer Spaceways, Incorporated!

I wonder if I really do want to do this live performing/touring group thing forever? This trip should help me know... More will be revealed. Touchdown!

Then on the plane flying to Paris.

Interesting synchronicities: In the Richmond airport we met Lonnie Liston Smith who was just arriving from Paris, having performed the night before on a show with the Temptations. Also, I spoke on the phone with Drummie Zeb, an ex-student of mine who performs with The Wailers. He tells me they are performing in Paris on Thursday night and wishes me a successful tour. I tell him I will try to go see them in Paris. It seems that Richmond is "representing" in Paris this week.

Flight landing notes: From above, the patterns of modern real estate development and lifestyles become apparent. Schools, recreation, neighborhoods, transportation centers are sited and arrayed and create interesting and discernable patterns. Early civilizations that created giant land drawings like in those in South America may have indeed used woven fabric and heated air to fly high above the earth to see those paintings; so man may have been flying for centuries. We're going from Richmond to Paris to perform; flying across the ocean to do a gig in the time it takes to drive from Richmond to Atlanta. Airplanes may be becoming the new transit for the masses, like buses. Flying and travel in general bring people closer together, makes us more familiar, more like family. Pretty soon all gigs may be local gigs!

Tuesday March 21, 9:00 AM. In my hotel bed.

We got through French immigration and customs with no hassles. Unfortunately, one of Asante's suitcases did not arrive. We got to the hotel, checked in and rested a bit before going to Radio Nova to do an interview. After that, I ate and crashed. The next day, Tuesday, was cold and rainy so I spent the day resting until sound check at 4:30 PM. We worked with the sound and tech crew until 8:00 PM. We ate in the dressing room. Then we painted up our faces, dressed, and did the gig.

The audience at the New Morning was very enthusiastic and intensely into the music and the show. I can definitely see possibilities for success here and in other progressive markets in Europe. Before the show I finally got a copy of the new DVD. I ripped it open, watched the documentary portion and I was completely blown away! That's all I can say. The documentary opens with footage of the Martin Luther King March on Washington and the

"I Have a Dream" speech. Then it continues with an extended interview of me. During the course of the 20-minute documentary there is rare archival footage of James Brown and his group with Bobby Byrd singing and Bootsy on bass and footage of Maceo Parker, Pharaoh Sanders, Fela Kuti all interspersed between shots of me walking around Paris and Plunky & Oneness of Juju playing live. The documentary is serious and of such a high quality technically that it is quite impressive!

Our show was tight and we rocked the house! The audience demanded two encores and we ended with Asante and Corey, and finally Asante alone, drumming them into a frenzy. They wanted yet another encore but I said that was enough. After the show we had a stream of visitors to the dressing room, including Patrick, the director of Nocturne Distribution, who is distributing the DVD and CD release in Europe. He seemed pleased with the performance and he said he was going to have some of his people come to the show in Marseilles on Friday and he himself would come down to Montpellier for the show on Saturday. After the show we came back to the hotel in the middle of the night and went to bed.

3:30 AM Thursday Morning in my hotel room.

The next morning we got up and had breakfast at the hotel and met a group called the Crawford Brothers, a gospel group from Upstate New York also staying in the hotel. They performed last night at another venue in Paris and are doing gigs in France and Holland over the next few days. We exchange contact information. They say they come to Europe several times a year, most times for a week or a weekend and for some one-nighters.

We spent the day in and around the hotel because it was again cold and rainy and we can all use the rest. I did an interview for a publication and another for an Internet TV site. I met with Daniel, the manager and Patrick, the DVD producer and we talked a little business. Tonya, Muzi and I ate dinner at a restaurant next door to the hotel. Muzi and I shot pool. Then I crashed until 3:00 AM. Now I am up and not sleepy…
Thursday 5:00 PM in my hotel room.

I finally fell asleep around 4:00 AM. I got up at 8:30 and did my yoga, even though at the start my body was so sore I wondered if age or arthritis is catching up with me and beating me down. After breakfast and Internet work and some more rest, I took a bus and a metro to go sightseeing. I walked the hell out of myself.

> I walk around Paris (the city of light and love)
> And I think of you
> I see posters and ads for haut-couture
> and I see you in those fashions looking so alluring
> I wish you were here

Friday morning in the room before leaving for Marseilles.

We are a modern-day menagerie, a troupe of troubadours, traveling from place-to-place to entertain, share ideas and amaze people. I wonder if it is worth the energy, the hassle and the concerns, boarding planes and trains, with bundles of instruments and costumes and artifacts from abroad. The circus is coming! Wow! What logistical complexities – just to entertain a few folks. But in this modern world what happens in the media is important, often more impactful than what happens on the stage. We're here getting media coverage and we're releasing new media product.

On the high-speed train to Marseilles.

We got out of Paris without too much hassle. We checked out of the hotel. Both Tonya and Asante had phone bills that they contested because they were using phone cards that they thought were toll free, but they were running up charges on the hotel phone. The hotel just waived the charges, which totaled about $100.

We took two minivan taxis to the Lyons Station in central Paris. In the confusion of loading up, Muzi left his suitcase in the hotel lobby and had to go back to retrieve it. It was a good thing we left with an hour to spare, so he had enough time to get back before the train left.

We have way too much luggage! We all agree that we could have brought much less stuff with us: fewer items of clothing, fewer artifacts and just less stuff. I am the main culprit though. I have one large suitcase of clothes, an even larger one with my sound effects processors and stands for my horns, plus my three saxophones, my briefcase, and my video camera. I have to have helping hands every time we move. I left one suitcase at the hotel in Paris until we return on Sunday, but I still have five things to carry and keep track of as we go for these two weekend dates down on the Riviera.

The high-speed train is a double-decker and it whisks us across the French countryside at 160 miles per hour. Still, even at that speed, the ride is relaxing. The Central France landscape is beautiful. Muzi says parts of it remind him of the mountains near Roanoke, Virginia. But the villages here are quaint and European, like the pictures in middle-school French grammar textbooks. The farmhouses and barns are all tan with clay tile roofs and they are aging gracefully. Trees and shrubs fence the parcels of land into neat rectangles. An ocean of flatlands, hills and valleys is punctuated by an occasional river, lake or train whizzing by in the opposite direction. A pensive and restful mood settles over the group and the whole train car.

Could we live in a cozy farmhouse out here in the middle of France? Or in Italy or Ghana or Venezuela? Probably friends, family and familiar things are too important to us. Maybe the two of us would be enough for us, at least for a short time. This is too far away from it all. But, boy, it is beautiful to pass through! It would be great for a change, for a week, but maybe no more than two. It could be a vacation spot. A rustic, isolated spa-like visit for relaxation, sex, meditation and longing to get back to our normal. I think I want to spend my old age doing what I know and being on the go as much as I am able. But then I'd like to think I could be content wherever there is beauty, comfort, access and you.

Saturday afternoon on the train to Montpellier. (The gig last night was da bomb!)

We got to Marseilles at 2:00 PM and the weather was sunny and warm. Finally a spring-like day to contrast to the wintry, dreary mix in Paris. Marseilles is too cute! Much more working class than the vibe of Paris. But Marseilles is right on the coast, the Riviera, and its port area and beach are breathtakingly beautiful. Tonya, Corey and I took a drive through the city with the wife of the promoter of the show here. We also drove over to and along the coast and we stopped to take some pictures and to ooh and aah at the views of the Mediterranean Sea, boats, cliffs, and the old buildings that border the beach. On a little cliff above the shoreline there is a large, impressive statue and monument to the Africans who came across the sea to Marseilles. The city is 2600 years old. And the Riviera is all it is cracked up to be!

We got back to the venue in time for the 4:00 PM sound check. The

Cabaret Aleatore is black box space in a converted tobacco warehouse. The venue accommodates a standing/dancing audience. The facility is part of a growing arts center, which has artists' studios, a theater space and indoor and outdoor exhibit spaces. The venue is super funky with lots of high-tech gear, lights, sound and decorations. Sound check lasted until 7:30 PM. It was thorough and effective. We walked to the band house, ate dinner, changed clothes and went back to the venue for the gig.

My French management and promotion team had been concerned about getting an audience for this gig. Advance ticket sales had been paltry. But we ended up getting a really good audience, 573 paid plus 75 comps in a venue that holds 700. With guests, press and crews we were near capacity. From the stage it definitely looked like a packed house, with a sea of smiling, grooving, mostly white faces from the edge of the stage all the way to the back of the room.

Plunky Paris show on tenor sax

The audience got into the music almost from the start, and they got more and more exuberant as we got funkier and funkier. By the end of the show and two encores, it was clear that we had triumphed and earned many new fans!

The night was revelatory. I had an epiphany or at least a series of revelations while lying in bed after the show: I could parlay my music, my experience, my history, my catalogue of recorded works and my current French connections into a successful, touring, music-selling career over the next few years. With my political/ spiritual bent, I could be marketed as a new Last Poets, Gil Scot-Heron, Pharaoh Sanders, Michael Moore, progressive act and media personality.

Young people could be drawn into our fold through hip-hop beats and my words. My show can be educational and engaging and enlightening and entertaining. I can use high-tech innovations for my stage shows and recordings. I have three DVDs that can be used for promotion. With all these things going for me, I could aspire to become an elder, cultural icon a la Fela, Bob Marley, Manu Dibango or George Clinton.

After the Saturday night gig in Montpellier

Tonight's gig and this mini-tour have demonstrated to me that this thing could happen! The performance tonight was quite good; we were a hit again. The venue, Le Jam, was small but well-designed with great sound and tech. Roy Ayers played here the night before. The likes of Archie Shepp, Dave Holland and Lonnie Liston Smith all play this venue, which is connected to a music school. We had no stands for Asante's conga drums but we improvised by using a platform for them. He was in fine form and he enjoyed moving the audience with his polyrhythms. Tonya had three keyboards and she had fun using all of them to work her show, manipulating the middle of the music, keeping it mellow, jazzy or funky as the songs required. She was super! Corey and Muzi were locked and grooving hard like Prince. The mostly college-aged young people in the audience were genuinely into it. We were teaching them the songs as we went along. The longer the night went on, the more they got into it and the more they wanted. It was really cool to watch and make it happen!

Plunky plays shekere

After the show, I met with Patrick, the distributor who had come down from Paris and I think he was impressed and is being won over. He seems committed to committing resources to the promotion of the DVD project and by inference I think he will help with our touring and other future projects. I inadvertently left his business card on the table in the dressing room and I forgot to give him a copy of the new album, but both those things can be corrected

We have the pieces in place and our foot in the door over here. We have a distributor, product, management, a good act, good songs, good press and an Internet buzz. Now we need a strong booking agent to complete our team.

Ideas and things to do:
- "Sax Machine" proclaims the headline for a review of our show in the Marseilles newspaper. A great concept, ad slogan or song title.
- How about props for one or two of the songs in the show; i.e., Plastic for "Plastic" a see-through flat sheet of Plexiglas, maybe with transparent peoplesilhouettes?
- Thank you notes to the venues.
- Get press, videos, pictures and recordings from all the gigs.
- Pick one song from the live DVD as a video.
- Try to get television airtime for the DVD and documentary: BET, TV One, African Television Network, etc.
- A new beginning or ending for the documentary segment to make it a doc film?
- Use the DVDs for multimedia displays and projections at all gigs where possible.

Plunky on alto sax

Vibe to use as the intro to the documentary: Where art meets science is near the same place where music is magic. The musician can be a minor character who plays a major role as change agent in the development of culture. The journey to become an impactful musician is similar to that of becoming a doctor, a teacher, a griot, a statesman, an ambassador, a wizard or a mystic. A musician can be part all these things. The way begins with study of the craft, history and culture. It continues with the development of greater self-awareness through introspection and meditation and the journeyman can be aided by guidance from a teacher or mentor. The candidate is steeled and completed through experience, work, travel, observation, experimentation and repeatedly renewing the entire process. A musician must travel, reach out, accumulate unique experiences and information and re-synthesize it all into a whole, then share it all with others to educate, effect change, and positively influence the culture and the people - using music as, and to convey, the message.

Plunky video shots to use: In Cuba receiving a Santeria blessing; in Cuba playing with Folkloyuma; in Brazil visiting the Christo Redentor statue, then soaring in a helicopter; performing with the choir at First Baptist Church; teaching children; on stage at the Arc de Triomphe in Paris; playing in NY Times Square; walking along the beach...

On the plane back to the USA.

On Sunday we took the high-speed train from Montpellier back to Paris. We checked back into the Mecure Hotel again for our last night in the City of Light. From the Bathroom window, Muzi's and my room had a great view of the Eiffel Tower with Parisian rooftops and buildings in the foreground. Muzi wants to come back in the future and reserve that room, #722.

Later we went out to dinner at a restaurant called Thanks Charlie and had a great meal - my best ever in Paris. After that I went to Samy's office/studio to try and change our plane seats online; but to no avail. I went back to the hotel to pack around 1:00 AM. Samy gave me a big suitcase with wheels to replace the big one of mine that has been the bane of the equipment moving all week because it was super heavy with no wheels. I made arrangements for two vans to pick us up at 6:45 AM to take us to the airport. I took some more shots of the Eiffel Tower from the bathroom window and finally got to bed around 2:00 AM.

The wakeup call came at 5:30 AM. I woke the others and we got downstairs just in time to meet the vans. We loaded up all our stuff for one last time in Paris and headed out into the dark, wet streets of Paris to the airport. We arrived early, 7:30 AM and our flight was not until 10:50 AM. Continental Airlines ticket windows didn't open until 8:00 AM. We were fourth in line. I was able to change Muzi's and my seats to a window and an aisle. We went through the security checkpoints without incident, except for the fact that Asante had a ball peen hammer in his carry-on bag. They searched him thoroughly both coming and now leaving. He went back to baggage check-in and put the hammer in his drum case.

We ate a light breakfast and then had to wait an extra hour before boarding at 11:00 AM and taking off at around noon. The flight was smooth and not at all uncomfortable.

After this tour, I have become a doctor of musical divinity, a Ph.D., Dr. Plunkenstein. I have earned my degrees through the school of living, performing and dreaming music and dues-paying. The school of mystic musings. The school of sacrifice and meditation and Hatha yoga and positive partying. I have bestowed the degree upon myself. Though I am "just a fucking musician" as I was once told by an angry club owner, I am also a producer, a critic, and empathizer and a counselor; and, I can justify my lack of employment by giving as much of my spirit to audiences who will listen and to those who seek me out or cross my path.

This tour has bought me another six months or so... Before it, I wondered if each gig was my last and if it were pure folly to continue to pursue a career in music. I am a lot like George W. Bush in my being tenacious to a fault, committed to staying the course at all costs, believing in the rightness of the calling and the cause. Those of our ilk take pride in our steadfastness and we could be martyrs. I hope and pray that I can attain and maintain balance and openness. That I can be a satellite dish receiving information and inspiration from the universe and then re-broadcasting it to my neighborhood and other parts of the known world...

I am amazed at how events can so dramatically influence attitude, even with so much study and training for self-control and actualization. I am amazed that such small things and trends can get me down and make me pessimistic about the future, especially when I have so many years of experience with receiving so many miracles! When will I get to the point that I have enough faith not to worry? Maybe I enjoy creatively working out worst-case scenarios that never come to pass?

This tour was a miracle! Another in a long, awe-inspiring line of just in the nick of time, life-saving miracles. It almost didn't happen. Then it was going to be postponed, again! But against all odds, it did come to pass, right on time to inspire me to keep on keeping on. As if God nodded his head to say, "Yes you can and you should stay on the path!"

I hope the others in the group, my fellow musician travelers, have also benefited. I know we all have bills waiting to be paid and families that have allowed us to take the time away from the day-to-day to go for the gold and the goal. Beyond the small amount of money made, and in spite of having to physically lug things around, I hope my bandmates enjoyed themselves, enjoyed making new audiences happy, and enjoyed expanding horizons.

I have had a group now for over 35 years. I have gotten to the point that I am kind of an institution through which a number of younger musicians get training and experience and then move on ever upward. I am like Roy Ayers, Lonnie Liston Smith, Pharaoh Sanders, Art Blakey, and Gil Scott-Heron; or at least I am trying to follow in their footsteps. I want to do some major touring, play bigger venues and have my show grow in size to be like George Clinton & P-Funk, James Brown, Sunny Ade, Fela Kuti, the Wailers, Maze, Earth Wind & Fire, Prince and Kool & the Gang. Is there enough talent and time? Time will tell.

Back at home. The plane trip back was long and tiring but not really that bad at all for me. Tonya had cramps; Corey was wedged in a middle seat on the long trans-Atlantic flight; Muzi had to prepare himself mentally to go to work the next day and Asante still had an hour's drive after we finally got to Richmond. But even with long waits and delays and an 8-hour flight plus a connecting flight, the trip wasn't that bad. Corey said, "Let's go again next week!"

We'll see…

Plunky eyes closed

V. Journal of the Drive-It Tour of France December 1-7, 2008

December 1, 2008 – On the flight from Newark to Paris…

I am not sure that I want to keep a journal on this trip. I am not sure I want to spend the time and the energy or share the introspection. My thoughts these past few weeks have been so personal that I am not sure if anyone else should be privy to them. I have been concentrating on promotion of my career, marketing my wares and pursuing personal and spiritual development so much that it seems I am self-absorbed. Maybe only others who are on a similar artistic journey or those in my personal *musiclan* – music clan – would be interested in a blog about my experiences on this tour.

I have been working on a theory of musiclans: groups of people responding to and influenced by the same music. Those of us who are fanatical about George Clinton and P-Funk are in the same musiclan. John Coltrane music worshipers are a musiclan. Patrons who come to the Martini Kitchen & Bubble Bar on a regular basis are a musiclan. These are "tribes" who share a common cultural experience based on musical interaction. Sharing excitement, movement, inspiration and valuation of a genre, recording, performance, or composition of music. Deadheads, Beatlemaniacs, hip-hoppers, jazz lovers, Old school R&B audiences, line dancers, and reggae groovers are examples of musiclans. Maybe this blog/journal will be for members of my musiclan – members of the I-Love-Plunky (& Oneness) Club. This one's for you.

We are going on our one week Drive-It Tour of France, to include two performances in Paris at the New Morning jazz club and in Montpellier in the South of France at Le Jam club. My seven-piece band includes my brother and long-time collaborator, P. Muzi Branch; keyboardist-vocalist Tonya Lazenby-Jackson; guitarist Carl Lester; vocalist Charlayne "Chyp" Green; New York based drummer John "Jozack" Zachary; and my son, Jamiah "Fire" Branch, on electronic percussion.

After days of preparation, a weekend of performances at our home base club, The Martini Kitchen & Bubble Bar, and packing, repacking and constant up-to-the-last-minute online marketing and management duties, it was finally time to embark on this, my next international performance excursion. I had been ready to go since last Monday, a week early; having my repertoire and set list planned out, my musicians passported, booked and ready, and my personal and business activities all lined up, budgeted and on auto-pilot for the duration of my trip. I was a little antsy, hoping that the final week of waiting to leave wouldn't allow for some mishap that would monkey-wrench our readiness to go. No last minute flu or traffic ticket or court case or medical emergency or family issues or foreclosure on property. Well, in fact all of those things had come up but they were all resolved before that last week of waiting to leave. I didn't want any new things to crop up.

This trip kicks off a December that is booked with a solid line up of gigs:

> December 3 & 4 – Paris, France, New Morning Club
>
> December 6 – Montpellier, France, Le Jam Club
>
> December 9 – Washington, DC, Zanzibar on the Waterfront Club
>
> December 12, 13 – Richmond, VA, Martini Kitchen & Bubble Bar
>
> December 17 – Richmond, VA, Toad's Place
>
> December 19 – New York, NY, Ashford & Simpson's Sugar Bar Club
>
> December 20 – Lynchburg, VA, Private Corporate Xmas Party
>
> December 26, 27, & 31 – Richmond, VA, Martini Kitchen & Bubble Bar Club

I got to the airport at 3:15 PM for our 5:30 PM flight and found that there would be delays. The ticket agent was going to try to get us on an earlier flight so we could get to Newark in time to be sure to make our connecting flight to Paris. Muzi and Carl were a bit late so we couldn't get checked in on time to be on stand-by for the earlier flight. So we had to wait until 6:40 to board for our original 5:30 flight.

The Richmond Free Press newspaper sent a photographer to get a shot of us getting ready to board our plane. It was a nice that they deemed it newsworthy that we local celebs were going to perform in Paris. In the recent days and weeks leading up to this trip, our community and fans from all over have voiced their approval and excitement for this confirmation of our musical success. So many folks have said things like "I'm so proud of you," or "It's been a long time coming," or "You really deserve this!"

It seems that getting to go on a tour on a tour in Europe or being submitted for a Grammy nomination are perceived as a validation of one's music; and they are, to be sure. But as often as not, these things are a confirmation of one marketing efforts and perseverance more than an indication of the quality of the music. Though I guess those things often go hand-in-hand. This period of success helps to validate one's whole career and the efforts of so many who collaborate and help along the way.

We board the plane at 6:30 and then sit on the runway for another 30 minutes before finally taking off for Newark Airport. Our flight to Paris was scheduled to depart at 10:00 PM so when landed in Newark we had only a little over an hour to get from Terminal A by shuttle bus to Terminal C. There we met up with Reynald DesChamps, my French connection with whom I have worked for over 10 years, and John Zachary, our drummer for this tour. They both live in New York. We were all smiles; happy we were all together and on our way to Paris.

The Paris flight was on time and uneventful, which is just the way I like them. The seats on this Continental 767 were smaller than on a Greyhound bus: a tight, barely comfortable fit for me, and an almost unbearable one for Tonya. Flying and especially landing in big cities always make me conscious of the magnitude of modern development: the highways and byways, the electricity and water requirements, the number of people and number of vehicles that have to be coordinated; are all impressive, if not overwhelming. So much energy, both physical and emotional. So much technology, both massive and micro. So many things working together to make things work together and so much of it unnoticed and taken for granted. The wiring of the runway lights and the wiring that make the airplane wing flaps go up and down and the wiring to the radar screens in the control towers and the wiring that run from the pilot's brain to his eyes and hands and the wiring between minds in synch moving toward the same goals. A lot of wiring indeed.

On the flight we ate a meal, watched movies, read books and did a lot of other things to pass the 6-hour, 11-minute flight. I brought my earplugs and mask to block out sound and light and proceeded to meditate and doze a little until the continental breakfast was served. Before too long we were landing in Paris. Entry and customs were a breeze. All our luggage and instruments arrived safe and sound. And we were here at last, ready to make music and good times happen.

Samy Elbaz, my main contact here in Paris, met us at the airport and we had a pleasant, post-morning rush-hour drive into the city. Paris is still a wonderful city: so vibrant, crowded, and quaint at the same time. It looks like Brooklyn, the Bronx, London, New Orleans and Manhattan all at once. It is old, having been here for 23 centuries; and new at the same time, constantly reinventing itself and being on the cutting edge of fashion, architecture, music, dance and all the arts. It is the quintessential European capitol. I just love it.

We got to the Cambrai Hotel and our rooms were not ready. In fact, our reservations were made incorrectly – we were not expected until tomorrow. The hotel staff was able to accommodate us but it took an hour to get the band's rooms ready one by one. I made sure everyone else was settled and it took two hours for my room to get straight. I was completely beat and bummed-out. I didn't like the hotel rooms because they were below our usual standard. I was really concerned about the ladies, especially Chyp, who is as particular, persnickety and as hard to please as anyone I know. But everybody went along with the program and settled in with no complaints. We were all so tired from the traveling we really just wanted to get some rest.

John Zachary and I walked around the neighborhood while waiting for my room to get ready. There were lots of stores, Africans, traffic and action all around. I went to exchange some money in order to have some Euros and I bought a phone card to be able to make calls back to the States.

By the time I got into my room, I had had to make three trips from lobby to take my horns, suitcase and other junk I had with me. I lay on the bed and nearly passed out with my clothes on. When I took my clothes off, I was too tired to fall asleep. I managed to get a couple of hours napping before it was time to get ready to meet our hosts to go out to dinner and sightseeing.

Samy and Reynald arrived to pick us up around 7:00 PM and we were driven to the New Morning, the venue where we would play tomorrow. We went to the club to make sure all the technical requirements would be met for our show. The sound engineer, Nadir, has done our sound mix for my previous shows at New Morning and he is really good as his job. Additionally, he really loves our music and respects what we do and he willingly does everything in his power to accommodate us. There is a band performing at the club this night as well, and Nadir says that he will work on getting the stage set up for us after that show. He will work late into the early morning hours so things will be ready for us when we come back for rehearsal and sound check tomorrow.

Then we go all the way across the city to a small café to have drinks and dinner. All total there are 12 of us: the seven band members, three promoters, the MC and an extra friend of Samy's. The café was very typical and very active. We spent several hours there drinking red wine, eating, talking and singing happy birthday to my son, Jamiah, who turned 27 years old today. I am not sure if it was the grandest way to celebrate his birthday in his world, but it was pretty special. I am sure he will remember 2008 as the year that he spent his birthday week touring in France.

Our driver for the night is Hugo, a friend of Samy's who is a professional tour guide. When we left the café he took us on one of his patented drives around Paris, showing first-time visitors Jamiah, Chyp, Jozack and the rest of us Paris, the City of Lights, decked out in all her Christmas decorations splendor. I had opted not to bring my video camera along on this trip because I have been here and done that before. But I forgot that this would be Christmas-time and the lights and decorations were truly spectacular. We went to the Eiffel Tower, the Champs d'Elysee, the Arc de Triumph, the Notre Dame, the Louvre, the red light district near the famed Moulan Rouge; and had an ooh la la sightseeing trip.

By the time we got back to the hotel it was midnight. Once again I was too tired to sleep. I lay awake going over the songs and the show in my mind. I meditated, looked at television and then closed my eyes for about two hours until finally I got up and took a Tylenol PM. Even so, I was awake for at least another hour. But then, the next thing I knew it was almost noon!

I got a croissant, yogurt, cheese and coffee for breakfast and then chilled out until 3:00 PM, when the driver, Stephan, came to pick us up to go to the club for sound check. Wow! Our ride was a black Mercedes-Benz minivan sitting on rims; classy and hip. What a nice ride! The band arrived at the venue in style.

The rehearsal went well. We went over the songs with Jozack, who hadn't played drums with us in years. I was a little apprehensive because I felt the tempos of the songs slipping or slowing down. This was largely due to his unfamiliarity with my show and his tentativeness caused by having to really listen to be prepared for all the changes I like to throw into the music without much warning.

At 5:30, we left the club to come back to the hotel to eat, rest and change clothes. We bought a lot of Chinese food right across the street from the club, took it back and feasted right in the hotel lobby.

The show was really quite special! The opening act was a Ghanaian singer, Sophia Nelson, who spent time in London but now lives in Paris. She sounds like a mature and sophisticated Sade. Her band was composed of excellent musicians from Africa, Cuba and Paris and a background singer from Atlanta, GA. Their show was quite good and Sophia's music was as diverse and international as her band and her own background.

After her hour-long set, the MC brought us on stage to a rousing ovation and we proceeded to funk things up. We opened with "More Than Meets The Eye," a jazz funk instrumental from my latest CD Drive It. Then we played "Follow Me" and "Hop Skip & Jump" from the Cold Heat CD. We performed old and new original songs and the audience seemed to really love the music. As we got funkier and funkier, they got more and more into it, dancing and screaming encouragement. By the time we ended the set they were screaming for more. We did an encore, left the stage again and thought that would have been the end of it, but five minutes later they were still screaming for more, so we went back out one more time.

After the second encore, when we attempted to leave the stage, one fan blocked the door to our dressing room, not letting us off the stage. He would not move. The crowd was still cheering. He begged us to play one more song and even got down on his knees and offered me the ring off his finger. I thought he was too funny, but he was so exuberant with his protest that I relented and went back on for a third encore. Too wild! After that one Reynald, our road manager, propped the door open so we could go right into the dressing room.

What a fun performance it was! The band really enjoyed themselves. Everyone was all-smiles and happy vibes ruled the dressing room as fans and friends and business people streamed through for picture-taking and congratulations and expressions of how much they enjoyed the show. It was emotionally satisfying to feel the energy, support and love of these fans, our Paris, France musiclan. After the wind-down and downing some red wine, our black Benz van drove us through the late-night, rain-wet reflective Parisian streets back to the hotel. All in all the night was a satisfying experience.

Breakfast at the hotel the next morning was right on time. Though it was a light continental style with just yogurt, coffee, croissants with cheese and jam, somehow it hit the spot. I spent the morning resting. I surmised that even at my age I could do multiple nights of gigs in a row if I could spend the days resting. I am blessed to be able to make a living solely through my various musical endeavors: record sales, commercial performances, licensing music, school lectures, etc. Some musicians also hold down a day job while gigging most nights and that is a wearying proposition. It is imperative that musicians have a plan for how to develop their careers and businesses.

I made phone calls back to the states, used the Internet on my laptop from my room and generally had a pleasant day. The weather was again cool, rainy and blustery. But by afternoon the sun peeked through and lightened the mood.

I had a photo session for a jazz magazine and the photographer was an older gentleman who used two old Nikon cameras, one for color and one for black and white film. Amazing, not digital, but film! I think the pictures will be like those old Blue Note Records album cover shots. I hope they will be cool. These days a photographer will often shoot 400-500 digital shots to get 10 good ones. This guy shot a total of maybe 30. We'll see how they turn out.

I bought a shirt and tie at a local shop on the block with the hotel. This is a bustling area with lots of inexpensive shops and restaurants. The neighborhood is right around the Gard Du Nord (North Train Station) and it teems with activity and a mix of races. We are comfortable here and don't have to spend a lot of cash to eat and pick up things we need.

Plunky painted up in dressing room with horns

Our driver picked us up to go to the New Morning around 7:30 PM and we already can see that the crowd will be bigger than last night. We are all relaxed and waited in the dressing room while Sophia Nelson and her band performed. I did go out to see some of their set, which was really polished, entertaining and urban. This second night confirmed my opinion that her international group with members from Africa, Cuba, France and Atlanta are all excellent musicians, and Sophia is experienced and attractive. Her warmth both on and off stage is readily apparent.

Our show was really hot, much tighter than the night before. Jozack on drums seemed a lot more relaxed and comfortable and funky. The crowd really loved the music and danced and swayed the night away. We took them on a journey through time and space and the music was our vehicle. Once again we had to do multiple encores. I had to really work my body to give the drummer a visual representation of where I wanted the energy level and the tempos. By the end of the night I was drenched in sweat. But everybody in the band felt like we did an incredible set.

Again fans came to the dressing room for autographs and photos. After a while all the flashes from the cameras started to blur my vision and I was happy when that part was done. I got so many comments from fans indicating that that they had been moved by the music and the show. One journalist whose name is Sheidia (which means Fragrant One) came both nights said she could feel our spirit and she was so impressed with our music.

Several people would clasp my hands or kiss both cheeks or hug me while giving heartfelt thanks for the music. I can usually sense when a person has been truly moved by the experience by the sincerity of their expression. I know how they feel because I have been that fan who has been truly moved by the music; like when I have heard Pharaoh Sanders or Sly and the Family Stone or George Clinton & P-funk or King Sunny Ade or a moving gospel performer in church.

Some people in the audience seem transfixed by the proceedings, like they are having a spiritual experience. It is interesting because in some ways that is exactly what I am trying to do. I am trying to give my energy, my emotion, my very all, to try to transcend the physical by a sheer act of willful surrender to the moment, to create a transcendent moment in time. I am sacrificing myself for the greater good to create a special, timeless happening. I try to give my best in the belief that whether it is good or not, the performance will be uplifting by sheer acts of will and surrender. Even in a nightclub the musical experience can and should be spiritual. Because everything is, or can be…

After the show Sophia Nelson came to me to say that she could feel our positive energy from the moment we hit the stage and she was moved by it. She said that pure musical energy could not be faked; and she and I agreed on that point. She is a beautiful lady with a beautiful spirit. We talked for a few minutes and shared smiles. She said the next time she comes to see us she would have on a Plunky tee-shirt.

One older French woman came both nights, bought a different tee-shirt each night and wore them both, one on top of the other. One guy asked me when we would be coming back to perform in Paris and when I told him maybe as soon as April or May he literally skipped out of the club, like he was a kid and I had given him a small toy or piece of candy.

Tonya and Chyp talked about a woman in the audience near the end of the show that proceeded to strip her clothes off and security had to come to stop her. After the show when I came out of the dressing room carrying two pairs of jeans a young women grabbed one pair and she and I were in a tug of war. She would not let go and I was determined to hold on to them because they belonged to the jeans company that was one of the sponsors and they had asked for the extra pairs to be returned. The girl even held on with her teeth. Then while holding on to the jeans with all her might with one hand, she proceeded to take off her pants, stripping down to her skimpy panties. So of course, at that point I let her have the sponsor's jeans. But when she put on the contested jeans they were way too large for her narrow hips. But I knew that they would be. She put her own pants back on while I and the few other people still in the place gave her a round of applause.

The ride back to the hotel was in the fly-est car I have ever been in. It was a black Mercedes-Benz limo that had been tricked out with $35,000 in extra accessories, including 22 channel televisions with 5.1 surround sound, individual temp controlled air-conditioning for each seat, Champaign bar, and assorted other high-tech goodies. What a ride! The driver made three trips back and forth to shuttle us to the hotel. The band was gassed and so impressed. A fitting end to the night.

The soundman gave me CDs of the night's performance and I started listening to it on headphones in my room. I was mesmerized by the sound and the grooves we had pumped out at the club. I stayed up until after 4:00 AM listening to it. I had a hard time falling asleep even then, replaying "Hop Skip & A Jump" in my head and silently writing new lyrics to the groove.

The next morning, Friday, I woke at 8:00 AM but lay in bed with my eyes closed trying to get rest even if I didn't get more sleep. I got the continental breakfast downstairs and came back to the room to get ready for a video interview at noon. The interview went well and we had the rest of the day free. That afternoon I roamed around with Jamiah in the neighborhood shopping. We bought some hip Italian casual shoes and had Kentucky Fried Chicken for lunch. The KFC was the Blackest place in town, filled with Africans of all persuasions from the front door to the behind the counter staff. Chicken is the universal Black food.

Tonya stayed in and rested all day. Muzi, Carl and Jozack went sight-seeing and Jamiah, Chyp and I went out on our own excursion. The weather was autumnal, but not at all unpleasant. We walked a couple of miles, then took a bus downtown to the Lafayette Galleries department stores area and did some shopping. There were bustling crowds shopping and sightseeing and watching the elaborate kinetic Christmas displays in the department store windows. We walked around some more, and then we took the Metro over to the Champs d'Elysee for more sightseeing and shopping and a lot more walking.

I was cold and tired and my knees were aching from pounding the cold hard pavement but it was rewarding because I know that Chyp and Jamiah were having their first Paris experience and I was happy to be their host and guide.

Finally, we decided to come back to the hotel around 9:30. We took the metro but got off at a stop that wasn't the closest one to our hotel, which meant we had to walk several more blocks. Chyp hadn't eaten and Jamiah hunted up a Chinese restaurant that turned out to be great; or at least it seemed quite good to us at that moment.

New Guestbook Entry on our Website – added Friday 5 Dec 2008 5:50:08am EST:

Name: Ben Still'a

Comment:

"Dude, guys, yesterday in Paris you simply FUNKED THE SHIT OUT'A ME!!!! I think it's the grooviest stuff I've ever seen on stage, seriously it was MIND BLOWING. I really really, really don't understand why the New Morning wasn't fully booked... THAT is unacceptable! Anyway we were there and we had sooo much pleasure feeling your groove. PLUS I'm a BIG fan of the old-school Chuck Brown style GOGO swings you gave us all night, that was the best thing ever. Hope you come back very soon in Paris. Peace."

We are scheduled to leave here at 9:00 AM in the morning to get to the train station for our 11:00 AM high speed train to Montpellier in the south of France, so I told everyone to pack before going to bed. I finally got to bed around midnight and slept only an hour-and-a-half before waking up and not being able to get back to sleep until after 5:30 AM! I worried that I was blowing my chance to get enough rest before the gig that night. I was also coming down with a cold and a sore throat and I was praying that I wasn't going to have any major physical problems for the final gig of the tour.

Tonya's call woke me up at 8:30 AM and that gave me just enough time to shower, shave and get a quick cup of tea before the driver arrived. Of course he was right on time, so I was rushed. It took two trips in the van to get all of us and our luggage and instruments to the train station. Then we had an hour's wait before boarding the high-speed train to Montpellier. Of course, our train car was the absolute farthest down the track from the station so we had to walk forever, hauling all our gear to it.

Once we got on board, the ride was really out of sight. Our seats were on the upper deck of the train, which afforded us the best views of the French countryside as we sped across the farmlands and through the occasional small town. The three-hour ride was smooth and pleasurable. I got a nap. Muzi took pictures. Carl talked to Reynald. We all had something to eat. The sun was out. And before too long we arrived in Montpellier where the weather was delightful and our spirits were lifted.

Plunky sings

Matthew, our driver for the day, met us at the station in a van large enough to carry all of us and all our gear. We went to the hotel, got settled in and I got him to take me to the pharmacy to buy some cold medication. An hour-and-a-half later we went to the venue for sound check.

Le Jam is a hot club. It is a concrete venue with a small amphitheater layout. The sound system is super and the engineers really know what they are doing. We had a really good sound check and everybody was feeling like we would have a good show. After sound check I did a taped interview with Ann, a young woman from Barcelona, which is surprisingly only three hours away by car. After that we all had a really good meal at the venue. We had great red wine, a salad, French bread, and a roast duck and gravy over rice, followed by cheese and more wine and capped with apple pear pie and coffee. We were stuffed and ready for a serious nap. But there was not enough time for one of those before the show.

By 8:00 PM, there were already people lined up outside, so we had a really good house when the doors opened. But the time we went on stage at 9:50 the place was full. It turned out to be not a good crowd, but an excellent one; definitely the best one this week. But then, it was a Saturday night, the weather was good and the people were ready for some funk. And we gave it to them!

Our show went extremely well. We were hot! The audience was pressed right up to the edge of the stage and the room pulsated with our grooves. They screamed and cheered more and more with each song. Our show flowed nicely and built in intensity and funkiness as the first set ended with them cheering for more.

Plunky in France

This performance was a hot example of what I have been saying for years: if we could just get to do our regular good shows that we do at home, in Europe, we could be an international smash hit. This was like one of our good shows at Martini Kitchen: hot and funky with good dynamics and making people move, but this time with the French fans going bonkers.

We did the second set and the audience was even more into it, cheering our every musical move. That only encouraged us to do more until it was better than a regular show; it became a series of really special musical moments. We did two encores, the second only after we had been in the dressing room and they continued screaming for more for almost 10 minutes. We had to do it. And even after that, they wanted more. We made lots of fans tonight. No doubt about it. We made converts.

They seemed to love us collectively and individually. They cheered and whooped and hollered for all of us. They really dug Chyp singing "Just Know That I Love You," and Tonya doing "Nevertheless" and her hip-hop rap. They dug Muzi and Fire and Jozack holding down the grooves and making things funky. But they really loved Carl's rhythm and lead guitar work. Carl was sizzling and when he went out into the audience and played, they went wild!

I think they liked me too! I think they appreciated my energy and my role as the leader of Plunky's band.

The repertoire and the pace of the show were nearly perfect. We have great original songs plus we quote or touch on enough cover songs that the combination creates a show that is both new and familiar at the same time. The lyrical content and comments about politics, positive vibrations and spiritually is uplifting food for thought and a powerful concoction is created when added to the group's musicianship and tightness. Our committed energy mixing with that of an audience that's really into it creates a synergy that is more powerful than the sum of its parts.

After the show we had to sign autographs on posters. We had fans that kissed my hands. The people who promoted the show and who worked in the venue were sincere in their accolades. People thought it was a great show. We did a photo session, drank wine, and packed up our stuff while people continued to express extreme gratitude for our show. Ann, the young deejay from Barcelona, said she hoped to try to get us a gig in Spain.

New Guestbook Entry on our Website – added Sun, 7 Dec 2008 7:19:58am EST:

Name: Paulie

Comment:

"Hi Plunkers!!!! We were at yesterday's concert in Montpeller!!!! It was absolutely fantastic!!!! I loved every minute of it; it took me way back to my funking roots!!! 3 hours of simple aural pleasure!!! thank you so much, for your energy, your talent and your music!!! Looking forward to seeing you guys again!! love plunks!!!"

Bruno, the head of the Cosmic Groove productions team who brought us to Montpellier, seemed genuinely pleased with both the show and the full house. One downer was that we didn't sell any CDs. I had mailed a box of 30 CDs to Bruno so we would have some to sell at the gig and so I wouldn't have to carry them with my luggage. The box hadn't been delivered to him until this morning, but he didn't bring the CDs to the club tonight. So although I kept telling the audience from the stage to "buy two of my CDs, one for yourself and one for your mama!" and people wanted to buy them, there were none to be had. That's so crazy because my gross revenues for the

Paris shows was reduced by 20%, so the 400 Euros from the sales here at Le Jam would have been welcomed.

But the good news from Bruno is that Cosmic Groove is doing a major festival here on the Riviera at an outdoor amphitheater right by the Mediterranean in August and he wants us to play at it. That would be so hot and really cool!

We got back to the hotel at 2:45 AM and the driver is supposed to come at 5:15 AM so we have said we might as well stay up. I am typing this blog. It's 4:00 AM now. Tonya and Chyp have taken showers and I guess I will get the others up around 4:30. We have 23 hours of traveling and layovers to do before we get back home to Richmond on Sunday night at 9:00 PM. Then we have a gig in DC on Tuesday at the Zanzibar Club, a Christmas party for a group of Black lawyers. I hope I get lots of rest before then.

Our trip back home was one of my most arduous ever. The flights, the layovers and delays made for 23 hours of rest-broken, butt-numbing tedium. We left the hotel right on time at 5:15 AM and got to the Montpellier Airport and went through the 45-minute process of getting us all checked in and our luggage checked through to Richmond. But the ticketing for three of us could not be confirmed from Paris to the States, so we had to do that in Paris.

vWhen we got to the Paris Airport, we had to go all around Robin Hood's Barn to get our tickets and boarding passes straight and to get to the right terminal and gate. Though that took us an hour, we still had four more hours to kill before the next flight at 1:00 PM. We napped, shopped, snacked, napped some more, medicated my increasingly bad cold, and dealt with the boredom and discomfort of the airport waiting area.

We finally boarded the Paris-to-Newark flight right on time. But once on the plane, we heard the pilot announce that we would be parked at the gate for one hour and the seven-hour flight would take eight hours and 40 minutes due to strong head winds. While it was long, the flight wasn't that uncomfortable, because it wasn't full and each of us were beside at least one empty seat.

When we landed in Newark for what would have been a three-hour layover, we had only a little over one hour to get through customs, recheck our bags and get to another terminal for the flight to Richmond. But before we could get through customs all their computers shut down, so we spent an anxious 30 minutes in that line and then had to rush to claim our bags. Muzi and Carl couldn't find theirs, so I rushed Tonya, Chyp, Fire, and Jozack on ahead.

We found the bags and literally make a mad dash to the train to get to the next terminal, get through security and get to the right gate, with 10 whole minutes to spare.

Once on this the final plane we had to wait parked at the gate for 45 more minutes due to high winds and the back-up of delayed planes. When we finally got back to Richmond, we were extremely happy to be home; however one of Muzi's bags and Fire's suitcase with his MPC instruments did not arrive. But those were delivered to our houses in the middle of the night.

It may be hard for people who are not directly involved to realize how much planning and effort that goes into even a short tour like this one. I think even some musicians themselves would be amazed. In my case I have been working with Reynald for over 10-15 years, aiming to do dates in France, in a relationship that started with him distributing some of my recordings both here in the U.S., Japan and Europe. This tour was the third time in the last five years that he and his friend, Samy, have promoted shows for us in France. In other words, it took five years and a lot of perseverance to get the first gig over there.

For this tour, we started planning nine months in advance, so it was like giving birth. There were lots of negotiations, emails, international calls; sending music, photos, web links; renegotiations; development of sponsors (like Edwin Jeans); working with publicists, journalists and photographers; arranging accommodations, airline tickets, flight changes, advertising, ticket sales, instrument and equipment needs; developing the repertoire; rehearsing; etc.

Then there are also the language and cultural differences. The French are often very excitable, argumentative, proud, edgy, and a little combative, even with each other, so any little misunderstanding can quickly escalate into a battle. A medium-size change might mean war. Promoters in general think that their part is the most important and everything comes in second place after money, PR and ticket sales.

But artists are the ones who make sacrifices of time, money, family relations and many other things to create music and put on a show. In preparing for this Drive It Tour of France we contended with: producing and shipping CDs, passport problems, threatened house foreclosures, major medical issues involving hospital stays, personnel changes, family issues, day job scheduling, luggage lost and found, diets and allergies, hang-ups, arrests and court appearances, and all manner of human interest stories and spin-offs.

On past tours I have kept notes and journals cataloguing the coincidences and synchronicities that happen along the way; noting how much luck, and how many interventions and blessings that happen just when needed to allow things to proceed as desired. These days I have also been realizing how much depends on my own efforts, my own planning, my marketing efforts, my sense of purpose and willingness to persevere and get the jobs done. If you don't sow, you won't reap. If you don't dream, pray and work; you are less likely to achieve, acquire and inspire.

Gotta keep Moving.

VI. JOURNAL OF A WEEKEND IN PARIS 2010
By J. Plunky Branch

March 25, 2010, Ivry, France, just outside Paris in the gallery apartment where I spent the night, 9:15 AM.

I am relatively well-rested, bathed, dressed and enjoying the morning in a rustic art gallery. Looking out through a sliding glass door across a wooden deck I can see a small courtyard surrounded by apartments in this suburb of Paris. Having spent the night here is a small wonder given the time and distance I have traversed since leaving the Washington, DC area so many hours ago. Let's see: I drove from Richmond, arrived at Dulles Airport, parked my car in long-term parking, took the shuttle bus to the terminal, checked in, went through security, waited three hours, took my flight to Montreal, waited two hours, then flew to Paris.

My airport experiences were quite pleasant, accustomed as I am to traveling alone and given the amenities of international airports. I rather enjoy being a quiet observer of the international community of journeyers and workers; alone with my thoughts, plans and whims and at the same time so much a part of the scene. At Dulles I had my *Washington Post* and the *USA Today* newspapers and their crossword puzzles to pass the time, and in Montreal I went online to check email and news of the world; so I was just fine.

My flights were just fine too. There were some short bits of turbulence on the trip to my Canada stop-over. But the transatlantic voyage on the Air Canada Boeing 777 was delightful. I re-selected my seat at the gate and managed to get a row of three seats to myself, giving me room to stretch-out for the sleep portion of my flight. The food was decent, the wine excellent, the in-flight touch screen entertainment was musical, and the flight crew cordial and unobtrusive. It was my "shortest" trip across the ocean ever.

Once on the ground in Paris luggage retrieval and customs were a breeze, and Sheidia, my publicist-hostess and erstwhile promoter of this weekend's two gigs, met me right outside the door of customs. Sheidia is a journalist of Algerian decent who is an avid funk music fan. She came to my last two gigs in Paris and since then she has communicated with me and worked tirelessly to get me a gig here in Ivry, France (just outside Paris) where she lives. Le Hanger is a city-funded venue that books groups from all over the place as a part of the town's cultural enrichment program. Funk, rhythm & blues, reggae, African and rock are mainstays of the music presented. Plunky & Oneness is considered quite a coup for the venue, and Sheidia and her colleagues are excited about our Saturday night show.

From the airport, Sheidia and I head straight to downtown Paris for an interview on Africa One Radio 105.7 FM. The station boasts a million listeners and we are happy to snag the interview at the 11 AM time slot. Everyone at the station is cordial and eager to take pictures with me and the interview goes well, with Sheidia acting as my translator. I was tired from my flights and baggage and everything, but I perked right up once the mikes were turned on. We were all smiles when we left the studio to head from downtown Paris out to Ivry to this gallery space where I would spend the night.

The drive out to Ivry was much shorter than I had imagined. There is little to designate the change from Paris to Ivry except a sign and perhaps a little less congestion. Plunky & Oneness are playing at the New Morning club in Paris on Friday night and the promoter for that gig has been complaining about the negative impact Sheidia's Ivry show has been having on his ticket sales. It was such an issue that a few weeks ago I had to lower my fee and then this week at the last minute he was going to cancel the show at New Morning which would have been devastating, to say the least. But given the proximity of the two venues and given that Le Hanger is subsidized, I can understand the problem with the competition between the two dates. Plus, because Sheidia is a journalist herself, she is really good at working the press for extra publicity for the Ivry gig.

At the gallery I had a lunch and a 30-minute nap and then it was back to Paris to do a 2:00PM interview on the Campus Radio Network. This one was taped for broadcast at 9:00 PM last night. Sheidia and I were even better this time with the pacing of my answers, the translating and interjections. The music would be interposed in post-production, so it was very professionally produced and satisfying. Once again the radio host was happy to have me in the studio and I was happy to be getting the promotion and media attention that can be so vital to generating and maintaining public support for my music.

We left that interview and headed straight back out to Ivry where we parked the city car and walked across the town to meet Stefan of the Soul Brothers Radio show, who would drive us 15 kilometers further out into the countryside to do another interview on his show from 7 to 8 o'clock. We got out to the rustic studio setup at about 5:45 so I took an hour nap in the car until 15 minutes before we went on air. Stefan is a record collector and a soul music connoisseur. He had his questions for me all printed out and translated. He and his crew of four deejays were genuinely excited to have me out there. They busy were taking pictures, plying me with snacks and juice, having me sign their records and saying that this day would go down in the annuls of the history of their radio shows.

Afterwards Stefan brought us back to Ivry and Sheidia and I had dinner at a Chinese restaurant. I was supposed meet Samy, my good friend and agent in France, but I was too tired. I got in around 10 and went to bed.

Now (10:30 AM) I am up waiting for Sheidia to get me downtown to meet my band members who have had their own long-assed trip from Richmond to Paris. They should be at the hotel by now and I need to get there to get them checked-in, and I have another interview in 90 minutes, at noon. Whew!

March 26, 1:15 AM Friday night after the New Morning gig; in my hotel room.

Yesterday Sheidia got to the gallery to pick me up just as I finished writing. I left all my things right there and we drove into Paris to the block where the New Morning club and the Best Western Hotel are located. When I got to the hotel, the guy who was to interview me was already there waiting, and Muzi, my bass-playing brother, was at the front desk getting ready to try to call me on Sheidia's cell phone. So it all came together quite nicely.

Muzi and the band had had a long and arduous trip, waiting in airports and most importantly flying on an older plane that was totally full with passengers for their trans-Atlantic flight. They were cramped in smaller seats with no room to spare. But they had no problems with baggage and customs and the driver had met them with a large van, right on time. Suffice it to say, they were happy to be checked in at the hotel and some of the band had already gone to bed for some much-needed rest.

I did my interview with a journalist for *Soul Bag Magazine*. He was an expert in 20th Century Black popular music and a saxophonist himself; so we were more than cool. The interview and photo session lasted over an hour and, though I enjoyed it, I was glad when we were done.

After that Muzi, Fire (my son) and I walked for about a mile to shop and sightsee. We went back to the area where we stayed the last time we were in Paris and went back to some of the shops where we had gotten good deals before. We bought some inexpensive, hip, casual shoes and then walked all the way back to the Best Western Hotel. Then we immediately went back out, this time taking the Metro further downtown to the more touristy area where the stuff is very expensive but quite nice. Most everything in Paris seems stylish and people of every ilk here seem to be aware of chic fashion.

We got caught in a rain shower. I bought a bag for my laptop computer and left it in a café and had to go back to get it. Muzi left his camera in a sushi shop and we went back to retrieve it too. We had fun taking the metro and we walked more than we should have, given our jet-lagged bodies; so by the time we got back to the hotel we were beat.

Samy, my agent, came by and we went out to dinner. Sheidia met us at the restaurant to bring me my luggage from the gallery and we had a tête-à-tête. The food was really good, the wine even better and the conversation was spirited, to say the least. We were two French persons, one Arab and one North African Jew, and me as the American mediator. I got in around 1:00 AM – worn out!

Today I got up around 10:00 AM and had the hotel's continental breakfast. Sheidia came to get me to take me to a 2:00 PM appointment with a big time promoter of Black music shows here in Paris. It was a good meeting and I am optimistic that we can make some business happen in the near future. I got back to the hotel in time to get ready for a five o'clock sound check.

The preparations for the sound check were running late, so we went to eat and then came back and got things ready for the show. The show went well. We got a decent house, perhaps with the promoter having a large number of invited guests. The audience was very enthusiastic and really into the music. There were lots of photographs taken and copious amounts of exuberant cheering to go along with the flashes. We sweated our way through two sets and two encores and then I went to the front lobby to sign autographs on the purchased CDs. I got me and my things back across the street to the hotel…

Now I am tired again.

Monday – On the plane headed to Toronto.

The next day we waited for Sheidia to come pick us up to go out to Ivry. Sound check was supposed to be at 3:00 PM but we didn't leave the hotel until 2:00 and by the time we got to Le Hanger and got a brunch the sound check wasn't complete until 6:30 PM, just time enough to check in the hotel, get dressed, get back to the venue, have dinner and do the show.

The Ivry show went really well too. Once we got started the audience warmed up to us and by the end of the first set they were enthralled with the music. The second set brought on more of the funk and more responsive energy and cheering. After a long encore medley we were spent and the show was over. Once again I signed autographs and took pictures with fans before being driven back to the hotel.

I slept well but not long before getting up to have the continental breakfast buffet. It was a cloudy Sunday with off-and-on showers but everyone (Muzi, Jamiah, Tonya, Chyp and Derrick) except José decided to take the Metro into downtown Paris for sight-seeing and shopping. We went to the Louvre Museum and then to the Arch of Triumph and down the Champs de l'Elysee. A pleasant day was had by all and then we took the metro back out to Ivry.

At 7:00 PM, Sheidia hosted a dinner for us with her family at the gallery where I spent the first night. I was apprehensive about a family dinner, but the event was casual, relaxed, arty, and cordial beyond my best expectations. The food was abundant and tasty. The hospitality was sincere and warm. The family members were all friendly and really into Black music. The wine flowed. The artwork was charming, commercial, and good. The whole affair was up-beat, unpretentious, simple, and satisfying – a fitting end to our weekend. We are really looking forward to coming back to Ivry!

VII. JOURNAL OF A TRIP TO MONTREAL

What a week of music and travel! Sunday I drove 75 miles from Richmond to Hampton, Virginia, to see Brides of Funkenstein featuring Dawn Silva. While that was a little bit of a distance for me, my colleague,

Sheidia, came all the way from Paris, France to catch the show.

Sheidia, my French publicist, had been trying set up a meeting between me and French hip-hop artist, Akhenaton of the IAM Band, in the hopes that we could explore prospects for collaborating on some music projects. When she found out that Akhenaton was doing a show in Montreal, Sheidia set up a meeting for me and my son, Fire, with Akhenaton and his manager at 1:30 on the afternoon of his Thursday night show.

I spent Monday and Tuesday in the Washington, DC-Baltimore area meeting with my distributor, promoters, gig venues and a video producer, Skipper Bailey, a friend of mine, who had me look at storefront space that he wants to develop into a video production facility. I got back to Richmond early Wednesday morning and spent the day clearing my desk of pressing items (bills and correspondences) and packing one carry on suitcase with my clothes, laptop, camera, CDs, etc.

I got up at 3:00 AM Thursday morning to get to the airport by 4:15 to take a 6:00 AM flight to Montreal. After a brief changeover in New York, Fire and I arrived in Canada at 10:30 AM and took the $8 shuttle bus into downtown Montreal. Because of the number of times I had to show my passport and travel documents, I had those things in a small plastic bag for easy access. When the shuttle bus reached the end of the line we had a five-minute stop before the bus would make a loop and head back toward the airport, taking a route that would pass nearer our hotel. I decided to go into the bus terminal to exchange some currency and it took a bit longer than expected. When I got back to the bus it had already taken off. Fire had removed our luggage but he didn't see the plastic bag I had left in my seat. So I lost my passport! And my little writing pad that had the contact information for the people we were to meet. All I knew was the rapper's stage name, Akhenaton, and his wife/manager's name, Aicha, but not their last name.

It was 11:30 AM. I jumped on the next shuttle bus at the station and had the driver contact his headquarters and they in turn called the other driver, who checked and said he didn't see my plastic bag or my documents on his bus. It was now 12 noon. Fire and I walked to our hotel but we couldn't check in until 3:00 PM; so we left our baggage there in storage and walked the eight or nine blocks to the Hyatt Regency Hotel to try to locate Akhenaton and his wife.

It is a 90 degree, sunny, muggy day in Montreal. Walking in the noon day sun, four blocks, then nine blocks, with the stress of losing my documents, feeling stupid, in a foreign country, with Fire complaining, with little sleep, took its toll. This is officially a downer.

In the meantime I am trying to contact Sheidia in Paris by cell phone, without success. We get to the Hyatt and it is a massive complex of shopping mall, food courts, business offices and more. It is so large that it takes lots of walking and forever just to find outlets to plug in our phones and my laptop to contact people by internet. I finally hear from Sheidia and get Akhenaton's name, Philippe Fragione. He is not in his room but I leave a message that we will be in the lobby.

Near 1:20 PM I go back out on the main street to try to intercept the shuttle bus we had taken as it made its return trip circuit. After five minutes I flag down the bus, jump on board and locate my plastic bag. Someone had put it on the large luggage rack and a suitcase had smushed and hidden my little bag. But I found it in ten seconds and my passport and papers were there and now back in my hand.

Fire and I hurry back to the Hyatt's fourth floor lobby and soon a bald-headed, thin, 42-year-old-white guy comes in looking and inquisitively asks, "Plunky?" It was Philippe Fragione, aka Akhenaton, the renowned French rapper.

Until recently I had never even heard of Akhenaton and his IAM band from Marseilles, France. From his videos on YouTube, I could ascertain that he has a legion of followers, he's been around for a while and that his impact has been international not just in France. Because I don't speak enough French I couldn't tell what his songs were about, gangster or positive, or if his celebrity was based on him being a pop icon like Vanilla Ice or having street and artistic cred like Eminem. But here I was in Montreal Canada having lunch with him and his wife.

He speaks English. Great. He was born of Italian parentage, grew up in France, spent several years in Brooklyn, NY, during 80s & 90s learning to speak English and meeting rappers and hanging-out. He moved back to France and started his hip-hop IAM band which over the years became immensely popular. During our 90 minute lunch he talked about his commitment to positive, political content, his healthy eating and lifestyle; his world touring and his productions. He loves the power of African rhythms, Afro-Brazilian music, and his Moroccan wife and manager is of West African descent so he is well versed in Black culture. He and his bandmates all have Egyptian stage names and he once did a concert in front of the Pyramids backed by the Egyptian orchestra. I was impressed, not so much by his accomplishments, as by his politics, his easy-going self-confidence and his casual grace.

We talked about collaborating on some music projects. He has done

Akhenaton and adoring fans in Montreal

things with a number of American soul artists, including, I think, Millie Jackson and the Dells. He was familiar with the rapper/producer Oh No from L.A. who produced a CD of tracks made of samples and snippets of songs from my early Oneness of Juju albums. So, we talked about Akhenaton rapping on one of the tracks from my latest CD, Plunky On Fire. We also talked about Akhenaton producing some tracks from some of my earlier recordings, like Oh No did; and perhaps us bouncing some new ideas back and forth via the internet. Akhenaton said that he was doing a club date in New York in November and perhaps Fire and I could do a walk-on appearance with him then. It was a very positive meeting.

Fire and I rode in the van with the group to the venue, the Metropole, for their sound check. We took pictures and checked things out as they prepared for the show that night. Then around 5:00 PM Fire and I left the venue and walked back to our hotel to rest a bit before the show. Around 8:30 we walked back to the area of the venue, had dinner in a café and went to the show at 10:00.

We had all-access backstage passes so we entered through the stage door. The place was packed. The energy was high. The show was incredible! Akhenaton and his rapper partner and two deejays held the sold-out crowd in the palms of their performing hands for a 90-minute show plus 30 minutes of encores. More than 25 or 30 New York style rap songs in French. They exhibited boundless energy on stage, spewing an astounding number of words to the delight of their Canadian fans. The four men onstage were an abbreviated version of the IAM Band but the show was a complete spectacle to behold. The audience response was exuberant and heartfelt. The respect for these artists was completely obvious by the ovations bestowed.

I knew Akhenaton had millions of views on YouTube and has sold bunches of recordings but sometimes those stats can be hyped or overblown. But on this night in Montreal I saw with my own eyes the true power of this artist. The group drew between two and three thousand fans who paid $46 each; that's a minimum of over $80,000! The people voted with their dollars. On this night Akhenaton could have be president of that sea of people.

Akhenaton

After the show we hung out in the dressing room with the group basking in the afterglow of a great show. At about 12:30 AM I walked the ten Montreal nightlife blocks to our hotel and Fire stayed to hang out with the deejays.

When Fire got back to the room at 2:18 AM we decided that we might as well take the 3:20 shuttle bus back out to the airport to make our 6:20 AM flight. So at 3:00 AM we walked the four blocks to the bus terminal and caught the bus (our $8 tickets were good for 24 hours, so that was a great deal). We checked in for the flight, went through security, spent some nervous moments going through the extra scrutiny and searches by U.S. Customs, and made our three-and-a-half-hour flight to Miami.

In Miami, we had to walk from Gate D1 to another terminal's gate J8 to take a two-hour flight to Charlotte, NC. Then we had a two hour wait for the 90-minute flight to Richmond which arrived at 5:10 PM. I had a 6:00 tennis match scheduled, but even though it was rush hour traffic and I had to change clothes in the car, I would have made the match had it not been rained-out while I was in route.

I then went to do my 9:30 gig at the Martini Kitchen & Bubble Bar: three full, hour-long sets. I had big fun making music with my band and was energized by the dancing crowd while we all partied with a purpose. I got home at 2:15 AM, stayed up until 3:00 AM and crashed until 7:00 AM.

At 8:00 AM the band gathered at my house and at 8:30 we took the three-hour drive in the van to do a gig out in rural Eastern Shore, Virginia, for a Juneteenth celebration. It was 90 degrees in the shade as we played from 1:00 to 2:00 PM and then got back on the long road home at 2:30. I got to my house by 6:30 PM totally beat. I was gratified by the week of music and business and new friends and new prospects, but I was totally spent. In fact, I think I set a new record for fatigue. However, by 9:00 AM the next morning, I was on the tennis court for three sets of doubles… Tennis anyone?

—Plunky

VIII. CAPITAL JAZZ SUPER CRUISE III

Day 1. 8:00 PM Saturday evening, October 10, 2009 aboard the Royal Caribbean Grandeur of the Seas for the Capital Jazz Super Cruise in my state room.

I have just returned to my room to rest a bit after seeing Jonathan Butler's solo guitar performance where he was joined by trumpeter Rick Braun for singular duo concert in the atrium of the grand ocean liner with the sunlight filtering from above and the Chesapeake Bay streaming pass the glass walls. People were hanging over the railings five floors up, lounging about, taking pictures and taking it all in. I felt blessed and happy to be there to witness the scene. I realized I am finally underway and this is what it will be all about: participating in a wonderful, relaxing happening, filled with music, scenic views and camaraderie. The audience already feels like family, knowing we are bonded in our love for music, culture and each other. I feel it. And I can feel that they feel it too. That's why most have paid around $2,000 to come on aboard and spend this week sailing from Baltimore to the Bahamas and Key West, Florida: to listen, party and be baptized in the company of world-class jazz and soul. It seems like these last few days leading up to this have taken forever. They have been filled with preparation and the expenditure of energy making music and madness. We performed at the Martini Kitchen last night (Friday) for our bon voyage party. The club was packed with beautiful hometown people, most of whom had come for their own reasons to celebrate. We jammed long and hard, sweating out the hits and making the room pulsate to the rhythms of the night. We played until 1:30 AM, our usual ending time, but that seemed a really late hour considering we were to gather at my house at 6:30 AM to load up and drive to Baltimore. By the time I got home at 2:15 and puttered around, wound down and got to bed at 3:00 AM, I had only less than three hours of closed eyes rest before making the wake up calls to the band and doing that final bit of packing. Of course, I had way too much stuff to bring and manage: three saxophones, video camera, digital recorder, 200 CDs, clothes, tennis racket, laptop, six musicians, their guests, five vehicles, boarding passes, passports, directions, headaches, worries and staying positive in the face of fatigue.

Before going to play the gig at the club last night, I spent a couple of hours assembling CD box sets and shrink-wrapping them to have them for sale on the cruise. At that time I lamented having even scheduled the club date on the night before the cruise. But in the end or the beginning, it had all worked out. We drove in our caravan at speeds of 80-90 mph up I-95 North, made it on time, got everything loaded in at the port and settled in on the ship along with the other musicians and tech people all before the noon arrival of the paying customers.

Now I am getting ready to go have a 9:00 PM sound check poolside on the top deck of the ship. We perform at noon tomorrow (Sunday), but since we are the first act in that setting, both we and the sound crew want to take advantage of the opportunity to tweak the system and get things right for our show.

12:47 AM Back in my stateroom

Tired as I don't know what! At 9:00 PM we went up to poolside for our sound check. The sound system, the engineer and the whole tech crew is first-rate and the equipment is state-of-the-art. We worked on getting the mixes just right and had a mini-rehearsal for about an hour. I think the sound was incredibly good, ringing out over the bay in the black of night. We drew a small crowd out to the pool to party to our sound check. I think it will be a hot show tomorrow. I think everybody in the band was satisfied and our crew of Jay, Jon and Al were on the case and happy to be along.

I came back to the room, changed clothes and went to see Najee in concert. He is a very special saxophonist who knows his music, plays modern changes and writes very smooth melodic compositions. I always enjoy listening to him. He was backed by Spur of the Moment band, instead of his regular touring group. Spur is an outstanding group who has lots of experience being a pro backup band. They nailed Najee's music, but the show lacked pacing and the tightness that comes from the comfort and nuances of a working unit. But the show did have its high points though. One was when alto saxophonist Candi Dulfer came out to jam with Najee on a song. And another happened when Najee was getting people from the audience to sing on mike and this lady really nailed her part of the song. I mean she really sang! And it turned out to be Silver, who was formerly a member of the group Chic. And that's one of the beauties of this cruise, once-in-a-lifetime pairings or unique musical moments.

After the show I went to the casino and learned how to play Three Card Poker. At one point I was down $90 and I was on what would have been my last hand, I hit a straight flush that paid $250! After 30 minutes I was up $100 so I quit while I was ahead.

Then at midnight we went up to the club to hear Chuck Brown, who was absolutely killing it! They were rocking that heavy go-go swing thing. After the first 10 minutes the whole place was partying like they wanted to prove something! The sound system was off the chain. The kick drum was thumping you in the chest. The whole group was grooving hard. And Chuck himself looked like he was really having the time of his life. As always. The music was a tremendous unifier. This older, largely black DC area crowd powered this big-assed ship right on down the Chesapeake Bay headed for the tropical zone. But it was already hot on this cruise, right where we are!

Day 2. Sunday morning 8:30 AM

I dreamed of my set and went over the repertoire for my show in my mind while the ocean gently rocked the boat. The dark drapes in the cabin did their job, covering the porthole window so thoroughly, I couldn't tell when the sun rose. I got up and crept out of the darkness of my stateroom and went up to the top deck to be greeted by a partly cloudy, warm and humid morning. Joggers and other early risers did their thing while the sound crew was already busy readying the system for today's music. I laid back on a deck chair to ponder the ocean and to write the song list for our concert at noon today. I think we'll get a good crowd given that it will be the first music of the day and before the football games start; and everybody onboard will be up and about, and ready to do something outside on the first full day of cruising. I am confident that the band will be ready to rock the whole ship and the passengers will enjoy our show.

A little bit of yoga. Shower. Breakfast. And then it will be time to get ready to do what we have come on this cruise to do – funk it up.

7:15 PM Sunday after my show. In the club listening to Ken Ford.

My show this afternoon ended up being a grand occasion! The weather was around 79 degrees with enough humidity to make it feel hotter. Folks all kicked

Grandeur Of the Seas cruise ship

back in the deck chairs, in the pool and the hot tubs, leaning over the railings of the top deck and digging our funk jazz and go-go grooves.

It didn't get off the best of starts however. After such a great sound check last night, when we kicked off the set there was an annoying glitch in the sound system that imitated the bass drum but in an off-time, so it was hard make the go-go groove happen.

I was almost distraught and I am sure it showed on my face. My son, Fire, even reminded me to smile. Once the engineer corrected the problem, it took me a while but I was finally able to relax and let the songs and the rhythms take me and the audience on an enjoyable excursion into music glory. We played for two solid hours, non-stop, and by the end we had turned it into a Plunky dance party! People jamming on the dance floor, sweating out the hits

Top: Plunky & Oneness jamming on the Capital Jazz Cruise; Middle: Plunky jams on boat; Bottom: Fire plays for cruise party.

Top: The audience at my pool side jam;   Bottom: Plunky playing to cruise loungers.

and converted into Plunky fans.

Afterwards, there was a line of folks who bought my CD. I signed autographs and took pictures with my new friends. After that, I spent the afternoon chilling out on the decks, watching the Redskins football game (they lost!) and winding down from the show.

I got so many congratulations, accolades and compliments! I don't think have ever had more positive feedback from any show I have done. In fact, it seems like everyone I run into has something nice or better to say. After several hours of repeated praises it is almost getting embarrassing. People genuinely were impressed or moved or converted; musicians, staff, crew, and mostly music lovers just gushed their approval.

I think the feedback is also a result of being up close and personal, artist and audience together in confined space, all be it a large space. We are seeing each other repeatedly on the various decks, in the venues onboard, in the corridors, elevators and lounge areas. People are taking pictures and conversing with the musicians to a degree that isn't normally possible when the performer might leave soon after the show. Here, we are all in the same boat and interacting is the norm.

Day 3. Monday morning 9:00 AM

Last night at dinner and beyond I was still meeting people who wanted to take photos with me and asking me questions about why they haven't heard more about me in the past and getting my autograph.

I spent the late afternoon and early evening roaming about, lounging about, watching a rainbow sail by and glancing at a glorious sunset.

After dinner I went to the casino and then I went to see Kem in concert. He was quite the consummate smooth crooner with a polished demeanor, a confident stage presence and a really good band. I stayed for the whole show and was quite impressed with his songwriting and his dynamic presentation of his new material.

After that show I went to the midnight jam session led by saxophonist Mike Phillips. It was a slamming affair with Mike calling various musicians to the stage. The audience was packed into the club setting, listening and rocking to the likes of Candi Dulfer, Joey Somerville, Brian Culbertson, Prince band alumni, two outstanding trombonists and saxophonists who played unbelievably ornate improvisations and combinations. When Mike called Chuck

Brown's drummer to the bandstand, the dance floor filled up and after a brief stint out there with the crowd I left to get some rest.

But I didn't get much. I got up early this morning to go up to top deck, get some juice, use the Internet and get my day started. I am still tired from this weekend and I hope I'll catch up on rest this week…

END PART I

Day 3. Tuesday, October 13, 9:00 AM in my cabin.

There may not be that much to blog about for the rest of the week. We don't have to perform again, so for me this will be a vacation cruise, now docked in Nassau Bahamas, then on to Key West, Florida, and finally back to Baltimore. I have finished my work portion of the week, though I have told the band that we will take some group photos to try and get a new promo shot of the group.

The band members are enjoying themselves. The music, entertainment and scenery have been really special. We had a group meeting to discuss the show and the business of this cruise and I think we shared several good ideas on improving the preparation and flow of our concert shows. They want fewer surprises in the repertoire for concerts and big shows. They suggest a strong opening fanfare groove to introduce me. I have got to remember to not let any distresses show on my face and to keep entertaining even when things go awry. We want to use more dynamics and contrasts in volumes of the songs. All good suggestions.

Yesterday we docked at Coco Cay, a private little island owned by Royal Caribbean Cruise line, where we swam, lounged about, and had a beach party. When we got back to the ship we went to see Spur of the Moment perform in the club. They are DC's finest urban jazz band and they were at their tightest last night. The place was packed and the people were right in the groove with the groove. Chuck Brown even came out and did a number with them. The crowd went wild.

After that show we went to the comedy show and were thoroughly entertained by AJ Jamal and Jay Lamont. AJ Jamal went on second and he was very funny, but Jay Lamont was absolutely the perfect act for this cruise because most of his show was performing parodies of songs, imitating soul and jazz stars and talking about the impact of our music on our lives. He was so funny! The audience roared its approval and stayed in stitches the whole hour he was on. Now I know why people say, "side-splitting" because I laughed so hard I had a pain in my left side. He nailed his impressions, sound effects, and had a great repertoire. He was a riot. And his impersonation of President Barack Obama was the best I've seen.

Later I played three-card poker in the casino, walked outside on deck five and then went to bed around 2:00 AM. Now this morning I'll go have breakfast, exercise and go out into Nassau.

9:30 PM Back in my stateroom.

I got up this morning, had breakfast and then went out into Nassau. We got a tour drive around the capital city of 200,000; seeing the sights, getting historical information and sampling local cuisine. After visiting the Paradise Resort and its casino I came back onboard in time for the 4:00 PM poolside sail away party featuring War.

I decided to watch the show from the hot tub. Wow, what a scene: hundreds of music lovers partying poolside to War's greatest hits. They played "Cisco Kid," "All Day Music," "The World Is A Ghetto," "Slipping Into Darkness," and so many others of their hits. People were dancing, singing along and whooping it up! The sound system was loud and clear, the band was jamming and the weather was almost perfect. Everybody seemed aware of the beauty of the setting and the conditions. Then after thirty minutes of the music reverberating all over the harbor, our Grandeur of the Seas cruised out of the harbor and on out to sea with the music pumping.

I was in the hot tub with several people including Jonathan Butler, and danced and waved and sang along loudly. There were three other hot tubs, a large pool, a surrounding balcony and people everywhere. Rich Braun, who got his start with War when he was right out of college, played with the group for the entire set. Candi Dulfer sat in as the first of a string of other great players who jammed with the group. War played for two hours, non-stop and the party didn't stop until the music did.

Day 4. 8:00 AM in the Windjammer dining area looking out to sea.

There is just something about the sea. Maybe its vastness symbolizes our small place in the universe and dwarfs our sense of self. But at the same time, looking out over the ocean gives us a perspective of limitless possibilities.

We are now headed to Key West. We should get there in a couple of hours and stay docked there all day. This gives us a chance to be back in the USA for a while. Hopefully our cell phones won't be in the roaming mode and things will be most familiar. One of the great things about international travel is seeing things, including yourself and your culture from a different perspective. Another good thing is appreciating what you have at home, even as you want to continually work to change it and yourself for the better.

Looking through the wall of windows of the casual dining area called the Windjammer the ocean drifts by under a mostly sunny sky. The few clouds give depth to the panoramic view that spans from the farthest left across the endless horizon directly in front to the widest right. The morning sunlight filters through one of the clouds brave enough to try to block the rays of our nearest star. A way off in the distance another ship passes as a tiny silhouette beneath its own set of clouds. But the ocean is an endless dark blue carpet beneath our very large ship. We float on the surface unconcerned about the 7,000 feet of water under it.

At the elevator I met a couple that I have gotten to know by sight and the woman says, "You know, Plunky, you are about the friendliest star on this boat! Some of the rest of them act kind of stuck up and stuff." And I responded "Oh, that's probably because they are just not used to being around their fans for such a long time and they are used to their privacy." And she said, "Oh well, I'll cut them some slack then."

A couple of things about that little exchange are interesting to me about me. I don't think of myself as being a star or as being friendly. From my perspective I am a musician putting my music and my views out there from the stage and on recordings. But I don't see me as a star; but I can see how someone seeing me from afar might. I am on stage, under the bright lights, with my sound and voice being amplified a hundred-fold until they ring out filling the whole space and commanding people to dance or listen or suspend belief for a moment in time. That could make me seem like a star.

Also, I don't think I am particularly friendly. Sure, I smile and I am genuinely happy that people appreciate and support our music. I don't have to fake that at all. It is amazingly gratifying to have people say they love my music or my sound or my band or my energy. Wow! How cool is that! Of course, I smile and blush and touch or hug them. But in reality I am a bashful loner. From the very first word of a conversation I am trying to end it. My every comment is designed to be the last sentence so I can make my escape back to my shell, back behind my façade and that could be perceived as me being aloof.

And so it is with a lot of artists. We may use our creative output as a way to communicate even our deepest feeling and most intimate thoughts, but we do it from a distance. And we just may be really uncomfortable being up close and personal. Some may even choose this type of profession because it allows us to do just that – communicate through the veil of the edge of the stage or on a screen. You can see us and be touched by us, but you can't really put your finger on us. Maybe lots of us performers are really masking our insecurities with bright lights and big sound and dancers and props. We are all, even we stars, children growing up into our dreams. Maybe everybody is a star, at least potentially so. Or maybe none of us are.

Day 6. 11:30 AM Thursday, October 15.

Deck 6 lounge facing east with the ship heading northwest. Just passing Cape Canaveral.

Last night I stayed up until after 2:00 AM checking the poolside midnight concert by Mike Phillips and the Unwrapped All Stars. The concert was loud and slamming and the folks were proud and jamming. It was billed as a Sadie Hawkins dance so there were several fine ladies showing their wares and their dancing skills. But it was the music and musicianship that were the stars of the night.

Mike Phillips is a killer alto saxophonist who loves hip-hop and neo-soul and he has serious jazz chops and lots of energy. He does a super funky job on the midi wind instrument with auto-tuned vocoder, and he is a really good master of ceremonies. The group he assembled was an aggregation of young lions of jazz funk and soul that consisted of two trombones, two trumpets, two saxes, drums, percussion bass, guitar, keyboard, and electric violin.

They were all killing it with high energy and high quality musical chops. The drummer, who looked to be about 12, was a funk fool who was polyrhythmic as hell! But the super nova of the evening was clearly electric violinist, Karen Briggs, who came to prominence performing with new age musician Yanni. That girl bowed that thing last night. She gave me goose pimples and made the crowd roar. Like I said, I stayed to the end. The whole show knocked me out! What a blast!

This morning at breakfast I saw Mike and I told him I thought the show

Island at sunset

was off the chain and he in turn paid me high praise, saying that he had loved my show, he had stayed to the end and that I had set the bar high. I told him that the bar had been duly raised by his show last night.

Earlier in the evening last night we had gone to see Patti Austin in concert. Young alto saxophonist Marcus Anderson opened the show and he was really sincere, more-than-competent and quite a showman. He has the skills and the smile to win over audiences and have longevity in this business of jazz and soul.

Patti Austin displayed true professionalism, stage presence, vocal prowess and a recently trimmed-down body. She looked good and sounded great with a pure, often vibrato-less voice and an impeccable sense of timing and pitch. Sometimes sounding a bit like Streisand, Nancy Wilson or Dionne Warwick, Patti explored the nuances and grand themes to be found in her repertoire of fantastic songs written by some of the best in the business. She has worked all over the world and recorded with giants in black pop music and all that experience showed in her concert performance last night, which was at times understated and but always luminescent.

When I see my band members at these shows I am gratified that they seem to be enjoying themselves being immersed in all this music. There is so much to be gleaned from seeing others in our profession doing what we do and at such a high level of proficiency, and in such quantities and variety. From the quiet self-assurance of Patti Austin to the exuberant boisterousness of Mike Phillips and his brash brass band, the range of sounds and personalities is really amazing. And all of it has its fans.

One of my vocalists, Chyp Page Green, stood transfixed in front of the stage at last night's pool party and said she just loved Mike Phillips' show! And this morning I realized that that are several factors in determining what music and musicians we love. Repertoire is important. What the songs mean to you, the personality projected by the artist, the style or genre of the music, the sound and lights and tech, the reaction of the rest of the audience, and your own mood, all influence the way and degree the music will impact you.

I think so much of the music and so many of these musicians are of such high quality that it could be hard for me to carve out a niche, much less excel in this talent-heavy environment. Yet even while Mike Phillips' group was killing it last night, a young lady came up to me to say how much she really enjoyed our show. And this morning at breakfast Wayne Bruce, the leader of Spur of the Moment, came past my table and did a fake kneel down and a fist bump and said to me, "I just wanted to kiss the ring." Wow, some high praise from several young lions for me, a funk veteran. Maybe I am due some accolades for my longevity in the game. Maybe I am an O.G. of Afro-funk jazz.

Yesterday, when we docked at Key West, my son Jamiah had to leave the ship, so I spent much of the hot October day making travel arrangements for him and his roommate to get back to Richmond to take care of business.

I did get to do some sight-seeing in the city with an old friend of mine, Elwood York, who not only took us to the airport, but also drove us around, giving up a guided tour of the place. Key West is the southernmost part of the US, only 90 miles from Cuba. If you take U.S. Route 1 South when you get to mile marker 0, you'll be in the center of Key West, Florida. It felt like it was 95 degrees in that beach town yesterday and that heat drained me enough that I needed a nap when I got back to the ship.

Today I am still being amicably besieged for autographs, pictures and even a few prospective gigs. People are still saying that they are surprised they had not heard of me, given the power of my performance way back then on last Sunday. I am amazed because so much music and so many great performances have happened since then. Some things make a deep enough impression to be timeless, at least for a minute.

End Part II

Day 7. 1:30 PM Friday afternoon in club on Deck 6.

The DC-based group 76 Degrees West is playing their hit song "School Days," a go-go jazz song that sounds so good when I hear on WHUR-FM. I always wish I had made that record as the follow-up to my song "Drop." The group had an uneven start to their set today, probably because the show, which was supposed to be poolside, had to be moved inside due to chilly, windy weather out on deck. They are rolling along now though, go-go swinging and with Eddie Backus on tenor sax, Marcus Anderson on alto and Joey Somerville on trumpet all sitting in. It has turned into quite a jam session and I am digging it. Right now Jonathan Butler is doing another solo session out in the main atrium and he is sounding so good. But you can't do everything on this cruise. And I promised 76 Degrees West I would catch their set and I love Eddie's playing.

3:00 PM Now I have moved to the atrium to catch the last part of Jonathan Butler's solo presentation. He is doing Q and A now. He has really enjoyed himself this week hanging out every day everywhere on the ship and being accessible and gracious.

Last night we saw Jonathan in full concert and he was fantastic. His backup group was Spur of the Moment and I thought it was their best work all week. Jonathan is so expressive with his voice and his guitar playing. He sounds like Stevie Wonder and Donny Hathaway but with a South African flavor and an L.A. twist. The audience loved him and Spur of the Moment seemed inspired by his music and the moment, especially their saxophonist, Skip Pruitt. At the end of the show, Jonathan went into his gospel mode, preaching and teaching and testifying, but the music still had that pop smooth jazz contemporary feel to it; very polished and improvised to fit that very moment in time.

Before that we saw an equally polished performance by Rick Braun in the nightclub venue. His show was very enjoyable, especially when he was joined on stage by Candi Dulfer, Brian Culbertson, and bassist Gerald Veasley.

So much music, so many good vibes, so much camaraderie and so many new friends and fans. So many learning and teaching moments. We are a family this week. Last night I did participate in the jam session. The music was hot and Mike Phillips and Karen Briggs were their usual superlative, powerful selves. When I went up to play along with five or six other horn players, they called a straight-ahead jazz tune on which I was barely able to hold my own with several young players who had the chops of old jazz heads. I would have much rather played some P funk, but you improvise, do your best and live the moment to the fullest. I learned I have to go back in the shed and practice a lot more and continue be dedicated to never stop learning, advancing, developing my art and myself.

12:00 midnight outside the CD store on board.

I am hanging out with several other musicians as I type this. We are all waiting for the gift shop and Capital Jazz reps to tally up our remaining CDs so we can determine how many we have sold. While we wait, the musicians are discussing how things have gone this week, comparing notes on other gigs and tours, and generally agreeing that this cruise has been a really positive experience. Mike Phillips is telling stories about touring with Prince and funny things that happened when he was touring with Jill Scott while I type away on my laptop. (The store sold 96 of my box sets and 8 single CDs.)

Now I am at home in my kitchen at 11:00 PM Saturday night October 17. Earlier on Friday night I had been a little seasick. The boat had more pitch and yaw, as the sea was more active beneath us than at any other time this week. In fact, the cruise had been super-smooth sailing up until that last day. I took some Dramamine and a nap and now move about slowly, feeling a bit woozy, like being drunk.

Before being outside the Gift shop that last night I had gone to see Candi Dulfer's show in the club at around 8:00 PM. She was hot and her repertoire was mostly straight up funk a la James Brown / Maceo Parker. She was a lot more than credible; she was spot on with her alto sax soloing, rapping, singing and the pacing of her show. Having toured with Prince and jamming over the years with a lot of funk heavy-weights, she is a powerful presence and a dominant force to be reckoned with, especially internationally where that brand of funk has a big audience. I really liked her show, her sincerity, and her command of her presentation.

The last show of the week was the Brian Culbertson concert at 10:30 PM Saturday night. Brian has been on all three of the Super Cruises and his show demonstrated why he is an award-winning festival favorite and why he will be back for Super Cruise IV. He has tremendous energy and an infectious smile and persona on stage. Playing the keyboard and trombone, he leads the band, and acts like he is having the time of his life with grand gestures, facial expressions and humorous posturing. He prances around the stage, striking poses, dancing and interacting with the band. Employing dynamics in the extreme, he alternates between funk and smooth jazz, using breaks, stops and sudden shifts in volume and textures. He creates a party onstage and the audience is invited.

Later that night there was a pajama party in the club from midnight to 3:00 AM. I did poke my head in for a second to see how the crowd was getting down with deejay Spinderella and they seemed to be having fun.

I went to the casino where I spent a lot of my spare minutes this cruise week and where I became friends with several ladies who also enjoyed Three-Card Poker. This last night I was mostly at the table alone with the dealers. Two days before I had been up for the week, holding on to six black $100 chips. One day ago I had lost three of those chips and on the last evening I had lost them all. So I was playing with my money at that point, down $200.

During the last hour from 1:30 AM until the casino closed down at 2:30 AM I had a great run of cards, hitting three-of-a-kind three times, trip 8s and three Kings, twice within three hands. Later I hit trip 8s again and several other good hands and finally ending up $1,125! What a great time to win, right at the end, with no chance to lose it back! I shared my winnings with the band.

I turned in at 3:00 AM after setting my phone alarm for 5:55 AM and got up at that time. I was squirrelly-eyed and tired but excited to be docking back in Baltimore. It was cold and rainy but still a wonderful time to be getting off the boat, even with the extreme contrast to the over 90 degrees weather in the Bahamas and Key West just hours ago.

We had breakfast; I collected the money from the CD sales (100 x $29.99 less 30% commission to the cruise line; wow!) and disembarked by 9:30 AM Saturday. We drove back to Richmond and I was so tired that I passed out for a deep-sleep nap almost right away. At 4:00 PM I was still feeling like I was still on the boat and using my sea legs. I was still almost drunk with sea motion even though I was well-inland, when I got a call to go play tennis. Crazily, I agreed and at 5:30 PM I was out on the court, "freezing," stiff, woozy and wondering about my own sanity, but warming up to play doubles tennis with three other wild and crazy tennis enthusiasts.

Even now at a quarter to midnight I am still feeling like I am on the rocking ship. And that's odd because for the vast majority of the hours on board you could barely feel the ocean's motion. But I do "feel" it now. Still.

Epilogue. 8:00 AM Sunday morning October 18, in my kitchen.

I slept good and hard for over seven hours for the first time in weeks. A week with a shipload of music and activities, sudden chilly weather and three sets of tennis after driving from Baltimore on three hours of sleep might knock you out! I am still a little bit tipsy but I can feel that today should be the last of that.

The Capital Jazz Cruise III was a fantastic voyage for me. The music, the musicians and the warmth of the audience inspired me. I learned so much from the experiences and I am charged up with determination to do and be better; and that's worth the price of admission to any gig or university master class. Of course I only had to pay with my time, energy and open mind.

And what great payoffs! I have never made so many sales and new fans from any one gig in my life. If you consider that there are six discs in the 2012 Collectors Box Set, then we distributed over 500 individual discs to music lovers who are likely to listen and in some instances, turn some of their family and friends on to our music. So many patrons on the cruise told us how much they loved our show and our music and our energy, and several said they would be coming to see us when we come to DC or Baltimore or New York or Texas and wherever they were from. And I got solid contacts for bookings in Baltimore, New York, London and Atlanta.

No doubt I will be contacting the Capital Jazz people to lobby for a slot on next year's Super Cruise IV already scheduled for the last week in October 2010 leaving out of Miami. I want my same performance slot, playing for the opening pool party.

In the meantime, I am committed to doing and getting more: more practice, yoga, strategic planning, marketing, chops, and more polished professionalisms. Instead of being discouraged by the great music coming out of my more youthful compatriots and competitors, I am inspired by my own wealth of experience and the respect given to what I do.

I am rededicated to giving up the funk and the best that I got, every time I have the chance to take it to the stage. Music is my ministry and my mistress. And the basis of my mysticism and magic. It is a source of inspiration for me and my shadow. I plan to continue to explore, develop and share the inner and outer workings of juju, funk, soul, world, African, blues, reggae, hip-hop, Latin, gospel and jazz. Understanding that they, like we, are much more alike than dissimilar is an essential step toward oneness.

⌘⌘⌘

C. Discography

Album Releases:
Juju - A Message From Mozambique (1973)
Juju - Chapter Two: Nia (1974)
Juju - Live at 131 Prince Street (1974)
Oneness of Juju - African Rhythms (1975)
Oneness of Juju - Space Jungle Luv (1976)
Oneness of Juju - Bush Brothers & Space Rangers (1978)
Plunky & Oneness of Juju - Every Way But Loose (1982)
Plunky & Oneness of Juju - Electric Juju Nation (1984)
Plunky - Tropical Chill (1988)
Plunky - Move Into the Light (1990)
Plunky - One World One Music (1992)
J. Plunky Branch - Spiritual Sounds Within My Soul (1993)
Plunky - The Oneness of Funk (1994)
Plunky & Oneness - I Can't Hold Back (1996)

Plunky & Oneness - Groove Tones (1998)
Plunky & Oneness - Saxy Mellow Moments (2000)
Plunky & Oneness - Got to be Phunky (2001)
Oneness of Juju - African Rhythms 1970-1982 (2-CD Compilation) (2001)
J. Plunky Branch - Instrumental Praise (2002)
J. Plunky Branch - Solo Journey Between Dimensions (2002)
Plunky & Oneness - Got to Move Something (2002)
Plunky & Oneness - Forever In A Moment (2004)
Plunky - Cold Heat (2006)
Plunky – Drive It (2008)
Plunky & Oneness – 2012 Collectors Box Set (5-CD Compilation) (2010)
Plunky – Plunky On Fire (2011)
Plunky & Oneness – Never Too Late (2014)

Singles:
"African Rhythms" (7" vinyl) Black Fire Records 1975
"Plastic"/"Got to Be Right On It" (7"Vinyl) Black Fire Records 1977
"Every Way but Loose" (12" vinyl) Sutra Records 1982
"Jackpot" (12" vinyl) N.A.M.E. Brand Records 1983
"Skeletons On Sax" (12" vinyl) N.A.M.E. Brand Records 1988
"Never Too Late" (CD singe) N.A.M.E. Brand Records 2014

Compilations:
DJ Food Volume 5 – "African Rhythms," Ninja Tune Records London
Sweet Emotions – "Just Know That I Love You," Instinct Records New York
The Soul of Smooth Jazz Vol.2 - "Just Know That I Love You," Jazz FM Records London
Totally Wired 14 - "African Rhythms," Acid Jazz Records London
Smooth Jazz for a Rainy Day – "Near the Castle at Elmina," Instinct Records, New York
Africa Funk – "African Rhythms," Harmless Records
Nova Classics 7 - "African Rhythms," Nova Records (Paris)
Club Africa – "River Luv Rite," Strut Records (London)
Funk Food Have It Your Way – "Plunkadelic," Soulciety Records (Germany) 1997
Jazz Cats Vol. 2 – "African Rhythms Part 1" P Vine Records, Japan 2003

Soul of the Holidays - "Silent Night" Howard University Records 2008
Living With It - Music and Poetry Compilation released by VCU-MCV Hospital Services
Under The Radar Afro-Cuban/ Afro-American Music Dialogues Compilation, N.A.M.E. Brand Records

With Other Artists:
Pharoah Sanders – Wisdom Through Music Impulse Records
Ndikho Xaba – Ndikho & the Natives
Okyerema Asante – Drum Message
Okyerema Asante – Ohene Kesee A Ebin
Okyerema Asante – Yes We Can
Shadiah & Plunky - Music Medicine for the Soul N.A.M.E. Brand Records
Dr. Ife – Illumination

D. Plunky & Oneness Musicians

1. P. Muzi Branch – joined in 1974, still with me after all these years, albums, album covers, songwriting,
2. Jamiah Fire Branch – percussion, co-producer
3. Derrick Simmons – drums, Chicken Grease
4. Jose Pomier – guitar
5. Tonya Lazenby Jackson – keyboards, vocals
6. Monica Jackson Smith – vocals (deceased)
7. Charlayne "Chyp" Green – vocals, songwriting
8. Okyerema Asante – master percussionist Hugh Masekela, Fleetwood Mac, Paul Simon
9. JL Harris – keyboards
10. Al-Hamel Rasul – piano
11. Babatunde Lea – percussion

12. Lon Moshe – vibraphone
13. Dennis Jalango Stewart
14. Ken Shabala – bass
15. Jacqueline "Lady Eka-Ete" Lewis – the voice of Oneness of Juju, African Rhythms, River Luvrite
16. Ronnie Toler – drums (deceased)
17. Ras Melvin Glover – guitar, went on to co-found Awareness Art Ensemble; the Wailers, Eddie Grant,
18. Weldon Hill – piano, VSU provost
19. Ronnie Cokes – drums
20. Virtania Tillery – vocals
21. Kevin Teasley – keyboards, L.A. producer, the Jacksons,
22. Chris Beasley – guitar, Visions Band
23. Carlton Blount – vocals, the Moments
24. Desiree Roots – vocals,
25. Carl Lester – drums, bass, guitar, Frens Band
26. Lance Dickerson – keyboards, Frens Band
27. Stan Scott – bass
28. Anthony Ampy Ingram – guitar, Waller Family
29. Peddie Maples – percussion, vocals (deceased)
30. Dick Watkins – percussion
31. Kevin Davis – percussion, drums, Ban Carribe
32. Rafael Solano – percussion
33. Alfredo Mojica – percussion
34. Simbo – percussion (deceased)
35. Oginga Tony Joyner – percussion
36. Cordell "Ngoma" Hill – poet
37. Linita Corbett – vocals, dance
38. Dwayne Calvin – bass, sound
39. Nat Lee Jr. – keyboards
40. Judy Spears – vocals
41. Veronica "Nilage" Jones – vocals
42. James Gates – sax student, Grammy nomination
43. Drummie Zeb – drums, ex-student, the Wailers
44. Hannon Lane – guitar
45. Marcus Macklin – guitar

46. James Banks – vocals
47. Rudy Faulkner – vocals, percussion
48. Miguel Pomier – percussion (deceased)
49. John Zachary – drums
50. Corey Burch – drums
51. Lester "Heavy" Kenny – drums
52. Debo Dabney – piano
53. Ken Friend – bass
54. Patrick Mamou – spoken word, Jazz Poets Society
55. Dovane Jefferson – Keyboards
56. Charlie Kilpatrick – piano
57. Lucy Kilpatrick – keyboards
58. Milton Marriott – organ
59. Larry Bland – keyboards
60. Adolphus Danja Mowf Maples – co-producer, Supa Friendz
61. Howard Bee Boisseau – keyboards
62. Shonda Davis – vocals, Chicken Grease
63. Jeremy Evans – drums
64. Marcus Parker – drums
65. Ashiki Branch – rap
66. Edward EJ Shaw – bass, drums
67. Francheska Sugah Davis – vocals
68. Rob Patterson – drums
69. Willie McWhite – keyboard
70. Kevin Pryor – drums
71. Wayne "Big Patt" Patterson – keyboards
72. Seandrea Earls – vocals
73. Erica Willis – vocals
74. Herbert Hop Pollard – keyboards
75. Brent Jones – drums
76. Ed Pentergast – bass
77. Martin Remy – spoken word
78. Moses Braxton – vocals
79. Deborah Bolden – vocals
80. Paris Ford – bass
81. Randall Cort – drums

82. D. J. Williams – guitar
83. Nikki Thomas – vocals
84. Larry Everette – vocals
85. Martina Taylor – vocals
86. Mike Hawkins – bass
87. Byron Tymas – guitar
88. Clarence Seay – bass
89. Marie Goodman Hunter – vocal
90. Brittany Hicks – vocal
91. Kris Marriott – vocal
92. Russell Wilson – piano
93. Johnny Peyton – sax
94. Rickie Cokes – drums
95. DJ Reese – deejay
96. Joe Taylor – flute
97. Janine Bell – shekere
98. Tony Green – drums
99. Carl Holland – drums
100. Ashby Anderson – piano
101. Scott Harlan – bass
102. Ram Bhaghat – percussion
103. John D – percussion
104. Martin Reamy – poetry
105. Gordon Jones – sax
106. Scott Frock – trumpet
107. Chris "Bam" Nevins – keyboards
108. Lee Graham – guitar
109. Cliff Fuller – keyboard
110. Al Campbell – keyboard
111. Ellis Tucker – keyboard
112. Kaila Valdez – Vocal

E. Momentous Gigs, Venues, Collaborations

Alice Tully Hall, Lincoln Center, New York, NY
Kennedy Center for the Performing Arts, Washington, DC
Capital Jazz Fest (2), DC
Capital Jazz Cruises (2)
New Orleans World's Fair
National Black Arts Festival (4), Atlanta, Georgia
Richmond Jazz Festival (3), Virginia
Ray Charles in RVA for 30,000
Hampton Jazz Festival (2), Virginia

Jazz Café, London, U.K.
JVC Jazz Festival, London
New Morning, Paris, France
Le Hanger Paris, France
The Homestead, Hot Springs, Virginia
Blues Alley Club, DC
New York Musicians' Jazz Festival, New York, NY
Ornette Coleman's Artist House, NY
The East, Brooklyn, NY
Cosmic Funk Festival, France
Richmond Festival of Arts, Dogwood Dell (25)
Artsplosure, Raleigh, North Carolina

Umoja Festival (5), Johnson City, Tennessee
Ashford & Simpson's Sugar Bar, New York City
Harborfest Norfolk, VA
Kappa's New Years Eve Balls, DC
2nd Street Festival, Richmond, Virginia
AFRAM Fest (4), Norfolk, Virginia
Carter Barron Amphitheater (4), DC
Fort DuPont Park (4), DC
CIAA Basketball Tournament (2), Charlotte, North Carolina
Virginia Museum of Fine Arts (4), Richmond, Virginia
National Museum of Africa Art, DC
Taste of DC Festival
Hoop City Jazz Festival Springfield, Massachusetts
Tour in Ghana West Africa for the Commission on Children
Tour in Europe with Bobby Byrd & Soulciety
African Liberation Day demonstrations (10), DC
Lake Arbor Jazz Festival, Maryland
The Mosque, RVA
Richmond Coliseum, RVA
June Jubilee, RVA
Virginia Museum of Fine Arts, RVA

Clubs – Richmond, Virginia
Third World
Blues Alley Restaurant (Richmond)
Ellington's
Ebony Island
Ovoutee's Club
The Devil's
Richmond Jazz Society Club
Lucky Strike
Ivory's
City Lights
Scandals
Scoundrels
Humphreys'
Armani's
Glenn's Restaurant

Crossroads
Alley Cats
Flood Zone
Canal Club
Capital Ale House
Bayside
Military Retirees' Club
Martini Kitchen & Bubble Bar
Aqua Lounge
Posh
Lucille's
Bliss
Elliot's
Brickstone Grill

Clubs – DMV
Ed Murphy's Supper Club
Harambe House
Kilimanjaro Club
Blues Alley, DC
Zanzibar, DC
Mckenzie's (Baltimore, Maryland)
Takoma Station
Half Note Restaurant
K2 Restaurant
Bethesda Jazz and Blues Club
Lowell's (Roanoke)
Talk of the Town (Durham, North Carolina)
House of Jazz (VA Beach, Virginia)
Basin Street Club (Sterling, Virginia)

Clubs – New York
The Cheetah
The East
Studio Rivbea
Slug's
Sugar Bar
Mikell's

Colleges & Universities
Columbia University, New York City
New York University
Howard University DC
Yale University
Hampton University
Virginia State University
Virginia Commonwealth University
University of Virginia
Virginia Union University
Norfolk State University
Old Dominion University
NC A&T University
Savannah State University
Wesleyan College
Morgan State University
James Madison University
John Tyler Community College
Baltimore City Community College
J. Sargeant Reynolds Community College
Wytheville Community College
Southside Virginia Community College
Danville Community College
Virginia Western Community College
Northern Virginia Community College

Impactful Collaborations
Pharaoh Sanders
Gil Scott-Heron
Brian Jackson
Hamiet Bluiett
Asante (Ghanaian Master Percussionist)
Akhenaton (French rapper)

Ornette Coleman
Bobby Byrd
Soulciety
Original Last Poets
Mike Phillips
Jackie McLean
Fela Kuti
Craig Harris
Danja Mowf
Oh No
Lonnie Liston Smith
Paris Ford
Norman Connors
Don Blackmon
Cuban Saxophone Quartet
Folkoryuma
Ilu Drummers
Elegba Folklore Society
MCV
VCU-South African Jazz Exchange
Virginia Commission for the Arts
National Endowment for the Arts
US-Aid/ Ghana Commission on Children

Record Companies
Strata-East Records
Black Fire Records
N.A.M.E. Brand Records
Sutra Records
Strut Records (UK)
Blues Interaction Records (Japan)
Stones Throw Records

F. CREDITS

Photographs by Lew Harrison, Jerry Bass, Dennis Harvey, Collis Davis, Plunky, Willie Redd, Kathy Branch, Zeke Robinson, Patrick Mamou, Adolphus Maples, Sheidia Badja, Al Dokes, and Jamiah Fire Branch

Album cover paintings by Philip Muzi Branch, Mary Greer Album cover designs by Philip Muzi Branch, Adolphus Maples, Mary Greer, Denny Williams, Sue Ying, Patrick Mamou, Collis Davis, and Jimmy Gray

Book cover portrait painting by Daniel Bussiere of France (www.dan23.com) Book cover design by Vee Cee and Patrick Mamou. Back photo by Stella K.

Newspaper clippings from Richmond News Leader, Richmond Times-Dispatch, Richmond Afro-American, Federated Arts Council News, New York Times, Billboard Magazine.

www.ingramcontent.com/pod-product-compliance
Lightning Source LLC
Chambersburg PA
CBHW071328080526
44587CB00017B/2767